"Between these covers, psychoanalysts, feminists, rabbis, and a variety of writers on queer life and theory enter into a crucial, luminous, and downright astonishing conversation with one another. Who would have thought that such a project could be accomplished? Slomowitz and Feit, the editors, bring together a group of wonderful writers who, in turn, bring their clinical, theoretical, and spiritual resources to bear on questions that have never before been simultaneously considered. This is a work of the greatest social and moral imagination. Those who are directly involved with the issues addressed will read the book and profit from it; and so will we all."

– **Donnel B. Stern, Ph.D.,** Training and Supervising Analyst, William Alanson White Institute, New York City; Adjunct Clinical Professor of Psychology and Clinical Consultant, New York University Postdoctoral Program in Psychotherapy and Psychoanalysis

"In this wise and compassionate book, an ancient religious and hermeneutical tradition engages a very current dilemma, one that is shattering traditional assumptions about identity. It brings together psychoanalytic, rabbinic, feminist, and queer voices in addressing sex and gender in the Orthodox Jewish community; but, obviously its implications are relevant to a much larger community. The lead editor, Alan Slomowitz, an interpersonal psychoanalyst and an orthodox Jew, in the very best of both traditions, sets the tone for the subsequent chapters, exploring the conflictual and painful issues involved, without recourse to glib solutions. I heartily recommend this book. It will be of great interest to anyone, professional or lay, attempting to come to terms with our socio-cultural upheaval."

– **Edgar Levenson, M.D.,** Fellow Emeritus, Training and Supervisory Analyst and Faculty Member, William Alanson White Institute, New York City; Honorary Member, American Psychoanalytic Association; Life Fellow, American Academy of Psychoanalysis; Distinguished Life Fellow, American Psychiatric Association; 2006 Mary S. Sigourney Award winner; author of *Fallacy of Understanding, The Ambiguity of Change, The Purloined Self,* and *Interpersonal Psychoanalysis and the Enigma of Consciousness*

Homosexuality, Transsexuality, Psychoanalysis and Traditional Judaism

Homosexuality, Transsexuality, Psychoanalysis and Traditional Judaism explores the often incommensurable and irreconcilable beliefs and understandings of sexuality and gender in the Orthodox Jewish community from psychoanalytic, rabbinic, feminist, and queer perspectives. The book explores how seemingly irreconcilable differences might be resolved.

The book is divided into two separate but related sections. The first highlights the divide between the psychoanalytic, academic, and traditional Orthodox Jewish perspectives on sexual identity and orientation, and the acute psychic and social challenges faced by gay and lesbian members of the Orthodox Jewish world. The contributors ask us to engage with them in a dialogue that allows for authentic conversation.

The second section focuses on gender identity, especially as experienced by the Orthodox transgender members of the community. It also highlights the divide between theories that see gender as fluid and traditional Judaism that sees gender as strictly binary. The contributors write about their views and experiences from both sides of the divide. They ask us to engage in true authentic dialogue about these complex and crucial emotional and religious challenges.

Homosexuality, Transsexuality, Psychoanalysis and Traditional Judaism will be of great interest to psychoanalysts and psychoanalytic psychotherapists as well as members and leaders of Jewish communities working with LGBTQ issues.

Alan Slomowitz, Ph.D., is a supervisor of psychotherapy and on the faculty of the William Alanson White Institute. He is on the Editorial Board of *Contemporary Psychoanalysis*, and an internet editor of the Contemporary Psychoanalysis in Action blog. He edited *Interpersonal Psychoanalysis and the Enigma of Consciousness* (2018) by Edgar Levenson and the new Routledge release of Levenson's book *The Purloined Self* (2016). He is in private practice in psychoanalysis and psychotherapy in New York City, USA.

Alison Feit, Ph.D., teaches at Stony Brook University, St. Louis Psychoanalytic Institute, and at the China American Psychoanalytic Alliance. She is an associate editor of the journal *Contemporary Psychoanalysis* and a member of the Artist Group, the Sexual Abuse Service, and the Trauma Service at the William Alanson White Institute in New York. She maintains a private practice in Manhattan, New York City, USA.

Psychoanalysis in a New Key Book Series
Series editor
Donnel Stern

When music is played in a new key, the melody does not change, but the notes that make up the composition do: change in the context of continuity, continuity that perseveres through change. *Psychoanalysis in a New Key* publishes books that share the aims psychoanalysts have always had, but that approach them differently. The books in the series are not expected to advance any particular theoretical agenda, although to this date most have been written by analysts from the interpersonal and relational orientations.

The most important contribution of a psychoanalytic book is the communication of something that nudges the reader's grasp of clinical theory and practice in an unexpected direction. *Psychoanalysis in a New Key* creates a deliberate focus on innovative and unsettling clinical thinking. Because that kind of thinking is encouraged by exploration of the sometimes surprising contributions to psychoanalysis of ideas and findings from other fields, *Psychoanalysis in a New Key* particularly encourages interdisciplinary studies. Books in the series have married psychoanalysis with dissociation, trauma theory, sociology, and criminology. The series is open to the consideration of studies examining the relationship between psychoanalysis and any other field—for instance, biology, literary and art criticism, philosophy, systems theory, anthropology, and political theory.

But innovation also takes place within the boundaries of psychoanalysis, and *Psychoanalysis in a New Key* therefore also presents work that reformulates thought and practice without leaving the precincts of the field. Books in the series focus, for example, on the significance of personal values in psychoanalytic practice, the complex interrelationship between the analyst's clinical work and personal life, the consequences for the clinical situation when patient and analyst are from different cultures, and the need for psychoanalysts to accept the degree to which they knowingly satisfy their own wishes during treatment hours, often to the patient's detriment. A full list of all titles in this series is available at: www.routledge.com/series/LEAPNKBS

Titles in this series include:

Vol. 50 *The Emergence of Analytic Oneness: Into the Heart of Psychoanalysis* Ofra Eshel

Vol. 49 *Homosexuality, Transsexuality, Psychoanalysis and Traditional Judaism* Edited by Alan Slomowitz and Alison Feit

Vol. 48 *Psychodynamic Perspectives on Asylum Seekers and the Asylum-Seeking Process* Barbara K. Eisold

Homosexuality, Transsexuality, Psychoanalysis and Traditional Judaism

Edited by Alan Slomowitz and Alison Feit

Routledge
Taylor & Francis Group

LONDON AND NEW YORK

First published 2019
by Routledge
2 Park Square, Milton Park, Abingdon, Oxon OX14 4RN

and by Routledge
52 Vanderbilt Avenue, New York, NY 10017

Routledge is an imprint of the Taylor & Francis Group, an informa business

British Library Cataloguing-in-Publication Data
A catalogue record for this book is available from the British
Library

Library of Congress Cataloging-in-Publication Data
A catalog record for this book has been requested

ISBN: 978-1-138-74946-7 (hbk)
ISBN: 978-1-138-74949-8 (pbk)
ISBN: 978-1-315-18015-1 (ebk)

Typeset in Times New Roman
by Swales & Willis, Exeter, Devon, UK

Alan Slomowitz:

To my family. My heartfelt thanks, appreciation, and love to my wife Elaine. Thank you for your love, advice, and guidance throughout. I could not have done this book without your being in my life. To our children and their spouses: Shira, Boaz and Aviv; Rebecca and Gidon, Rivka, Joshua and Yonah, Dovid and Judah. Thank you for the joy you all bring to our lives.

To my late father, Rabbi Shlomo Slomowitz (Yehi Zichro Baruch, Of Blessed Memory) and my mother Lillian Slomowitz: Thank you for your wide-ranging intellectual breadth, depth, and curiosity which provide me with the intellectual foundation for all that I do.

Alison Feit:

To Betty and Jack and Hattie and Dudley who sowed their seeds in their time and encouraged me to plant my very own. To Jacob, David, Micah, and Elisha who continue the tradition. And, of course, to Jordan, a most extraordinary companion for the journey. But mostly, to Joseph and Surella, without whom I would not have found my way at all.

Contents

Acknowledgments

Alan Slomowitz

I wish to express my thanks to Kate Hawes and Charles Bath at Routledge for their invaluable help and support in publishing this book.

I want to express a special heartfelt thank you and appreciation to **Donnel Stern**, for encouraging me to publish this book. As editor of the book series, *Psychoanalysis in a New Key*, Don's unflagging support throughout enabled me to assemble a unique and talented group of psychoanalysts and psychotherapists, rabbis, and Jewish scholars for this important book. I could not have completed, let alone published, this book without your special, unique, and unflagging support and advice. Thank you Don.

The contributors to this book made this unique publication possible. I would like to thank each of you personally and publicly. The relationships I have built through this book are personal and meaningful ones. Through your writings, our discussions, and the editing process itself, each one of you had an impact on me that goes beyond the content itself. Your clear, insightful, and authentic conceptions of sexuality, gender, Judaism, and spirituality have left an indelible mark on me. My selves as clinician, Jew, spouse, and parent have been changed. I am fortunate to have met you and worked with you. Thank you.

Seth Aronson, Psy.D.
A mentor and a colleague, a key clinical supervisor in my own training, his personal support and encouragement enabled me to expand in important ways my vision of this book and the contributors to this unique book. Seth's insightful and multi faceted commentary on Ben

Badder's lyrical writing incorporates psychoanalytic theory, Kabbalistic echoes and literary allusions that complement Ben's beautiful chapter.

Ben Baader, Ph.D.

Ben has become a spiritual friend. His warmth and lyricism combined with his ability to see light in the spaces of *halakhah* (Jewish law) demonstrate his unique ability to literally stand in the "Brombergian" (more in this later) spaces of his different selves. When you read Ben's chapter you will be transported to a light filled world while at the same time feeling the darkness and yet not being consumed by it.

Mark Blechner, Ph.D.

Mark is also a mentor and a colleague. His influence as a clinical supervisor continues with me years later. His speaking at our conference in 2015 and writing this chapter on Collateral Damage are critical in highlighting the dangers of societal and cultural oppressiveness, especially with regard to sexuality. The individual, the family, and the community all needlessly suffer.

Elaine Chapnik, J.D.

Thank you for your learned analysis of a disregarded set of Jewish laws about lesbian women, written over 1,000 years ago. I greatly appreciate your working with me to edit your original chapter, "Women known for these acts", first published in *Keep Your Wives Away From Them* (2010).

Rabbi Mark Dratch, L.M.S.W.

Rabbi Dratch is the Executive Director of the Rabbinical Council of America (RCA), the largest Orthodox rabbinic organization in the US. I truly appreciate his authentic engagement as an Orthodox rabbi with me and his meaningful chapter in this book on this important subject, Orthodox Judaism, and the LGBTQ community.

Jack Drescher, M.D.

I want to express my appreciation and gratitude to Jack for approaching and suggesting we organize a first of its kind conference (in 2015) on Gender and Sexuality and the Orthodox Jewish Community. For the first time, Orthodox Jewish LGBTQ activists, rabbinic leaders, and psychoanalysts and psychotherapists met and presented together. Much thanks to Jack for his moving introduction in the book and for encouraging

Dr. Feit and myself to write our original paper, "Does God make referrals" (Slomowitz & Feit, 2015), which was the basis for the conference and this book.

Anne Fausto-Sterling, Ph.D.
I greatly appreciate Dr. Fausto-Sterling granting us permission to publish her important article on gender development and variability. Her scholarship is a crucial chapter in our book. Thank you to Taylor & Francis for permission to republish this key article.

Michelle Friedman, M.D.
Thank you Dr. Friedman for your advice and input as I was assembling this book. Our discussions have helped shape the book. An extra thank you for writing about the older LGBTQ Orthodox community because they go unnoticed and even forgotten in today's Orthodox community (see Chapter 5) and for the detailing the training needed by Orthodox rabbis today.

Hillel Gray, Ph.D.
Thank you to the journal *Nashim*, for giving us permission to republish Dr. Gray's original and scholarly article on a major Orthodox Jewish legal work on transgender issues, *Dor Tahapuchot* (*A Generation of Perversion*). (See the introduction to Section II for more details.) Thank you to Dr. Gray for adding an updated introduction to his chapter.

Rabbi Steve Greenberg
A special thank you to Rabbi Greenberg for agreeing to work with me to edit and republish his path-breaking chapter on envisioning an Orthodox Jewish gay wedding. His chapter adds an important religious and spiritual dimension to this book. This is consistent with his vision as the founding director of Eshel, the Orthodox LGBT community support, education, and advocacy organization. Thank you for your friendship.

Miryam Kabakov, L.M.S.W.
Thank you for writing about a crucial and another often forgotten group, the parents of Orthodox LGBTQ children. Ms. Kabakov does them justice in making their voices heard. She works tirelessly supporting the Orthodox LGBTQ community through Eshel and other important LGBTQ organizations.

Joy Ladin, Ph.D.

My heartfelt appreciation and gratitude to Dr. Ladin for agreeing to include a chapter (edited) from her new book, *The Soul of a Stranger*. Thank you for working with me so we could include such a unique gloss on the Torah from a transgender perspective. Her writing is inspiring, scholarly, and a significant contribution to Jewish scholarship.

Thank you to the University Press of New England for permission to republish the edited version of this chapter.

Ronnie Lesser, Ph.D.

Thank you for your thoughtful and important comments on our original article. You made sure we were authentic in our understanding the Orthodox LGBTQ community.

Jeremy Novich, Psy.D.

A special thank you to Dr. Novich for agreeing to contribute a summary of his important research on gay men in the Orthodox Jewish community. Your research is crucial in giving voice to this community. I am honored that we can provide a wider forum for your work.

Oriol Poveda, Ph.D.

My special thanks to Dr. Poveda for summarizing his path-breaking dissertation and research on the Orthodox transgender community. His study is a first in this area. Many thanks for introducing me to Drs. Baader and Ladin. And for introducing me to the book *Dor Tahapuchot*.

Rabbi Hyim Shafner, L.C.S.W.

Thank you Rabbi Shafner for contributing your personal experiences, insights, and practical *halakhic* perspectives on transgender issues. He understands what it means to deal with real people.

Thank you to my colleagues who helped me edit my own writings. To Drs. Helen Quinones, Michael Singer, and Gudrun Opitz, and Rachel Altstein. Any errors are mine alone.

Overview

Alan Slomowitz

This book brings together psychoanalytic, rabbinic, feminist, and queer voices in addressing sex and gender in the Orthodox Jewish community. The book is divided into two separate but related sections. The first section is focused primarily on sexual orientation, highlighting the challenges faced primarily by gay and lesbian members of the Orthodox Jewish world.[1] The second section focuses primarily on gender identity, especially as experienced by the Orthodox transgender members of the community as they confront their lived gendered selves, which appear to be incoherent in the strictly binary gendered religious practices and beliefs of Orthodox Judaism. The narratives of the Orthodox LGBTQ member create, in turn, personal, social, and clinical challenges for the psychoanalysts, rabbis, and educators who engage with them in therapy, Jewish law and pastoral counseling. Their narratives challenge us to put aside stereotypes and prejudices so we can create for them clinical and lived spaces to grow and thrive.

A key goal in publishing this book is to create an ongoing dialogue while knowing that it will be messy. Although the different perspectives may well be irreconcilable, I believe we must find ways to live in the mess of this "irreconcilability." We must find the actions and words (which are actions) that cross the chasm, and are authentic and humanizing, even if we are not ready or able to bridge, let alone close, that chasm. We must find ways to discuss these matters without allowing the very real differences to harm what is essential about being an Orthodox Jew, an Orthodox LGBTQ Jewish community member, a psychoanalyst, a rabbi, or an educator.[2]

This book has been a challenge to and for me: A personal challenge, a religious challenge, and a professional challenge. These challenges are representative of different "selves" that I believe exist within me, and perhaps within you the readers as well. We will attempt to struggle with, negotiate with, and hopefully find the spaces to live within these incommensurable viewpoints. This book attempts to establish a dialogue of multiple voices, each spoken to and listened to with a seriousness and respectfulness that may enhance each of us who has written and each of us who will read the many important contributions.

I was raised from a young age in a traditional Orthodox Jewish home and school, where biblical injunctions, whatever they may be, are inviolable edicts, where one is taught that questions are welcomed as long as the final answers follow in a particular path. This may work for some because their minds feel at home in a community that provides structure, comfort, and support. However, when your mind feels differently in a fundamental way with long-accepted traditions and interpretations about certain behaviors and identities, you feel the anxiety and unsettledness of perceived danger and loss of acceptance and love.

My psychoanalytic self is trained to look for the gaps in the narratives, into what is not being talked about, into what is selectively in-attended or dissociated and split off from awareness.[3] This self sometimes runs into my Orthodox self, raised in a traditional Orthodox Jewish home, educated in traditional Orthodox Jewish schools. The collisions of these selves, sometimes split off in ways I am not aware of, hold potential danger if acknowledged. I may find myself feeling dismissive of the Orthodox community and not acknowledging the numerous individuals who might feel as I do. Or, in a clinical setting, I may miss a lesbian or gay patient's terror at the loss of her or his connection with family and the only life she or he knows. I believe I am usually aware of such deep feelings, but the subtle details their unique connections may escape my notice or attention.

The contradictions abound. As a psychoanalyst, raised in an Orthodox tradition, I explore, with Orthodox lesbian and gay patients, their attempts to reconcile sexual desires that appear clearly forbidden yet feel natural and part of themselves. What if you are a male Orthodox yeshiva student who finds himself having a crush on his study partner? That can't be you, yet it is you. If you are a ninth grader in an all-girls Orthodox high school, what self are you if your felt sense of self is male, yet your assigned-at-birth body/gender is female, and you want to

perform an explicitly gendered ritual, such as putting on tefillin (phylacteries) or leading the morning services, that does not match your
assigned-at-birth gender? The different parts of your self must be
disavowed or hidden – your observant self, communal/social self,
desirous sexual self, gendered self – male, female, non-binary selves:
All potential and often unacknowledged parts of whom we are or might
be. When they are, disavowed danger looms.

In addition to a yeshiva education my parents also valued literature
and reading. My parents were proud there were "Jewish" writers, such as
Saul Bellow, Bernard Malamud, and Philip Roth and welcomed their
writings into our home. Although Roth was the object of much criticism
by the Orthodox Jewish community his writing embodied the raw
conflicts between the then traditional Jewish world and the emerging
Jewish secular world. Philip Bromberg (personal communication)
describes Roth as one who writes most clearly about dissociative
experiences; in fact he writes poignantly about dissociative experiences.
This is clearly depicted in his early story, *The Conversion of the Jews*
(Roth, 2005, pp. 109–124). Roth captures the conflicts and splits about
religion, sex, and Judaism, as experienced by the main protagonist,
Ozzie. Ozzie is a smart and curious 12 year old, raised by a single
mother, holding on to their Jewishness in a culture that is encouraging
assimilation and adherence at the same time. Rabbi Binder is 30, and so
had to have been trained in America, not Europe, and represents modern
American Orthodox Judaism. He believes he knows what the truth is
about Judaism and God and its chosen-ness, its superior morality. And it
this rabbi's job to impart these important truths to the children he is
teaching. He is sincere and knowledgeable. He is willing to hear all
questions – he even has a free Q&A period before class starts.

However, sincerity is not authenticity. Edgar Levenson, in *The Purloined Self* (Levenson, 2003/2017, pp. 8–9), distinguishes between
sincerity and authenticity. Sincerity comes from the Latin word *sincerus*,
meaning clean, pure, without decay. Authenticity comes from the Greek
authentikes, meaning either one who does things himself or a murderer.
What does that all mean? Levenson writes (p. 9):

> The sincere man is without rottenness; the authentic man takes
> action. The internalized effort to be one's best is replaced by the

interpersonal effort to be, with others, oneself with all its imperfections and shortcomings. Authenticity tries to match being and action, sincerity tries to perfect being and consequently action.

Our struggle and challenge as therapist, rabbi, LGBTQ member of the community, are to authentically meet each other with all of our imperfections, with all of our humanness.

The young rabbi is sincere, but he is not prepared for the messiness of authenticity. He is not prepared for the messiness of the clashes between religion and sexuality, between curiosity and religious doctrine and dogma. He is not prepared to meet Ozzie where he is: A Jewish, pre-adolescent boy, full of rebelliousness and vulnerability, emerging sexuality and independence. Ozzie wants to know: If God can do anything, why couldn't he make Mary pregnant? Ozzie enrages the rabbi directly attacking the rabbi's sense of self: Shouting the rabbi doesn't know anything about God. Rabbi Binder slaps him and bloodies his nose. Ozzie curses him and flees to the roof of the synagogue. Once on the roof, suddenly Ozzie is confronted with a "not-me" experience: Can this be him on the roof who cursed the rabbi and may now jump? When did this become a life-and-death struggle for Ozzie and he didn't even know it? Were his seemingly innocent questions about Jesus and the virgin birth and the Jews so innocent? Who is the "me" who is asking these questions? Who is the "me" who just cursed the rabbi? Who is the "me" who was on the roof threatening to jump? And now suddenly is there a "me" that is part of "us": His friends, his community, his parents, his Jewishness?

Roth wrote this story in the late 1950s. Although the details of the times may have changed, the splits have not been resolved between the Orthodox Jewish community and the culture at large. At the margins, progress has been made (see below). However, the LBGTQ members of the Orthodox community often face the same Rabbi Binder as Ozzie did. Ozzie could have asked if God can do anything why couldn't he create gay, lesbian, or trans people and, if he did, what right do we have to not fully accept who they are? They ask the rabbi(s) about their/our sexuality and desires. They want to know how to find a way to be able to choose to continue the connection and membership within the observant community. However, are they expected to accept only certain answers?

Answers they likely knew before they asked. Why ask? Because we all need to announce who we are without feeling compelled to be Ozzie, to not find oneself up on the roof ready to jump. The questions and answers are not supposed to be life threatening but rather life affirming.

Edgar Levenson (2003/2017), in a paper titled "On seeing what is said," describes how even the most experienced analyst attempts to makes sense of what is being said. The level of abstraction rises as the anxiety levels of both analyst and patient increase. It is difficult to pressure a deconstructive inquiry, to not make sense of it all and allow the narrative to unfold. The subjects with which this book engages evoke controversy and anxiety in traditional religion, hence the motivation to find reasons (see below) that explain the laws – whether to forbid or permit such behaviors and identities. We try to make sense of it all when we might be better living in and through the no-sense of it all.

The explanations, often stated as "compassionate acceptance," may often (though not always) mask a felt experience of condescension: We all struggle in our observance, sorry this is your struggle. The recognition by the questioning LGBTQ member that she or he is uniquely expected to give up intimacy and love. A sacrifice no other member of the community is expected to make. At the same time rabbinic and community leaders have been trained to understand the world in a very specific way, through the lens of long-standing tradition that has read and interpreted biblical texts that not only outlaw same-sex activity but do not admit to the possibility that a person sees themselves through the lens of their sexuality and gender: That a person sees a core part of their identity as a lesbian, gay, or transgender person. To the rabbis, this cannot be. Hence, the irreconcilable differences. Given these differences how do we remain open and curious?

Donnel Stern (2003, p. 250) in *Courting Surprise* writes, "Curiosity is the imagination and discipline that lead to seeing what is questionable. To be curious is to be sensitive to the possibility of a question." However, it is not the answers to our questions that are most significant. The significances are the thoughts and feelings that arrive "unbidden" following the answers. Stern (2010), in his chapter "The eye sees itself," notes we can become frozen and curiosity may vanish. "The alternative patterns of relatedness are invisible to both participants ..." (Stern, 2010, p. 75). That's when dissociation occurs. This is what we are describing in the above paragraph: The dissociations between the "me" (what is acceptable) and "not-me" (what cannot ever be and if it is acknowledged, I may fall apart). This leads to an inability to consider a range of possibilities that might be articulated or formulated, and a shutting down of curiosity.

How do we unfreeze our curiosity? I am proposing we read this book, intimately and allow our moment-to-moment shifts in feelings and thoughts guide us. As Stern advises, pay attention to the affective snags and chafing as we read each chapter. Philip Bromberg's thoughts and insights provide an additional point of meeting for all of us. Bromberg (2017, p. 7) writes that our mental functioning is inherently relational. And psychotherapy is a relational experience, shaped by two people, and what makes it therapeutic is its *uncertainty*. These are the experiences of what he refers to as "safe surprises" between two people as they struggle with relational uncertainty – they "hang in there." We must read the different chapters and "hang in" while feeling what we are experiencing.

These safe surprises are authentic, yet safe, relational encounters. Bromberg quotes Levenson (1974, pp. 368–369) that, in an authentic (see above) therapeutic encounter, we as therapists risk our own identity. He adds an important component to this encounter: The "self-state" perspective. Without this perspective, "the recognition of who *feels* the authenticity and who *doesn't* is confusing and difficult to deal with in the here and now" (Levenson, 2003/2017, p. 11). The "safe, but not too safe" negotiation of individuality and otherness allows paradox to exist: "self-otherness" without being "someone else." Authenticity is how close one's self-state matches the other individual's experience of "me-ness." And, importantly, this "me-ness" will not be re-written to suit the other's desire or commands. We have to acknowledge the "messy" parts of the relationship and be open to a mutually personal process of relational self-reflection on our participation in this dialogue. The key perspective that Levenson, Bromberg, and Stern emphasize is to refrain from asking "What does all of this mean" and focus on "*What is going on around here?*"

With this question we may begin to explore how, within all of us (readers and authors), all too often reside unbridgeable self-states, certain "narrative truths" that are not points of view but states that have their own truths which are "not-me" states to the other states. An Orthodox gay man in synagogue listening to the biblical injunctions against same-sex sexual activity may find himself transported to a time of self-hate, whereas later that afternoon in intimate conversation with his male partner not understand how he could have not stood up and shouted during the reading. A straight Orthodox therapist in the consulting room with her young Orthodox lesbian patient may feel her patient's rage and non-recognition fully, yet, a few hours later, this same therapist trying to listen to her husband talk about his day may feel depressed and distant, and not be aware how her feelings might be connected to what happened in the consulting room with her patient. An Orthodox rabbi reading, in the second section of this book, Chapter 14, *Soul of a Stranger* by Joy Ladin, the transgender professor of English at Yeshiva University, may find himself contemptuously critical of her writing, yet somehow "knowing" that if he did not "know" who she was he would find himself admiring her insights.

We would do well to heed the words of the Jewish philosopher, Abraham Joshua Heschel, who writes in the opening chapter of his book *God in Search of Man* (Heschel, 1955/1983):

> Religion declined not because it was refuted, but because it became irrelevant .... When faith is completely replaced by creed, worship by discipline, love by habit ... when faith becomes an heirloom rather than a living fountain ... when religion speaks only in the name of authority rather than with the voice of compassion ...
>
> (p. 3)

My goal is that you read each chapter of this book as an intimate dialogue with the writer. Pay careful attention to your feelings and thoughts as they emerge through your engagement with the author. Don't allow your faith to become creed, your worship discipline, your love a habit. Try to match each author's authenticity and desire with your own.

Notes

1 Orthodox Judaism is made up of different groups, often known by such descriptions as ultra-Orthodox, modern Orthodox, Hassidic, open Orthodoxy. Each group differs in practices and customs. However, a common thread of

observance is the keeping of the Sabbath and its rules around work and physical creative activity, the keeping of kashrut (kosher slaughter of meat, not mixing meat and milk), and the belief in the divine revelation of the Bible and adherence to rabbinic authority in daily living. As with most religions in today's world, the boundaries are fluid and changing. In this book the term "Orthodox Judaism" is used generically and I expect readers may fill in their experiences and perspectives of what it means to be an Orthodox Jew.

2 There is an existing literature that addresses interaction of psychoanalysis and religion. Sochaczewski (2017) discusses Ian Barbour's four-typology classification describing the relationship between religion and science. She applies it to psychoanalysis and religion. The types are: Conflict, Independence, Dialogue, and Integration. These typologies might have meaning for our discussion and the book, but I do not have space to address these ideas at this time.

3 There is perhaps some irony in a historical parallel in the struggle for acceptance by the LGBTQ community in the Orthodox Jewish and psychoanalytic communities. Psychoanalysis itself has a complicated history with regard to the acceptance of the LGBTQ community into its training institutes, and in how it treated the LGBTQ community in the consulting room. That history has been discussed in other papers and books (see Drescher, 2008).

References

Bromberg, P. (2017). Psychotherapy as the growth of wholeness. In Solomon, M. F. and Siegel, D. (eds.), *How People Change: Relationships and Neuroplasticity in Psychotherapy (Norton Series on Interpersonal Neurobiology)*. New York, NY: W. W. Norton & Co..

Drescher, J. (2008). A history of homosexuality and organized psychoanalysis, *Journal of the American Academy of Psychoanalysis and Dynamic Psychiatry*, 36(3):443–460.

Heschel, A. J. (1955/1983). *God in Search of Man*. New York, NY: Farrar, Strauss & Giroux.

Levenson, E. A. (1974) Changing concepts of intimacy. *Contemporary Psychoanalysis*, 10, 359–369.

Levenson, E. A. (2003/2017). On seeing what is said, in *The Purloined Self*. New York, NY London: Routledge.

Roth, Philip (2005). *Goodbye Columbus and Five Short Stories, Letting Go*, Library of America Edition. New York, NY: Penguin Books.

Sochaczewski, J. (2017). Psychoanalysis and religion in the 21st century: Examining the possibility of integration, *Contemporary Psychoanalysis*, 53(2):247–268.

Stern, D. B. (2003). *Unformulated Experience: From Dissociation to Imagination in Psychoanalysis*. New York, NY, London: Psychology Press.

Stern, D. B. (2010). *Partners in Thought: Working with Unformulated Experience, Dissociation, and Enactment*. New York, NY, London: Routledge.

Preface

Alison Feit

The headline of the *Jewish Press* on August 10, 2018 stated: "20,000 March for Immorality, Stalwarts Defend Honor of Holy City." It was accompanied by a picture of a large group of men carrying signs. The caption below it states that the protest is against the annual gay pride parade in central Jerusalem (www.jewishpress.com/in-print/e-edition/390536/2018/08/10/). One man holds a sign that reads "Your rainbow-colored balloons are more dangerous to youth with sexual identity confusion than the rockets that fire on us from Gaza! The psychological and bodily damage to youth cannot be repaired!"

Such sentiments are not uncommon. A few weeks ago, Jerusalem's Chief Rabbi Aryeh Stern stated that children raised by gay couples have "strange and unnatural lives" (*The Times of Israel*, July 27, 2018, www.timesofisrael.com/200-rabbis-slam-lgbt-rights-groups-for-aggressive-terror-brainwashing). A letter signed by 200 rabbis in defense of Rabbi Stern claimed that LGBTQ advocates employ "aggressive terror accompanied by nonstop media brainwashing" and turn "perverts into heroes." The Coalition for Jewish Values (CJV), which represents more than 1,000 ultra-Orthodox American rabbis endorsed the letter, solidifying mainstream ultra-Orthodox rabbinic leadership for such rhetoric.

In marked contrast to these ultra-Orthodox positions, some modern Orthodox Jews have begun to grapple with the specific issues facing LGBTQ community members. This has been particularly evident with regard to young adults. JQY (Jewish Queer Youth), a long-standing Orthodox LGBTQ youth organization, achieved the milestone of attaining nearly $100,000 in funding this year. Next month they will open their second "drop-in center" where Orthodox Jewish teens can receive help in navigating the complexities of identifying both as LGBTQ and as an Orthodox Jew. In addition, LBTQ clubs and support groups have opened in several modern Orthodox high schools – referrals for mental health providers for LGBTQ Orthodox Jewish youth have quadrupled since 2014 in this new culture of relative openness.

This marked difference in attitude between ultra-Orthodox and modern Orthodox Jews toward LGBTQ community members has come about quite suddenly. In 2014, when the idea for this book was conceived, the schism within the Orthodox community was not yet visible. At that time, very few modern Orthodox or ultra-Orthodox Jewish communities openly discussed LGBTQ issues. Just a year before the landmark civil rights case of *Obergefell v. Hodges* (in which the Supreme Court of the United States guaranteed the fundamental right to marry for same-sex couples) few synagogues or schools of any religious denomination acknowledged the issues facing the queer community –- acceptance of LGBTQ marriage was *never* considered.

Today's reality is quite different. Increasing legal efforts to eliminate conversion therapy have made it impossible for most Orthodox Jews to envision sexual orientation change as a possible solution to the LGBTQ crisis. A successful law suit against the most widely utilized conversion therapy clinic, JONAH (Jews Offering New Alternatives for Healing), and a subsequent court order for JONAH to cease operations have left Orthodox Jews without a place to send community members who want to change their sexual identities. (Most medical, psychiatric, and psychological associations have also refuted the efficacy of conversion therapy during this same period of time.) In some communities, mounting frustrations have led to a backlash against LGBTQ community members and communal acceptance of unusually vitriolic rhetoric.

More modern communities have begun to adapt to a changing culture that embraces openness towards sexual identities/orientations, and have begun to address the various issues of concern within a religious framework. However, more rigidly traditional communities are experiencing a growing communal anxiety about the inability to find solutions to the LGBTQ "problem," and are experiencing a growing frustration about their inability to rid their communities of things considered antithetical to religious values. A changing legal and cultural landscape, along with mounting scientific evidence that sexual orientation cannot be changed at will, have led many ultra-Orthodox Jews to feel "dis-oriented" themselves. They are quite suddenly faced with a vastly new reality, where same-sex marriage is legal and there is little hope that individuals can conform sexual preferences and identities within long-held beliefs about religious obligations and norms.

This discomfort is evident in other aspects of contemporary life. In the era of "me too," uncomfortable conversations have become increasingly hard to avoid. Communities are forced to deal with many potentially shame-inducing issues such as drug addiction, sexual abuse, eating disorders, and other mental health problems. Although treatment and therapeutic interventions have increased a great deal over the past few years, open conversation about difficult topics is still not culturally accepted within ultra-Orthodox populations. Although sexual orientation has not been considered a mental disorder for more than 40 years, many still conflate queer issues with both mental and moral disease. This book, an edited volume, which represents the different viewpoints of clinicians, theoreticians, and rabbinic and religious leaders, is intended as a resource for those who are navigating the complicated terrain of religious and sexual identities. It is our hope that the many different perspectives and ideas will help in the creation of solutions that do not deny or negate aspects of self, but are, at the same time, also religiously coherent and spiritually meaningful.

Author biographies

Seth Aronson, Psy.D. is Director of Training, Fellow, Training and Supervising Analyst at the William Alanson White Institute. He is (adjunct) Professor at Long Island University, where he teaches child psychopathology and psychotherapy. At Yeshivat Chovevei Torah, as part of the pastoral counseling faculty, he leads process groups for rabbinical students. His publication topics include wearing a yarmulke and working as a psychoanalyst, the analyst's mourning, and analytic supervision. He is the co-editor, with Craig Haen, of the *Handbook of Child and Adolescent Group Therapy*, published by Routledge in 2017. Dr. Aronson is in private practice in New York City.

Benjamin M. Baader, Ph.D. is Associate Professor of History at the University of Manitoba, where he also headed the Judaic Studies Program for some time. He teaches, writes, and lectures on European history, Jewish history, historiography, gender studies, and feminist theory, and much of Baader's work focuses on nineteenth-century German Jewry. Among other publications, Baader is the author of *Gender, Judaism, and Bourgeois Culture in Germany, 1800–1870* (Indiana University Press, 2006), together with Sharon Gillerman and Paul Lerner, co-editor of *Jewish Masculinities: German Jews, Gender, and History* (Indiana University Press, 2012), and most recently guest editor of the special issue of *Journal of Jewish Identities*, vol. 11:1, 2018 on Gender Theory and Theorizing Jewishness.

Mark J. Blechner, Ph.D. is Training and Supervising Analyst at the William Alanson White Institute, and Professor and Supervisor at New York University. He has published four books: *The Mindbrain and Dreams: An Exploration of Dreaming, Thinking and Artistic Creation* (2018), *Sex Changes: Transformations in Society and Psychoanalysis* (2009), *The Dream Frontier* (2001), and *Hope and Mortality* (1997). He is former Editor-in-Chief of the journal *Contemporary Psychoanalysis*.

Elaine Chapnik, J.D. has been involved with organizing LGBT Orthodox communities since 1995 as a founding member of the New York City Orthodykes support group for Orthodox and previously Orthodox, lesbian, bisexual, and transgender women. Elaine sat on the LGBT Committee of the Jewish National Fund. Recently, she was on a national book tour with Miryam Kabakov as the author of the chapter on Jewish law and lesbianism in *Keep Your Wives Away From Them: Orthodox Women, Unorthodox Desires*. She is a graduate of the University of Michigan, where she received a BA in Philosophy and a Juris Doctorate. A member of the New York State Bar, she began her association with Eshel as a pro-bono lawyer, giving advice on various legal issues before becoming a Board member. For the last two decades, she has worked in public health, and is currently working for New York City's municipal hospital system, providing legal expertise on procurement and information technology contracts and managed care reimbursement.

Rabbi Mark Dratch, L.M.S.W. is the Executive Vice President of the Rabbinical Council of America. He was ordained at the Rabbi Isaac Elchanan Theological Seminary of Yeshiva University. He earned a Masters in Jewish Education and an MSW from Yeshiva University. He founded JSafe: The Jewish Institute Supporting an Abuse Free Environment. Rabbi Dratch served as a pulpit rabbi and Instructor of Jewish Thought and Ethics at Yeshiva University.

Jack Drescher, M.D. is a psychiatrist and psychoanalyst in private practice in New York City. He is Clinical Professor of Psychiatry at Columbia University, College of Physicians and Surgeons, and a Faculty Member at Columbia's Center for Psychoanalytic Training and Research and Division of Gender, Sexuality, and Health. He is Adjunct Professor of Psychiatry, New York Medical College, and Clinical Supervisor and Adjunct Professor at New York University's Postdoctoral Program in Psychotherapy and Psychoanalysis. He is a Training and Supervising Analyst at the William Alanson White Institute. Dr. Drescher served on APA's DSM-5 Workgroup on Sexual and Gender Identity Disorders. He serves as a member of the World Health Organization's Working Group on the Classification of Sexual Disorders and Sexual Health addressing sex and gender diagnoses in WHO's forthcoming (2019) revisions of the *International Classification of Diseases* (ICD-11). He served on the Honorary Scientific Committee revising the second edition of the *Psychodynamic Diagnostic Manual* (PDM-2). Dr. Drescher is author of *Psychoanalytic Therapy and the Gay Man* (Routledge) and Emeritus Editor of the *Journal of Gay and Lesbian Mental Health*. He is an expert media spokesperson on issues related to gender and sexuality.

Anne Fausto-Sterling, Ph.D. is the Nancy Duke Lewis Professor Emerita of Biology and Gender Studies in the Department of Molecular and Cell Biology and Biochemistry at Brown University, and founder and former director of the Science and Technology Studies Program at Brown University. The author of three books that are referenced widely in feminist and scientific inquiry and over 60 scholarly articles, she is also a Fellow of the American Association for the Advancement of Science. She is currently focused on applying dynamic systems theory to the study of gender differentiation in early childhood. Her ambition is to restructure dichotomous conversations in order to enable an understanding of the inseparability of nature/nurture. She asserts that dynamic systems theory permits us to understand how cultural difference becomes bodily difference. Dr. Fausto-Sterling regularly writes blog posts for the *Boston Review, The Huffington Post*, and *Psychology Today*.

Alison Feit, Ph.D. teaches at Stony Brook University, St. Louis Psychoanalytic Institute, and the China American Psychoanalytic Alliance. She is an associate editor of the journal *Contemporary Psychoanalysis* and a member of the Artist Group, the Sexual Abuse Service, and the Trauma Service at the William Alanson White Institute in New York.

Her most recent work appears in R. Gartner's *Trauma and Counter-trauma, Resilience and Counterresilience: Insights from Psychoanalysts and Trauma Experts* (2016) and R. C. Curtis' *Psychoanalytic Case Studies from an Interpersonal–Relational Perspective* (2018). She maintains a private practice in Manhattan.

Michelle Friedman, M.D. is a psychiatrist and psychoanalyst in private practice, the chair of Pastoral Counseling at Yeshivat Chovevei Torah Rabbinical School (YCT), and Associate Professor of Psychiatry at the Icahn School of Medicine at Mount Sinai Hospital in New York City. A graduate of Barnard College, NYU School of Medicine, and the Columbia University Center for Psychoanalytic Study and Research, Dr. Friedman has been involved in bridging religious life and mental health issues for over 30 years. She has spearheaded educational initiatives on a variety of topics, including religious identity, postpartum depression, and sexuality. In 1998 Dr. Friedman was invited to develop a pastoral counseling curriculum for YCT in order to prepare modern Orthodox rabbis to meet the challenges of contemporary community leadership. Her recent book, *The Art of Jewish Pastoral Counseling: A Guide for All Faiths*, co-authored with Dr. Rachel Yehuda and published by Routledge, comes out of her teaching experience and her ongoing contact with graduates of YCT and other rabbinical seminaries.

Rabbi Steven Greenberg received his BA in philosophy from Yeshiva University and his rabbinical ordination from Rabbi Isaac Elchanan Theological Seminary. He is a faculty member of the Shalom Hartman Institute of North America and a Senior Teaching Fellow at the National Jewish Center for Learning and Leadership. Rabbi Greenberg is a founder of the Jerusalem Open House, Jerusalem's first gay and lesbian community center, advancing the cause of social tolerance in the Holy City. In 2001 he appeared in "Trembling Before G-d," a documentary about gay and lesbian Orthodox Jews, and joined the film-maker, Sandi DuBowski, carrying the film across the globe as a tool for dialogue in 500 post-screening dialogues. He is the author of the award-winning book, *Wrestling with God and Men: Homosexuality in the Jewish Tradition* (University of Wisconsin Press) for which he won the Koret Jewish Book Award for Philosophy and

Thought in 2005. Rabbi Greenberg is currently the Founding Director of Eshel, an Orthodox LGBT community support, education, and advocacy organization. He lives with his partner Steven Goldstein and daughter Amalia in Boston.

Hillel Gray, Ph.D. received his Masters in Theological Studies (MTS) from the Harvard Divinity School and his PhD in Religion (History of Judaism) from the University of Chicago. His focus was on Jewish bioethics. He is currently a Lecturer with the Department of Comparative Religion and Coordinator of the Jewish Studies Program at the Miami University of Ohio.

Miryam Kabakov, LCSW is the Executive Director and a founding board member of Eshel, an organization that supports and advocates for LGBTQ Orthodox individuals and their families. Before being a leader at Eshel, Kabakov was the New York and National Program Director of AVODAH: The Jewish Service Corps, Director of LGBT programming at the JCC Manhattan, social worker at West Side Federation for Senior and Supportive Housing, and the first social worker at Footsteps. Miryam attended the Ramaz Upper School, Stern College for Women, and received her Masters' degree in social work from the Wurzweiler School of Social Work. She also received certification in a fundraising program from the University of St. Thomas, in program evaluation at the University of Washington, and from the Institute for Informal Jewish Education at Brandeis University. She founded the New York Orthodykes, a support group for lesbian, bisexual, and transgender Orthodox women, and is the editor of *Keep Your Wives Away From Them: Orthodox Women, Unorthodox Desires* (North Atlantic Books, 2010), a collection of writings about the challenges and joys of LGBT Orthodox Jews and winner of the Golden Crown Literary Award.

Joy Ladin, Ph.D., the first openly transgender employee of an Orthodox Jewish institution, is the author of *The Soul of the Stranger: God and Torah from a Transgender Perspective*, due out in 2018 from Brandeis University Press. Her memoir, *Through the Door of Life: A Jewish Journey Between Genders*, was a 2012 National Jewish Book Award finalist. She has also published nine books of poetry, including

Lambda Literary Award finalists *Impersonation* and *Transmigration*. Her work has been recognized with a National Endowment of the Arts Fellowship and a Fulbright Scholarship, among other honors. She holds the Gottesman Chair in English at Yeshiva University.

Ronnie Lesser, Ph.D. is a psychoanalyst in private practice in Lyme, NH and Norwich, VT. With Thomas Domenici, PhD she co-edited *Disorienting Sexuality: Psychoanalytic Reappraisals of Sexual Identities* (Routledge, 1995), and with Erica Schoenberg, PhD she co-edited *That Obscure Subject of Desire* (Routledge, 1999). Dr. Lesser is a graduate of the NYU Postdoctoral Program in Psychoanalysis and Psychotherapy. She has written on the subject of psychoanalytic theory and lesbian desire.

Jeremy Novich, Psy.D. is a licensed clinical psychologist in private practice in New York City. He earned his doctorate from Long Island University, Post Campus, and completed a postdoctoral fellowship at Stevens Institute of Technology. Dr. Novich has worked on LGBTQ concerns as a clinician, researcher, and community educator. In addition to his clinical work relating to sexuality, identity, and LGBTQ issues, Dr. Novich specializes in harm reduction psychotherapy for substance use. He can be contacted through his website: www.jeremynovichpsyd.com.

Oriol Poveda, Ph.D. is originally from Barcelona, Spain. In 2017 he obtained his PhD in sociology of religion at Uppsala University, Sweden. His doctoral thesis was the first study of the intersection of gender and religion in the lives of transgender Jews with an Orthodox background. His dissertation is titled: "According to whose will: The entanglements of gender and religion in the lives of transgender Jews with an Orthodox background." Since 2015 Dr. Poveda has been working for Paideia, the European Institute of Jewish Studies in Sweden, in one of its educational programs.

Rabbi Hyim Shafner, L.C.S.W. is the Rabbi of Kesher Israel: The Georgetown Synagogue, in Washington, DC. Previously he served as rabbi of Bais Abraham Congregation in St. Louis, Missouri, as rabbi of the Hillel at Washington University in St. Louis, and as the rabbi of India for the American Jewish Joint Distribution Committee. He has rabbinical ordination, an MSW in social work, and an MA in Jewish philosophy, from Yeshiva University. Rabbi Shafner holds a Certificate in Advanced Psychodynamic Psychotherapy from the St. Louis Psychoanalytic Institute. He is the author of the *Everything Jewish Wedding Book* (2008), a founding writer of *Morethodoxy*, and a periodic contributor to the *Journal of Jewish Ideas and Ideals*.

Alan Slomowitz, Ph.D. is a supervisor of psychotherapy and on the faculty at the William Alanson White Institute. Dr. Slomowitz edited the book *Interpersonal Psychoanalysis and the Enigma of Consciousness* (2018) with Dr. Edgar Levenson, and the new release of Dr. Levenson's book *The Purloined Self* (2016). He is on the Editorial Board of *Contemporary Psychoanalysis*, and internet editor of the Contemporary Psychoanalysis in Action blog. Dr. Slomowitz is in private practice in psychoanalysis and psychotherapy in New York City.

Section I

Sexual identity, psychoanalysis, and traditional Judaism

Preface to Section I
Moving the conversation along

Jack Drescher

LGBTQ Orthodox Jews are coming out of their closets. Once invisible, or simply relegated to the status of oxymoron, their lives were revealed in Sandi Dubowski's poignant 2001 documentary, "Trembling Before G-d." *Trembling*, as the film came to be known, was seen by millions of Jews and non-Jews around the world. The film portrayed the conflicting desires of *frum* gay men and lesbians attempting to reconcile devotion to cherished traditions with a modern gay identity. Having cast off invisibility and broken the silence, the film (and the internet) allowed hidden Orthodox LGBTQ Jews around the world to find each other.

One day they found me as well. Although raised in a kosher Jewish home in which my mother lit *shabbat* candles, we were not *shomer shabbos* (as *frum* Jews were called back then). I attended Orthodox *Talmud Torah*, learned to *daven*, entered Bible contests, sang songs, and earned academic accolades. Yet by age fifteen, I was no longer observant. Except for weddings and *bar* and *bat mitzvahs*, I had not attended *shul* for decades.

However, I was writing about treating gay patients with compassion and respect (Drescher, 1997, 1998a, 1998b, 2002). Which is why, in November 2003, I was invited to speak about gay and lesbian psychosocial development and so-called conversion therapies at a secret conference for Orthodox Jewish therapists on Manhattan's Upper West Side. Fifty clinicians from North America and Israel came to learn contemporary scientific thinking about homosexuality. Although historic, the event was not widely publicized. In a process parallel to the subjectivity of closeted LGBTQ Orthodox Jews, the therapists who came feared being shunned by their religious communities if they were outed for doing so.

The conference began with introductions. As they proceeded, I felt out of place. I could not stop thinking about my father, a Polish Jewish Holocaust survivor who had died only a few months earlier. Was my being here a sign? Was this God's way of reconnecting me to *yiddishkeit* now that one of my most important connections to it was gone? Who knew?[1]

More involvement followed. In 2004, I chaired a symposium at an American Psychiatric Association meeting: "Gay and Lesbian Orthodox Jews: A Primer for Clinicians." In 2008, editing the *Journal of Gay and Lesbian Psychotherapy* (now the *Journal of Gay and Lesbian Mental Health*), I published papers by Orthodox therapists Abba Borowich (2008) and Naomi Mark (2008) about their perspectives on homosexuality and Orthodoxy. Then, in 2011, I was invited to speak at an Eshel *Shabbaton* attended by 150 LGBT Orthodox Jews.[2] In 2017, I was again invited to an Eshel *Shabbaton* organized for the Orthodox parents of LGBT children. In 2015, I spoke at a conference on "Desire, Faith and Psychotherapy: Psychoanalytic Perspectives on Sexual Orientation and Gender Identity in the Orthodox Jewish Community." And now, here I am writing an introductory chapter in a groundbreaking volume on *Conflicting Desires: Psychoanalytic and Rabbinic Discourses on LGBTQ Issues in the Orthodox Jewish Community.*

Reading the chapters in this volume, I recalled my experience at the first *Shabbaton.* The workshops included "Rabbinic Texts on Lesbianism," "Religious Approaches to Gay Relationships," "Gender Identity and Judaism," and "Why did G-d make me gay?" At the time, I was reminded of openly gay and lesbian analysts first coming out in the 1980s and 1990s writing about "traditional" heterosexist, antigay orthodoxies of psychoanalysis (D'Ercole, 1996; Domenici & Lesser, 1995; Drescher, 1998a; Isay, 1989; Lewes, 1988; Magee & Miller, 1997; O'Connor & Ryan, 1993; Schwartz, 1993). I distinctly remember feeling sorry for this generation of Orthodox rabbis, whom I imagined to be totally unprepared to meet with the proud and *frum* LGBTQ men and women who studied and revered the same texts they did.

Much has changed since my early involvement with the *frum* LGBTQ community. At that time, Rabbis routinely referred congregants to conversion therapists to "cure" homosexuality. They wanted to believe pseudo-scientific offerings tailored to their pre-existing prejudices, rather than listen to what science says (Drescher, 2009, 2015). Eventually, rabbis, as they do in other life situations, were asked to approach issues of sexual orientation and gender identity with the knowledge of modern science (Slomowitz & Feit, 2015—reprinted in this volume). They were asked to heed the counsel of mental health organizations warning of the harm of conversion "treatments"

(American Psychiatric Association, 2000, 2009). According to Rabbi Mark Dratch (in this book), "The Rabbinical Council of America [RCA], the leading membership organization of Orthodox rabbis in North America, which once endorsed conversion therapy as a tool to recommend to congregants, is on record for several years now opposing it." However, the RCA's 2011 statement is more nuanced, leaving room for multiple interpretations:

> On the subject of reparative therapy, it is our view that, as Rabbis, we can neither endorse nor reject any therapy or method that is intended to assist those who are struggling with same-sex attraction. We insist, however, that therapy of any type be performed only by licensed, trained practitioners. In addition, we maintain that no individual should be coerced to participate in a therapeutic course with which he or she is acutely uncomfortable.[3]

Although change is happening slowly, it is nevertheless happening. The Orthodox community is now speaking aloud about *frum* LGBTQ people, which is always better than what happened in the past when they only talked about them in condemnatory whispers. As occurred in secular society, open conversations demystify uncomfortable and awkward feelings associated with the subject (Drescher, 2012; Drescher & Byne, 2017a, 2017b). Toward that end, the editors and contributors to this book are to be congratulated for their participation and contributions in moving this important dialogue further along.

Notes

1 Old joke: Why does a Jew answer a question with a question? Answer: Why shouldn't a Jew answer a question with a question? The same joke is told about psychoanalysts.
2 I wrote about this experience on a Psychology Today blog: www.psychology today.com/us/blog/psychoanalysis-30/201102/when-love-fights-faith
3 www.rabbis.org/news/article.cfm?id=105665

References

American Psychiatric Association (2000). Commission on Psychotherapy by Psychiatrists (COPP): Position statement on therapies focused on attempts to change sexual orientation (Reparative or conversion therapies). *American Journal of Psychiatry*, 157:1719–1721.

American Psychological Association. (2009a). *Report of the Task Force on the Appropriate Therapeutic Response to Sexual Orientation*. Washington, DC: American Psychological Association.

Borowich, A. E. (2008). Failed reparative therapy of Orthodox Jewish homosexuals. *Journal of Gay and Lesbian Psychotherapy*, 12(3):167–177.

D'Ercole, A. (1996). Postmodern ideas about gender and sexuality: The lesbian woman redundancy. *Psychoanalysis & Psychotherapy*, 13(2):142–152.

Domenici, T. & Lesser, R. C., eds. (1995). *Disorienting Sexuality: Psychoanalytic Reappraisals of Sexual Identities*. New York, NY: Routledge.

Drescher, J. (1997). From preoedipal to postmodern: Changing psychoanalytic attitudes toward homosexuality. *Gender & Psychoanalysis*, 2(2):203–216.

Drescher, J. (1998a). *Psychoanalytic Therapy and the Gay Man*. New York, NY, London: Routledge.

Drescher, J. (1998b). I'm your handyman: A history of reparative therapies. *Journal of Homosexuality*, 36(1):19–42.

Drescher, J. (2002). Ethical issues in treating gay and lesbian patients. *Psychiatric Clinics North America*, 25(3):605–621.

Drescher, J. (2009). When politics distorts science: What mental health professionals can do. *Journal of Gay & Lesbian Mental Health*, 13:213–226.

Drescher, J. (2012). The removal of homosexuality from the DSM: Its impact on today's marriage equality debate. *Journal of Gay & Lesbian Mental Health*, 16 (2):124–135.

Drescher, J. (2015). Can sexual orientation be changed? *Journal of Gay & Lesbian Mental Health*, 19(1):84–93.

Drescher, J. & Byne, W. (2017a). Homosexuality, gay and lesbian identities, and homosexual behavior. In B.J. Sadock, V.A. Sadock & P. Ruiz, eds. *Kaplan and Sadock's Comprehensive Textbook of Psychiatry* (pp. 1982–2013, 10th edn. Philadelphia, PA: Wolters Kluwer.

Drescher, J. & Byne, W. (2017b). Gender identity, gender variance and gender dysphoria. In B.J. Sadock, V. A. Sadock and P. Ruiz, eds. *Kaplan and Sadock's Comprehensive Textbook of Psychiatry* (pp. 2023–2039, 10th edn). Philadelphia, PA: Wolters Kluwer.

Isay, R. A. (1989). *Being Homosexual: Gay Men and Their Development*. New York, NY: Farrar, Straus & Giroux.

Lewes, K. (1988). *The Psychoanalytic Theory of Male Homosexuality*. New York, NY: Simon & Schuster.

Magee, M. & Miller, D. (1997). *Lesbian Lives: Psychoanalytic Narratives Old and New*. New York, NY: Routledge.

Mark, N. (2008). Identities in conflict: Forging an Orthodox gay identity. *Journal of Gay & Lesbian Mental Health*, 12(3):179–194.

O'Connor, N. & Ryan, J. (1993). *Wild Desires and Mistaken Identities: Lesbianism & Psychoanalysis*. New York, NY: Columbia University.

Schwartz, D. (1993). Heterophilia—The love that dare not speak its aim. *Psychoanalytic Dialogues*, 3:643–652.

Slomowitz, A. & Feit, A. (2015). Does God make referrals? Orthodox Judaism and homosexuality. *Journal of Gay & Lesbian Mental Health*, 19(1):100–111.

Introduction to Section I

Sexual identity, psychoanalysis, and traditional Judaism

Alan Slomowitz

In the opening chapter of this section, originally published as a paper titled "Does God make referrals" (Slomowitz and Feit, 2015), the question is raised: What are the respective roles of the rabbi and the psychotherapist when dealing with LGBTQ members of the Orthodox Jewish community? On a broad level, the expected roles of the Orthodox rabbi include being an expert in deciding Jewish law, giving classes in Jewish law, and, to an increasing extent, providing pastoral counseling to congregants in crisis (see Chapter 5 for a more detailed discussion of rabbinic roles and training). Psychoanalysts are trained to question and clarify and to view different sexual behaviors and identities as normative. Rabbis and psychoanalysts sharply clash when it comes to LGBTQ issues.

The clashes in roles, beliefs, and motivations are highlighted in Chapter 1. In fact, the social landscape has changed even more since the 2015 publication of this paper. Same-sex marriage is now legal in the United States. The social and cultural state of affairs that provided a cultural and legal cover for leaders of the major religious groups to continue their opposition to same-sex couples in their communities, congregations, and schools has disappeared. Jewish schools actively attempt to be sensitive to and accepting of their LGBTQ students. To this end, note the pledge against bullying of LGBTQ students, at Shalhevet High School in California and promoted by Eshel (www.eshelonline.org/pledge).

Nevertheless, even with the cultural and political changes that have occurred I believe we still face the quintessential psychoanalytic question: "What is going on around here?" We may have rational theories of why Orthodox Judaism denies the reality of its LGBTQ members even as it proclaims to accept them (a contradiction that is explicated in

Chapter 1): theories include essentialist thinking, God ordained binary identities, and sin as pathology; each appears to make "sense" when seen through the lens of traditional rabbinic interpretations of biblical injunctions and Orthodox Judaism. We also have counter-arguments why these laws may have been promulgated when they were (see below).

We cannot escape the millennia of cultural and legal influences and rulings. Many find it difficult or impossible to escape the literal wordings of biblical injunctions forbidding same sex sexual acts. We could look to Mary Douglas, the renowned anthropologist, who writes in *Leviticus as Literature* (2009, p. 236): "These laws are about defilement by idolatry." The laws listed in Chapters 18 and 20 of Leviticus are not about everyday affairs or guidance about marriage; they are about the defilements associated with idol worship. They appear more to do with sexual acts, such as homosexual acts, associated with temple prostitution. The idea of homosexuality as a condition of person was not envisaged (Douglas, 2009, p. 238). Douglas states that punishment for homosexual acts is the same as for adultery. She writes: "no one who would tolerate an adulterer in the community would be able consistently to persecute a homosexual" (Douglas, 2009, p. 239). Her point of view seems sensible and rational. Nevertheless, we (even today) cannot escape the long-held religious (and cultural) views that non-heterosexual sexual activity and/ or orientation or gender identity is wrong and sinful if not pathological.

The above example, a sensible attempt to "explain away" the prohibitions, may still miss the point for today's LGBTQ Orthodox Jew. The attempts at tolerance are not fully accepted and incorporated into current Jewish law. They miss the point because it is still considered news when an Orthodox Jewish community recognizes its LGBTQ members or organizes a conference devoted to the LGBTQ community. One such conference was held in Efrat, Israel on June 3, 2018 (Video interview, in Hebrew, about the conference: www.facebook.com/story.php?story_fbi d=2164483720449200&id=2137029799861259&refsrc=https%3A%2F% 2Fm.facebook.com%2F2137029799861259%2Fvideos% 2Fvb.2137029799861259%2F2164483720449200%2F). It is still front-page news, for example, when the grandson of the late Sephardi chief rabbi of Israel, Rabbi Ovadia Yosef, publicly announces he is gay and marries his boyfriend (www.timesofisrael.com/grandson-of-former-israeli-chief-rabbi-to-marry-boyfriend/?utm_source=The±Times±of

±Israel±Daily±Edition&utm_campaign=3e9f85869e-EMAIL_CAM
PAIGN_2018_06_02_11_24&utm_medium=email&utm_term=0_adb46
cec92-3e9f85869e-55284201). It is still considered newsworthy when
Rabbi Michael Moskowitz, a rabbi ordained by the ultra-Orthodox
yeshiva in Lakewood, becomes a rabbi in the oldest LGBTQ synagogue,
Congregation Bet Simchat Torah, in New York City (http://jewishweek.
timesofisrael.com/this-orthodox-rabbi-just-took-a-job-at-an-lgbt-
synagogue).

Perhaps Tamar Ross, a noted Orthodox Jewish feminist scholar,
provides a Jewish legal beginning for the rabbinic and LGBTQ community. She delivered an important speech at the JOFA (Jewish Orthodox
Feminist Alliance) conference in NYC in 2016 (T. Ross, 2016, personal
communication) and published an important chapter in Jewish law:
"Halakha contextualized: The Halakhic Status of homosexuals as a test
case" (Ross, 2016, in Hebrew) about homosexuality from an Orthodox
legal and philosophical perspective. Ross lays out the legal parameters of
the debate about homosexuality and explains that, although Orthodox
rabbis use many classical Jewish legal strategies to limit the severity of
laws, such as the distinction between sexual orientation and sexual
activity, they still work from a biased perspective. She highlights this
especially with regard to feminist issues, such as the *Augunah* (the
chained or abandoned wife) issue (only the man may initiate the divorce
in Jewish law), when the rabbis say "Oh, nothing we can do." So
Orthodox feminists need to be sensitive to excluded groups, such as the
LGBTQ community. What Ross explains is that at its core the challenges
of accepting LGBTQ members cannot be viewed only through the lens
of *halakha* (Jewish law).

Ross (T. Ross, 2016, JOFA speech, personal communication) notes
that the ongoing relative success of, what she calls, the "learning
revolution" of Orthodox women and their increasing entrée into positions of leadership and authority in Jewish legal decision-making, as
well as growing acceptance of single motherhood, cannot be explained
as based on any formal rabbinic authority or rulings. This success
appears more likely based on the growing disparity between the
women's equality in general society and their secondary status in
Jewish tradition. Her conclusion is that *halakhic* tradition is not passive.
Even the language of biblical texts undergoes reinterpretations.

One of her conclusions is that *halakhic* tradition is not always internally consistent or monolithic. She writes "halakha sometimes allows for a variety of positions to exist side by side in self-conscious and contentious disagreement." I interpret her conclusion from a psychoanalytic perspective: How to create a dialogue of dissociated (opposing points of view) self-states? For example, a rabbi is confronted with an allegiance to a "self" that believes in unbending application of objective *halakha*, and, at the same time, a self that is committed to be a father who loves his son dearly, though his son is in love with his study partner. This rabbi/father is forced into a confrontation: the clash between his Jewish legal self and his personal truth father self.

Ross (T. Ross, 2016, JOFA speech, personal communication) writes that, given today's cultural changes, rabbis must address questions that apply not only to an individual's private life but also to dilemmas that hold in the public sphere and the community at large. She believes that the status of the LBGTQ Orthodox community will not be settled by *halakhic* fiats and rulings. In her opinion, what will settle these debates will be the:

> degree to which the new understanding of homosexuality (and I would add all LGBTQ members) and its revolutionary implications can be absorbed by mainstream Orthodoxy, aided and abetted at least in part by insights that stem from joint experience shared halakhic space.
>
> (pp. 11–12).

She continues: "more fluid views of the male–female divide, calls for a less binary approach in the theological realm as well, one that will soften the divide between human insights and divine command." Ross concludes with an important statement:

> in a dynamic and fluid age such as ours, religious feminists might argue that it is precisely the intensification of negotiation between formal considerations of text and precedent, the predispositions of traditional poskim (religious decisors) regarding the nature of truth and justice, and the demands that come up from the field that is the best guarantee of worthy pesika (religious decision making).[1]
>
> (pp. 13–14).

I believe that Ross's words implicitly ask the psychoanalytic question: "What is going on around here?" The conscious, explicit, rabbinic self-state cannot see or experience the questions and answers as anything other than "strict halakha." They miss, as described above, the lived experiences of the LGBTQ members of their own community. The chapters in this section, as you will see below, attempt to bridge the dissociative gap in unique and creative ways. Bromberg (2011), in *Shrinking the Tsunami*, gives important advice. He writes that the process (in analysis) of collision and negotiation is about developing the capacity to move from experiencing the other as an object to control, or be controlled by, to be able to play with each other, to experience each other as a subject. Although Bromberg is writing of the analytic relationship, what he says feels especially valuable for us as we engage with chapters in this book.

Mark Blechner's chapter (Chapter 2) highlights the "collateral damage" of forcing Orthodox Jewish gay men to live secret and closeted lives. Blechner, a training and supervising analyst at the William Alanson White Institute, shares his insight based on his decades-long clinical and supervisory experiences working with the LGBTQ community. He writes about a family man who believed he had banished his "gay me" forever. He had indeed banished that part of him to a "not-me," a state that cannot be, but somehow still is. And once his last child leaves home a change occurs and the disavowed not-me collides with his "Orthodox straight husband/father me." And the collision proves disastrous for him and his family. Thus, this man's journey from consciously gay to disavowing gayness and taking on a pseudo-identity, and then back to gay seriously damaged not only his life but his entire family. The other part of this is the family and community believing this man cannot be gay, because there aren't any gay women or men among us. Furthermore, his wife seamlessly participated in the dissociation because (as Levenson explained) he was not who she wanted or expected him to be. Yet, despite Blechner's negative clinical experiences, he points out the growing possibilities of being gay and Orthodox. He expresses hope in his chapter. Still, the questions remain unanswered.

Ronnie Lesser, a psychoanalyst in private practice who writes about psychoanalytic theory and lesbian desire contributes an important critique (Chapter 3) of Chapter 1. She criticizes our use of self-states to reassure the Orthodox gay person when she or he is in synagogue or at home. I think she perceptively catches our own enactment here, doing what we claim we are trying not to do: banish the person's gay identity from the synagogue and religious ritual. Ross's views would appear to coincide with Lesser's views, and are further reiterated in Chapter 8 (see more below) which addresses that very issue. Rabbi Greenberg is transforming Orthodox ritual and enriching Orthodox Judaism as Lesser poignantly demands.

There is change occurring within the mainstream Orthodox Jewish community. The articles from rabbinical thinkers point to a continued shift toward acceptance of personal truth that cannot be hidden from sight. In this way the LGBTQ community is being seen and not being made to disappear. Rabbi Mark Dratch, the executive director of the largest organization of Orthodox American rabbis (Rabbinical Council of America) describes (in Chapter 4) the inherent difficulties rabbinic leaders face in attempting to change Jewish law, especially with regard to what are determined to be biblical injunctions. However, Rabbi Dratch writes, change and acceptance are occurring within the community. The change is slow and uneven and clearly for many not enough. Rabbi Dratch also explains that, in Jewish legal theory, change is quite slow and even the change we note today may be considered rapid. Dratch's chapter (Chapter 4) at least implicitly agrees with Ross's point of view. Change in *halakha* is not even or consistent, and is responsive to changing cultural views.

However, I believe our distinction between the different self-states an Orthodox gay man might experience when in synagogue or yeshiva, on the one hand, and with his male partner, covertly, on the other, most likely capture a lived reality among closeted Orthodox gay men. This may be both consciously experienced as well as strongly dissociated. This is highlighted in a study by Kissil and Itzhaky (2015, p. 385): "The participants expressed a strong sense of duality in their relationship with the community." They did show an appreciation and love of the stable and consistent community providing for many of their religious and personal needs. They also simultaneously experienced "a sense of pending doom, of possible persecution and intense fear of losing their world by being excommunicated if their sexual identity was revealed" (Kissil and Itzhaky, 2015, p. 385). They recommend we keep the conversation alive as part of the gradual process of acceptance and find ways that enable these gay men to remain in the only world they have ever known.

An equally important issue involves the lack of training or under-standing of sexuality and gender among religious leaders. These (mostly male) congregational, educational, and *halakhic* (Jewish legal scholars) leaders are expected to counsel pastorally as well as make Jewish legal judgments, even as they lack a basic understanding of gay identity, gay relationships, gay sexual activity, or the changing culture that influences many of the younger congregants – the children, the parents, and their extended families. Michelle Friedman identifies an important group, a forgotten cohort of older gay men and women, who grew up during the 1960s to 1990s. Gay Orthodox Jewish life (as much of gay life in the US) had to be lived underground, in fear and self-loathing. They lived in fear of being "outed" in a community that did not believe they actually existed, as well as in fear of infection with HIV/AIDS. These gay men and women were at multiple disadvantages, because they could not turn to their traditional sources of advice and knowledge: their rabbis and educators. Many did not know where or to whom to turn to obtain even basic sexual, medical information and treatment.

Friedman (in Chapter 5) creates and provides important advice with real-world scenarios that Orthodox rabbinic and educational leaders face regarding sexual orientation and identity. She addresses, in clear and practical terms, how a rabbi meeting with his gay congregant and family must be aware of his own reactions and feelings to the people in his office, to his stated allegiance to his Orthodox teachings, and to his congregations and group membership in an Orthodox rabbinic organiza-tion that holds power over his career and livelihood.

Jeremy Novich's chapter (Chapter 6) is a summary of his doctoral dissertation (Novich, 2014). Novich's dissertation is one of the few academic studies of gay Orthodox men and an important contribution to our understanding of them. His chapter brings the struggles of gay Orthodox men to the foreground and provides important practical clin-ical advice for therapists. Novich points out the communal and cultural pressures that influence gay Orthodox men to dissociate their sadness and depression over their non-acceptance within the community and the potentially negative impacts on their families of origin (loss of marriage prospects for other siblings, ostracism of parents). They dissociate the self that feels "this can't be me" causing all these problems. How could that be possible? Chapter 6 is a warning to clinicians to inquire carefully and in detail what is going on in their Orthodox gay patient's life that even the therapist perhaps cannot see?

Miryam Kabakov, Executive Director and a founding board member of Eshel, an organization that supports and advocates for LGBTQ Orthodox individuals and their families, eloquently explains (in Chapter 7) the impact on parents when their children come out as gay or transgender. As mothers and fathers, they want to protect their children and keep them close. As members of Orthodox Jewish communities they also face the challenge and dilemma of "coming out" and then potentially facing, in partnership with their children, ostracism from communities who have had little if any education on sexuality and gender, and from their religious and educational leaders as well.

Rabbi Steven Greenberg, founding director and head of Eshel, the organization dedicated to providing support for LGBTQ Orthodox individuals and their families, highlights the type of change that is occurring. His chapter (Chapter 8) lays out the structure for a *halakhically* (Jewish legally) binding gay marriage ceremony. Drawing on biblical and rabbinic sources Rabbi Greenberg integrates them in a unique and scholarly text that creates a meaningful and legally binding, Orthodox Jewish wedding ceremony. Rabbi Greenberg's innovative chapter demonstrates the power of combining classic rabbinic thinking with the power of integrating culture and real people's desires and needs. Dissociation is not required.

Elaine Chapnik, an attorney, addresses the issues (in Chapter 9) from a different perspective. She too underwent the "historical dissociation" that Jewish lesbians did not exist. As readers may notice, although there are only a few academic studies of Orthodox gay men, there are perhaps none of Orthodox lesbian women. Chapnik's chapter is a detailed *halakhic* study of the laws of women's sexual behavior. Through her analysis of rabbinic laws and guidelines about female same-sex sexual behavior, she demonstrates the historical presence and communal knowledge, in the Orthodox Jewish community, of lesbian women and their sexuality from Talmudic times onwards. These were women living in plain sight. However, over the centuries these women and their identities became the "not-me" of Orthodox Jewish communities. It took 1,000 years for these women to be rediscovered and written about. Although Orthodox lesbians disagree with the laws, their very existence establishes their lesbian existence and their influence on their communities.

As I write in the Preface, my goals for this collection are for the reader to engage with chapters in authentic dialogue, to connect as closely as possible with the content, the author, and the points of view, even if they radically disagree with the reader's own. I believe we will all benefit from such an engagement.

Note

1 Current research shows much more sexual fluidity than previously recognized. See Savin-Williams (2017) in his recent book, *Mostly Straight: Sexual Fluidity among Men*. This updates previous research that claimed women were more likely to be sexually fluid than men (Diamond, 2008).

References

Bromberg, P., (2011), *In the Shadow of the Tsunami* (pp. 17–18). Hove and New York: Routledge.

Diamond, L., (2008). *Sexual Fluidity: Understanding Women's Love and Desire*. Cambridge and London: Harvard University Press.

Douglas, Mary, (2009). *Leviticus as literature*. Oxford and New York: Oxford University Press.

Edelstein. (2013). http://nleresources.com/2013/05/a-traditional-jewish-approach-to-homosexuality/#.WxqhSi-ZNo4

Kissil, K, and Itzhaky, H. (2015). Experiences of the orthodox gay community among orthodox Jewish gay men. *Journal of Gay and Lesbian Social Services*, 27:371–389.

Novich, J. (2014). The experiences of gay Jewish men in the orthodox community: Social justice, oppression and Winnicott. Doctor of Psychology Dissertation, Long Island University.

Ross, T. (2016). Halakha contextualized: The Halakhic status of homosexuals as a test case. In A. Rosenak (ed.), *The Halakhah as Event* (pp 375–430, Hebrew). Jerusalem: Van Leer Institute.

Savin-Williams, R. C., (2017). *Mostly Straight: Sexual Fluidity among Men*. Cambridge and London: Harvard University Press.

Slomowitz, A. & Feit, A., (2015). Does God make referrals: Orthodox Judaism and homosexuality. *Journal of Gay & Lesbian Mental Health*, 19(1):100–111.

Does God make referrals?

Orthodox Judaism and homosexuality

Alan Slomowitz and Alison Feit

An Orthodox Jewish man walks into his rabbi's office and says: "Rabbi, I seem to be only attracted to other men. This is prohibited! What should I do?" The rabbi says "What? Do I look like a therapist? Hold on, I've got Dr. Goldstein on speed dial."

Although not the best of jokes, this vignette illustrates an interesting phenomenon about Orthodox Jewish life and its relationship to the mental health field. It asks its audience to ponder some serious questions: Why does the man want to talk to his rabbi about being gay? Is it a problem? Whose problem is it? His or the rabbi's? What is it that he hopes to gain from such a conversation? What is it that the rabbi feels unequipped to say? What does he hope Dr. Goldstein will offer? And why is Goldstein on the rabbi's speed dial? In short: What is the role of a psychotherapist when dealing with homosexuality and men and women with same-sex feelings and attractions in the Orthodox Jewish community?

Mental health resources are not uncommon in Orthodox Jewish communities. Organizations such as Ohel, Relief, and The Jewish Board of Family and Children Services are several among many that specialize in providing mental health services to the Orthodox community. Most Orthodox groups are not closed off to advances in science and health-care. In medical, financial, and political areas, Orthodox Jews are generally encouraged to engage with secular cultural expertise (Soloveitchik, 1964). This is true across the spectrum from modern Orthodox through ultra-Orthodox populations. Orthodox rabbinic medical ethics are usually rooted in the most contemporary findings in science and research. Jewish law as to what is and is not permitted takes on a technical/legalistic nature and application once scientific authority and clinical best practices have been established. This is true of many medical and ethical decisions such as end-of-life decisions surrounding brain death and organ donations, where Orthodox Jewish law must be integrated with the latest medical knowledge (Tendler, 1990).

In contrast, controversial psychological–cultural issues within the Orthodox community that have to do with mental health have become major points of disagreement and opprobrium when it comes to diagnosis and treatment. This is most notable with regard to homosexuality and the concept of sexual orientation.

The joke at the beginning of this chapter points to a serious question in contemporary Orthodox Jewish society: What are the clinical and cultural meanings of a referral from a member of the clergy to a clinician? This issue is not only about treating a perceived "illness" but also potentially preventing a sin.

For sexual orientation issues, clinicians used to have a clear-cut answer for Jewish Orthodoxy. Until 1973, homosexuality was considered a mental disorder (Bayer, 1987), so the rabbi (and his congregant) could both conceptualize being gay as a "disease," and the referral was simply to a doctor who could provide a "cure." In other words, the cultures of Orthodox Judaism and official mental health practice were aligned. But for the past 40 years this has not been the case. In the differing views of the ultra- and modern-Orthodox communities, although over the past 10–15 years the cultural divide has both widened and narrowed, the impact of this divide is still significant. Although Orthodox Jewish culture has continued in its opposition to open expressions of homosexuality, it has also split into two divergent paths within Orthodoxy. The ultra-Orthodox point of view maintains that not only is homosexuality a forbidden practice, but the concept of identifying as gay or homosexual is also not recognized. Believing oneself to have a gay sexual orientation is regarded as a false, willful, and rebellious act. As Rabbi Avraham Edelstein (2013), an ultra-Orthodox rabbi puts it: "Judaism is opposed to defining people as gay . . .. There is, in fact, no word in Judaism for a gay person per se . . .. Judaism doesn't define people based on sexual desire." In essence, gays do not or cannot exist in Rabbi Edelstein's brand of Judaism. There are homosexual actions that are forbidden, but the possibility or concept of a homosexual identity or orientation does not exist in the ultra-Orthodox community.[1]

However, there is a modern Orthodox viewpoint, as represented by Rabbi Yuval Sherlo,[2] which does not see things in the same way. The culture of the modern Orthodox community has shifted in the past two decades and offers the potential for dialogue and engagement. For example, Schweidel (2006) explains that, although Rabbi Sherlo believes homosexual activity is strictly forbidden and that there is no way for Orthodox Jewish law to permit such practices, Sherlo also maintains that a person who identifies as homosexual cannot and should not be excluded from the community and the synagogue. He can be a fully functioning member of the synagogue. Sherlo is one among many modern Orthodox rabbis who recognize the existence of a gay identity and the conflict experienced by gay men and women between their sexual orientation and Jewish law.

Despite the growing internal cultural conflicts within the Orthodox Jewish community, both of these religious viewpoints conflict with current mental health understanding. Contemporary mental health professionals are trained to accept a wide variety of sexual orientations and desires. In contrast, Orthodox Jewry consults such professionals for a "solution to the homosexual problem" and continues to believe that this solution is found in the world of mental health.

The most recent iteration of this conflict surrounds sexual conversion "therapies" and whether they are valid, effective, or ethical.[3] Despite the growing body of literature that argues against any scientific validity for the efficacy of sexual orientation conversion efforts (SOCEs)[4] and the position statements of both the American Psychological Association (2009)[5] and the American Psychiatric Association (2000) that such treatments don't work, the rabbinic world has continued to support these types of therapies as the solution for "the gay problem" (Torah Declaration, 2011). For the ultra-Orthodox, this is consistent with their viewpoint that there is no underlying sexual orientation that needs changing. Their only measure of cure is the cessation of any homosexual acts. If there are "therapies" that can stop such activities, they are considered to be successful and ethical.

Although a referral to a mental health professional may be helpful, if suggested in an empathic and nonstigmatizing fashion, the often unstated (and perhaps unconscious) wish within the Orthodox community is that whatever magic therapists pull off in helping with self-esteem, family issues, personality issues, eating disorders, and drug addictions can and should be accomplished with regard to unacceptable homosexual behavior. The implicit request made of the clinician is, however, to stop the unacceptable desire itself. That is, if a patient wants it enough and a clinician is talented enough, perhaps a queer cure of biblical proportions can be performed.

Does "fluid" sexuality imply an ability to "change" or "choose" sexuality?

The Orthodox point of view is an essentialist one with regard to gender and sexuality. It is captured by Englander and Sagi's (2013) recent book, *New Religious-Zionist Discourse on Body and Sexuality.*[6] The majority Orthodox Jewish point of view believes in a particular God-given essentialist core identity that is either male or female. This essentialism is also exemplified by another ultra-Orthodox rabbi, Rabbi Aharon Feldman (2012). Feldman writes about drives and bodily desires (think Freudian Id) that try to overcome the soul (think Freudian Ego). According to Feldman, it is critical that one become Other-centered and not Self-centered, and the reproductive drive is the most powerful determinant of this process. Only if the reproductive drive is used to effect a sexual relationship between a man and a woman can the person become Other-centered and therefore "healthy." Any other sexual relationship, such as between same-sex couples cannot be Other-centered, is unhealthy, sinful, and therefore cannot exist or be tolerated.

The ultra-Orthodox community believes that, as male and female are different biologically, they must be different cognitively and emotionally. According to this viewpoint, humans who act or feel differently from this way of being are by definition violating their "true" self and role in the world. Any attempt to legitimize a different role identity, such as a gay identity, is not only going against this essentialist philosophy but is also seen as a purposeful act of sin.

Many decades of research have made it clear that some individuals vary a great deal in the potential fluidity of their sexual attractions. There are also gender differences in such fluidity as well, because at least some women experience a greater variety in their sexual attraction to others over their lifespan than men (Diamond, 2009). Yet the implications of this research are not immediately clear. Should an Orthodox therapist focus on sexual conversion in therapy for female patients to a greater degree than when treating male patients? Are reported changes of sexual behavior or attractions of either gender merely a function of "wishful thinking" on the part of both the patient and the clinician? At this moment in psychological research and practice, these questions have no clear answers. In contemporary life, this uncertainty has led to a strange fusion of mental health and religious authority structures.

There does appear to be significant confusion within the modern Orthodox world about sexual orientation and the potential to change it. Even those who attempt to write about this topic in a factual, sensitive, and caring manner express views that demonstrate a certain lack of clarity and understanding. Debow (2012), an Orthodox clinical psychologist who trained at Bar Ilan University in Israel, wrote one of the best English language books on the Orthodox approach to sexuality. *Talking About Sexual Intimacy: A Guide for Orthodox Jewish Parents* addresses its subject within the normative conversations that Orthodox Jewish parents have with their children. Yet when attempting to answer the question, "Can people learn not to be homosexual?," even Debow gets caught up in the current religious climate of obfuscation around clinical efforts to change sexual orientation. At one point she states that conversion therapies are highly controversial in the academic field and that there are few long-term successes (Debow, 2012, p. 237). A few lines later she notes, "on the other hand, there are a number of religious organizations (Jewish and Christian) that offer conversion therapies ... who claim to have much success" (Debow, 2012, p. 237). Debow does not attempt to make sense of this current state of affairs. It is easy to see how a parent who turns to this book for a definitive view about how to help their child might come away confused.[7]

It is easy to understand why such puzzlement occurs. If some people are sexually "fluid" then why can't they be helped to "swim" towards the heterosexual end of the swimming pool? Diamond (2009, pp. 252–253) attempts to explain how such fluidity does not imply that SOCEs can actually change sexual orientation. She quotes Beckstead's (2006, pp. 75–81) research:

at the end of therapy, they could still be aroused erotically by the body shape of same-sex individuals …. Participants reported that therapy helped them change their thinking about and expression of homosexuality and sexuality but not their actual sexual orientation.

Diamond explains that "sexual fluidity does not imply individuals can mold either their sexuality or someone else's into a pattern of their choosing. Variability does not equal choice …" (Diamond, 2009, p. 15). It is precisely this understanding of the complexity of same-sex and other-sex sexuality that is lacking in both ultra- and modern-Orthodox Jewish culture. It has led to the misguided push towards trying to change anyone who wishes to, despite the small odds of change for most people.

The clinical conundrum

To return to the question about the referral by an Orthodox rabbi of a lesbian, gay, bisexual, transgender, and queer (LGBTQ) person to a therapist, what is the implicit meaning in making such a referral? That the person is not normal? After all, heterosexual people are not referred to therapy because they are straight. Or perhaps there is something about not only the sinful nature of homosexuality itself, but also a person who might identify as "gay" that leads to a referral? Such an identity would be viewed as either defining oneself as a nonentity that cannot exist or as a member of a group to be either pitied or, at best, treated with compassion but looked upon as inferior and troubled.

In contrast, would this rabbi make a mental health referral if a straight person came to him and disclosed he was experiencing strong sexual attractions to married women – which is also a "sin?" Would a referral be made if this man came to him and said he wanted to marry a non-Jewish woman? Would he prefer this man marry a non-Jewish woman rather than a Jewish man? In any of these other cases would the rabbi speed dial Dr. Goldstein?[8] What about other sins? Are we living in an age where therapy is seen as a first-line tool in combatting the *yetzer harah* (literally translated as the evil inclination, the religious equivalent to the Freudian Id)? If so, where will this all lead? Rabbis suggesting mental health counseling for the Orthodox Jew who has trouble keeping kosher and is compulsively drawn to McDonald's double cheeseburgers?

Given the above, there is concern that clinicians may not question the Rabbi's implied assumption that an Orthodox Jew who is interested in others of the same sex has "something to work out." Does the Orthodox clinician unconsciously buy in to the notion that, on some level, a gay person is unwell, both spiritually and psychologically? An individual can have psychological difficulty reconciling a gay identity within the Orthodox Jewish lifestyle and feel anxious or depressed as a result (perhaps this is best seen as some type of social trauma), but not necessarily because there is something inherently mentally disordered about that attraction. Anxiety or depression around sexual orientation can be a good reason to seek treatment but perhaps a particular person is not emotionally troubled by their sexual desires. Is it ethically possible to treat a gay man referred by an Orthodox rabbi who believes the goal of therapy is sexual behavior or orientation change? What obligations do clinicians have and how will these differences affect the way a treatment is conducted?

Bridging "incommensurable" differences

In an effort to grapple with these questions and find some common cultural ground, certain aspects of psychoanalytic theory and praxis may be helpful. Edgar Levenson (1988) attempts to highlight and struggle with a parallel problem in psychoanalytic theory: two psychoanalytic perspectives that each purport to explain human motivation. He noted this problem in reference to questions where each psychoanalytic perspective establishes a different order and each ideological framework claims to explain everything. He uses the term "incommensurable" to describe worldviews that rest on fundamentally different *a priori* assumptions and offer two paradigmatically different views of the world. For Levenson, conflict has always been the nature of human discourse. This concept is well known to Jewish thought and learning as well as to psychoanalysis.[9] Levenson's problem of "incommensurability" has been intrinsic to discussions within psychoanalysis for decades, because there are many psychoanalytic models that attempt to explain all of human experience to the exclusion of any other psychoanalytic model. Greenberg and Mitchell (1983) draw attention to this psychoanalytic problem in their side-by-side comparison of many psychoanalytic theories. Mitchell (1988) later wrote that:

> the history of psychoanalytic ideas has developed not smoothly and linearly but in jumps and lurches in a dialectical field of conceptual possibilities created by sets of polarized concepts: fantasy/reality, insight/relationship, conflict/developmental arrest, oedipal/preoedipal, and intrapsychic/interpersonal. They arise as dichotomies ....
>
> (p. 494).

For Levenson and Mitchell, conflicts are mainly expressed in theory and not always in practice. For the Orthodox Jewish clinician, the conflict about homosexuality is intensely fundamental. One side sees homosexuality as a problem in itself and the other does not. It is a dichotomy between illness and health, virtue and sin. The binary essentialism of this Orthodox Jewish point of view may make it difficult, if not impossible, to acknowledge a competing theory of mind and being that might lead to a plurality of orthodoxies (as oxymoronic as that may sound). Can radically different perspectives be viewed through the lens of complementary views of a common experience? Or are Orthodox Jewish clinicians trapped within a never-ending battle for an essential truth that will always prove to be elusive?

Nevertheless, change is occurring. The change going on within Orthodox Judaism is most likely happening out of the community's conscious awareness. Although there are innate aspects to human development, according to contemporary interpersonal and relational psychoanalytic theory, individuals cannot help but be influenced and changed by the culture around them. Even the most insular groups of Orthodox Jews are not immune to outside influence. In this context, Orthodox Jewry will need contemporary, new, and different ways to formulate categories of illness and health, as well as virtue and sin. One cannot predict how Orthodox Judaism will resolve these apparently incommensurable conflicts, although the following is a potential opening through which one might begin.

One way of opening discussion is to consider the problems a person who identifies as an Orthodox Jewish gay person might face. Rather than seeing a gay orientation as an internal battle of Superego versus Id, contemporary psychoanalysts view individuals as composed of many shifting self-states, which leave room for the individual to have wholly elaborated emotional lives with different states of experience that might be quite disconnected from one another. As Bromberg (1998, 2011) notes:

> a noticeable shift has been taking place with regard to psycho-analytic understanding of the human mind … towards a view of the self as decentered, and of the mind as a configuration of shifting, nonlinear, discontinuous states of consciousness in an ongoing dialectic with the healthy illusion of unitary selfhood.
>
> (Bromberg, 2011, p. 270).

Stern (2010, p. 139) writes "the mind is therefore theorized not as a vertical organization of consciousness and unconsciousness, but as a horizontally organized collection of self-states, states of being, or states of mind, each in dynamic relation to the others." Through these lenses, Orthodox Jewry could have a different perspective on understanding human experience. The Orthodox community may need to acknowledge that thoughts, feelings, and behaviors that interfere with their traditional framework often occur out of awareness and cannot be looked at by the community itself. The key process active in this theory of mind is dissociation, a kind of splitting of the mind (Sullivan, 1956).

Such conceptions of the way the mind works can lead to important steps in understanding the Orthodox Jewish gay experience and the Orthodox rabbinic understanding of such experiences. For example, if such an individual is in synagogue and his emotional and spiritual core are engaged, part of him is fulfilled, yet the parts of him that are focused around gay identity are less accessible, because there is little space for such self-reflection in a religious environment. However, if the same person is at an LGBTQ event on a Friday night, part of him may be engaged and feel at home with similarly identified peers, but other parts of himself and his religious experience may not be fully available to conscious thought and experience. Similarly, Rabbi Sherlo's attempts at engaging the Orthodox gay individual as he is and accepting his identity as well as welcoming him into the synagogue demonstrates a less binary and more nuanced grasp of what an embodied gay person experiences as opposed to a disembodied concept of how one ought to be.

Stern (2010, p. 140) notes that some self-states are bearable but uncomfortable (e.g., one is able to admit that one is envious or competitive with others). These states of mind may not be "fun" but they are tolerable. Drawing on the work of Sullivan (1953), he calls such states "bad me." However, there are states of mind that cannot be tolerated; these are dissociated and cannot be "experienced simultaneously" and "remain sequestered from the others." These states of mind are experienced as alien to the individual and are defined as "not-me." It is these "not-me" parts of self that are defended against actively and unconsciously and remain what Stern calls "unformulated." These feelings cannot be experienced as one's own without severe psychic consequences.

Such is the state of mind of many young Orthodox individuals at the cusp of marriage who cannot bear to formulate the hazy sexualized attraction to same-sex others because the notion of "being homosexual" is so horrific, so "not-me" that it cannot be tolerated. In a broader cultural framework, it is this cultural dissociation that led to an "anti-internet" rally attended by more than 60,000 people, which was sold out to ultra-Orthodox communities, yet was sponsored by an internet company where most of the attendees used their smartphones during the event.

In terms of same-sex attraction, in Rabbis Feldman and Edelstein's world, the gay person is a "not-me," an intolerable impossibility. In Rabbi Sherlo's world, a gay identity approaches a "bad-me," a state that at least can be acknowledged and articulated. Although the mental health community may not agree with such a conception, at least it becomes possible to discuss and formulate the different viewpoints across the divide.

One may now circle back to the young Orthodox man in the rabbi's office where Dr. Goldstein is on speed dial. Through a contemporary psychoanalytic lens it would appear that both the young man and the rabbi are mutually enacting and dissociating what for them is an unbearable and intolerable experience: the possibility that there is anything normal or acceptable about the congregant's same-sex attraction. It must therefore be conceptualized as a sign of illness, a status of "not-me." The notion that an essential queerness is not something to be cured and may be lived with is simply unbearable in this context.

Because the biblical prohibition is so direct (it is written twice, called an abomination, and in the second reference a heavenly death penalty is decreed), this attraction must be completely contrary to nature and one's being. It quite literally cannot be me. And so it must remain dissociated and unformulated.

However as culture changes, these not-me states are increasingly difficult to keep unformulated. This might be a stretch of Stern's concepts, but no person in today's electronically connected culture (no matter how many times the rabbis try to ban the internet) is completely removed from queer culture. It is becoming increasingly difficult to keep a powerful attraction such as sexuality from remaining unformulated. The enactments will multiply and the rabbis, along with their followers will have no choice but to face what was relegated to the not-me and somehow come to terms with, at the very least, the bad-me.

One might be pessimistic and say, "Yes this change may well occur, but it could take two or three generations." The authors are certainly not prophets (nor do they wish to be) but change today occurs so quickly that it truly is impossible to predict either the timeframe or the actual nature of the change. A recent article by Lefkowitz (2014) demonstrates how significantly many people within the Orthodox community are already changing. Lefkowitz appears, from his stated practice, to be an Orthodox Jew. Yet he also states that he is not certain of the divine authorship of the commandments, and is willing to pick and choose from the menu of Jewish rituals he will observe, without fear of divine retribution. He is not only comfortable with but clearly supports the accommodation of gay and lesbian students in day schools. As he states, he is not alone. Change is occurring. The challenges, however, are still there. The fractures in the Orthodox community are real and are not diminishing.

As psychoanalysts who are identified with the Orthodox Jewish community we need to be acutely aware of implied messages about referrals around gay or queer issues. If we allow ourselves to be open to and search for the potential not-me (in ourselves and our patients) that cannot be acknowledged, such as the sexual identity and orientation that by its definition appears to be beyond the pale, then we can begin to explore and address the "unbearableness" of the state. The challenge is to allow these various self-states, some contradictory and incommensurable, to exist, to come into conflict, and thus into our awareness. This will allow us to make whatever choices make sense with a fuller sense of whom we are. And yes, one choice may well be to call Dr. Goldstein.

Acknowledgments

The authors want to thank Jack Drescher, MD, and Mordechai Levovitz, LMSW, for their thoughtful and important advice as well as their careful reading of our chapter.

Notes

1 This is similar to the beliefs of many conservative Christian communities in the Southern Baptist and Evangelical traditions.
2 Rabbi Sherlo is the head of an Israeli yeshiva and is a member of the Israel National Board of Medical Ethics.
3 See also Drescher (1998, 2002) and Shidlo, Schroeder and Drescher (2002).
4 Sometimes known as "conversion therapy" or "reparative therapy."
5 Also in Glassgold et al. (2009).
6 There they quote two similar viewpoints (translation ours): "Basically, naturally and normally, there is no reason that a man and woman would want to sit next to each for even one minute, because their basic nature is so essentially different from each other. They are two types that are so different essentially, intrinsically and self-interests …. They have no choice but …. It is actually more natural that a man would want to build his life with his male friends and the woman would want to build her life with her female friends" (p. 120). Also: "A man and woman are two different types of creations, not only physiologically but also spiritually and mentally ….. The most logical we can be is to warn the woman that there are areas which are limited for her, she will not succeed in them" (p. 122).
7 A similarly mixed message is conveyed when Debow (2012, p. 245) writes about dealing with children who have come out to their parents. She says that people with a homosexual orientation are by Jewish law exempt from the commandment to get married and be fruitful and multiply. But in the next paragraph she writes: "Any homosexual who seeks to enter into a marriage with a member of the other gender is halakhically (legally) required to fully inform the potential spouse of his sexual orientation. Parents should be fully supportive and encouraging of these behaviors."
8 Even if the answer is yes, the questions we just posed are really not as parallel as they might first appear for two reasons: (1) sexual identity and attraction patterns

are core aspects of self and (2) there is not an implied "mental illness" component to the other referrals.
9 Psychoanalysis has sometimes been referred to disparagingly as "the Jewish science."

References

American Psychiatric Association. (2000). Therapies focused on attempts to change sexual orientation (reparative or conversion therapies) position statement. Retrieved from http://web.archive.org/web/20110407082738/ and www.psyc.org/Departments/EDU/Library/APAOfficialDocumentsandRelated/PositionStat-ements/200001.aspx

American Psychological Association. (2009). *Report of the Task Force on the Appropriate Therapeutic Response to Sexual Orientation.* Washington, DC: American Psychological Association.

Bayer, R. (1987). *Homosexuality and American Psychiatry: The Politics of Diagnosis.* Princeton, NJ: Princeton University Press.

Beckstead, A. L. (2006). Understanding the self-reports of reparative therapy "successes". In J. Drescher & K. J. Zucker (eds.), *Ex-Gay Research: Analyzing the Spitzer Study and It Relation to Science, Religion, Politics, and Culture* (pp. 75–81). Binghamton, NY: Haworth Press.

Bromberg, P. M. (1998). *Standing in the Spaces: Essays in Clinical Process, Trauma and Dissociation.* New York, NY: Psychology Press.

Debow, Y. (2012). *Talking about Intimacy and Sexuality: A Guide for Orthodox Parents.* Jersey City, NJ: Ktav Publishing House.

Diamond, L. M. (2009). *Sexual Fluidity: Understanding Women's Love and Desire.* Cambridge, MA: Harvard University Press.

Drescher, J. (1998). *Psychoanalytic Therapy and the Gay Man.* Hillsdale, NJ: The Analytic Press.

Drescher, J. (2002). Causes and becauses: On etiological theories of homosexuality. *Annals of Psychoanalysis*, 30:57–68.

Edelstein, A. (2013). A traditional Jewish approach to homosexuality. Retrieved from http://nleresources.com/2013/05/a-traditional-jewish-approach-to-homosexuality

Englander, Y. & Sagi, A. (2013). *New Religious–Zionist Discourse on Body and Sexuality.* Jerusalem: Shalom Hartman Institute.

Feldman, A. (2012, Fall). A Torah view of homosexuality. *Dialogue*, 3:9–23.

Glassgold, J. I., Beckstead, J., Drescher, J., Greene, B., Lin Miller, R., Worthington, R.L., & Anderson, C. W. (2009). Report of the American Psychological

Association task force on appropriate therapeutic responses to sexual orientation. Retrieved from www.apa.org/pi/lgbt/resources/therapeutic-response.pdf

Greenberg, J. A., & Mitchell, S. A. (1983). *Object Relations in Psychoanalytic Theory*. Cambridge, MA: Harvard University Press.

Lefkowitz, J. (2014). The rise of social orthodoxy: A personal account. *Commentary*, 137(4):37–42.

Levenson, E. (1988). Real frogs in imaginary gardens: Facts and fantasies in psycho-analysis. *Psychoanalytic Inquiry*, 8:552–567.

Mitchell, S. A. (1988). The intrapsychic and the interpersonal: Different theories, different domains, or historical artifacts? *Psychoanalytic Inquiry*, 8:472–496.

Schweidel, Z. (2006). On the place of religious homosexuals and lesbians in the religious community. *Akdamot*, 29:85–114 (Hebrew).

Shidlo, A., Schroeder, M., & Drescher, J. (2002). *Sexual Conversion Therapy: Ethical, Clinical and Research Perspectives*. Boca Raton, FL: CRC Press.

Soloveitchik, J. B. (1964). Confrontation. *Tradition: A Journal of Orthodox Thought*, 6(2):5–29.

Stern, D. B. (2010). *Partners in Thought*. New York, NY: Routledge.

Sullivan, H. S. (1953). *The Interpersonal Theory of Psychiatry*. New York, NY: Norton.

Sullivan, H. S. (1956). *Clinical Studies in Psychiatry*. New York, NY: Norton.

Tendler, M. (1990). Halakhic death means brain death. *The Jewish Review*, 3(3):6–7.

Torah Declaration. (2011). Declaration on the Torah approach to homosexuality. Retrieved from www.TorahDec.org

Chapter 2

Collateral damage in the battle to change sexual orientation[1]

Mark J. Blechner

Drs. Slomowitz and Feit have described some of the problems of the relationship of Orthodox Judaism, homosexuality, and psychotherapy. I would like to expand on what they have so ably outlined.

First I would like to bring to your attention the notion of collateral damage, a term that most of us have learned from news reports. Collateral damage is frequently used as a military term, meaning the destruction of innocent lives as the result of their being near to someone who has been targeted. As a euphemism, it allows the military to describe the murder of innocent people with a term that sounds neutral, avoiding the normal human reaction of horror.

Attempts to convert homosexuals to heterosexuals must be considered in light of the collateral damage that they cause; they destroy not just the lives of the men subjected to such treatment, but the lives of their wives and children. In order to illustrate this process, I am going to tell you about one of my patients, a man whom I will call Yossi.

Yossi came to me when he was 55 years old. He knew he was primarily attracted to men from his early teen years. He had one very close male friend through college whom he loved, but the friend was straight and didn't return the romantic feeling. Thus Yossi never had a single sexual experience with another man leading to orgasm. Then, at the age of 25, Yossi met Chana. They spent a lot of time together and were the best of friends. Yossi told Chana he was gay. Then Yossi began psychotherapy with Dr. Avram, a psychoanalyst. Dr. Avram suggested that Yossi should marry Chana. He would have a much happier life that way; after all, he wasn't having any meaningful romantic relationships with men, and he and Chana enjoyed each other's company. Yossi told Chana that he was no longer gay. They started dating and married. They had three children, whom they raised in a stable home. The children developed well and went off to college.

It looked fine to all the world. Yossi developed a public identity as a stable married man, a good father, and a successful professional. In the literature on sexual orientation-change therapy, Yossi would probably be counted among the "rare long-term success stories" that Debow (2012) discusses.[2] But inside, Yossi was burning. He worked in a school with young adults, some of whom he found very attractive. He fantasized about them often, although he never acted on these desires.

Finally, when Yossi was 53, his last child went off to college. Faced with the "empty nest," he snapped. His true sexual desires, banished for so long to the not-me, rushed into his consciousness like a tidal wave. He felt tremendously sad that he had never lived out his sexuality. He told his wife that he was gay. She was furious and told him to move out immediately. He was surprised at her fury; after all, hadn't he told her in the beginning that he was gay? But hadn't he also told her that he had changed? Such is the power of dissociation that they both could claim to be shocked, surprised, and hurt by the other's reaction. In a way, both were innocent of wrong-doing – they both had the best intentions, but were innocent victims of the pressures of society, religion, and an old-school psychotherapist.

Yossi came to me for a consultation. He was severely depressed and anxious, and was troubled about Dr. Avram. He alternately spoke highly of Dr. Avram as a "good man" but was also furious that he did not try to help him work out his conflicts about his sexuality; instead, Dr. Avram pushed Yossi to suppress his homosexuality and falsely promised him that his life would be better. Yossi was in agony, his wife was miserable, and the children were confused and angry. They felt that their upbringing was filled with fakery and falsehood, and questioned their relationships with their parents and their own confused identifications.

Now here is the trouble: Dr. Avram probably thought, and may still think, that he successfully converted Yossi to heterosexuality and might tell people that it can be done. He may never hear about the long-term disastrous consequences of his treatment approach. Neither Yossi nor Chana is likely to let him know.

In the 40 years I have been in practice, I have seen many patients like Yossi. In the 1980s and 1990s, their numbers peaked, and I thought that, maybe, with more accepting attitudes toward homosexuality, such cases would disappear. Men who were primarily attracted to other men would not be encouraged to marry women, and then come to severely regret that choice, causing havoc in the lives of their wives and children. So I hoped; but I continue to see such men in psychotherapy, right up to the present day, who seek to undo the damage done to them by conversion therapy. They know they cannot undo the past, but can they have hope for the future? And how are they to live with their guilt towards their wives and children (J. Isay, 2014)?

Yossi's story captures the question of the stance of Orthodox Judaism toward homosexuality, and its interaction with psychotherapy. You may be able to get some men with a bisexual potential to have sexual intercourse with a woman; some combination of urging and subtle pressure can have an effect. I have heard of therapists who also suggest to their gay patients that they fantasize about an attractive man while in bed with their wives, and some men are able to achieve an erection in this way in order to impregnate their wives. But is this success? Enough pressure and encouragement may get the man to marry and have intercourse with his wife, but the homo-sexual desires do not go away, and the marriage becomes a ticking time bomb. So the question of "conversion therapy" must be considered in the total context of the family. If you manage to get someone like Yossi to marry and have children, you are not just harming him. You are harming his wife terribly. Think about what it means to be such a woman, married to a man who is not really attracted to her, who needs to think about another man while making love to her. This, to me, is an abomination. Is this a fate you would like for your daughter?

Think about what it is like to be a son or daughter growing up in such a family. You realize that your parents' marriage was a sham. You feel shame and confusion. Can you ever trust someone in a romantic relationship?

There is another kind of collateral damage, a danger to society. Yossi has sworn to me that he has never acted on his sexual attraction to the young men in his school, but he knows other men in his situation who do. They use their positions of power to seduce their younger students (Neustein & Lesher, 2008; Satlow, 1994). I want to make clear that most of these men are not intrinsic pedophiles (Gartner, 1999). If they were allowed to have a decent romantic relationship, there is no reason to think that they would ever abuse a student. There is no inherent connection between homosexuality and pedophilia. However, there is a connection between sexual frustration and impulsive sexual behavior. Jewish law recognizes this; a heterosexual man, single or married, is barred by Jewish law from being alone with a woman who is not his wife, and yet a gay man, who is barred from sexual satisfaction, is freely subjected to temptation. It is an impossible situation.

Thus, if you consider homosexuality a sin, you must balance your attitude toward that sin by considering that a futile attempt to "cure" that sin leads to other, perhaps worse sins – severely damaging the life of an innocent woman and her children, and also potentiating the problem of sexual molestation of young men.

There is also the danger of suicide. Orthodox Jewish men who recognize that they are gay, yet fear the condemnation of their family and community, can become severely depressed and have a high risk of suicide. A meta-analysis of data from 25 international studies found that gay and bisexual men were four times more likely to report lifetime suicide attempts than heterosexual men, and lesbian and bisexual women were twice as likely to attempt suicide as heterosexual women (King et al., 2008; Marshall 2016).

There is still one more danger: when Orthodox rabbis condemn gay people, they are exacerbating the risk of those gay people contracting HIV or other sexually transmitted infections. If a young gay man cannot integrate his sexuality into a committed relationship, he is much more likely to have furtive encounters with strangers and risk contracting AIDS. The White Institute ran the first program at a major psychoanalytic institute, dedicated to helping people with AIDS and HIV, and their families and relatives (Blechner, 1997). During the worst years of the epidemic, from 1980 to 1997, we often shared stories of Hassidic and Orthodox Jewish families who had children with AIDS. It was tragic to see them both trying to keep their sons alive and trying to hide the nature of their illness from families and friends. The advent of same-sex marriage has brought the promise that gay men and lesbians can form committed, monogamous relationships that are recognized, blessed, and supported by their families and communities, and this can have beneficial effects not just on their mental health, but on their physical survival as well.

I describe one other case with a somewhat different collateral damage. Shimon was an 18-year-old Jewish man who realized in college that he was in love with his best friend, Chayim, who also felt same-sex desire.

They spent all their time together and were delighted in each other's presence. Chayim was happy to continue the relationship, but Shimon felt tremendous guilt, so he sought psychoanalysis with Dr. Binyamin. Dr. Binyanim had been trained in psychoanalytic self-psychology, and thought that homosexual feelings were "disintegration products" of an inadequate self-structure (Kohut, 1977). He used his influence to push Shimon to explore a heterosexual relationship. Shimon found Leah, who was Chayim's cousin. He started to date her, and she fell in love with him. He never stopped seeing Chayim and started to panic. He broke up with Leah, who was very upset and did not understand why he left her so suddenly. Meanwhile, Dr. Binyamin continued to interpret Shimon's actions in self-psychology terms and pushed Shimon to go back to Leah. Shimon did so and continued to date Leah for another five months. Again, he panicked and broke up with her. This time, Leah was devastated. She attempted suicide and was sent to a psychiatric hospital. Chayim was put off by what Shimon did and stopped talking to him. All three were traumatized, and Shimon stopped his psychoanalytic treatment.

Shimon felt that Dr. Binyamin had acted unethically. He felt that, in his pursuit of changing Shimon's sexual orientation, he had ignored the terrible damage inflicted on Leah, who nearly died, and on the lives of Shimon and Chayim. About twenty years later, Shimon saw Dr. Binyamin on the street and ran to speak to him about what had happened. Dr. Binyamin jumped into a cab and sped off.

I am not a theologian, but I have a religious question for our rabbis. If enforcement of one Jewish law leads to the breaking of another Jewish law, how do you decide which one to enforce? I think this is a basic question behind the religious view of homosexuality. If you manage to push a gay man into marrying a woman, but, in doing so, you seriously damage the lives of his wife, children, and the man himself, is that the right way to go? You may accept that, according to the Torah (Bible), male homosexuality is a sin, or at least anal intercourse between men is a sin, which was Rashi's interpretation. But if enforcement of the ban on homosexuality causes suicides, misery, and physical illness, should you still enforce the ban? We know that the Torah says the Sabbath must be kept; yet if a man is sick, a doctor is permitted to break the laws of the Sabbath to save the life of the sick man. Shouldn't we be able to modify edicts about sexuality to save lives? It is the principle of *pikuach nefesh*. Lives can be saved; and we must balance the modification of some laws to save lives.

Also relevant is the principle of *kevod habriyot*, the dignity of the individual. Rabbi Eliezer Waldenberg, the well-known expert on medical matters and Jewish law, held that some rules of the Sabbath could be modified under the principle of *kevod habriyot*. For example, a nearly deaf person may carry a hearing aid on Shabbat, so that he will not in any way be demeaned in his own eyes or the eyes of others. Rabbi Waldenberg wrote in *Tzitz Eliezer*: "there is no concern about *kevod ha-beriyot* greater than the one that arises in connection with ensuring that a deaf person does not suffer embarrassment because of being unable to hear what people say to him." I would say, "*kal vachomer*," all the more so. If you can adjust the Sabbath to prevent humiliation to a deaf person, would you not adjust *halakha* (Jewish law) to avoid not only humiliating a gay person, but depriving him of many of the basic joys of life?[3]

These are religious questions, but the rabbinic decisions about these matters can be affected by the rabbi's psychology, and here psycho-analysis has a potentially major contribution to make. Psychoanalysis is the science of the irrational. It is the task of psychoanalysis to identify and analyze the irrationality of religious leaders in relation to homosexuality.

There are at least two factors: one is that rabbis are more inclined to be lenient toward situations that are likely to apply to themselves and their relatives. They allow breaking the Sabbath for someone who is hearing impaired because they know many people who are hearing impaired, and there is a good chance that they will become hearing impaired themselves if they live long enough. Because, until recently, most gay Orthodox Jews kept their homosexuality hidden, the rabbis mistakenly believed that there weren't many gay people in their communities. Today we know that 5–10% of all people are gay, no matter what their religion, ethnicity, or nationality.

A second factor is disgust (Blechner, 2009, 2016a, 2016b). Many heterosexual men, rabbis included, feel dread and disgust about male homosexuality. Is it that they fear the security of their own masculinity? Is it disgust about anything they feel compromises male privilege? Is it disgust on a more visceral, bodily level about certain sexual acts? There is much to be discovered here.

The combination of selective empathy and unconscious disgust may lead to skewed religious decisions. It is not only Jewish clergy who have these unconscious psychodynamics; they probably extend to many, if not all, religious decision-makers. For example, Catholic clergy have dismissed many Old Testament laws: their parishioners may eat pig and the men do not need to be circumcised. Yet, when it comes to the Old Testament ban on male homosexuality, the Catholics say: "Oh, that law we will retain."

As trying to change one's sexual orientation or gender identity has so many severe consequences, in terms of mental and physical health, it is especially important for Jews to reconsider laws related to sex and gender, and make sure that excessive hurt and humiliation are avoided. So let us consider the bans on same-sex relations in the Bible. *Leviticus* 18:22 says: "Thou shalt not lie with mankind, as with womankind: it is abomination."

Notice that this refers to men having sex with men. There is no overt reference to women lying with womankind. In case you think this is an oversight, look at the next verse in *Leviticus*, 18:23: "Neither shalt thou lie with any beast to defile thyself therewith: neither shall any woman stand before a beast to lie down thereto: it is confusion."

So when it comes to having sex with animals, men are forbidden, but so, too, are women. One must conclude that when the Bible means to include women, it does so. Same-sex sexuality between women is not mentioned in the Hebrew Bible.

Apparently, rabbis (in the *Sifra*, an early rabbinic commentary on the book of *Leviticus*) banned lesbian sex on the grounds of the verse, in *Leviticus* 18:3, that prohibits what are called Egyptian and Canaanite practices: "After the doings of the land of Egypt, wherein ye dwelt, shall ye not do; and after the doings of the land of Canaan, whither I bring you, shall ye not do; neither shall ye walk in their statutes." This is a thin basis on which to ban lesbianism, considering the serious consequences of banning lesbian sex on the mental health of lesbian women. It needs to be reconsidered.

Similarly, with transgender individuals, the attitude of many rabbis is based more on prejudice than deep knowledge. I have consulted with Orthodox Jews who feel they are transgender. When they consulted a rabbi, they were almost always told to stick to their own gender and overcome their feelings. As with overcoming same-sex attraction, we know that ignoring transgender feelings doesn't work, and can lead to severe depression and suicide. But, also, there are discussions in the Jewish Talmud about the tumtum and the androgyne, people with mixed genitalia or ambiguous genitalia. These passages are surprisingly open-minded and should be related to the understanding of transgender people and other atypical gender identities. The forward-thinking Rabbi Eliezer Waldenberg not only has thought through the implications of sex-reassignment surgery for Jewish law (*halakha*), but has written new prayers for transgender people.[4]

In summary, religious decision-making needs to be examined for its unconscious determinants. Prejudice needs to be replaced with knowledge. This was something we learned during the difficult history of gays and lesbians in relation to psychoanalysis, which has some striking parallels to the relationship between gays and lesbians in Orthodox Judaism today. Fifty years ago, psychiatry and psychoanalysis considered homosexuality to be a diagnosable disease. The psychoanalytic writings about homosexuality from that era were filled with falsehoods and prejudicial pronouncements that said more about the psychology of the homophobic psychoanalysts than about the gays and lesbians they were describing (Blechner, 1992, 1995, 2008).

If you were gay and you wanted to train as a clinician at that time, you either had to hide your sexuality or give up being trained at any of the most reputable institutions. You were not eligible and not wanted, no matter how skilled you were. Those in power attempted to cut out gays and lesbians from the psychiatric community.

Nevertheless, gay men and lesbians in mental health banded together. Many of us developed our identities as clinicians of integrity, even if we were told it could not be so. We formed organizations of fellow clinicians, did research, shared our strategies for how to understand prejudice psychologically and combat it, and developed our own unique kinds of clinical expertise, not just about homosexuality itself, but about many clinical issues. We formed study groups to support each other and share our insights, so that we could learn from our experience and contribute back to the psychoanalytic world (R. Isay, 1991; Lesser, 1992; Schwartz, 1992; Trop & Stolorow, 1992; Schaffner, 1995; Vaughan, 2015).

Eventually, the psychoanalytic establishment saw what we had to offer and changed their minds. They welcomed us into their institutes, appointed us to their faculties, invited us to speak on issues on which we had developed expertise, published us in their journals, and asked us to edit their journals. We went from being outcasts to being pillars in the psychoanalytic community.

Today, one can see a similar movement developing among gay and lesbian Orthodox Jews. It is thrilling how the younger generation is breaking the bounds set by the older generation (Shilo et al., 2016). The younger generation is not accepting the rules of the elders, that homosexuality is a sin, that they must suppress it or give it up in order to retain their participation in religious community and family life. "No," they are saying:

> We will form our own groups, our own families, our own *minyanim* (prayer groups) and synagogues, and our own social organizations. We will live as open gays and lesbians in committed couples with a rich religious, social, and family life. We will form study groups where we can learn together and work out our own understandings and modifications of Jewish law. If existing organizations of Orthodox Judaism will not embrace us, then we will take Orthodox Judaism for ourselves; we will create our own Orthodox Judaism, where we can feel welcome, and develop lives of religious and ethical integrity.

The list of such organizations is large – I will mention just a few. In the United States, there are:

Eshel, an organization to create community and acceptance for LGBT Jews and their families in Orthodox communities;

Jewish Queer Youth (JQY);

Orthogays;

Orthodykes;

GLYDSA, the Gay and Lesbian Yeshiva and Day School Alumni Association;

Keshet, which works for the full equality and inclusion of lesbian, gay, bisexual, and transgender Jews in Jewish life;

the *Dina Listserv* for Orthodox and formerly Orthodox transsexuals;

Tirzah, a community of *frum* (pious) queer women;

Temicha, an online support group for Orthodox Jewish parents of gay children;

Or Chayim, an independent monthly *minyan* (prayer group) in New York for Orthodox lesbian, gay, bisexual, and transgender Jews.

In Israel, there are other organizations:

Bat Kol, for Orthodox gay women;
Chavruta, for Orthodox gay men;
The Pride Minyan, a prayer group for Tel Aviv's Orthodox LGBT community;
And the website *Homo'im Datim*, religious gays.

This is the way for the future. When the psychoanalytic establishment at first rejected gay and lesbian analysts, we worked to develop ourselves independently until they recognized what we had to offer them and welcomed us. I predict that the same thing will happen for Orthodox Jews who are gay, lesbian, bisexual, and transgender. LGBT Jewish scholars will reexamine, in the most precise way, the religious understanding of same-sex feelings and behavior, and atypical gender identities. LGBT Orthodox Jews will reformulate religion and will make Orthodox Judaism richer and more welcoming to many minorities. They will not judge others so quickly without first examining their own sins in being judgmental. Already, the congregation Beit Simchat Torah in New York, although not Orthodox, has been a pathbreaker. It is the only major congregation in Manhattan I know of that does not charge admission to High Holiday services. Because of this, more than 3,000 people attend their Kol Nidre service – many of them heterosexuals who cannot afford to pay to pray. In this way, the LGBT community has created an innovation in synagogue practice that is a shining example for all Jews.

The messiah is not an individual being who will come once and for all to fix our world. Every one of us has a little bit of the messiah in us, and it is our task in life to realize that small bit of messianic revelation to the world (Ross, 2004). LGBT Orthodox Jews need to stop being supplicants to the prejudices of the old establishment, and need to recognize what they have to offer Judaism. They need to be trailblazers who show the way for Orthodox Jews to widen their humanity, embrace the variety that God created, and help each person develop his or her integrity, and ability to love and contribute to society. In this way, LGBT Jews will make the organizations of Orthodox Judaism not just better for themselves, but better for everyone.

Notes

1 Earlier versions of this chapter were delivered at the conference "Desire, Faith and Psychotherapy: A psychoanalytic perspective on gender and sexuality in the Orthodox Jewish community," New York, April 19, 2015, and at the American Psychoanalytic Association, January 20, 2017, New York.
2 Yossi stayed in treatment with Dr. A on and off for most of his marriage, which kept the pressure on him to keep his homosexuality under wraps. This was not uncommon is such treatments. See, for example, R. Isay (2001).
3 On November 29, 2016, the Rabbinical Council of America (2016) passed a resolution demanding that gay people practice "lifelong abstinence as well as the absence of companionate love."
4 For example, according to Tzitz Eliezer (Volume X, Part 25, Chapter 26, Section 6), a transgender man should say the prayer: "Blessed are you, Lord our God, Ruler of the Universe, who has changed me into a man."

References

Blechner, M. (1992) Homophobia in psychoanalytic writing and practice. *Psychoanalytic Dialogues*, 3(4):627–637.

Blechner, M. (1995) The shaping of psychoanalytic theory and practice by cultural and personal biases about sexuality. In: T. Domenici and R. Lesser (eds.), *Disorienting Sexuality* (pp. 265–288). New York, NY: Routledge.

Blechner, M., ed.. (1997) *Hope and Mortality: Psychodynamic Approaches to AIDS and HIV.* Hillsdale, NJ: Analytic Press.

Blechner, M. (2008) Selective inattention and bigotry. *Journal of Gay and Lesbian Mental Health*, 12:195–204.

Blechner, M. (2009) *Sex Changes: Transformations in Society and Psychoanalysis.* New York, NY: Routledge.

Blechner, M. (2016a) Disgust in emotion theory, development, and clinical work. *Psychoanalytic Dialogues*, 26:427–436.

Blechner, M. (2016b) Psychoanalysis and sexual issues. *Contemporary Psychoanalysis*, 52:502–546.

Debow, Y. (2012) *Talking about Intimacy and Sexuality: A Guide for Orthodox Parents.* Jersey City, NJ: Ktav Publishing House.

Gartner, R. (1999) *Betrayed as Boys: Psychodynamic Treatment of Sexually Abused Men.* New York, NY: Guilford Press.

Isay, J. (2014) *Secrets and Lies: Surviving the Truths that Change Our Lives.* New York, NY: Doubleday.

Isay, R. (1991) The homosexual analyst: Clinical considerations. *Psychoanalytic Study of the Child*, 46:199–216.

Isay, R. (2001) Becoming gay: A personal odyssey. *Journal of Gay and Lesbian Psychotherapy,* 5:51–67.

King, M., Semlyen J., Tai S., Killaspy, H., Osborn, D., Popelyuk, D., & Nazareth I. (2008) A systematic review of mental disorder, suicide, and deliberate self harm in lesbian, gay and bisexual people. *BMC Psychiatry,* 8:70.

Kohut, H. (1977) *The Restoration of the Self.* New York, NY: International Universities Press.

Lesser, R. (1992) A reconsideration of homosexual themes: Commentary on Trop and Stolorow's "Defense analysis in self psychology". *Psychoanalytic Dialogues,* 3:639–641.

Marshall, A. (2016) Suicide prevention interventions for sexual and gender minority youth: An unmet need. *Yale Journal of Biological Medicine,* 89(2): 205–213.

Neustein, A. & Lesher, M. (2008) A single-case study of rabbinic sexual abuse in the Orthodox Jewish community. *Journal of Child Sexual Abuse,* 17:270–289.

Rabbinical Council of America (2016) Resolution: Principled and Pastoral Reflections on Sanctity and Sexuality. November 29. www.rabbis.org/resources/

Ross, T. (2004) *Expanding the Palace of Torah: Orthodoxy and Feminism.* Lebanon, NH: Brandeis University Press and University Press of New England.

Satlow, M. (1994) They abused him like a woman: Homoeroticism, gender blurring, and the rabbis in Late Antiquity. *Journal of the History of Sexuality,* 5:1–25.

Schaffner, B. (1995) The difficulty of being a gay psychoanalyst during the last 50 years. In T. Domenici & R. Lesser (eds.), *Disorienting Sexuality*(pp. 243–254). New York, NY: Routledge.

Schwartz, D. (1992) Heterophilia: The love that dare not speak its aim. *Psychoanalytic Dialogues,* 3:643–652.

Shilo, G., Yossef, I., & Savaya, R. (2016) Religious coping strategies and mental health among religious Jewish gay and bisexual men. *Archives of Sexual Behavior,* 45:1551–1561.

Trop, J. & Stolorow, R. (1992) Defense analysis in self psychology: A developmental view. *Psychoanalytic Dialogues,* 2(4):427–442.

Vaughan, S. (2015) The dignity of one's experience: Dignity and indignity in the lives of LGBT people. In S. Levine (ed.), *Dignity Matters*(pp. 101–117. New York, NY: Routledge.

Chapter 3

Discussion of "Does God make referrals?"

Orthodox Judaism and homosexuality

Ronnie Lesser

When Alan asked me to contribute to this book I turned him down. I was certain I didn't fit in because I'm an atheist who approaches the issue of orthodoxy, in both religion and theory, from a social constructivist perspective. I'm cynical of all claims to Truth, whether they are biblical or scientific. I'm also a lesbian psychoanalyst and have worked with LGBTQ patients who carry deep scars from their encounters with orthodoxy, both religious and psychoanalytic. My anger about my patients' suffering makes me want to strike back. Surely Alan wouldn't want me to write a diatribe against Orthodox Judaism's perspective on homosexuality, I told myself.

After sitting with Alan's offer a little longer, I became intrigued by the challenge; is there a way that I can discuss the Orthodox belief that homosexuality runs counter to religious law and God, and therefore should be prohibited, without being disrespectful? Is there a space from which to speak about two incommensurable ideas without trashing one or the other (see Levenson, 1988, in Chapter 1)?

The question holds particular significance because I write this discussion less than one week before the 2016 Presidential election. During the interminable campaign, the clash between incommensurable perspectives has given rise to vitriolic speech and actions. Simultaneously, western Europe is awash in xenophobia and the rise of right-wing parties, Brexit recently won the referendum in Britain, the civil war in Syria continues unabated, terrorist attacks are frequent and terrifying, and clashes between religions and ethnic groups grip many other regions of the world. It is a frightening, disheartening time to be alive. No leader has emerged with the ability to bridge the chasms that make people hate each other. It seems presumptuous for me to think that I can carve out a space to be respectful of Jewish Orthodoxy's treatment of homosexuality while vehemently disagreeing with it. Does a third space exist anywhere other than on the page in someone's theory?

What is clear to me is that such a space must begin with both sides being willing to listen respectfully and empathize with each other's positions. So let me start by recognizing and respecting the sanctity of the writings in *Leviticus* that regard sex between men as abhorrent. I also understand that homosexuality has been viewed as running counter to the pillars of Jewish society's reproduction and family. It follows that rabbis would both want to follow God's word and ensure the propagation of the Jewish people. For a people who have faced the specter of annihilation throughout their history, ensuring survival must be paramount.

But there are times when flexibility in interpretation of the Bible has to hold sway because it alone ensures survival. I see this as one such time. Orthodox Jews might try to understand that viewing the Bible as a living, breathing instrument that has to adapt and be reinterpreted in different cultural settings doesn't mean destroying it. As Alan and Alison point out, in the age of the internet, young Orthodox Jews are acquainted with the growing acceptance of homosexuality throughout the western world.

And it is here that Orthodoxy runs into a huge problem: the fear that congregants will be contaminated by profane ideas about sexuality that are globally disseminated. In closed societies all over the world governments attempt to lock down access to the internet, fearing the collapse of traditional values and ideas. But we who live in western democracies have the right to freedom of speech. When it comes to homosexuality and Jewish Orthodoxy it is as though rabbis believe that being exposed to gay people and ideas will infect the community and cause its collapse. It's rather comical, in a way, that people are so afraid that there are homosexual impulses in all of us that could come tumbling out that they have to go to such extreme measures to batten down the hatches. I suspect that as homosexuality becomes more accepted more people will try it, but only some will become gay. Whether this is because homosexuality is biological or just speaks to some people more than others, I don't know. I do know that the fear of sexual experimentation and contamination is vastly out of proportion.

As the general population, particularly young people, are already more accepting of homosexuality, I can imagine a time in the (hopefully) not too distant future when some heterosexual and homosexual members of the Orthodox community will protest its prohibition. It would be more honorable if Orthodox rabbis initiate these changes themselves.

The notion of an orthodoxy not keeping up with change gives me a feeling of déjà-vu, because I'm a lesbian psychoanalyst who went into psychoanalytic training in 1991, many years after the American Psychiatric Association (APA) had de-pathologized homosexuality. But psychoanalysis, save for the lone voices of Richard Isay (arguably the first psychoanalyst to come out in a publicized way) and Stephen Mitchell, had not paid attention, so sure were they that they knew the Truth. When I started training at the New York University Postdoctoral Program in Psychoanalysis and Psychotherapy, I sat through classes in which instructors would opine that all homosexuals were sick. I was assigned readings that excoriated gay men. Encouraged and supported by our own psychoanalysts, a group of gay and lesbian candidates began meeting, came out to the postdoc community, and organized a conference. No longer intimidated, we found our voices and gained power. The anti-homosexual tenor in psychoanalytic institutes began to change. How much this had to do with economics (gay and lesbian patients began to insist on seeing gay and lesbian or gay affirmative analysts), changing cultural attitudes toward homosexuality, and/or gay and lesbian activism, is impossible to determine.

Based on my own experiences I would encourage Orthodox clinicians who treat gay and lesbian Orthodox patients to support them in coming out, organizing, and being heard. To this suggestion you might ask, "but aren't clinicians supposed to be neutral?" I believe there is no neutrality when it comes to treating gay and lesbian patients; a clinician sees homosexuality either as a normal variant of human sexuality or as a pathology in need of a cure. You can be sure that your perspective will be communicated to the patient even if you think you're keeping it to yourself. There is no way that a clinician can avoid being political when it comes to this subject.

I feel sympathetic toward Orthodox therapists who are caught between two vastly different paradigms, the Orthodox one that proclaims that homosexuality doesn't exist or is, at best. a pathology and the "new" psychoanalytic one that recognizes sexual diversity as normal. But let me add here that clinicians might consider the biblical injunction to "love thy neighbor as thyself." Enormous suffering is caused by forcing gay and lesbian people to commit to heterosexual relationships in the name of God. To use the notion of sexual fluidity as an argument for the viability of conversion therapy doesn't make sense. Conversion therapy has been banned in most places as harmful and ineffective. Fluidity is an interesting concept, and it has always been fun to argue about whether sexuality is universal, essentialist, or culturally determined. In real life it is destructive to use the concept of fluidity as if its something that is true for all people, when it certainly is not. Countless people, both homosexual and heterosexual, experience their sexualities as fixed.

When Alan and Alison use psychoanalytic theory about multiple self-states to reassure Orthodox Jews that gay men and women use different parts of themselves when they are in synagogue than when they are in private spheres, I can't help but feel that they are themselves partaking in the "contamination" position. Is what gay people do in private so profane and "catching" that it has to be kept out of sight? In my opinion, gay and lesbian Orthodox Jews carry their devotion to God into every sphere of their lives, including the sexual. Orthodox rabbis and communities need to be familiarized with the fact that Jewish men and women who are gay are committed to their marriages and families in the same way that heterosexual Jews are. With the passage of gay marriage laws throughout the nation this commitment now has legal approval.

This will further strengthen gay and lesbian relationships and families. Hopefully this will mitigate the fear that homosexuality threatens the survival of the Jewish people.

I thank Alan and Alison for giving me the opportunity to discuss their important and passionately argued chapter. I tried to be respectful in my arguments for changes in Orthodox Judaism's treatment of gay and lesbian congregants and patients. I hope I succeeded in doing this.

Chapter 4

The challenges faced by LGBTQ Orthodox Jews

An Orthodox response

Rabbi Mark Dratch

The challenges faced by LGBTQ Orthodox Jews, described by Drs. Marc Blechner and Ronnie Lesser in Chapters 2 and 3, are real, as are the challenges that LGBTQ Jews pose to Orthodox Judaism and to non-LGBTQ Orthodox Jews. For many, the issues are raw, personal, theological, principled, and emotional. They reach to the core of who we are as humans, as God-fearing religious adherents, as friends, and as families. They call on us to examine some of the fundamental narratives we have created that explain who we are, what we believe, and how we interact with others.

I believe that many in the Orthodox community and the Orthodox rabbinate today are in a different place in terms of sensitivities and understandings of the religious nuances and human complexities related to issues around homosexuality than were some of the families and therapists described in Chapters 2 and 3; some are not. The Rabbinical Council of America, the leading membership organization of Orthodox rabbis in North America, which once endorsed conversion therapy as a tool to recommend to congregants, is on record for several years now opposing it. Discussions among rabbis and at rabbinic conventions have focused on how to respond in pastorally adaptive ways to congregants and their families. Books, such as Orthodox Rabbi Chaim Rapoport's book *Judaism and Homosexuality: An Authentic Orthodox View* (2004) have helped to change the conversations and attitudes of many. These responses are not sufficient for some; they have gone too far for others.

Drs. Blechner and Lesser's assumptions and suggestions about the particulars of rabbinic responses deserve analysis. To do so, one must understand the fundamental assumptions of Orthodox Judaism including: the divine authorship of the Torah, the binding and eternal nature of its

613 commandments, the significance of Talmudic explications of law, and the authority of rabbinic law. This is not the place to go into detail. Suffice it to say that, for advocates of greater inclusion and acceptance of LGBTQ of the Orthodox community to achieve the success in the Orthodox community they seek, they need to work within and respect these assumptions. Otherwise, Orthodox adherents will suspect and resist what they will judge to be an attack on the fundamentals of traditional Judaism.

Some of the values posited by the authors—*piku'ach nefesh* (saving a life) and *kevod ha- habriyot* (human dignity)—as correctives to the perceived harshness of biblical and rabbinic proscriptions of homosexual behavior are essential elements in formulating *halakhic* (Jewish legal) and social responses. However, depending on the consideration given and weight assigned to each of these and other values, and legal principles with which they may stand in tension, rabbinic authorities may reasonably hold positions that will fall short of Drs. Blechner and Lesser's expectations. This is because these considerations are based on centuries of detailed and complex legal precedents and analyses, as well as codified law and response literature. They cannot be facilely invoked. *Pikua'ch nefesh* overrides most, but not all, biblical commandments. The immediacy and proximity of a threat is a controlling factor, as is the nature of the potential compromised act. Further, *kevod ha-beriyot* is a mitigating consideration in rabbinic legislation, and applies only in very limited ways in cases of biblical law.

Complicating matters are rabbinic decisors' sense of responsibility for protecting and championing the *Masorah*—the traditions of Jewish life and community character. This includes safeguarding the centrality of traditional family structure as well as championing a sexual ethic based on traditional norms and *tzeni'ut* (modesty). In addition, they are responsible for advocating compliance with religious law and practice. Furthermore, concerns that now stem from the legal arena over religious freedom of expression, in such matters as hiring and providing services that are considered violations of religious doctrine, impact considerations as well.

At the same time, Jewish law is sensitive to the consequences that its demands have on individuals and communities, and legal rulings may be adapted due to these and other considerations. The history of *halakhic* analysis and interpretation is filled with nuance, deep understanding of the human condition, and sensitivity to the spiritual, emotional, financial, and physical well-being of religionists. Concern for the physical and emotional well-being of an LGBTQ member of the community is a significant *halakhic* consideration, as is their ability to pursue meaningful religious lives.

As the conversation over acceptance and accommodation of LGBTQ Orthodox Jews evolves—and for all intents and purposes it is still a rather new conversation for this traditional, conservative religious community (it is only a few decades old in the general community despite seismic changes in law, policy, and attitudes)—these and other issues will be weighed and balanced. In some ways it is not unlike the struggles and debates that took place in the nineteenth and twentieth centuries over the status and inclusion of those who were not compliant with the laws of Shabbat. For millennia, strict observance of the Sabbath rules including, in particular, rest from certain work-related activities, was a controlling factor in a Jew's standing, inclusion, and participation in the community and religious life. When the norm changed, due to a host of social, economic, and demographic factors, and many Jews abandoned strict Sabbath observance, decades-long debates concerning legal, theological, social, and communal policy-related principles ensued, until some widely accepted theories of accommodation emerged. Although some will reject the comparison outright as insensitive and inappropriate, those schooled in the dynamics of Jewish law will understand that a rabbinic decisor must work within the established categories of Jewish law and base decisions on precedent. In some cases, it is the resulting policy decision and not the means of analysis that is more important.

As the conversations concerning the place of LGBTQ Orthodox Jews ensues there are several factors that need to be considered carefully:

- Torah law and its observance are prerequisites in the Orthodox community.
- LGBQT are created in the *tzelem Elokim*, the image of God.
- LGBQT Orthodox Jews are our children, cousins, aunts and uncles, parents, and friends. Loving them, supporting them, and maintaining close ties are family values.

- For many Orthodox LGBTQ, the Orthodox community, family, and synagogue are their homes, the loci of their identities, and the places they want to live, grow, raise families, and to which they desire to contribute. The threat of loss of family and community is so important in how it affects behavior.
- Many LGBTQ Orthodox Jews are sincerely committed to the observance of Torah law. Lack of acceptance of them in the Orthodox community often impacts negatively on their commitment and observance.
- LGBQT Jews must be seen as holistic human beings and, therefore, understood, appreciated, and engaged for much more than specific sexual acts in which they may or may not engage.
- The alienation and sense of rejection of LGBTQ Jews is real and may impact significantly on their psychological and physical well-being.
- Rates of depression and suicide are disproportionally higher in the LGBTQ community than in the larger community.
- Evolution of ideas in the Orthodox community is slow and uneven.
- Many rabbis sincerely and sensitively struggle with the need to understand and provide pastoral support to LGBTQ Jews, and with their own sense of fidelity to Jewish law and their responsibility to maintain community standards as they understand them.
- Some of the suggestions offered to LGBTQ Jews in the past—marriage, conversion therapy, repentance—have not only failed, but have also caused significant harm to many (see RCA, 2011, 2012).

Through the vignettes presented in Chapter 5, Dr. Michelle Friedman successfully describes many of the personal, rabbinic, and communal dilemmas and struggles that are faced and correctly assesses that there are currently no simple resolutions. She focuses on, among other issues, communal policy and pastoral care.

It is important to consider the contexts in which communal policy issues play out, locally and beyond. Members of congregations are often strongly invested in their synagogues and their policies, and have conflicting visions and needs. They are concerned about their local needs and accommodations, as well as the policies and opinions of the larger Orthodox and Jewish communities with which they identify.

Although this is true with regard to minor ritual and policy concerns, it is certainly true when confronting larger social and religious issues.

Change comes with *machloket*, a Hebrew term for heated debate and divisiveness. The rabbi and lay officers, charged with the burdens and demands of leadership, must balance the demands of Jewish law, principle, community tradition, and the diverse, competing, and often incompatible interests of congregants. The integrity, unity, and stability of the congregation, along with the needs of individuals and families, are important factors in their considerations. In addition, other important factors include the policies and positions of the larger community, individuals, and organizations, which, by dint of the nature of modern communication, are not only aware of local activity, but also often express pressure and opinions on local communities. Thus, for example, the issue of public acknowledgement of life cycle events, as raised by Dr. Friedman, is not a simple matter: the Jewish legal issues must be clarified as to whether extending such greetings is appropriate; the pastoral needs of the individuals and their families, and friends must be weighed; the opinions and needs of the members of the larger community must be factored in; and the positions of the larger Orthodox community and the community's standing must be considered. Different rabbis and lay leaders, and different communities, will balance these demands in different ways.

Opportunities for gay men to receive *kibbudim* (honors during the service) may differ from congregation to congregation as well. Many congregations have long histories of welcoming and providing honors to Jews with diverse levels of observance and circumstances, and in many congregations gay men are also honored. This may not be the case in congregations in which the people honored are more limited.

Dr. Friedman outlines the tenets of pastoral care: "active, compassionate, non-judgmental listening, taking one's own emotional pulse, respecting boundaries and borders, and maintaining confidentiality." These tenets define the pastoral support provided by many Orthodox rabbis, regardless of the issue brought to them. However, many view their silence in matters that affect proper religious practice as complicity and will use counseling sessions as opportunities to teach about proper observance and to try to influence their counselees to abide by Jewish law.

We are in a dynamic time concerning the place and opportunities for LGBTQ Jews in the Orthodox community. Some are influenced by the shifts in the larger population toward greater understanding, welcoming, and accommodation. Others react to those influences with strong rejection. Nevertheless, across the spectrum, rabbis and communities are giving creative thought to how to meet the needs of both individuals and Jewish law, the desideratum of the Orthodox Jewish community.

References

Rabbinical Council of America (RCA). (2011), RCA reaffirms policies regarding same sex attraction and marriage, while clarifying its position on reparative therapy. Available at: www.rabbis.org/news/article.cfm?id=105665

Rabbinical Council of America (RCA). (2012), Rabbinical Council of America's statement regarding JONAH (Jews Offering New Alternatives to Homosexuality). Available at: www.rabbis.org/news/article.cfm?id=105723(accessed July 2018)

Rapoport, C. (2004), *Judaism and Homosexuality: An Authentic Orthodox View.* London, Portland, OR: Valentine Mitchell.

Chapter 5

Pastoral counseling and LGBTQ Orthodox Jews

Michelle Friedman

Introduction

This chapter explores pastoral counseling between Orthodox clergy and their gay constituents. Pastoral counseling refers to how rabbis and other Jewish spiritual leaders help congregants navigate their lives including everyday matters, major milestones, and unexpected turmoil or trauma. Sound pastoral counseling is informed by religious and psychological wisdom, and anticipates complexity and nuance. This is especially important with regard to homosexuality because the present climate in the Orthodox world is fraught with religious and political tensions. Orthodox Jewish law *(halakha)* does not permit sexual intercourse between two men (and, to a lesser degree, between two women), and the Orthodox community, even its more modern manifestations, is by and large not hospitable to gay relationships and life. In contrast, twenty-first-century western culture promotes acceptance of non-heteronormative identities and cultures. This highlights the growing cognitive and emotional gap between values and behaviors of contemporary society and those of Orthodox Jewish life. People of all sexual identities expect acceptance, equality, and dignity in personal matters and the milestones of their lives. In the Orthodox world, such acceptance is often seen as a challenge to both Orthodox Jewish values and traditional social norms. Every day, however, rabbis, educators, and other Jewish communal leaders confront urgent human issues which, although not explicitly invoking infractions of Jewish legal code, carry great social and emotional significance. Such interactions demand pastoral attention, the focus of this chapter.

For the purpose of organization, I have divided the text into sections entitled "policy and education," "pastoral issues," and "education for rabbis." However, these issues are never fully disentangled from each other and arise in each section. Fictional vignettes illustrate key points and raise additional questions. These examples acknowledge the diversity of the gay community and the pastoral, social, and psychological issues that clergy inevitably face in the contemporary Jewish world. Although it would not be possible to answer the many questions raised, the goal of this chapter is to highlight some main topics that rabbis confront and to suggest approaches informed by pastoral sensitivity.

An additional demographic clarification is that the focus will be the relationships between North American clergy and men and women who identify as Orthodox and gay. Although bisexual, transgender, and queer (BTQ) identities pose important issues, these are beyond the scope of this discussion (issues about transgender and queer Orthodox Jews are discussed in the second section of this book) Readers should also appreciate how rabbis need to parse the meanings of terms such as gender, sexuality, and identity in order to help congregants navigate such labels. So, too, clergy need to appreciate nuances across being gay in the Orthodox community, identifying as gay in the Orthodox community, and identifying outwardly as gay in the Orthodox community. The same can be said about the framing of "gay Orthodox Jew." What does "Orthodox" identity mean in the context of whatever "gay" identity means? Does it reflect the person's past or current communal affiliation, past or future observance, or family life?

The chapter posits a divide between older and younger populations of Orthodox Jews who are gay. In most communities, "over 50" gay Jews are a forgotten, invisible generation. Some older gay Jews from observant backgrounds have left the religious community. Those who remain live in ongoing heterosexual marriages or are single, possibly with such marriages behind them. The "over 50s" often lead closeted lives and in general are not activists. When older gay Jews vocalize their requests, these tend to include asking for recognition, respect, and support from the larger community. Further, some older, gay men may be HIV positive and have lived with this, perhaps in secret, for years. Gay men who were adults in the 1980s are likely to know people, perhaps good friends and partners, who died of HIV.

In contrast, the younger generation of gay Orthodox Jews is impatient with the "compassion for gays" attitude. Millennials and post-millennials expect recognition of their identity, changes in Jewish law, and social and communal inclusion. Members of this generation are more likely to join self-advocacy organizations. Activism by Orthodox gay Jews evokes discomfort, ambivalence, or anger in the rest of the Orthodox community. However, younger Orthodox Jews are vocal about wanting to live out the core components of their identities as religious and gay. As one slogan proclaims, "We're here, we're queer, and we're *machmir* [scrupulous in religious observance]."

Two vignettes illustrate aspects of gay life in older and younger populations.

> Max, a 67-year-old retired public school principal, lives a closeted, single life. He comes from a traditional Orthodox family. Distressed by his attraction to boys and men, Max dated and married a female college classmate. The marriage lasted two years, disintegrating in bitterness and shame for both Max and his wife. Following the divorce, Max had some brief, clandestine relationships with men but could never reconcile his same-sex longings with his sense of religious guilt and family shame.

Traditional Orthodox society rests on the bedrock of heteronormative family life. From early childhood on, observant culture inculcates values of marriage and child rearing. This poses obvious challenges for gay Jews, for whom marriage to an opposite-sex partner is untrue to a primary aspect of their identity. Rabbis are in the position to help navigate the moral issues and rabbinic responsibility of closeted gay Jews, with respect to them heterosexually dating, maintaining a heterosexual marriage without informing the spouse, coming out to children, and not being fully truthful in relevant positions such as counselors and youth authority figures. But in order to serve gay and straight constituents, rabbis must first recognize these realities and be prepared to discuss them with clarity and honesty.

> Lila, a 29-year-old marine biologist, struggled in her teenage years with her strong attraction to girls in her all-girls religious high

school. She pushed herself to go out on *shidduch* (matchmaker-arranged) dates in college. They felt miserable and false. Lila worried that her highly traditional, observant family would reject her if she voiced any doubts about her sexuality. Finding JQY (Jewish Queer Youth), a Jewish peer support group for LGBTQ youth, helped her clarify her identity and come out to her parents. Lila's dad was fully accepting of her as a gay woman early on. Her mom was devastated. She cried for months over the loss of the life she imagined for her daughter. After a few years, Lila's mom agreed to meet Shlomit, Lila's girlfriend. Lila's parents now occasionally attend events sponsored by Eshel, a support, education, and advocacy organization for LGBTQ Orthodox Jews and their family members.

In addition to issues of dating and marriage, rabbis have a crucial role in guiding elementary, middle schools, camps, and high schools on the treatment of and policies concerning gay youth and issues affecting their families. Clergy and educators need to be informed as to resources such as JQY and Eshel.

Policies and education

This section addresses communal and individual policy and educational concerns. Most of these hot button topics do not elicit weighty or intricate Jewish legal responses. Rather, the main challenges exist in pastoral and communal dimensions. Although a growing number of rabbis aim to convey acceptance of gay individuals they meet or counsel, they are reluctant to challenge what they deem to be societal norms or family structure. Rabbis feel anxious that allowing changes in the traditional status quo will implicitly condone impermissible behaviors or lifestyles, and initiate a slide down a slippery slope in the powerful, unsettling arena of gender and sexuality. Many congregants, especially those of an older generation, fear that allowing openly gay Jews to participate in rituals as they exist now, such as being called to the Torah *(aliyot)* on the occasion of a gay couples' child, or designing new rituals, such as wedding ceremonies for gay couples (see Chapter 8 by Rabbi Steve Greenberg: Envisioning an Orthodox gay wedding), at best attenuates and at worst corrupts their community's religious values and its Orthodox Jewish identity.

The religious, social, and political climate of each community impacts decisions about policy and educational matters. Clergy must take into account how the local congregation/school/institution will react to questions or situations that threaten to split the community. If the rabbi is open to pursuing change, the rabbi must consider whether to personally lead the charge to carry out and support that change. This involves enlisting the support of key congregants who will in turn mobilize other members. If, after serious consideration, the rabbi determines that change on a matter concerning gay issues is not appropriate or that it is premature for the community, the rabbi needs to convey this decision to congregants invested in the decision. This includes the gay congregant(s) and their allies, as well as the rest of the community. The rabbi needs to anticipate disappointment and possibly anger on the part of these congregants and their supporters. If their alienation leads to them severing the relationship with the rabbi, the rabbi should remain available and express concern as to how the gay congregant(s)'s pastoral needs will be met.

Membership in synagogues and schools

A basic matter in synagogues, schools, and other communal organizations is the criteria for membership. The question of whether same-sex couples can be counted as a family unit has catalyzed many heated debates in Orthodox synagogues. A vignette illustrates this issue.

> Lila and Shlomit, now married with a toddler son, Yakov, relocate for work purposes to a small coastal city where there is one synagogue. They apply for a family membership.

Recognition as a family unit is fundamental to dignity and standing within a Jewish community. The conventional argument against granting this recognition to gay couples (and their children) is that doing so confers tacit approval of homosexual acts and implicitly condones this as an acceptable family unit within Jewish tradition. Some synagogues have eased this tension by offering individual or household memberships, thereby sidestepping the question of what constitutes family status. A related situation is that of gay parents who apply for admission to the local Orthodox day school for their child(ren). Here an additional concern may be the school's worry about children receiving mixed messages just as they hesitate to accept children from non-Sabbath-observant or non-kosher homes.

Honors (kibbudim)

Another fraught arena in some communities is that of giving ritual honors (*kibbudim*) to men who are openly gay. These include being called up to the Torah (*aliyot*), leading public prayer (*davenning*), and serving as witnesses (*eidim*). This is not, by and large, an issue for observant gay women, as the conventional Orthodox world does not give public ritual honors to women altogether. For synagogues that allow female officers, the issue of being gay might come up in the same way – some members' concerns as to whether a woman who is openly gay serving as a synagogue president, for example, would cast aspersions on the religiosity (*frumkeit*) of the community.

Equal standing for public events

Public classes, symposia, and articles that address homosexuality are also viewed with ambivalence. People working toward greater openness confront hesitancy and sometimes frank refusal from rabbis who have control over who may be invited to address a public gathering, what venue will be used, which stories will be published, and what events may be advertised. A vignette illustrates.

> Members of a large synagogue organize a panel on challenges of being gay and Orthodox. The rabbi and synagogue officers support the project but insist that the panel take place in the gym rather than the main sanctuary where large forums are usually held, because others members voice protest that a panel on homosexuality take place in the same space where the Torah scrolls are kept.

Although it is commendable to hold a public symposium that offers the opportunity to learn about gay Orthodox experiences, the negative message sent by relegating the event to an alternative, less dignified space registers loudly. Gay congregants and their families and friends cannot be but offended or hurt by such actions.

Educational messages

Content of traditional Jewish educational materials and activities is largely organized around heteronormative narratives that are also Ashkenazic, white, and masculine centric. Children with gay parents or relatives, as well as children who are struggling with their own sexuality, are likely to experience confusion and alienation when feeling excluded from Jewish tradition as depicted in this next vignette.

> Yakov, Lila and Shlomit's 4-year-old son, remarks to his nursery school teachers that having a Shabbat *ima* (mother) and *abba* (father) is not what happens in his house.

Children of all ages are highly attuned to feelings of belonging and not belonging. Rabbis and educators need to be attuned to obvious as well as latent heteronormative messages in texts and rituals, as well as biases on the part of other faculty, children, and parents. Similar sensitivity applies to feminist concerns as well as Jewish families who are Sephardic, of color, or non-traditional for other reasons such as children being raised by single parents or other relatives.

Coming out to clergy and teachers

As boys and girls are acknowledging their gay identity at younger ages, rabbis and educators increasingly experience teens coming out to them in school, synagogue, and camp. Clergy must be prepared to deal with the multiple levels of sensitivity inherent in this situation. Staff need training to deal with their own reactions so that they may then respond appropriately to issues of vulnerability on the part of the student coming out, and discomfort or bullying by peers.

Educators must also anticipate issues for gay students who plan to spend the year after high school in Israel. North Americans studying in

Israel frequently report messages of intolerance from members of their programs' faculties that conflict with other faculty members or with those of their American high schools. It is important to support these teenagers' desire to study in Israel as well as to find the right place for them. In addition, these teenagers will need proactive and regular contact from friendly teachers or clergy at home who can help them deal with the diverse experiences they are likely to encounter which may be quite different from those they are used to.

Ceremonies and lifecycle events

Lifecycle events present an array of challenges to Orthodox rabbis and congregations. This chapter does not deal with efforts to reinterpret Jewish law or develop new religious rituals. Rather, it raises awareness of social, political, and pastoral aspects of milestone ceremonies for gay Jews who affiliate with an Orthodox community such as in these next two vignettes of birth and bar mitzvah.

> Lila, with Shlomit by her side, gives birth to a second baby boy who is conceived via donor sperm.

The birth or adoption of a new baby is a profound milestone in the life of any individual or couple. This watershed moment offers the opportunity for new parents to connect to the Orthodox community. Will the rabbi publicly announce and celebrate the birth or arrival of a new baby to gay parents? Will the rabbi allow a gay couple to hold the circumcision *(bris)* or welcome for a newborn girl *(simchat bat)* in the synagogue or other communal space? What about the redemption of the first-born son *(pidyon haben)*? If the decision is made to hold the ceremony for a newborn in a home or other private setting, will the rabbi attend? If two dads adopt a non-Jewish child, will the rabbi agree to convert the baby? Will the rabbi celebrate the baby's conversion and entry into the community? Going forward, when a blessing for these children is made from the pulpit, will both their gay parents' names be announced?

> Lila and Shlomit's sons grow up. Their older boy, Yakov, attends the local community day school and will become a bar mitzvah in

several months. He prepares to lead the morning service, chant his Torah portion and give a speech. Yakov's mothers want to follow this with a kiddush and luncheon in the synagogue's social hall. They also expect that their family's joyous occasion will be announced from the pulpit by the synagogue president and printed in the synagogue bulletin, as is the custom of the synagogue.

Ceremonial and ritual issues raised by the birth of a baby to gay parents come up again with *bar/bat mitzvah*. Any aspect of conventional celebration such as acknowledging the family's milestone by wishing *mazel tov* to gay parents from the pulpit, announcing events in written/email publications, or holding a party in the synagogue social hall will be interpreted by some congregants as the rabbi condoning homosexuality as a "valid Jewish lifestyle." This also applies to engagements, wedding commitment ceremonies, funerals, and burials. Clergy also need to make a series of decisions – will they participate in lifecycle events of gay Orthodox Jews? If they will not participate in a rabbinic capacity, will they attend such events? Each of these events poses challenges for rabbis in navigating a delicate path that conveys respect for traditional values while affirming the dignity of gay congregants and their right to celebrate lifecycle events in a Jewish manner.

End-of-life matters with gay congregants are another lifecycle event that requires rabbinic and pastoral skills as illustrated here.

> Brad and Gideon met at work and lived together for two decades before getting married in a civil ceremony. They also made out their wills, filled out advance life directives, and purchased adjoining plots in the local Jewish cemetery. Brad died three months ago. Their rabbi visited him in the hospital a few days before his death. At that time, Brad and Gideon told the rabbi their wish for an Orthodox funeral as well as for a headstone that expressed their union.

Dying, death, funerals and burials are intensely private as well as public experiences. The rabbi is called on to provide comfort to those at the end of life and their loved ones and also to negotiate and conduct final ceremonies that involve family, friends and the larger community.

The officiating rabbi has decisions to make: how direct will he be in his eulogy in acknowledging the nature of Brad and Gideon's relationship? How will he handle any objections raised as to the burial of a gay couple in a Jewish cemetery? How will the community support Gideon in mourning rituals such as *shiva* and anniversaries of the death?

Pastoral issues

Each of the above vignettes depicts lifecycle moments packed with pastoral significance. Regardless of the rabbi's religious–philosophical views, pastoral sensitivity and interpersonal skill skills are of the utmost importance in such matters that occur in the regular course of life.

Family counseling

Just as heterosexual individuals have unresolved issues lingering from their families of origin, so too Orthodox gay Jews deal with family conflicts. Small and large relationship problems easily become magnified when an individual is struggling to be fully authentic with his or her family members, who are in turn denying or adjusting to the fact that their relative has come out as gay. Rabbis have a position of unique authority to encourage and mediate family dialogue. Gay Orthodox Jews may become estranged from their families. Although Orthodox gay individuals increasingly speak out, join support groups, and form alternative families, there is still pain and loss in these transitions within their families of origin and communities. Sound pastoral counseling skills are necessary for clergy to mitigate or prevent family estrangement.

Similarly, just as straight Orthodox Jews struggle with finding spouses and then negotiating the demands of marriage and raising children, so too do gay Orthodox Jews. Rabbis must be prepared to counsel gay couples struggling with typical relationship issues such as religious differences and family pressures as well as divorce and its aftermath. Gay Orthodox Jews may also pose unusual pastoral questions to their rabbis. For example, should gay women in a committed relationship go to the *mikvah* (ritual bath)? Although these questions raise Jewish legal issues as well, it is important that clergy not miss the deep emotions latent in these questions.

In order to be fully available to their straight and gay congregants, rabbis need to understand the anxiety generated in their own hearts when confronted with such issues. In addition, they need basic skills to navigate emotional conversations with congregants and families. Rabbinic education must dedicate time and resources to help future clergy unpack their own assumptions and feelings about homosexuality, as well as other contemporary issues. Rabbis must be prepared to serve all congregants and be careful of the pull to "take sides" in emotionally charged situations. Classes, reading, and personal exploration will prepare rabbis for assessing Jewish legal and pastoral concerns going forward (Friedman, 2016).

In addition, rabbis need to be mindful of the impact a family member's gay coming out has on his or her family of origin. The rabbi will often be the first person parents will turn to for support and guidance on finding out that their child is gay. Some Orthodox families will try to recruit the rabbi in a campaign to convince their beloved family member to pursue any treatment that will make them straight. Families of gay Orthodox Jews may face communal censure in the form of children not getting invited over for dinner or sleep-overs or siblings not getting set up on dates (*shidduchim*). For many Orthodox Jews, the experience of a child or other relative coming out creates a paradigm shift in their worldview. They become advocates for their loved one and begin to challenge aspects of Jewish life that they may not have considered as deeply before. This may affect how they view their role in the community, and their relationship to the Jewish legal system and to religious authority. It may result in increased distance or alienation from their members of their communities, teachers, and leaders who seem oblivious to or critical of the plight of gay Orthodox Jews. Once again, pastoral competency on the part of clergy will help families negotiate the delicate balance between tradition and personal expectations.

Religious struggle

Rabbis should also be prepared for pastoral counseling around religious conflict and theological issues. Recall Max, the character from the first vignette in this chapter. Observant gay men and women struggle with shame and guilt stemming from long-held attitudes that homosexuality is inherently sinful. A natural extension is probing into theodicy. Jews who are gay grapple with the question of why God created them with desire for unacceptable sexual lives and why religious texts seem to reject this core aspect of their humanity. Orthodox gay men may feel that they must choose between keeping religious law that restricts same-sex activity and achieving sexual fulfillment.

Clearly there are no easy answers to any of these challenges. The tenets of basic pastoral counseling continue to apply – active, compassionate, non-judgmental listening, taking one's own emotional pulse, respecting boundaries and borders, and maintaining confidentiality. These principles, as well as many other aspects of pastoral counseling, are explicated with extensive vignettes in *The Art of Jewish Pastoral Counseling: A Guide for All Faiths*, written by me and Rachel Yehuda. The rabbi needs to be mindful of the rabbinic role and repeatedly define who needs care in these complex situations. Often, the rabbi has multi-layered rabbinic and personal connections to various members of a family, all of whom clamor for the rabbi to take their side (see Chapter 1).

Education for clergy

Rabbis and educators need and deserve specific preparation in order to meet the needs of gay and lesbian congregants and their families. Educational programs in rabbinical school and beyond are needed to provide up-to-date information and opportunities for personal exploration so as to educate rabbis as to current knowledge about the challenges faced by Orthodox gay men and women and their families. Rabbinical students need to be assigned readings on relevant Jewish legal and pastoral matters. All of this must be discussed in classes where confidentiality is respected, because students must first examine their own feelings towards gay Jews before they can be effective as rabbis.

Educational curricula for rabbis in yeshiva and continuing education must consider specific mental and physical health issues associated with the struggle of being gay and Orthodox. Many gay Orthodox Jews, especially ones who grew up in the *frum* community, have dealt with issues related to depression, suicide, and bullying. Rabbis also need basic sexual education pertaining to gay men and women. As mentioned earlier, rabbis should be aware that congregants might be HIV positive. It is of lifesaving consequence that sexual education in day schools cover relations between same-sex couples. When a man comes out to a rabbi, the rabbi should be mindful as to whether the man is practicing safe sex with a man. Although this is awkward for rabbis who may not know technicalities about sex between men and/or feel that the Torah forbids it, the medical urgency of preventing HIV should motivate rabbis to be prepared to ask those questions and, if necessary, direct the person to appropriate local resources. Every city in America has places that offer free HIV testing services. These can be accessed through LGBT community centers and Planned Parenthood, among others.

Pastoral programs should facilitate encounters with Orthodox Jews who are gay and their families so that rabbinical students meet real people and get first-hand understanding of their lives. Rabbinical schools can draw on resources for gay Orthodox Jews or people looking to learn about gay Orthodox life. These include the organizations mentioned earlier in the chapter, JQY (Jewish Queer Youth) and Eshel, and the film *Trembling Before God*. CBST (Congregation Beit Simchat Torah), although not Orthodox, in New York can provide many resources about being Jewish and gay.

In addition to the issues of gay congregants, the contemporary Orthodox rabbinate must acknowledge the reality of both closeted and openly gay peers and students. Most rabbis are reluctant to take positions that might ostracize them from the Orthodox establishment. This hesitancy results in a paucity of written material and limits public discourse on issues relevant to gay individuals who are living an observant Jewish life. Rabbinical schools need to support and model forums of appropriate written and spoken discourse.

Rabbis will face enormous political pressure from their local community and from the larger Orthodox world in the area of gay observant life if they attempt to adopt a sensitive and inclusive approach. Just as a gay inclusionary stance can come with costs, so too can the opposite. It is important that rabbis be prepared for consequences of gay congregants and their families getting offended if they deny a request, for whatever reason. For the rabbi to get defensive or upset will serve neither the rabbi nor the congregant, who is offended by an exclusionary stance the rabbi has taken, however legitimate. The same can be true of family and friends of gay

Jews, who may also be offended by the stance of the rabbi. Yeshiva and post-ordination education is needed to prepare and support rabbis to meet the challenges that they will face, consider strategies for addressing them, and develop structures for self-care and peer-support.

YCT (Yeshivat Chovevei Torah) Rabbinical School addresses these needs in several ways. From a curricular perspective, all students take a foundational course in pastoral counseling class. This class prepares them to explore and apply active, compassionate, non-judgmental listening from a Jewish religious perspective, as well as to identify personal strengths and vulnerabilities that are elicited by pastoral encounters. A follow-up course on conducting lifecycle rituals integrates the Jewish legal and pastoral components of these milestone events. All along, the curriculum, starting with ceremonies for newborn babies and closing with issues of death and dying, YCT includes issues specific to gay Jews and their families. Several sessions are devoted exclusively to the challenge of being LGBTQ and Orthodox. LGBTQ panelists come in to share first person accounts, as do Orthodox parents of LGBTQ youth. From the personal perspective, all YCT students attend process group meetings where students, together with a designated facilitator, meet in a confidential setting to share feelings and reactions elicited by the experience of becoming a rabbi.

RIETS, the rabbinical school of YU (Yeshiva University) discusses issues relating to gay Orthodox Jews in several classes, starting with Pastoral Psychology 1, and continues into advanced pastoral care classes. Here too students are encouraged via discussion and role play to explore feelings that may be triggered in them in dealing with these complex issues. The program's goal is for rabbis to be open and welcoming to all members of their communities. RIETS students think through situation in which they might engage with gay congregants and empathize with challenges that Orthodox gay persons encounter.

In summary, all Orthodox rabbis encounter gay Orthodox Jews. Although different sub-communities and individuals acknowledge this reality to varying degrees, twenty-first-century life demands that rabbis prepare to care for the religious and pastoral lives of their gay congregants.

Acknowledgments

With thanks to Daniel Atwood, Rachel Fried, Rabbi Steven Greenberg, Mordechai Levovitz, Rabbi Dov Linzer, Naomi Mark, Dr. David Pelcovitz, Miriam Schacter, and Rabbanit Devorah Zlochower.

Reference

Friedman, M. and Yehuda, R. (2016), *The Art of Jewish Pastoral Counseling: A Guide for All Faiths*. London: Routledge.

Chapter 6

Gay Jewish men in the Orthodox Jewish community

Striving for selfhood

Jeremy Novich

Introduction

This chapter aims to provide a glimpse into the day-to-day challenges experienced by gay Jewish men in the Orthodox community and draws from my doctoral dissertation (Novich, 2014).[1] A brief description of the methods is followed by the results of my study and a discussion of how they can inform clinical conceptualization. Based on the analysis, the experience of this population can be understood as existing in the four domains of social, family, community, and self. The discussion contextualizes the data and proposed model through the lenses of social justice and psychoanalytic theory, to provide a multilayered framework of this complex experience. Clinical approaches and interventions to promote wellness in this population are discussed.

The study

Twenty-four cisgendered, gay-identified men were recruited from the New York City metropolitan area to participate in focus groups to discuss their experiences. The experiences of women, transgender individuals, and people who identify as bisexual were expected to diverge from cisgendered, gay men, and were beyond the scope of this study. Participants needed to consider themselves "part of the Orthodox Jewish community." This included people of all observance levels because the study was focused on the experience in the community and not personal religiosity.

Participants varied with regard to their religious backgrounds and current levels of observance. Twelve participants (50%) identified as observant from birth; they were raised in an observant family and were observant at the time they participated in the study. Five participants (20.8%) endorsed the item: "I grew up in an observant home but I am no longer observant today." One participant (4.2%) indicated that he fell between those two options, suggesting that he grew up in an observant home and that he was between observant and not observant at the time of the study. Six participants (25%) identified as *ba'alei teshuvah*, meaning they did not grow up in an observant home but became observant later in life. The participants ranged from 18 years to 66 years with an average age of 37 years.

Participants were asked to speak about different aspects of their experiences in a group format. The goal of the focus groups was to gather information about the experiences of the participants in an open-ended, semi-structured format.

Results

Data analysis

Analysis of the interview transcripts was completed according to the method detailed in *Qualitative Data* (Auerbach & Silverstein, 2003) to extract relevant text, organize them into repeating ideas, themes, and theoretical constructs, and then construct a theoretical narrative. The coding team consisted of three individuals, all of whom were doctoral candidates in the Clinical Psychology Doctoral Program at Long Island University, Post Campus. The coding team then met and reached consensus on a master list of repeating ideas. The list of repeating ideas was organized into themes and theoretical constructs. Together, the theoretical constructs yielded a theoretical narrative that organized the focus group data into a coherent story of the gay Jewish man's experience in the Orthodox community.

Theoretical narrative[2]

When the gay Jewish men in the Orthodox community related their stories during the focus groups, they spoke of their experience as occurring in four distinct but overlapping domains: the SOCIAL, FAMILY, COMMUNITY, and SELF (see Table 6.1 for the hierarchical data organization).

Table 6.1 The different levels of hierarchical organization

	Number of participants	Percentage of participants	Number of groups	Percentage of groups
SOCIAL.				
Social problems	15	62.50	6	100
"I always thought I was just different socially in general"	6	25	5	83.33
"It's just a tension I feel toward some of the people in Judaism"	4	16.67	4	66.67
"And like everybody has to fit into a cookie cutter"	5	20.83	3	50.00
"Unfortunately I lost several friends once I realized I was gay"	6	25.00	3	50.00
To come out or not to come out?	13	54.17	5	83.33
"We don't walk around saying, 'Hi everyone, I'm gay and by the way, my name is [name of P16]'"	6	25.00	4	66.67
"I'm afraid that I would lose what I have there [if I come out]"	6	25.00	4	66.67
"I don't want to lose jobs"	4	16.67	3	50.00
"To what extent do I want to come out?"	2	8.33	1	16.67
Possible positives of coming out	2	8.33	1	16.67
Positive social experiences	15	62.50	5	83.33
"Almost all my friends [had] positive responses [to my coming out]"	13	54.17	5	83.33
"I choose my friends carefully"	4	16.67	3	50.00
"And everyone knows and like no one cares"	3	12.50	2	33.33
Strengthened relationships from coming out	2	8.33	1	16.67
"Everyone knew that I was gay, and I was totally out and I was totally welcome"	2	8.33	2	33.33
FAMILY				
Marriage and family building challenges	19	79.17	6	100.00
"All of this focus on dating and getting married, so, I don't want to deal with that."	16	66.67	6	100.00
"What kind of wedding ceremony" and family "would I have?"	7	29.17	5	83.33
"I think if the Orthodox community was more welcoming to begin with, I would probably be more selective about who I date"	2	8.33	2	33.33
"It's a very small pool of potential partners and there's no one in the Orthodox world helping you"	4	16.67	2	33.33

(Continued)

Table 6.1 (Cont.)

	Number of participants	Percentage of partici-pants	Number of groups	Percentage of groups
Difficulties of singlehood	5	20.83	3	50.00
Negative aspects of experience with family	21	87.50	6	100.00
"When you come out publicly, it affects a whole family"	16	66.67	6	100.00
Negative family reactions: "Family is always a big challenge"	14	58.33	5	83.33
Negative impact on relationships with parents	3	12.50	2	33.33
Unsafe family environment: "You never made it safe for me to tell you"	7	29.17	4	66.67
Family support	9	37.50	5	83.33
Support from family. COMMUNITY	9	37.50	5	83.33
Moderators of experience	17	70.83	6	100.00
"It depends where in the Orthodox Jewish community you are"	11	45.83	5	83.33
Age and generation matters	7	29.17	5	83.33
People adjust over time: "They both come a long way since"	8	33.33	4	66.67
Unmet needs	14	58.33	6	100.00
"I think that there's a lack of resources at an institutional level"	4	16.67	2	33.33
"What the Orthodox community did not provide . . . is role models for guys like us"	3	12.50	2	33.33
"There's only one real narrative," so what's mine?	6	25.00	3	50.00
"There isn't this movement yet to actually take steps"	3	12.50	2	33.33
"There's no sex ed"	3	12.50	1	16.67
Understanding	10	41.67	5	83.33
"There's really a lack of awareness"	8	33.33	5	83.33
"I want you to understand the issues that I'm going through"	4	16.67	3	50.00
Acceptance	14	58.33	6	100.00
Tolerance and acceptance: "Have a place for us I guess"	12	50.00	6	100.00
"On a communal level, there's no real acceptance"	4	16.67	3	50.00

(Continued)

Table 6.1 (Cont.)

	Number of participants	Percentage of participants	Number of groups	Percentage of groups
Discussion	11	45.83	5	83.33
"I'm sad it isn't discussed more"	8	33.33	4	66.67
"Have a conversation"	6	25.00	4	66.67
I'm treated differently	12	50.00	6	100.00
Double standard: "We're not afforded that same consideration that the straight couples are afforded"	8	33.33	4	66.67
Straight privilege: "When you're gay, you don't necessarily cash in on those incentives"	5	20.83	3	50.00
I don't always feel welcome or safe	11	45.83	6	100.00
"Gay people are not welcome in the shul"	11	45.83	6	100.00
Negative types of re/interactions	18	75.00	6	100.00
Outed and confronted	8	33.33	6	100.00
Omissions: "We don't really talk about it"	6	25.00	5	83.33
"They're [family and friends] in denial"	13	54.17	4	66.67
How gay people are viewed	15	62.50	6	100.00
"If you're single, you're a kid"	6	25.00	3	50.00
"There's this notion that we're predatory"	4	16.67	2	33.33
"The whole idea that we're defined by one sexual act that we may or may not do . . . is ridiculous"	6	25.00	4	66.67
"If they would just change their language"	4	16.67	2	33.33
"There's still this massive stigma against queer people"	5	20.83	3	50.00
"There's obviously a negative stereotype from a social perspective"	3	12.50	3	50.00
Positive social/communal experiences	8	33.33	5	83.33
"There has been some effort [to improve the situation for gay men]"	5	20.83	4	66.67
"It's good that a lot of people are coming out"	3	12.50	2	33.33
SELF				
Satisfaction and identification with Orthodoxy and the community	20	83.33	6	100.00
"But I get those things out of the gay Orthodox community that I have here"	8	33.33	4	66.67
"The Orthodox part is still part of our identity"	13	54.17	6	100.00
"We're all one big family. I like that aspect"	9	37.50	4	66.67

(Continued)

Table 6.1 (Cont.)

	Number of participants	Percentage of participants	Number of groups	Percentage of groups
"It [Orthodoxy] provides structure, and I think structure is good in any context"	3	12.50	2	33.33
Returning to observance	1	4.17	1	16.67
Rabbinic successes: "It's people like that who we want to keep"	3	12.50	3	50.00
My disconnections	18	75.00	6	100.00
"There are a bunch of rebbeim that I kind of lost respect for since coming out"	8	33.33	4	66.67
"The more I have accepted who I am as a gay man, the more . . . I have felt uncomfortable in the Orthodox community"	10	41.67	6	100.00
"The external is important and the internal is not important"	6	25.00;	3	50.00
Internalized stigma	9	37.50	5	83.33
Internalized stigma	9	37.50	5	83.33
Duality	14	58.33	5	83.33
"I'm leading a double life"	10	41.67	4	66.67
"A lot of people have asked me like, 'how do justify being gay and frum?'"	7	29.17	5	83.33
Coming to peace	13	54.17	5	83.33
"Once I started coming out, I just started embracing everything about me"	4	16.67	3	50.00
"I don't feel like they have to change their core beliefs to accommodate" me	5	20.83	3	50.00
Benefits of being gay	5	20.83	2	33.33
Communal participation: "I think it's so much up to me"	2	8.33	2	33.33

Being a gay man in the Orthodox Jewish community was a SOCIAL experience for participants. The men spoke about various social problems resulting from being gay. They reported a general sense of being different, and conveyed dissatisfaction with what they felt was a norm of needing to fit a particular mold or risk being criticized. Losing friends as a result of being gay was another reported experience. However, participants distinguished their social experience from their experience of the religion itself. As one person remarked: "*It's just a tension I feel toward some of the **people** in Judaism*" [emphasis added].

Some participants also reported positive social experiences. Some denied negative social consequences of their gayness, whereas others reported feeling welcome even when out as gay. They reported positive responses to their gayness from many friends with some potential for *strengthened relationships from coming out*. Others reported being selective about whom they chose to be their friends.

An important part of the social experience of the participants was deciding when, where, to whom, and at what risk they should come out or be out. Several acknowledged not coming out without a reason, and expressed hesitancy about coming out in their communities and/or synagogues. They reported a fear of damaging their standing in the community by coming out. Another important concern was financial—as one participant stated: "*I don't want to lose jobs.*" Despite the general negative anticipations of coming out, several participants saw some *possible positives of coming out*, such as gaining an opportunity to serve as a role model for other gay people.

FAMILY was another domain of experience for participants. When it came to their families of origin, participants reported a variety of negative experiences. Some of the gay men felt unsafe in their family well before coming out, increasing the challenging nature of the experience. Coming out to family elicited negative reactions, and being gay had a *negative impact on relationships with parents* for some participants. Last, participants reported that their gayness made them a burden on their families. For example, one participant remarked that, after coming out, his family was concerned that his sexual orientation may negatively impact the marriage prospects of members of the extended family. On the other hand, some participants reported receiving family support, such as maintaining an accepting stance.

Also within the FAMILY domain, participants reported marriage and family building challenges. First, they struggled with the focus on dating and marrying women, and the subsequent pressure. When considering dating other men, they discussed some unique challenges to being gay in the Orthodox community. They talked about being unsure how to get married and build a family and expressed dissatisfaction with the Orthodox community's disapproval of civil same-sex marriage. Not only did participants reflect on not having the institutions of marriage and family available to them, but they also reported a dearth of potential partners and no assistance from the Orthodox community in finding a partner (see Chapter 8). This is in contrast to the general eagerness of the Orthodox community to facilitate opposite-sex matchmaking. As a result of the lack of recognition of same-sex couples in the Orthodox world, some participants reported being less selective about whom they date. For example, one participant explained that, because of the lack of acceptance of his future partner, no matter who he is, he expanded his pool of potential partners to include non-Jewish men. Finally, participants who were not able to find a partner for whatever reason described the *difficulties of singlehood*, such as fitting in with neither same-aged peers who are married and have families, nor single people who are substantially younger.

A third component of the experience of gay Jewish men in the Orthodox world is the domain of COMMUNITY. This domain includes aspects of experience that occur at the societal level or are parts of experience that do not fall strictly into the SOCIAL, FAMILY, or SELF domains. First, participants identified variables that affect their experience. They explained that the experience of being gay in the Orthodox world is influenced by geography as well as the religious outlook of the person's particular community. Participants recognized the importance of the era in which they grew up. They stated that being a gay man in the Orthodox community is easier now than it was years and decades before, and that younger age predicts a more positive experience.

They specified a number of unmet needs. First, as one participant put it: *"there's a lack of resources at an institutional level."* They reported not having role models, making it difficult to plan a life given that the single narrative for Orthodox Jewish men (i.e., marrying a woman) is not an ideal option for many gay men. Despite recognizing an overall improvement of the situation for gay men in the Orthodox community, participants complained of a lack of action to make further improvements. There was also dissatisfaction with the lack of sex education that participants received over the course of their lives. One participant attributed his contraction of HIV, at least in part, to this lack of sex education.

Participants identified three major lacks on the communal level in need of remedy: first, they pointed to the lack of discussion about homosexuality and expressed a desire for the community to *"have a conversation."* They highlighted a lack of understanding, and conveyed a desire for increased understanding. As one participant put it: *"I want you to understand the issues that I'm going through.*" Finally, participants reported a lack of communal acceptance and indicated a desire for improvement in this area. In addition, participants stated that they did not always feel welcome or safe in communal spaces.

Participants discussed being treated differently because of their gayness. This unequal treatment took two forms: first, participants reported the idea of a double standard. They described the double standard of gay people being held to a stricter standard of behavior than straight people. For example, participants pointed to the fact that opposite-sex couples are presumed to observe the Torah laws of family purity, whereas same-sex couples are presumed to violate the specific Torah prohibition of anal intercourse between men. The second aspect of unequal treatment can be thought of as straight privilege, the unearned benefits an individual receives because he is straight. For example, one participant mentioned that, for straight people, the benefits of having a family and fitting in with community may mitigate doubts in God or other theological questions. However, for a gay man, theological doubts may be felt more acutely because of the lack of social benefits received.

Participants pointed to three types of negative interactions they have with others in the community. Some participants had been outed— meaning the fact that they are gay had been disclosed to others without permission. Some participants were confronted about their gayness by family or friends without their having first come out to them. Others reported people in their lives who knew that they were gay but would not talk to them about it. This relates to participants' experience of a denial of their gayness by others.

Participants described how they experienced being stereotyped and stigmatized. They explained how they are viewed in an infantilized fashion, such that: "*if you're single, you're a kid.*" The men linked their gayness to being viewed as sexual predators. Participants complained of being pigeonholed such that being gay is viewed as their defining characteristic, focusing on their sexual activity not on who they are. This was related to participants expressing dissatisfaction with the derogatory language employed by community members when referring to gay people.

Several participants reported positive communal experiences. Specifically, they acknowledged that "*there has been some effort [to improve the situation for gay men]"* in the Orthodox community. They added that the increasing number of people coming out is helpful.

Finally, the men in the study discussed the impact their social, family, and community experiences, have on them. This domain is called SELF. Participants, both those who were out and those who were not, described experiencing a duality in their lives. One participant was closeted to his wife and managed to attend gay events, whereas another participant who was out returns to using his Jewish name only when he visits family. Participants also experienced duality with regard to how they can be observant and gay. This experience was often triggered by the comments of others, such as: *"A lot of people have asked me like, 'how do [you] justify being gay and frum [observant]?'"*

Participants reported various ways in which they felt disconnected from the community. There seemed to be a trade off; the more participants became comfortable with themselves as gay men, the less they felt comfortable in the Orthodox community. They felt disconnected from the values of the community, particularly with their experience that *"the external is important and the internal is not important."* Another source of disconnection for the participants was rabbinic failures. As one participant put it: *"there are a bunch of rebbeim* [rabbis] *that I kind of lost respect for since coming out."*

Participants made comments that suggested an internalization of the negative statements communicated to them either explicitly or implicitly by the Orthodox community. For example, there were comments comparing homosexuality with an addiction, comparing same-sex marriage with interspecies marriage, viewing being gay as being "in everybody's face," and stating that "there are worse people out there"—as if being gay itself makes the individual bad.

Despite these negative experiences, many of the participants also reported positive outcomes with regard to their personal development and their relationship with the community. One participant said: *"Once I started coming out, I just started embracing everything about me."* Others expressed a comfort with Orthodoxy maintaining its central religious beliefs instead of changing to accommodate them. Some participants saw some *benefits of being gay*, such as developing a sensitivity to other marginalized groups in Orthodoxy. Some participants came to the conclusion that their participation and membership in the Orthodox community is, in the end, up to them.

Participants expressed satisfaction and identification with Orthodoxy and the community. The men discussed the important positive influence gay, Orthodox, Jewish infrastructure has on their lives. They reported that: "*The Orthodox part is still part of our identity.*" The men enjoyed the communal aspect of the Orthodox world, as one participant put it succinctly: "*We're all one big family. I like that aspect.*" Some participants stated that they appreciated Orthodoxy because "*It [Orthodoxy] provides structure, and I think structure is good in any context.*" Some participants reported positive interactions or experiences with rabbis. There was even the potential process of *returning to observance* as a result of positive experiences in the community, including having children.

Discussion

Social justice

Although the constructs SOCIAL, FAMILY, and COMMUNITY were presented as aspects of experience, they can also be thought of as forces that act on the individual and affect his view of self, his relationship with Orthodoxy (beliefs, practices, and values), and his relationship with the community. The gay man's family and his perception of what type of family building experience he might have also affects his view of self, Orthodoxy, and the community. Finally, the community force is both similar to and different from the other two forces. It is similar in that it has direct impact on the individual, his relationship with Orthodoxy, and his relationship with the community. It does so by communicating norms and messages that are either affirming or marginalizing of the gay man's identity. However, the community force is unique in that it is the contextual force in which the social and family forces lie. As such, the community force influences the social and family forces. For example, as mentioned earlier, a family was concerned that their son being gay would impact their other family members' marriage prospects. The community force impacts the gay man both directly and as mediated through the social and family forces (see Figure 6.1 for a visual representation). This makes the gay Jewish man's experience subjectively multi-dimensional and objectively over-determined.

The idea that the individual's experience is influenced, if not determined, by his surroundings is not new. In fact, Prilleltensky and

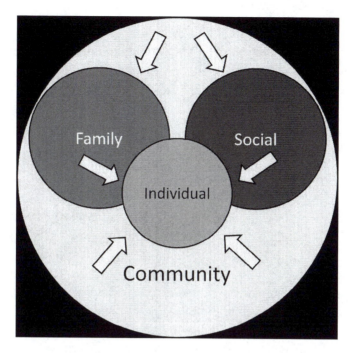

Figure 6.1 Visual representation of the experience of the gay Jewish man in the Orthodox community

Nelson (2002) presented a similar schematic of the context of the individual. They described the concept of well-being as multidimensional and hierarchical. They presented a figure that features the individual nested in the family, which is nested in the community, which is nested in society. In other words, the individual is impacted by the multilayered context in which he lives. The model proposed in this project adapts Prilleltensky and Nelson's model to the phenomenon under study and shows the experiences of gay Jewish men in the Orthodox community to be determined by their community, both directly and as transmitted through families and social groups. This argument is similar to that of Carrion and Lock (1997) that societal intolerance trickles down from larger institutions to the local environment of children.

Psychoanalytic lens

Countertransference

Transcribing between 10 and 12 hours of audio with 24 participants was a difficult experience for me. Many of the participants are my friends or acquaintances, some of whom I look up to or view as windows into my future as a gay man in the Orthodox community. Most of them are high functioning, some of them are well accomplished either financially or professionally, and many of them seemed to me to be comfortable, or at least comfortable with their discomfort, in the Orthodox community. But as I heard their stories in person, replayed them over and over again as I transcribed them, and then read the transcriptions repeatedly, I felt hopeless and sad. I looked at the stories of my participants, members of my group, and I saw that they had not achieved the life that I hoped for myself. Many were single, even if they had enjoyed long-term relationships in the past. Everybody was somewhat on the fringe and an outsider in some way. The participants became a window into my past, present, and future, and the view was dark and dreary. "Will this be my lot in life?" I asked myself. "Will *my* dream of finding a life partner and raising children remain unfulfilled?" I felt pain as I looked into my future because it looked challenging at best.

At the same time, I felt surprised. Many of the participants, though not all, displayed a strong, deep-rooted, positive connection to Orthodoxy and to their communities. They praised many aspects of Orthodoxy, from good values and critical thinking skills to ancient rituals and a sense of engaging one's history. Despite their dissatisfaction, they expressed a desire for the community to maintain its practices and traditions. It became clear to me that most participants wanted the same things that straight members of the Orthodox community want: an Orthodox community that embraces them and celebrates them and their families.

So, although many participants did not explicitly report intense negative affect during the focus groups, I believe that the sadness and hopelessness I felt in reaction to their stories may have reflected an aspect of their experience that was not verbalized and perhaps unconscious. So it is in the spirit of what I understand to be the difficulties experienced by participants, along with their adoration of their faith and communities, that I review and apply a psychoanalytic lens to the data.

True and false selves

Concepts pioneered by Donald W. Winnicott, an object-relations-oriented psychoanalyst and pediatrician, can help enhance the conceptualization of the experiences of gay Jewish men in the Orthodox community. According to Winnicott (1964), a baby's psychological development, healthy or not, is highly influenced by the mother. The mother's repeated successes at meeting the child's needs lead to the development of the True Self. The False Self, on the other hand, is created by the mother's failure to meet the needs of the infant, instead meeting her own needs. The infant interprets this as a demand for compliance. The False Self, characterized by compliance, is the baby's reaction to demands from the environment. Through this False Self, the child builds false relationships that may appear real. The False Self is defensive in that it serves the function of hiding or protecting the True Self from the overwhelming anxiety of the potential loss of the mother's love by complying with her demands.

False Self organizations fall along a continuum with the least healthy at one end and the most healthy at the other (Winnicott, 1964). At the most extreme end of the unhealthy side of the spectrum, the False Self sets up as real, and others see the False Self as the real person. The False Self fails, however, in various interpersonal relationships, particularly when the person needs to be his whole person. In a less extreme organization, the False Self protects the True Self, which is acknowledged and is allowed a private life. The most healthy version of the False Self is one that is represented by politeness and appropriate social behaviors, such as not expressing every emotion that is experienced by the individual. In this case, the individual gains a place in society through this False Self.

Attributing much of the child's development to early mothering, Winnicott certainly believed in environmental influence on the individual. He discussed the concept of the facilitating environment which, although it does not "make the child" (Winnicott, 1964, p. 85), it allows the maturation process to occur, and "enables the child to realize potential" (ibid). For Winnicott, facilitation means "that there is adaptation to basic need" (Winnicott, 2002, p. 51), referring to the mother's adaptation to the child's needs. Winnicott also coined the phrase the "good-enough mother" (Winnicott, 1964, p. 145) to describe the parenting needed for healthy ego development. Winnicott (2002) emphasized the human aspects of facilitation and not mechanical perfection.

Winnicott's theory of development and the False and True Selves has the potential to lend a useful perspective from which to view the experiences of gay Jewish men in the Orthodox community. However, Winnicott wrote about his concepts of the facilitating environment, good-enough mothering, and True and False Selves in reference to infant development. In order to apply these concepts, I broaden his theory in two ways: with regard to time and with regard to people. First, I suggest that the development of the False Self and of the True Self need not develop only in infancy. Instead, I see the True Self and False Self as developing and existing dynamically throughout the lifespan. In this case, an infant who eventually turns out to identify as a gay man may not develop a compliant False Self until his gayness emerges, whether unconsciously or consciously. The need to satisfy the other while protecting both one's True Self, and one's gay self in this instance, may arise much later than infancy. If a False Self can emerge later in development, it follows that the need for a facilitating environment and good-enough mothering extends beyond infancy and childhood as well. In fact, if True and False Selfhood are seen as dynamic aspects of personhood that have the potential to wax and wane throughout life, a facilitating environment becomes a lifelong, human necessity to facilitate authentic and spontaneous living.

In addition to Winnicott's focus on infancy and younger years, he also focused on the mother as the almost exclusive facilitator of the development of the False and True Selves. Father and other family members play a role in development, according to Winnicott, but not until later (1964, 1986), and they do not impact the True and False Selves of the individual. Still, Winnicott acknowledged the influence of non-mother entities on the individual, even beyond the family. For example, Winnicott wrote that "the family leads on to all manner of groups, groups that get wider and wider until they reach the size of the local society and society in general" (1986, p. 140). Clarke, Hahn, Hoggett, and Sideris (2006) wrote that Winnicott's concept of the facilitating environment has been useful in understanding the therapeutic nature of professionals and institutions in helping the individuals hold and consider overwhelming emotional experiences. In light of this literature and Winnicott's acknowledgment of the importance of family and society in development, I extend his concept of False and True Selves to the dynamic, life-long aspects of the self, and that each person depends on an ongoing facilitating environment, or good-enough mothering, as provided by social circles, communities, and society, to attain and sustain healthy, authentic living.

This expanded version of Winnicott's theory of development contributes a rich and helpful understanding of the experiences of gay Jewish men in the Orthodox community. The data suggest, then, that the Orthodox community does not constitute a good-enough facilitating environment to encourage True Selfhood for gay men. Instead, this community often conveys disappointment, disapproval, and dissatisfaction. Given this "un-facilitating," if not hostile, environment, a False Self develops in gay men to protect their True (gay) Selves. The idea that communal expectations lead to two versions of the self is also written about by Greenberg (2004, p. 217): "Gender expectations split us into the desiring, feeling, expressing self and the censoring self." The best example of this in the data is the theme of duality, which speaks to the necessity of gay men having two existences: their gay existence and their Orthodox existence. Fear of losing friends, disappointing or burdening family, and being stereotyped are all some of the ways in which the Orthodox community fails to sufficiently facilitate the continual existence of authentic selfhood of gay men.

To be sure, the False Self is an unconscious and automatic defense of the True Self rather than a conscious mechanism (Kitron, 2001). The fact that some of the participants spoke about the duality of their lives in terms of concrete and presumably deliberate behaviors, such as pretending to be single in synagogue while in a committed same-sex relationship or having to hide participation in this study from straight friends, does not appear to fit with the unconscious nature of the False Self. However, the sadness and hopelessness I experienced while listening and analyzing the focus groups in combination with some of the participants' positive evaluations of Orthodoxy can be seen as examples of projective identification and reaction formation and as evidence of unconscious False Self processes. If unconscious False Self processes are understood to be present, the fact that participants were conscious of some of their efforts at compliance can be seen as high levels of self-awareness of what once was a more unconscious process.

Clinical implications

Caution is warranted in discussing the clinical implications of this study. Viewing the data and the model presented through a clinical lens can be problematic because doing so could mislead rabbis, community leaders, and community members to think that the path to alleviating the suffering of gay men in the Orthodox community is primarily through psychotherapy. Although therapy is one excellent method for alleviating psychic pain and problematic coping behaviors, it should not be viewed as the primary solution for this problem, the cause of which is socio-religious.

Still, mental health clinicians (and rabbis when serving as pastoral counselors) play an important role in helping individuals heal and communities transform (see also Chapter 5 in this book). This is true for several reasons: first, unfortunately, the Orthodox community is not currently in a place where the maturational, personal, religious, and identity developmental processes of gay men are widely understood, let alone supported. As such, mental health clinicians often bear the responsibility of filling in where the community falters. Using the data from this study and the application of Winnicott, several principles are presented to guide clinicians in providing culturally sensitive and effective therapy for gay men seeking assistance in navigating their sexuality, their families, their communities, and themselves.

It is important that psychotherapy constitute a facilitating environment that encourages the development of the authenticity characteristic of the True Self. This involves being non-judgmental and cautious not to induce compliance, particularly with regard to sexuality and gender, and the exploration and experimentation thereof. This may involve redirecting a patient to voice his own wishes, desires, and reactions when he appears focused on what others in his life want from him. Another way to communicate acceptance might be to wonder aloud a behavioral strategy that might be seen by the patient as religiously forbidden or frowned upon. For example, a therapist may wonder why the patient has not tried to meet up with a man via an app or website. Simply showing that such an exploration strategy is in the realm of possibility, helpful behaviors communicate to the patient that the goal of therapy is to help him be him. This type of intervention may be particularly powerful when performed by an Orthodox Jewish therapist who is known by the patient to be observant. In this case, the intervention would serve as an emotionally corrective Orthodox experience for the patient who is primed to be guarded and compliant in Orthodox settings.

Therapists will be better equipped to provide helpful therapy if they are familiar with concerns and aspects of experience common to gay men from the Orthodox community. Some, if not many, of these issues have been written about in this chapter. Awareness and basic understanding of these issues will allow the therapist to normalize such experiences reported by their patients.

Therapists are advised to consider the conceptualization of the four domains of experience as a potentially powerful clinical tool in two ways: first, knowing that the self experience is influenced by the social, family, and communal experience can guide a therapist to target the improvement of quality of life in some domains when other domains are characterized by suffering and challenges. A patient struggling in the domain of family may find solace in strengthening his social supports. Second, keeping the four domains and themes in mind may help a clinician remain vigilant to omissions, what the patient is not talking about, so that important clinical material is not overlooked. For example, a patient who speaks about difficulties with his family of origin and theological challenges may forget to explore his social experience. The therapist may wish to call attention to this omission in the interest of exploring all potential areas for therapeutic exploration and personal healing.

One of themes in the theory was unmet needs, which contained the ideas of there being insufficient institutional resources, sex education, and role models. As such, it is incumbent upon the therapist to address each of these needs as appropriate. Refer patients to organizations that cater to the intersection of LGBT identities and Orthodox Judaism, two examples of which are Eshel (www.eshelonline.org) and JQY (Jewish Queer Youth, www.jqyouth.org). These organizations can help patients find sensitive religious guidance, social support, and mentors and role models. Third, it is critical that therapists have competency in safe sex practices, with regard to preventing sexually transmitted infection (STI) contraction, assaults, and trauma. Be sure to bring up health, safety, and also pleasure with regard to sex if the patient does not do so on his own.

An important—and perhaps the saddest—phenomenon of the gay man's experience in the Orthodox community, according to the data, is the impact the environment has on the individual's view of himself and his sexuality. Participants received continuous, repeated messages, both implicit and explicit, that their sexual orientation is simply not OK. Weddings will not be officiated, partnerships will not be celebrated, and children of gay parents may have a limited selection of Orthodox day schools they may attend. The data suggest that gay men internalize the messages from their families, social groups, and larger community. For example, one participant compared his attraction to men with an addiction, another saw his sexual orientation as being "in everybody's face," and a third viewed himself as guilty of a crime. It is usually a sign of healthy modesty for individuals to recognize their own weaknesses and understand that they are imperfect. However, in the case of gay men in the Orthodox community, according to the data, their gayness is often seen as a cause of their imperfection. This internalized sexual stigma is consistent with the concept of internalized homophobia, as described by Mark (2008) and Hartman and Koren (2006). This internalized stigma, also called internalized homophobia, can be an important target for discussion in treatment. Addressing internalized stigma is best done from a stance that balances acceptance of the patient's present view of himself and his gayness, given his background and environment with guiding and assisting the patient to develop a less stigmatizing view of himself and his sexual identity.

Remarkably, most of the gay men in the study maintained strong, often positive, connections to their religion, culture, and communities. Despite significant challenges, even suffering, many sang the praise of Orthodoxy. They liked the family feel and the ability to go anywhere in the world and simply "plug right back in," as one participant put it. They still strongly identified with the community. And, with this strong connection, a number of the participants came to terms with Orthodoxy and their relationship with the community. Whether they comfortably concluded that neither they nor the Orthodox community needed to change or they ended up believing that their involvement in the community was up to them, their negative feelings often came to some kind of resolution. They maintained surprisingly positive connections to their Orthodox identities and communities with varying degrees of observance. Though this may not be the case for all gay men in the Orthodox community, maintaining a connection with the community was ubiquitous among participants, and a somewhat positive connection was common as well. As such, it is important that therapists help their patients maintain positive connections to the Orthodox community to the degree that it is healthy and enriching. Therapists will best serve their patients by helping them become aware of and embrace their ambivalence toward the Orthodox community. Much like our closest family members, it is possible—indeed healthy—that we feel both love and anger toward them—so too, the Orthodox community.

Coming out

When, where, and to whom to come out is an ongoing question for gay men generally, as well as for men in the Orthodox community. Orthodoxy can be distinguished from other branches of Judaism by its focus on its strict behavioral and ritualistic system of laws. Because Orthodoxy views male-to-male anal intercourse as a biblical transgression, and other male-to-male sexual acts as rabbinic level prohibitions, when a person says, "I am gay," he is seen as publicly acknowledging forbidden sexual behaviors. The gay man is treated like a straight man who walks around announcing to his fellow community members all of the various sexual transgressions in which he engages with his wife. Straightness represents love, family, and fulfilling God's commandments, whereas gayness may be perceived as equaling forbidden sexual behavior and only that. In such an environment, patients and therapists may benefit from a reframing of what it means to come out.

Minton and McDonald (1983) acknowledged that concealing one's gay identity may have negative psychological effects. de Monteflores and Schultz (1978) applied Jourard's (1971) theory of self-disclosure to coming out to others. Jourard saw disclosure to others as a necessary part of achieving self-knowledge, and without self-knowledge, an individual "will sicken" (Jourard, 1971, p. 6). Cass (1979) emphasized the importance of cognitive and affective congruency with regard to a gay person's view of his gayness, his gay behavior, and his perceptions of others' view of his gayness. For Cass, coming out to others affirms one's own gay identity and makes one's public identity in line with one's private identity.

The literature on gay identity development consistently points to the importance of public versus private identities and the importance of personal authenticity. Coming out as gay in the Orthodox community is, therefore, hardly about reporting one's sexual behaviors. Instead, it is about claiming an identity that runs in contrast to the expectations of the community and about being authentic and honest with others about one's life. Coming out in the Orthodox community need not be viewed as a confession of sin or a flaunting of transgression and might, instead, be more helpfully and accurately understood as an individual's attempt to be his whole self with others. Figure 6.1 depicts the various social forces as they impact the gay man. The drawing shows the family, social, and individual resting within the community context. The community impacts the individual both directly and as mediated through the family and social forces. The overlap shows the individual's experience to exist in the community, his family, and his social circle.

In Table 6.1, different styles of text are used to indicate the different levels of hierarchical organization. The 68 repeating ideas (*italics*) were categorized into 21 themes (underlined) which were organized into four theoretical constructs (ALL CAPS). The theoretical constructs were then used to create a theoretical narrative.

Notes

1 See the full dissertation for a literature review, detailed explanation of the methods, limitations and critique, and implications for further research.
2 Different styles of text are used to indicate the different levels of hierarchical organization. Repeating ideas are in *italics*, themes are underlined, and theoretical constructs are in ALL CAPS. Quotation marks are used to indicate direct quotes from participants. Brackets contain additional information to facilitate understanding.

References

Auerbach, C. F., & Silverstein, L. B. (2003). *Qualitative Data*. New York and London: New York University Press.

Carrion, V. G. & Lock, J. (1997). The coming out process: Developmental stages for sexual minority youth. *Clinical Child Psychology and Psychiatry*, 2(3):369–377.

Cass, V. C. (1979). Homosexual identity formation: A theoretical model. *Journal of Homosexuality*, 4(3):219–235.

Clarke, S., Hahn, H., Hoggett, P., & Sideris, T. (2006). Psychoanalysis and community. *Psychoanalysis, Culture & Society*, 11:199–216.

de Monteflores, C. & Schultz, S. J. (1978). Coming out: Similarities and differences for lesbians and gay men. *Journal of Social Issues*, 34:59–72.

Greenberg, S. (2004). *Wrestling with God and Men: Homosexuality in the Jewish Tradition*. Madison, WI: The University of Wisconsin Press.

Hartman, T. & Koren, I. (2006). Between "being" and "doing": Conflict and coherence in the identity formation of gay and lesbian Orthodox Jews. In D. P. McAdams, R. Josselson, & A. Lieblich (eds.), *Identity and Story: Creating Self in Narrative* (pp. 37–61). Washington, DC: American Psychological Association.

Jourard, S. M. (1971). *The Transparent Self: Self-disclosure and Well-being*. New York: Van Nostrand Reinhold.

Kitron, D. (2001). Secluded lives: The shelter of false selves in sociocultural contexts. *Psychoanalysis & Contemporary Thought*, 24(1):67–79.

Mark, N. (2008). Identities in conflict: Forging an Orthodox gay identity. *Journal of Gay and Lesbian Health*, 12(3):179–194.

Minton, H. L. & McDonald, G. J. (1983). Homosexual identity formation as a developmental process. *Journal of Homosexuality*, 9:91–104.

Novich, J. (2014) *The Experiences of Gay Jewish Men in the Orthodox Community: Social Justice, Oppression, and Winnicott*. Brookville, NY: Long Island University.

Prilleltensky, I. & Nelson, G. (2002). *Doing Psychology Critically: Making a Difference in Diverse Settings*. New York: Palgrave Macmillan.

Winnicott, D. W. (1964). *The Maturational Processes and the Facilitating Environment: Studies in the Theory of Emotional Development*. New York: International Universities Press.

Winnicott, D. W. (1986). *Home is Where we Start From: Essays by a Psychoanalyst*. New York and London: W. W. Norton & Co..

Winnicott, D. W. (2002). *Winnicott on the child*. Cambridge, MA: Perseus Publishing.

Chapter 7

The parents are our future[1]

Orthodox communities' openness to their LGBT members

Miryam Kabakov

Parents as catalysts for change

When Orthodox parents find out that their child is LGBT (lesbian, gay, bisexual, transgender), their hopes and dreams for their child's future—which are usually based on the presumption of the child's heterosexuality—are often shattered. Orthodox parents of LGBT children report experiencing: loss, grief, fear, isolation, depression, and alienation from community, rabbi, and friends; threats to quality of life for themselves and their children; and fear for the future of their child. Some of these challenges are particularly acute because Orthodox families are part of religiously (and often socially) conservative communities. Yet precisely because Orthodox families with an LGBT member face these specific challenges, they are also presented with unique opportunities to create a more open space for their child within those communities. My work with such parents as the executive director of Eshel (www.eshelonelin.org), a support and advocacy organization for LGBT Orthodox Jews and their families, has suggested that, when parents of LGBT children receive support, they are empowered to advocate for themselves. In doing so, they become key players in opening or widening the door to their communities' acceptance of their children. In this chapter, I argue that parents of LGBT children, more than those children themselves, serve as catalysts for change in the Orthodox community. This chapter is based on my work with parents of LGBT children. Very little, if any, research has been done on this topic.

Coming out: for parents too

"Coming out" is a term that usually applies only to a person with a minority sexual or gender identity who publicly acknowledges that identity. But it is a term that also accurately captures the difficulties that family members of LGBT individuals face when they reveal that they have an LGBT person in their close inner circle. Wherever parents fall on the spectrum of acceptance, once they start to grapple with their children's coming out, they all eventually have to form a new identity as the parent of an LGBT person. If Orthodox parents decide to share their new identity with their community, thereby reestablishing themselves as a family with an LGBT member, they place themselves on the frontlines of the constantly negotiated tension within Orthodox communities about the extent to which they are inclusive.

This is no small decision; to come out about one's child has grave consequences. For example, the "marriage-ability" of their other children can be compromised if the parents reveal they have an LGBT child. Yet being in the closet about their children is a painful experience. As one mother writes:

> My son had come out to me as transgender (female to male) a few years back and the fallout from what felt like a nuclear explosion was still very much impacting my life and all around us. So the landscape was such that I was "in the closet" in my very black hat community about my son. Every time someone inquired about the well-being of my "daughter," I answered in a deceptive but truthful manner . . .. However, it never felt right, and I was living a life that felt deceptive—I felt like a fraud.

Although some parents choose to remain closeted, others—however painful, as in the account above—do develop the courage to come out to their friends, community members, rabbis, and other community associates about their children. In fact, some of the challenges Orthodox parents face when they "come out" about their children have prompted these parents to work for systemic change within their communities.

One of the coping mechanisms of Orthodox LGBT people, when they understand themselves as lesbian, gay, bisexual, or transgender, is to move away from the Orthodox community in which they grew up. Most Orthodox LGBT Jews of various upbringings, from modern to Hasidic to yeshivish, find moving to a different location and community, in which they feel relatively comfortable, a better alternative than staying within their community of origin. For such Jews, leaving the fold is often the preferred choice, even if it is a painful one.

The typical path for parents of those who choose to leave the community differs from that of their children: parents of late-adolescent or adult children are less likely to leave their Orthodox community when they discover they have an LGBT child. Usually in their 40s or older, they are deeply rooted in their community, jobs, and homes. Staying rooted forces a conversation in their communities that may not otherwise happen. As a result, some of these parents—some who are leaders within their communities—can counter the negativity with dialogue and discussion among their peers.

The good news is that the opinions of Orthodox community members have changed over the past several years about including LGBTQ members in their synagogues. A recent study by Nishma Research (2017) explores the connection between trends in secular society and shifting beliefs occur concurrently within modern Orthodoxy.

Possibly as a reflection of marriage equality and a more open attitude to LGBTQ individuals in American society in general, "U.S. society has experienced a shift toward greater acceptance of gays." As a tenet of modern Orthodoxy is interaction with secular society, it is interesting to see if the secular society's attitudes have permeated modern Orthodoxy. In fact, modern Orthodoxy has similarly become more open to gays. Overall, 58% support Orthodox shuls in general, accepting gays as members with 12% opposed (29% are not sure) (https://forward.com/news/breaking-news/383902/modern-orthodox-jews-are-mostly-observant-wealthy-and-gay-friendly/) (Nishma Research, 2017).

Communal challenges: rabbinic responses

In many Orthodox communities, people turn to their rabbis with a range of questions about life choices and situations from large to small. When parents learn about their LGBT child, their first impulse may be to tell their rabbi to seek support and advice. This places the rabbi in a unique position as a first responder. Yet, the rabbi is often the last person who the parent reaches out to.

In February 2016, Eshel sent a confidential survey to approximately 300 Jewish Orthodox and traditional parents with LGBT children. Over 100 parents completed the survey. One significant finding was that synagogue rabbis are among the last resources parents seek out for help when their child comes out. Nearly 20% of respondents did not seek outside help at all. For the remaining parents, they approached a psychologist outside of school first (17%), an Orthodox support group, such as Eshel, second (16%), other parents of an LGBT child third (12%), and a rabbi outside their synagogue fourth (9%). Synagogue rabbis and school principals or counselors were the last resources parents reached out to in the Orthodox community.

When parents do tell their rabbis, many parents report feeling let down and disappointed with the response of their spiritual leaders. Although the rabbi may give *halakhic* (legal–practical) or *hashkafik* (normative–theological) advice on how to treat the child, as they would with regard to any nonconforming child, many rabbis feel at a loss and admit to not having enough information to help the parents understand their child's sexual or gender identity. A systematic dearth of information on LGBT issues from a modern psychiatric and medical perspective remains typical of Orthodox rabbinic education. As a result, many rabbis remain in the dark about current thinking with regard to being LGBT and are unable to provide adequate responses to members who come to them seeking advice about their child. As one mother put it, "the rabbi in *shul* has been trying to understand but he does not get it." (See Chapters 4, 5, and 16 in this book on different approaches and attempts to focus on and educate rabbinic leaders.)

Parents have reported that their rabbi has confessed to them this lack of knowledge and awareness on how to deal with an LGBT child. As one father reflected:

> I think the Rabbis are not knowledgeable about the LGBT situation regarding Orthodox Jews. They don't know what to answer them or how to guide them. They are ignorant of many basic facts about LGBT people and react based on stereotypical and false premises.

Some parents have reported that their rabbis suggested they consider having their child undergo "reparative" therapy, even though the Rabbinical Council of America withdrew its support of JONAH (Jews Offering New Alternatives to Homosexuality) in 2012 after a lawsuit was brought against the organization (see Chapter 4 which explicitly opposes "reparative" therapy).

Orthodox rabbis who are relatively open to hearing news of an LGBT family member often do not know how to convey acceptance. At a variety of levels, they often do not feel comfortable welcoming the child back as a fully fledged member of the community. For reasons related to Jewish law, the rabbi may not feel willing or able to have the child participate fully in synagogue rituals. In not fully accepting the child, clergy are asking parents to choose between their community and their child. For example, a parent of a transgender child told me that the rabbi asked that the child not come back to the synagogue because he feared it would be a hostile environment as a result of the reaction of other congregants. Although having good intentions, the rabbi has created an untenable situation for the family.

Another effect this rejection has is that LGBT children are more likely to walk away from Orthodox Judaism. For an Orthodox parent, the prospect of their child leaving Judaism can be more disturbing than their being LGBT. As one parent put it:

One of the parents at the regional meeting said what was most painful is not the fact that their child was gay or trans but that their child was leaving Judaism .... This comes back to our rabbis, they do not realize that we are losing wonderful Jews because—to put it mildly—they are apathetic about our children.

Without fully realizing the impact of their words, rabbis can make stinging comments from the pulpit that have a great impact on the family. Parents often hear derogatory language about LGBT people from the pulpit or while being a guest in a friend's home at a Shabbat meal. One mother lamented:

Our rabbi said [Hurricane] Katrina happened because there were so many gay people in New Orleans .... You hear something like that from the bima (pulpit) ... and think if there are any teenagers here who are struggling ... you push them away.

In these moments parents feel the tension of the choice before them: if they admit to being offended by such comments, this identifies them as an ally, parent, or friend, or as someone who has more "liberal" views than their friends, which might ostracize them from peers. If they choose to remain silent they experience a complicit betrayal of their child.

Although it is extremely difficult to stand out and speak up in public, for fear of being ostracized by peers, the power of this act can create opportunities toward change. In one case, one parent walked out of his synagogue for the last time after his rabbi made an offensive comment during a sermon. As he was a long-time member of the synagogue, the leaders of the community took notice when he decided not to return to the congregation until after the current rabbi left his position. This resulted in a community-wide conversation about how the synagogue treated LGBT people. In another case, when siblings experienced teasing and bullying because of their LGBT brother, the family decided to move to a more hospitable community. They were able to find an Orthodox community where they knew the rabbi and members would be welcoming.

From rabbinic authority to peer support

Another finding from the Eshel report is that synagogues and synagogue rabbis have remained largely silent on the issue of LGBT Jews with little or no public discussion. Over 73% of parents report no public forums or classes on the topic of LGBT Jews, with only 18% of parents reporting that their synagogue has held a public discussion on the subject.

As community leaders (rabbis, educators) have for the most part remained silent on this issue, and are often at a loss as to how to counsel parents about their LGBT child or, worse, reject these families, parents must draw on their own internal strengths and resources. Many rely heavily on their intuition about their child, and this, in turn can affect their religious beliefs. As one mother said about her experience in her community and her attitude toward her child: "All the people have been amazing.... I know in my heart that *Hashem* wants us to love our children. No child would choose this."

In addition to shoring up their own internal resources, parents look for friends who will not turn them away. More than two-thirds of parents report their friends are generally supportive when their children have come out, according to the Eshel study.

Finding supportive friends enables parents to form a ring of allies around them. These are people in their community whom they know they can rely on, turn to, and not be worried that they will be ostracized. When parents have a group of friends, these allies can and do support them in their inclusion efforts, thus broadening their community of support. For example, one couple felt particularly excluded when the birth of their daughter and her partner's newborn was not announced in the same way as was done for other members' grandchildren. When the parents shared this experience with their friends, a number of community members were quite upset on behalf of the new grandparents. Since then, the rabbi has become more attentive to the parents' concerns and, during one Shabbat, the rabbi of the synagogue provided a forum to discuss LGBT issues in the Orthodox community by having the couple teach on the topic on a Saturday afternoon.

Through the various emotions of disbelief, grief, confusion, and hope, parents are able to mentor each other in the process of accepting their new reality. They eventually learn, from each other, how to advocate most effectively for their children. They compare notes on how their children have been treated by their community; they share how they have handled similar situations with community and clergy. Through mutual support, a transformation occurs: parents become a part of a larger community they did not know previously existed.

Some parents have expressed that, although they have sought out support from non-Jewish or non-Orthodox support systems, these systems do not adequately address their unique challenges; they need other Orthodox parents to draw from as they navigate the inclusion of their new family construct in Orthodox community. As in most support groups, when parents find each other, they expand their community to include not only others in a similar situation but also allies who can provide solace and support; these allies eventually become friends and like family.

Often anonymously, parents have used the internet as a tool to share their process and progress in their relationships with their children and community. Through blogs, articles, and opinion pieces, Orthodox parents have been outspoken about their and their families' needs, challenges, and struggles. For example, the anonymous blog, "Frum Gay Kids Mom," began in December 2013; here is an excerpt from the first post:

> I'm hoping this blog will evolve over time. Right now I'm writing it for myself. So I can get my feelings out in writing. In the future, I hope this can be a resource for anyone else dealing with a similar situation.

A post from June 2014 testifies to the importance of advocacy and locates its beginning in the support of peers:

> Over the past eight months I've gone out of my comfort zone in so many ways. This blog takes me out of my comfort zone. Not the writing, but the writing so many personal things (even though I do it anonymously). I've gone out of my comfort zone to contact people I may not have otherwise met and contacted. I went to a retreat with 30 people I NEVER met before and I had an amazing time. I can't stress enough how not "me" that is. I'm mostly proud that I have figured out that if I want change, I need to be part of it. And I'm willing to be part of it. Can't say it doesn't frighten me on a daily basis because I really prefer not to put myself "out there." But if I want change, I can't sit back and think that everyone else will make it happen.

Gaining rabbinic support

As seeking rabbinic advice is a high priority for many Orthodox people, parents help each other navigate this relationship so that it benefits them and their families. When approaching clergy for support or advice, parents need to know what they are asking for and what they hope to receive. Framing the conversation can be vital to a positive outcome.

When one couple began a conversation with their rabbi about their LGBT children, they asked him to listen as a parent and not as a rabbi. Thus, before they asked for any advice, the parents guided the rabbi in taking an empathetic response. The subsequent communication between parent and rabbi was effective because it drew on the rabbi's ability to empathize and respond as a parent.

As Orthodox leaders are often neither informed about nor equipped to deal with the needs of their LGBT members, parents are in the unique situation of being the ones to educate their clergy toward understanding their children. Similar to how LGBT children have had to educate their parents or point them to resources, parents have the opportunity to educate their rabbis or suggest how they can gain the needed information to better help their congregants.

Last, parents have learned that, with controversial topics like this one, Orthodox leaders are vulnerable when voicing their opinions. Their peers often marginalize those rabbis who are outspoken on behalf of LGBT people, and rabbis who do speak out may divide their congregation. They risk their jobs or losing credibility as a leader and as an authority figure.

Rabbis must realize that, when a parent tells their rabbi about their LGBTQ child, they are coming out in similar ways to when their child came out to them. By coming out to their rabbis as parents of an LGBTQ child, parents report feeling vulnerable, scared, and at risk of losing their friends and community. They fear rejection from their religious leaders, and know that their other children are under the threat of being stigmatized.

Resources

Parents are often left leaderless with no rabbinic authorities helping them holistically navigate the challenges of having an LGBT child. Thus parents have relied on other sources of support. Eshel and Temicha are two groups that provide resources to them and their children.

Temicha: operating under the auspices of JQYouth, an organization that focuses on serving the needs of LGBT Jewish youth and their families, has a Listserv for parents. In the New York area it runs JQY's Long Island Teen Group, a support group for local teens from Orthodox backgrounds.

Eshel conducts regular monthly meetings on the phone for parents of LGBTQ children. Over the past 5 years, over 300 parents have reached out for support. Through an annual retreat and local gatherings, Eshel has developed a national parent support network. Eshel has also developed a parent mentoring program.

Through Eshel's Welcoming Shuls Project, a network of 120 Orthodox pulpit rabbis have been identified as being welcoming in some way toward their LGBTQ members. This project serves as a resource to anyone who calls Eshel's warmline in search of a community to which to belong.

In the last year, Eshel has launched a Pledge campaign (www.eshelon line.org/pledge/), which consists of alum of Yeshivah Day schools urging the leadership of these schools to take a pledge of inclusion for their LGBTQ students. Although many school administrators will not, for political reasons, be able to fully proclaim inclusivity, this Pledge project will get the conversation going, hopefully, at board and lay leader levels.

A spiritual journey

Many parents report that the challenge of having an LGBT child has put them on path to a spiritual quest. They wonder why this particular parenting challenge is happening to them, why God has given them this challenge.

Rabbis are in a unique position to serve as a spiritual guide for parents on this journey—to recognize that this is a spiritual journey for the parents as well as the child. Their approach should include taking in the totality of the child; sexual identity is not just about a sex act but rather about the growth of an individual who may care deeply about integrating his or her religious and sexual or gender identity. Ultimately, how the child is treated in the community can determine whether he or she will leave Orthodoxy. For the parents, the rabbi can use this opportunity to guide them to make positive parenting choices that do not push the child away. As some parents wonder what the spiritual message is that they should be receiving from this challenge, rabbis are in a position to help parents make meaning out of their new reality, thereby helping them grow as Jews as well as parents.

Key leaders within Orthodoxy have expressed a new openness to hearing from LGBT people. In some communities the time is ripe for change and dialogue on how to support families with an LGBT child. Parents can rely on leaders trained and educated about the needs of LGBT individuals for guidance that combines current knowledge with wisdom and fidelity to *halakha*—which is what Orthodox individuals should expect from their religious leaders.

Although Orthodox communities tend to move much more slowly on controversial topics than their non-Orthodox counterparts, now is a particularly potent time for opening up dialogue about their LGBT members. As youth in America come out to their families more frequently and earlier than ever before, traditional Jewish communities will, over time, encounter more members whose gender and sexual orientation do not conform. According to the 2013b Pew study, *A Survey of LGBT Americans*, "12 is the median age at which lesbian, gay and bisexual adults first felt they might be something other than heterosexual or straight. For those who say they now know for sure that they are lesbian, gay, bisexual or transgender, that realization came at a median age of 17."

Another 2013a Pew Research Center survey, *A Portrait of American Jews*, found that 27% of Jewish children are being raised in Orthodox households. It is clear that, in the next 20 years, the make-up of the traditional Jewish family will be changing. Traditional Jewish communities need to be equipped to deal with these changes.

As executive director of Eshel, I am often asked whether I feel hopeful about the future for Orthodox LGBT people and their families. I have seen how parents occupy a unique position in the quest for LGBT inclusion in the Orthodox community, and it is parents' involvement that makes me feel hopeful. Dr. Kenneth Prager (2010) in his article, "The answers lie in our love for our daughter," wrote that the "process of re-examining the Orthodox position on homosexuality has begun—and there is no turning back. A proud and outspoken parent, I am a part of a growing community of parents who are partially responsible for animating this process of reexamination. It is for them, as much as for their children, that this process must continue."

There is no turning back because of the chilling statistics that have emerged recently in a study in the *Huffington Post* about the correlation between religious beliefs and suicide attempts and suicidal ideation in youth in April of 2018.

The study surveyed 21,247 students aged 18–30 years. Five percent of heterosexual youth reported attempting suicide in their lifetimes, compared with 20% of bisexual youth, 17% of questioning youth, and 14% of gay or lesbian youth.

Each increase in the level of importance of religion among straight youth was associated with a 17% reduction in recent suicide attempts. For lesbian and gay youth, however, increasing levels of religious importance were associated with increased odds of recent suicidal ideation. In fact, lesbian and gay youth who said that religion was important to them were 38% more likely to have had recent suicidal thoughts, compared with lesbian and gay youth who reported religion was less important. Religiosity among lesbians alone was linked to a 52% increased chance of recent suicidal ideation (Federal Bureau of Investigation, n.d.; Eisenberg & Resnick, 2006; Ryan et al., 2009).

Finally, the answer to depression, alcohol and drug use, and suicide is communal, religious, and family connectedness and acceptance. According to a 2009 study done by the Family Acceptance Project, the factors that contribute to lower likelihood of exhibiting suicidal ideation and suicide attempts are family connectedness, caring teachers, and safe schools. Parents, more than anyone, are in a position to make major changes for their children within Orthodox synagogues, schools, and communities. The answer lies within the family, and the parents are the change agents of the larger Orthodox communities in which they belong.

Note

1 An earlier version of this article appeared in: *Journal of Jewish Communal Service*, Volume 89, No. 1, Fall 2014. Reprinted by permission of the journal.

References

Eisenberg, M. E. and Resnick, M. D. (2006). Suicidality among gay, lesbian and bisexual youth: The role of protective factors. *Journal of Adolescent Health.* 39:662–668.

Eshel (2017). Confidential study. Available at: www.eshelonline.org/about-new/our-mission/

Federal Bureau of Investigation (n.d.). Available at: socialexplorer.com. Census Bureau, Pew Research Center, Williams Institute

Huffington Post (2018, April). Chilling study sums up link between religion and suicide for queer youth. Available at: www.huffingtonpost.com/entry/queer-youth-religion-suicide-study_us_5ad4f7b3e4b077c89ceb9774.

Nishma Research (2017). The Nishma Research profile of American modern Orthodox Jews. Available at: http://nishmaresearch.com/.

Pew Research Center (2013a). *A Portrait of Jewish Americans*. Philadelphia, PA: Pew Research Center.

Pew Research Center (2013b). *A Survey of LGBT Americans*. Philadelphia, PA: Pew Research Center.

Prager, K. (2010). The answers lie in our love for our daughter. *The Jewish Standard* October 29. Available at: http://rabbicreditor.blogspot.com/2010/11/nj-jewish-standard-opinion-answers-lie.html

Ryan, C., Huebner, D., Diaz, R. M., & Sanchez, J. (2009). Family Acceptance Project™, Family rejection as a predictor of negative health outcomes in white and Latino lesbian, gay, and bisexual young adults. *Pediatrics.* 123(1):346–352.

Chapter 8

Envisioning an Orthodox gay wedding

A Jewish ritual of same-sex union and an inquiry into the meanings of marriage

Rabbi Steven Greenberg

Although the mood in the US had been moving slowly toward marriage equality for a generation, the Orthodox communal leadership joined a chorus of religious denominations that resisted any such liberalization. After more than two decades of intense social and political conflict, on June 26, 2015, the US Supreme Court legalized same-sex marriage in all 50 states much to the dismay of conservative religious voices. In response to the vote the Orthodox Union released a statement that reiterated their standard position that the Bible, Talmud, and Codes all forbid homosexual relationships and condemns "the institutionalization of such relationships as marriages."

None the less, over the past few years, especially among the rank-and-file Orthodox laity, a growing tolerance can be discerned. A recent survey of modern Orthodox attitudes in the US found that 58% of those interviewed (a broad swath from open Orthodox to modern, centrist and right centrist Orthodoxies) support Orthodox shuls in general accepting gay people as members.

Over the past two years Eshel, a support, education, and advocacy organization for LGBT Orthodox Jews and their families, conducted a survey of 110 Orthodox rabbis. The research suggests that nearly all centrist and modern Orthodox rabbis (and even some rabbis in the Haredi world) have become demonstrably sympathetic to the realities faced by LGBT people. These rabbis can now associate names and faces with "LGBT." As people have come out of the closet at younger ages and as more queer people seek to remain in the midst of religious communities, the emerging human encounter refutes the "old time" presumption that LGBT people are willful sinners. Real-life encounters have shaped a powerful empathy, and, in some cases, an alliance, with those who wish to live, worship, celebrate, and learn in observant communities.

Remarkably, this ground of empathy tends to falter when gay people find companionship and wish to comport themselves as couples. In only half the synagogues surveyed can gay couples join synagogues as families or, using a more amorphous category, as households. Two-thirds of the rabbis had no appetite for penalizing the children of gay parents and so they supported lifecycle celebrations for such children. But whether both parents could be recognized as such and stand together on the bima during the baby naming or the bat mitzvah was a more challenging question for the rabbis. Even in the most welcoming of communities we continue to find a concern for the appearance of "normalization," of "married" gay couples.

Given this social context, it should not be surprising that actively supporting and even passively attending the marital rituals of gay couples is a flashpoint in many Orthodox communities. Attitudes to such ceremonies can be a litmus test of loyalty to the tradition and its values. The legalization of same-sex civil marriage has further polarized communities and families, dividing between the religious progressives and the stalwart formalists. Among younger open and modern Orthodox rabbis who have grown up with gay family and friends, there is a growing sense that their refusal to perform or even attend commitment ceremonies feels increasingly like a moral failure.

Understood in this way, same-sex marriage has become a defining frame of reference, a way to open up religious questions that have been percolating for some time under the surface with regard to gender, sexuality, love, family, and, more broadly, the theoretical underpinnings of *halakha* (Jewish law). What are the moral and religious meanings of gender, of sexual pleasure, of reproduction? Is marriage a fixed and "natural" institution or is it a sociocultural one, open to change as society changes? How might the biblical creation story and its various interpretive strands resist or make room for same-sex marriage? Open-minded religious Jews are trying to decide whether the invitation to the commitment ceremony of their nephew is a victory for love, an over-coming of gender by justice, or a threat to the very foundations of Jewish law, and maybe even a harbinger of societal corruption and decadence.

One of the ways explore these deeper questions is to bracket the fundamental *halakhic* concerns with homosexual sexual relations (specifically anal intercourse for men and, at a rabbinic level, "rubbing" for women) and begin instead by exploring the ritual frameworks of traditional marriage in light of the growing desire to expand its embrace to include gay couples. If it is determined that homosexuality is not a perversion, but a normal and healthy minority variant, then what resources from within the Jewish tradition might be available for the celebration of a committed gay love? From the perspective of the Jewish law, what ought a same-sex wedding look like?

My hope is that by exploring the details of praxis—in this case, those of the traditional Jewish wedding—and by considering their relevance (or lack thereof) to same-sex coupling, we may be able to tease out some interesting insights with regard to both homosexuality and marriage. At the very least, by beginning with the formal and liturgical questions involved in the creation of a same-sex wedding ritual, we will be able to clarify our terms, deepen our questions, and provide a much richer frame for the consideration of same-sex marriage.

It bears admitting that an exploration that jumps over the question of the legitimacy of gay sex to interrogate the possibilities of gay marriage will seem to many of my colleagues to be counter-intuitive at best and a dangerous exercise of willful denial at worst. The traditional Orthodox perspective, to date, is essentially univocal in its condemnation of same-sex sexual expression (if somewhat more vociferously for males than for females). There are even a few midrashic texts that explicitly decry same-sex marriage, the most famous being that of Rav Huna, the Babylonian rabbi who tells us that the generation of the flood was not obliterated from the world until they wrote nuptial songs for [unions between] males and [between humans and] animals. Beyond the midrashic material associating same-sex marriage with corruption and divine retribution, the rabbis explicitly prohibited such rites. In *Leviticus* 18:3 the Torah prohibits copying the practices and customs of the Egyptian pagans. Which practices may not be copied? Those, say the rabbis, that were given legal force from the time of the fathers and their fathers' fathers. "What would they do? A man would marry a man, a woman a woman, a man would marry a woman and her daughter, and a woman would be married to two men" (*Sifra* 9:8).

Exploring whether and how these legal restrictions can be overcome is not the aim of this chapter. Instead it is an inquiry into the process of ritual imagination to ask the key question, but backwards. Not how can gay people meet the expectations of *halakha*, but how can *halakha* meet the present-tense needs of gay people. Were it not for the growing voices of gay Jews who wish to remain religiously observant, who, when they find partners are creating such celebrations, were it not for the willingness of parents to support such weddings and the growing eagerness of a couple's religious friends to dance and celebrate at such weddings, then none of the innovation described here would make any sense. Unfolding human realities are reshaping the normative practice of a small but growing cadre of progressive Orthodox Jews who are creating old/new rituals for themselves and for those whom they love. These ritual frameworks have begun to feel authentic (or authentic enough) to those in attendance and especially to the couples who are being celebrated. As one couple shared, in this ceremony they feel themselves "becoming the change that they wish to see." This exploration is consequently for those who, despite the explicit normative challenges, still believe that listening to the needs of people is where *halakha* must always begin. Whether, as Rav Kook so boldly suggested in *Arpelei Tohar*, this "transgressive" moment is an invitation to *halakhic* renewal remains to be seen. At very least, it is a way to honor the question of every gay and lesbian person coming to age in Orthodox communities. When they ask us "what future can I hope for?", what shall we say?

Deconstructing the dish

There are two rituals and *one* legal document that make up a Jewish wedding. They are the espousal ceremony called *erusin*, the nuptial celebration called *nisuin*, and the marriage contract called the *ketubah*. Formally speaking, *erusin* made a woman prohibited sexually to the world and *nisuin* permitted her to her husband. Once *erusin* was contracted, no other man could preempt the husband. Initially, *erusin* and *nisuin* were distinct rituals commonly separated by a full year, during which time families devoted themselves to preparing the dowry, the wedding banquet, and the couple's future home. Sexual relations were not permitted to the espoused couple until the completion of the *nisuin*, which was essentially the accompaniment of the bride into the domicile of the groom where a colorfully decorated room was provided for the consummation of the marriage. The rabbis commonly referred to the *erusin* ceremony as *kiddushin*, (sanctification) and the *nisuin* ceremony as *huppah* (tent or covering). In the twelfth century, the time lapse between the espousal and the nuptials was removed and these two rituals were fused together into a single matrimonial ceremony. Originally, the *huppah* was a colorful tent or a bed chamber in the groom's home where consummation would occur. In the sixteenth century the *huppah* became a canopy on four poles under which the combined *kiddushin* and *erusin* took place. The original seclusion and intimacy of the *huppah* is preserved at the end of the ceremony when the couple is ushered to a private *yichud* room where they are formally permitted (and *halakhically* required) to be alone together for the first time. After 20 minutes of seclusion the now married couple is danced into a banquet hall for dancing, feasting and celebration.

Erusin

Erusin begins with two blessings: the first is the standard blessing recited upon wine (*bore pri hagafen*) and the second is the espousal blessing (*birkat erusin*).

> Blessed are you Lord, ruler of the universe, who has sanctified us by his commandments, and commanded us regarding forbidden relations and has forbidden us those who are merely espoused, but has permitted to us those lawfully married to us by *huppah* and *kiddushin*. Blessed are you, O Lord, who sanctifies his people Israel by means of *huppah* and *kiddushin*.

This blessing recited by the officiant appears to have been instituted as a warning to couples not to have sex during the original lag time between the two ceremonies.

The betrothal or *erusin* consists of an act by which the groom gives an object of value to his bride. Traditionally, he puts a ring (which he owns) on the right forefinger of the bride and recites the following statement: "Behold you are sanctified to me by this ring according to the laws of

Moses and Israel." By accepting and so acquiring the ring, the bride gives to her groom exclusive access to her sexual body. She is now sexually off-limits to all other men. Were the couple to recant at this point, a legal divorce would be required.

The act must be initiated by the man and responded to freely by a woman before witnesses. The legal means by which the betrothal is contracted is acquisition. The word used in *Deut.* 22:13 for taking a wife (*kihah*) is the same word used in *Gen.* 23:13 for Abraham's "acquiring" the Cave of Machpelah. The Mishna introduces the tractate of *kiddushin* by telling us that "a woman can be acquired by money, written document, or sexual intercourse." Witnesses were required for all three methods. Because of the immodesty of arranging for witnesses, sexual intercourse was essentially eradicated by later authorities as a means of realizing a marriage contract.

The standard marriage ceremony was initiated by the transfer of an object of value, typically a ring, from one party to the other. The act is unilateral and the man is the sole initiator of the transaction. Were a woman to "take" a man by the same ritual formula (reciting the formula of "Behold you are sanctified to me . . ." and the giving of a ring), the act would have no legal efficacy. It is clear that he is buying and she is selling—but exactly what is up for sale and what is meant by ownership in this circumstance?

As, formally speaking, ownership is about rights, one might say that the husband acquires certain rights in relation to his wife's body. Following the *erusin*, he "owns" access to her body (which he cannot partake until after the *nisuin*). However, this is a very unusual sort of ownership. When one owns an object, one has the right to do with it what one wants, to restrict others from its use, to loan it to someone, or to give it away. This is not the case with a wife. A wife is not like a loaf of bread that may be shared with others. Moreover, the law does not permit a husband to force his wife to engage in sexual intercourse. If she refuses, he may try to seduce her, but he is not permitted to force her. Indeed, it is his obligation to satisfy his wife's sexual needs up to once a day if he is of independent means and twice weekly if he is a laborer. The ownership that *erusin* confers is hardly conventional.

The question to ask at this point is why the sages of the Talmud employed the language of acquisition in the first place. Liberal theologians have rejected the framework on both aesthetic and moral grounds, but perhaps their critique, understandable as it is, has been superficial and hasty. Might the metaphor of acquisition and ownership be more than a remnant of patriarchal domination? Despite the moral pitfalls of the language, it may be that marriage is bound up in ownership because, for all its uncomfortable associations, it still comes closest to what couples intend. The giving of oneself and especially one's body to another in love is often articulated as a belonging. "You are mine" is what we mean when we give a ring. "I am yours" is what we mean when we let our partner place it on our finger. Different couples imagine different sorts of relationships when they marry. They may or may not share their finances; they may or may not be able to live full-time in the same city; they may or may not have other families demanding their time and money. But whatever couples may mean by their commitments in marriage, they are always committing to an exclusivity of a sort. Or to put it another way, although loving one person does not preclude loving another, in marriage we delineate a sort of access to our heart and to our body that cannot be shared with others outside the marital relationship. Marrying is not like making a best friend or acquiring the perfect business partner. It is about a relationship that demands my service in ways unique and unlike all others. Although various cultures (and individuals) have marked the violation of exclusiveness at different points on a continuum from eye contact to sexual intercourse, the meaning of marriage is surely bound up in some mix of sexual and emotional exclusivity that is akin to ownership.

None the less, because the marital bond could in fact not be understood as an ordinary form of chattel ownership, the rabbis themselves sought and found another ritual metaphor to associate with the woman's change of status, that of the sanctification of property. Any person was free to make a pledge to give an object or animal to the Temple by means of simple statement. Once uttered, the object becomes *hekdesh*, and the sanctified property could now not be used for any secular purpose. It is forbidden to the owner or any individual to use and permitted only to the custodians of the Temple. *Kiddushin*, like *hekdesh*, is a method of transformation, a formula for the creation of something holy, set aside, and beyond the reach of ordinary persons. *Kiddushin* makes a woman's sexual body forbidden and out of bounds for all other men. At the biblical level, nothing about the man's body is limited by *kiddushin*. Her status changes but his does not. Adultery is only the wife's sexual disloyalty. A married man may be branded a degenerate or a cad by the community, but his extramarital affairs with unmarried women are not formally considered adultery.

The one-sidedness of *kiddushin* is most obvious in the biblical acceptance of polygamy. Men with the means to support and sexually satisfy more than one wife could do so if they wished. Despite the formal permission, the norm throughout Jewish history was essentially monogamous. The obvious conflict between co-wives is built in to the arrangement and attested to in the biblical narrative. This, along with the economic challenge of sustaining two or more wives, if not multiple households, was enough to make the phenomenon fairly rare. There is no evidence of a single rabbi in either the Jerusalem or the Babylonian Talmud having had more than one wife. At the first millennium, the year 1000 CE, under the influence of Christian custom and around the time that the ideals of romantic love were being popularized by troubadours in France, the leader of diaspora Jewry, Rabbenu Gershom, prohibited Ashkenazi Jews from the practice of polygamy and the divorce of wives against their will.

Consequently, today, when a groom gives his bride a ring, he too is formally limited to a single partner. So, although the act is technically unilateral, the consequences are not. Still, the fundamental legal roots of *kiddushin*, even if they have been largely reduced to a metaphor, are deeply morally troublesome if not offensive to the egalitarian sensibilities of many in the contemporary social context.

The ketubah

Following the *erusin* and before the *nisuin*, a marriage contract, called a *ketubah*, already drafted, signed, and witnessed, is read and then given by the groom to the bride. The *ketubah* roughly delineates the duties of both parties in the marriage but its main role was to protect women from the unfettered male powers embedded in the inherited institution. Both prerogatives, that of marriage and that of divorce, were to be initiated by men. One needed a woman's consent to contract a marriage, but originally a divorce could be effected by a man even against a woman's will. Until quite recently, for those women without extraordinary family wealth, virginity was a key financial resource. Once her virginity was sold, a woman was particularly vulnerable to a husband's whims. If divorced, a woman could easily find herself alone, destitute, and practically without hope for remarriage. This problem so deeply concerned the rabbis that they created a disincentive for husbands to summarily divorce their wives by binding them to a contract to pay a sizable sum of money in just such a case. The same sum was provided her, as well, in the case of the husband's untimely death, protecting her from the interests of the husband's family that may not always be aligned with hers. After the *ketubah* is read and handed over to the woman, the second portion of the wedding ceremony, the *nisuin*, begins.

The nisuin

The *nisuin* is a public accompaniment of the couple to their shared domicile, an affirmation of the beginning of their intimate life together, and a celebration of their union with family and friends. The *nisuin* is marked by seven blessings that speak of the creation of human beings in God's image, Adam and Eve brought together in the Garden of Eden, and the future restoration of Zion in joy and delight. After the wedding blessings are recited, the groom breaks a glass to signify that the joy of the wedding does not completely erase the sadness of the destruction of Jerusalem and the Holy Temple, and with this gesture to the brokenness of life, the music, dancing, and celebration begin.

Following this ceremony, as specified earlier, the couple is ushered into a private room where they can be alone together, unchaperoned, for the first time. It is a symbolic beginning of their now fully sanctioned sexual intimacy. This is the essential format of the traditional Jewish wedding.

Erusin/kiddushin revisited

As we have noted, the central legal engine of *kiddushin* is unilateral acquisition. Liberal rabbis who use *kiddushin*, as well as some modern Orthodox rabbis, make efforts to mask the one-sided nature of the ritual. Traditionally, the man places the ring on the woman's finger and says, "By this ring be thou sanctified unto me according to the laws of Moses and Israel." In order to create a greater sense of equality many modern rabbis innovated a double-ring ceremony. Non-Orthodox rabbis generally ask the bride to repeat the same line as is traditionally recited by the groom, with relevant changes in the gendered words.

Orthodox rabbis motivated to accomplish greater female agency within the given ritual have resisted the typical double-ring ritual for two basic reasons. *Kiddushin* is effected by the act of the groom giving the bride a ring and, as such, it changes her status into a married woman. When rings are exchanged in sequence the parties have simply traded gifts, a ring for a ring, but no *kiddushin* has been effected. Some modern Orthodox rabbis have tried to retain the legal clarity of *kiddushin* while providing a sense of mutuality by adding a second ring ceremony later in the service, during which the bride gives the groom a ring and says a beautiful, if legally inconsequential, line from the Song of Songs. Some rabbis even further separate the ceremonies by suggesting that the bride give the ring to her husband when they are secluded in the *yichud* room after the ceremony.

Double-ring ceremonies suffer from another problem. As mentioned above, the imbalance is biblical. If one takes formal elements of a marriage seriously, then it is strange to pair a legally transformative gift with one that accomplishes nothing. Adding an element that appears mutual, but is legally a sham, may look nice, but for some members of the Orthodox community it can lend an air of false pretense that mars the serious nature of the commitments being undertaken.

For the most part, despite the potentially alienating if not morally troubling imbalance in the ceremony, Orthodox Jews have remained strongly attached to the traditional ceremony. Even couples who in every other way have adopted more egalitarian views, have largely chosen to retain *kiddushin* as it has been for millennia. Rituals often function long after their symbolic origins have faded from literal relevance. Moreover, it can be argued that the well-worn rituals, despite their original patriarchal context, still connect us to the past and constitute a moving pageant worth preserving.

But, even if this is true for straight couples, can the same be said for gay couples? Without the gorgeously striking oppositions, the white wedding dress and the black tuxedo, the groomsmen and bridesmaids all reinscribing and celebrating the fruitful energy of gender polarity, how does *kiddushin* make any sense?

But there is an even more basic reason for gay couples to reject *kiddushin*. *Kiddushin* works, as we have noted, by providing a specific ritual context shaped by the rabbis of late antiquity to accomplish a biblical change in status. By analogy, biblical marriage is the electrical current; *kiddushin* is just the switch that turns it on. Without the biblical reference point to inaugurate, *kiddushin* by itself is mere theatre, having no legal efficacy. Where there is no biblical warrant for marriage, *kiddushin* just doesn't work. What becomes clear when the roots of traditional Jewish wedding rituals are laid out is that they are simply not relevant for gay couples.

In the absence of *kiddushin* there are other *halakhic* resources, legal frameworks for relationship and obligation that function more broadly which could be honed to fill the gap. Rachel Adler has innovated the use of a simple partnership, in Hebrew, *shutafut*, as the primary legal framework for a non-*kiddushin* marriage. *Shutafut* can be engaged between any to two people who wish to be bound to each other in service of a shared enterprise for which each bears responsibility. Although *shutafut* was originated for the creation of business partnerships, it can be employed for inauguration of any entity that two people wish to create which demands their investments and offers them benefits. A gay couple then can become partners in the creation of a shared household. Adler's suggestion to employ the rabbinic framework of legal partnership will require the couple to write a binding partnership document, a *shtar shutafin*, instead of a *ketubah*, which will describe the investments and duties of each party and the intended goals of the shared enterprise.

Shutafin

At first blush, legal partnership may seem lackluster and business like. However, it is remarkably open to the specifications of its framers, mutual in its structure, legally binding, and beyond gender. Partners in an economic enterprise are bound to each other and can obligate themselves in specific ways as determined by their agreement. The partnership document stipulates the duties and expectations that both enjoin upon each other. Partnership was traditionally accomplished by each party putting a coin or any valuable object into a bag, and then lifting it together, symbolizing the joining together of their individual contributions to a single enterprise. In a few recent ceremonies one groom purchased a beautiful *mezuzah* housing and the other a parchment to put inside it. These two objects were placed in a bag and the grooms then lifted the bag together to effect the partnership contract, the complete *mezuzah* symbolizing their aim of building a shared household together.

The document is signed by the couple and by the witnesses who saw the moment of effective commitment in the lifting of the bag. The writing of the *shtar shutafin* provides couples with an opportunity to discuss in advance the many sensitive concerns around their planned future with regard to finances, domicile, future or existing children, and their education. It offers couples an opportunity to discuss and express in words the spiritual and moral vision of the shared life they are intending to build together.

Shutafut is a model for formally and legally delineating what a union demands of each partner. In theory the document can include a disclosure of the assets and duties each partner is providing for the accomplishment of the shared endeavor. Most couples prefer an open framework, putting all their assets and energies on the table, in ways open to ongoing renegotiation which jointly they deem fair.

Although modeling marriage after a business partnership may seem superficial, some *halakhic* authorities considered business partnership to be a form of mutual servitude. A medieval authority, Rabbi Abraham ben David Zimri (referred to as the Ra'avad), uses astonishing language to describe business partnership. Each party in a partnership, he suggests, becomes an *eved ivri*, a Jewish slave, to the other. Conceptually, Jewish slavery was a world apart from its harsh Roman counterpart or from the brutality of the European colonial slavery of Africans. The *halakha* obligated a master to give a slave food and lodging that was qualitatively similar to his or her own. Although the notion of partnership as servitude is surely jarring, the mutuality of service transforms the very notion of a servant into something very different. Each party enters into such a relationship knowing that he or she will serve and be served in love.

In practice, to situate this ritual in a more personal rather than a business context, couples have opted to recite an Aramaic phrase from the traditional *ketubah*, a phrase that paradoxically marks the "servitude" of the husband to the wife. Before they lift the bag together each partner says to the other: "I will serve, honor, support and maintain you in truth."

However, although the *shtar shutafin* functions well to create a container for mutual partnership, it is still missing spiritual depth for two reasons. First, God has not been brought into the union in any formal way. The shared enterprise of building a business or a household does not convey purposes beyond the overlap of interests. Second, one may make multiple partnerships in business, but, in *erusin*, the exclusivity of relationship is paramount. Adler's use of *shtuafut* is inadequate to these tasks.

In order to articulate these elements, we have chosen the power of a formal oath (*shevuah*) to supply a sense of holiness and uniqueness to this one partnership. Each partner takes an oath conditional upon receiving a ring from the other. This oath binds each partner to the other exclusively in an intimacy that is theirs alone and to which God is witness. The spouse who is first receiving a ring takes the oath after which her partner places a ring on her wife's finger. Then the ritual repeats in the other direction.

הרי אני נשבע[ת] שבועה פרטית שמרגע שאקבל ממך טבעת זו אקדיש את עצמי
נפשי וגופי ליחודיות זיווגינו

Behold I swear a personal oath that from the moment I receive this ring from you I will dedicate myself, spirit and body, to the exclusive uniqueness of our relationship as a couple.

Once this *shevuah* is spoken and the ring is given, the partner is bound to explicit physical and emotional loyalty. Taken together, this double vow ceremony binds both partners to build a household together and to guard the sharing of intimacy with each other in an exclusive fashion. It should be clear that such a ritual is not effective if a couple wishes to have an "open" marriage.

Originally this ritual included a second statement, a declaration uttered by the partner prior to placing the ring on the finger of the oath-taker. This line is similar to the line spoken by the groom in a traditional wedding.

הרי את[ה] מוקדש[ת] לי בקבלת טבעת זו בתוקף השבועה אשר נשבעת

Behold you are dedicated to me by receiving this ring according to the oath that you have sworn.

Although this line has a familiar resonance with the traditional ceremony, I prefer to remove this line for a number of reasons. The most salient reason is that, although it adds no legal strength (indeed some feel that it makes the ritual weaker *halakhically*), in practice couples have found it confusing. The simple oath accompanied by the giving of a ring, repeated sequentially for both partners, accomplishes the task.

Legal partnership (*shutafut*) with the addition of vows (*shevuot)* then completes what is typically accomplished by *erusin*. The decisive act of marriage begins with the closing off of a myriad of potential lives in order to actually live one life. *Erusin* is the formal relinquishing of the infinite possibilities that are entailed in marriage. This sort of commitment is a reckoning with mortality and a welcoming of finitude. Of course, there is, as well, a new—and in its own way infinite—territory born by the decision to commit to the lifelong love of one person. The joy of this new world is at the center of *nisuin*.

Nisuin revisited

The *nisuin* is the joyous part of marriage. It is the ceremony that formally permits the bride and groom to be physically intimate with each other. If *erusin* is about sexual restriction, then *nisuin* is about sexual expression.

The *erusin* moves from the public toward the private, while the *nisuin* moves from the private back to the public. The *erusin* is a segregation, the *nisuin* an inclusion, a weaving of the personal into the communal, by public acknowledgment and joyous celebration. This inauguration of the most intimate element of a couple's shared life is celebrated with family and friends amid dancing, music, and a lavish feast.

Last, the *nisuin* provides the cosmic frame for the whole affair. A wedding is about much more than the romantic joining of two lovers. It is about marking the love of two people as part of heaven's greater purposes. At the center of the *nisuin* is a story, a narrative that holds the power of what we are doing. If we are celebrating the love of two people, then a party will do. If we are tracing the lines in some grander plot in which the love of two is situated, then we have more solid ground for spiritual depth. The master story of the traditional wedding is conveyed with the seven blessings chanted under the *huppah* before family and friends. They are arguably the most beautiful part of the service.

1. Blessed are You, Lord our God, Ruler of the universe, who created the fruit of the vine.
2. Blessed are You, Lord our God, Ruler of the universe, who created everything for your glory.

3. Blessed are you, lord our god, ruler of the universe, shaper of humanity.

4. Blessed are You, Lord our God, Ruler of the universe, who has shaped human beings in his image, an image patterned after his likeness, and established from within it a perpetuation of itself. Blessed are You, Lord, shaper of humanity.

5. May the barren one exult and be glad as her children are joyfully gathered to her. Blessed are You, Lord, who gladdens Israel with her children.

6. Grant great joy to these loving friends as You once gladdened Your creations in the Garden of Eden. Blessed are You, Lord, who gladdens the groom and bride.

7. Blessed are You, Lord our God, Ruler of the universe, who created joy and gladness, groom and bride, merriment, song, pleasure and delight, love and harmony, peace and companionship. Lord, our God, may there soon be heard in the cities of Judah and the streets of Jerusalem the voice of joy and the voice of gladness, the voice of the groom and the voice of the bride, the rapturous voices of grooms from their bridal chambers, and of young people feasting and singing. Blessed are You, Lord, who gladdens the groom together with the bride.

The first blessing over wine is the way the tradition inaugurates joyous celebrations. The second and third blessings introduce the theme of creation. The second blessing is surprisingly apt for a same-sex wedding. It affirms that everything, perhaps even same-sex love, was created for the glory of God. The third blessing honors the creation of the human being. This blessing surely could be contextualized to apply well enough to gay weddings. However, we will soon see that the themes of creation are particularly relevant to straight weddings. The next four blessings open up increasingly larger circles of relationship, carrying the love of two into ever more expansive frames of reference.

Blessing 4 is about planting within the human body the power to reproduce. One of the obvious ways that marriage expands the love of two is through family. The duty to reproduce is the first commandment of the Torah. It is considered an affirmation of God's creation to participate in the refurbishment of humanity. Blessing 5 is both about children and about the redemptive renewal of Zion in the end of days, when our mother Sarah, the once barren one, will rejoice in the return of her children to the land of Israel. Especially for Jews, family is the foundation of the covenantal promise. God takes Abraham outside and says, "Look up to the heavens, and count the stars if you can ... so shall be your children" (*Gen.* 15:5). The Jewish people are a chain of generations all bearing an ancient covenant with God, which began with Abraham and Sarah. Jesus made disciples to carry his message; Abraham and Sarah made a baby.

Marriage extends the love of two outward, beyond the family to the community. The stability of community is aided by the fact that the disruptive power of sexual self-interest has been largely neutralized by marriage. Communities of singles are much more unstable, much more transient and less prone to sinking roots in a particular place or building lasting institutions. Although this is surely a generalization to which there are exceptions, monogamous marriage is how sexuality can be given its due so that other socially constructive efforts can proceed more smoothly.

The focus of romantic love is narrow. In its most frantic tropes, romantic passion utterly abandons the world. Jewish marriage rituals articulate the love of two not only as a turning inward, but also as a reaching outward toward others.

It is a pious custom for brides and grooms to walk down the isle toward the *huppah* reciting psalms and praying for the needs of others. The turning away from the self at this moment is deemed so powerful that heaven cannot help but answer these prayers.

The last two blessings draw an even wider circle beyond the Jewish people to include the world. Blessing 6 refers to the bride and groom as loving friends. It is a beautiful expression that suggests an emotional bond quite distinct from the patriarchal role divisions of the *ketubah*. The blessing continues and reminds us that every groom and bride are Adam and Eve in Eden. They reframe every straight wedding as a return to Paradise. Were the world to end and leave only the bride and groom, humanity could begin again. The wedding ritual marks every straight wedding as a reenactment of the beginnings of humanity. Mystically, to witness a wedding is to see a glimpse of Eden, the very beginning when human loneliness was healed in the union of Adam and Eve.

Blessing 7 is based on the prophecy of Jeremiah following the destruction of Judea in 586 BCE. Amid the ruins of the destroyed capital city, he promises that a day will come when there will again be singing and dancing in the streets of Jerusalem. He tells of wedding revelry and the sounds of children playing in the street. In Jeremiah's mythic frame, every straight wedding becomes a promise of a rebuilt Jerusalem, of a perfected world, more real and more attainable because it speaks not only of the lives present, but also of the generations to come that will be born out of this very moment. At every heterosexual wedding we are witnesses to the beginning and the end of time; we are carried back to Eden and forward to a Jerusalem rebuilt in joy and gladness, pleasure and delight, love and harmony, peace and companionship.

As beautiful and moving as these marital narratives are, they cannot be appropriated for a gay wedding because they do not constitute a gay story. The first few blessings might be salvaged, though by themselves they do not tell us what a gay wedding is, and the last four blessings do not seem right at all for same-sex weddings. Though gay couples are able to raise families, gay unions do not revisit Adam and Eve and the birth of life itself, nor do they promise the physical continuity toward the redeemed Jerusalem that Jeremiah envisioned. The linking of the generations past and future to a same-sex couple underneath the canopy is, at best, much less obvious. We must find more apt images and metaphors for gay love and commitment, not only for the love of truth, but for the realness and power of the moment that we are celebrating. The poignancy of the moment for straight couples works because the metaphors are experientially genuine, mythically alive, and emotionally compelling. To employ them when they are not cheapens what is actually true and wondrous about same-sex marriage.

In straight marriage, God is linking the generations, connecting us all to our ancestors and to our future progeny, to Eden and Jerusalem. What is God up to in gay marriage that could be honored and celebrated? In fact, the question may be asked even more boldly: What are homosexuals here for? What larger purpose do we suppose God may have in mind for gay people? Of course, there is no ready-made biblical narrative. A historically reviled sexuality cannot easily find its holy way. However, there is a sliver of the creation story, an interpretive midrash of the rabbis, and a mystical ritual that may offer a possibility.

In the beginning

Before creation, God alone fills existence. God's oneness is without division or separation. One is always all-powerful without needing any power-over to be so. One is stable and sure, unchanging, and whole. The seed of creation is the idea of more than one. At the moment of creation, the magisterial oneness of God, according to Jewish mystics, concentrated itself to leave room for an-other. Creation begins with the possibility of two.

Two are a rickety thing, a temptation, a suspicious thing, an ecstatic, thrilling, dangerous thing. Two always have a history. The pain and pleasure of difference, the tragedy and glory of the lines that separate things are the subtext of the first chapters of Genesis. Separation between things inaugurates creation. Light and dark, day and night, the waters below and above, the dry land and the seas are all separated. It is by these separations that creation unfolds. Much as the infant separates first physically and then psychically from its mother, little by little, the world comes to be by separations amid the chaos.

However, twos pose a problem. Separation is a birth pang that passes, but, once there are two, how are they to relate? On the third day of creation, two great lights are created. The Hebrew word for lights (*meorot*) is missing a letter in the plural ending. The missing letter is not crucial for the meaning of the word, but the irregularity seems to suggest that something is wrong.

The sages explain that the pair of lights, the sun and the moon, was unstable in a way related to their being two. These twin creations became so highly problematic that God had to alter the original plan. On the third day, we are told, God made the sun and the moon. "And God made the two great lights, the greater light to rule the day and the lesser light to rule the night, and the stars" (*Gen.* 1:16). Thus, after introducing the sun and the moon both as great, the text adds that, actually, one light was great and the other was lesser. The contradiction between the verses generated a legend that is recorded in the Talmud.

> "And God made the two great lights," but later it says: "the great light and the lesser light"! The moon said before the Holy One: Master of the world, is it possible for two kings to share (literally: to use) one crown? God said to her: Go and diminish yourself! She said before God:

Because I asked a good question, I should diminish myself? God said: Go and rule both in day and in night. She said: What advantage is that? A candle in the daylight is useless. God said: Go and let Israel count their days and years by you. She said: They use the daylight [of the sun] to count seasonal cycles as well. . . . Seeing that she was not appeased, the Holy One said: Bring a (sacrificial) atonement for me that I diminished the moon! This is what R. Shimon ben Lakish said: What is different about the sacrifice [lit. ram] of the new moon that it is offered "for God" ["And one ram of the flock for a sin offering for God" (*Num.* 28:14) meaning for God's sin]? Said the Holy One: This ram shall be an atonement for me that I diminished the moon.

The problem of two great rulers sharing a single crown is a problem that God does not anticipate. The problem is raised by the moon, and the Creator solves the problem with a fixed hierarchy. The moon complains that she got the raw end of the deal just for asking a tough question, one that ostensibly might have been thought out in advance by the Creator. Failing to appease her, God accepts the duty to offer a sin offering on the occasion of every new moon, a monthly atonement for the lesser status he forced on her.

The moon's diminishment is understood by the sages as a sin committed against the moon for which God asks to atone. The midrash is an invitation by the rabbis to project a world of restored harmony and equality. A liturgy of sanctifying the new moon was begun in Talmudic times and embellished by later mystical traditions. If God brings a sacrificial atonement for the diminishment of the moon, then there must be some desire on high to truly repent of the wrong done to her. The laws of repentance require it. We learn that there is no forgiveness for sins between parties until the offended party has been appeased. A sacrifice alone cannot right a wrong done. Implicit in the midrash of the first century is Rabbi Isaac Luria's prayer for the moon's restoration.

Restoring the moon: the ritual of *Kiddush Levanah*

The monthly Jewish ritual of the sanctification of the new moon, *Kiddush Levanah*, is recited during the waxing phase of the lunar cycle. Commonly, the prayer is said at the conclusion of the Sabbath falling during this period. On this Saturday evening after the end of the prayer service, the congregation files outdoors and, underneath a visible moon, chants *Kiddush Levanah*. The main sources of the ritual are essentially biblical and rabbinic, but the messianic prayer that follows is pure Jewish mysticism:

> May it be your will, O Lord, my God and the God of my fathers to fill in the darkness of the moon that she not be diminished at all. And let the light of the moon be as the light of the sun, and as the light of the seven days of creation, just as she was before she was diminished, as it is said: "the two great lights." And may we be a fulfillment of the verse: "And they shall seek out the Lord their God and David their king. Amen."
>
> (*Hosea* 3:5).

This tradition of the moon's diminution and its future restoration in the world to come is explicitly understood by Rashi, the most famous of medieval Jewish exegetes, as a veiled reference to women. He says that, in the world to come, women will be renewed like the new moon. This prayer, chanted before a waxing moon, imagines an increasing feminine light that will some day be restored to its full equality with the masculine light. If God atones for diminishing the moon and for the subjugation of Eve to Adam after the sin in the garden, then the way things are is not the way things ought to be or ultimately will be. The disharmonies that attended the banishment from Eden, the conflict between humans and the natural world, and the hierarchy of the sexes, these are just the beginning of a great drama, the last act of which will include God's joyous restoration of the moon.

Perhaps the place to end our same-sex marriage narrative is with the restoration of the moon and the healing of the hierarchy between men and women so apparent in the traditional wedding service. The ancient story of the moon's diminution and our monthly prayer for her renewal and restoration is already an established and venerable ritual introduced into Jewish custom by R. Yitzhak Luria in the sixteenth century. It is a beautiful ritual, full of dramatic imagery and power of its own. Its relationship to gay marriage is twofold.

The moon is a veiled reference to the feminine in the world, or perhaps, as mystics might say, to the feminine face of God, the *Shekhinah*. Our prayer for its restoration is our hope that we have indeed learned how two can rule with one crown, the sharing of power without hierarchy. Perhaps this is what God ought to have said to the moon in the first place, unless, of course, this is the sort of knowledge that can be acquired only over time, a great deal of time, and at great cost. Only the fullest of loves makes it possible for two to rule with one crown. In this midrash we are offered an image of a love beyond gender that embodies neither submission nor domination, but equality and partnership. Might it be that gay relationships are a harbinger of the moon's restoration, a forward guard to the coming redemption?

Remarkably, this text provides a narrative that also carries us back to both themes of creation and redemption. Although gay unions may not recapitulate creation and redemption in the same way that heterosexual unions do, it appears that the same two tropes are there after all. Straight unions are about the love of Adam and Eve that bears new life. Gay unions are about the flaws of the creation that we are called on to fix. Gay couples, who by definition cannot employ the scaffold of patriarchy to work out their power arrangements, have little choice but to learn how to share a single crown. Whereas straight unions offer a promise of a future redemption in flesh and blood, gay unions help to pave the way for us to heal the very problem of difference, and in a gesture no less redemptive than the rebuilding of Jerusalem, to restore the moon to her former glory.

In practice, the ritual of *Kiddush Levanah* includes the giving and receiving of peace. Under the faintest sliver of the moon's white crescent, each of those assembled blesses the new moon and then they turn to each other and say, *shalom aleichem*, "peace be unto you," to which a reverse greeting is returned, *aleichem shalom*, "unto you be peace." This greeting of peace is shared with three different people so, although one is seeking three different people to greet, one is being greeted by others. The effect is a moment of communal bonding that is overtly mutual and about the interplay between giving and receiving. What better way to articulate the communal effect of marriage than to spread out its hope of peace and love between two toward the whole community.

The mystical prayer for the restoration of the moon serves as a foil to the degradations of the biblical creation story that unconsciously inhabits the traditional wedding. Before the first couple leaves the garden, Eve's destiny is set in both desire and subjugation: "Your urge shall be for your husband and he shall rule over you" (*Gen.* 3:16b). For thousands of years, the ongoing punishment of Eve has become Adam's abiding interest prettified by gowns and flowers. *Kiddush Levanah* reveals the fractures of the story, grasps them as a challenge to God's goodness that will in time be fixed, and calls on us to insure that the love we honor at a wedding will be shared with the wisdom of heart by which two can rule with a single crown.

This ritual of partnership, vows, and vision is not nearly the final note of gay ritual creativity. Rituals are shaped over many years as attempts to find the right touchstones of text and law, metaphor and meaning, poetry and purpose are honed by successive generations. By creating new *halakhic* frameworks for enacting the formal relationships of couples and seeking a unique narrative to undergird and remythologize the ritual, we may be able to offer gay couples an avenue of marital commitment that sustains their love of the tradition. As important, the inquiry itself may not only offer a fuller account of gay sexuality to Jewish tradition, but also help to demonstrate what is at stake in the content of our all our wedding rituals, straight or gay. For many heterosexual couples, a ceremony that accomplishes the aims of kid-dushin while shaping a fully mutual commitment, and that does not entail the possibility of a withheld divorce bill, is an upgrade worth considering. Whether this particular ceremony for gay couples, the canopy and the rings, the legal frameworks of partnership, and personal oaths and finally the mythic vision of relationship without gender hierarchy, are absolute necessities or not, a clearer understanding of what marriage means to us all surely is.

Appendix: marriage document

שְׁטַר שׁוּתָּפִין

בְּאֶחָד בְּשַׁבָּת ט״ו תמוז שנת חמשת אלפים ושבע מאות ושבעים ושבע לבריאת העולם למניין שאנו מונין כאן בווֹשינגטון די. סי. החתנים נשבעו להקדיש את עצמם לזוגיות מיוחדת ואישרו את שטר השותפין הזה בפני עדים להודיע את כוונתם לבנות בית משותף ונאמן בישראל. החתנים זהודיעו:

אנו מקדישים את עצמנו ,נפשנו וגופנו, לקיים זיקה ייחודית זו זה עם זה ולא עם אף אחד אחר.

אנו מקבלים על עצמנו את כל הדרישות והזכויות החלות על בני זוג, לטפל ולספק
זה את זה. ואם נזכה בחסדי שמים לילדים אנו מקבלים על עצמנו לגדל, לחנך
ולקיים אותם יחד באהבה.

אנו מבקשים לבנות בית שיוקדש לחסד ולאמת, לצדק ולשוויון, בית של תורה
מצוות ועבודת ה' בדעת המעורבת עם הבריות ומקדישים עצמנו יחד לתיקון
הכלים השבורים.

אנו מתכוונים לחלוק את משק ביתנו באופן הוגן, ולשעבד כל אחד את נכסיו
לקופה משותפת להיות אחראיים יחד על תשלום כל חוב ועל רכישת טובין.

אנו מתחייבים לתמוך זה בזה בשעת מחלה, ברגעי צער, ועד ערש דווי להיות
נאמנים זה לזה כל ימי חיינו כדי לקיים את הכתוב: "שימני כחותם על ליבך
כחותם על זרועך כי עזה כמוות אהבה" (שיר השירים ח:ו).

אנו בוחרים זה בזה כבני זוג וכחברים כדאמרו חז"ל: "קנה לך חבר כיצד מלמד
שיקנה אדם חבר לעצמו שיאכל עמו ישתה עמו יקרא עמו וישנה עמו ויישן עמו
ויגלה לו כל סתריו סתרי תורה וסתרי דרך ארץ" (אבות דרבי נתן ח). החתן
שמואל בן ברוך והחתן זכריה נתן בן אריה התחייבו בכל הכתוב והמפורש לעיל.
הכל שריר וקיים.

**On the first day of the week, the fifteenth day of the month of
Tammuz 5777**, according to the Jewish calendar, in **Washington, DC,
Name 1 and Name 2** vowed to dedicate themselves to a unique
relationship and confirmed this document of *Shutafin* in the presence of
witnesses to declare their joint commitment to building a faithful household among the people of Israel. **Name 1 and Name 2** announced:

We dedicate ourselves, our bodies and our souls, to sustain this
relationship with one another and have vowed that we will share such
intimacy with none other.

We each accept upon ourselves all the rights and responsibilities that
apply to spouses, to attend, care, and provide for one another, and
together to raise, educate and sustain in love all the children that we
may be blessed with in the future.

We seek to build a household dedicated to mercy and truth, justice
and equality, a home of Torah and mitzvot, working together in
serving Hashem, contributing to the community, and healing a broken
world.

We intend to equitably create and sustain this household and have committed all of our financial resources to do so, acquiring each other's assets and debts.

We will support each other in times of illness, in moments of pain, and until death, remaining loyal to each other all our lives fulfilling what has been written: Set me as a seal upon your heart, and as seal upon your arm, for love is as fierce as death (*Shir HaShirim* 8:6). We have chosen one another as spouses and companions as our rabbis taught: Get yourself a companion: This teaches that a person should get a companion to eat with, to drink with, to study Torah with, to sleep with, to confide all one's secrets, secrets of Torah and secrets of worldly things (*Avot D'Rabbi Natan* 8). **Name 1 and Name 2** have committed to all the terms of this document. Everything is valid and confirmed.

חתן
חתן
עד
עד

Chapter 9

"Women known for these acts"

A review of the Jewish laws of lesbians

Elaine Chapnik

In 1999 I became involved in Orthodykes, a support group in New York for Orthodox lesbian, bisexual, and transgendered women, both as an organizer and as a participant. For the holiday of *Shavuot* in 2000, we held a *tikkun leil Shavuot*, a traditional program of all-night text study, but on a very untraditional subject: how Jewish law views sexual activities between women. At this quietly revolutionary event, Jewish lesbians, Orthodox but far from conventional, studied together until dawn, driven not just by religious duty or devotion but with the feeling that their prospects for happiness depended on these sacred Jewish texts.

Jews who are both lesbian and religiously observant are necessarily concerned about what *halakha*, Jewish law, says about their sexual behavior and life decisions. They seek to understand and interpret Jewish legal texts in ways that allow them to remain true to both themselves and the Torah. Study, interpretation of, and extrapolation from *halakhik* texts by traditionally agreed-upon methods comprise the archetypal Jewish responses to moral dilemmas, offering ways to make bearable the apparent conflict of being an Orthodox Jewish lesbian. Becoming versed in these sources enabled me to understand what the rabbis in fact said about lesbianism—versus the uninformed homophobia found in much of today's Orthodox world—and to give support to others in Orthodykes who were struggling to make peace with themselves. In this chapter I share my own discoveries from these texts and how they affected the lives of some of the women I knew.

At first glance, accepting oneself as a lesbian may seem incompatible with Orthodox Judaism. Indeed, some women in Orthodykes felt forced to leave the Orthodox community. As they were from a range of religious backgrounds, and on a continuum of non-heterosexual orientations from lesbian to bisexual to transsexual, their approaches differed as to how and whether they would continue to lead a religiously observant life. Some grew up modern Orthodox, some Hassidic, and some chose the Orthodox path later in life; others were conservative Jews and Jews by choice. Some had previously been married and squelched their attraction to women, and some remained mired in marriages entered into before they got in touch with their heterodox desires. Many had children; some had never been with a man and had no desire to be with one. Some needed to become comfortable enough to marry a man and some wanted to feel comfortable loving a woman. Many came with no particular agenda but knew they needed a place to think and talk through their feelings. The group was a place where they would not be judged and would receive support, whether they wanted to lead a homosexual or a heterosexual life, within or without the fold.

Many women in Orthodykes expressed feelings of anxiety, depression, shame, self-doubt, self-hatred, and internalized homophobia, often as a result of their families' rejection. Married women felt guilty for living a double life or cheating on their husbands. Some felt like failures for being unable to live lives consistent with the dictates of Jewish law. Along with emotional support for their struggles related to identity conflicts and rejection by their families and communities, these women sought insight into and information about *halakha.* Those who were able to resolve these feelings positively sometimes did so by studying the ancient and medieval commentaries on lesbian sexual activity[1] and understanding the rabbis' strictures and true concerns as they discerned them to be. Some felt comforted learning of lesbian antecedents in Jewish communities throughout the past, knowing that the tradition had not entirely abandoned them, even as they needed to be in dialogue with the disapproving aspects of the tradition. Some wanted to be able to challenge the invidious homophobia found in various Orthodox communities today. As they were *halakhically* observant, it was very important to them to know whether Jewish law was so strict or immutable as to doom them to a loveless, sexless, single life or staying married to men for whom they felt no physical attraction. They sought a way to feel comfortable living as lesbians within a general *halakhik* framework, instead of discarding the tradition altogether.

A word about myself: I did not have an Orthodox upbringing and often felt like a bit of an outsider in the group. My parents were Orthodox in eastern Europe but, having narrowly escaped the Holocaust and bearing grave psychic wounds, they assimilated quickly after reaching America. As an adult, I returned to my parents' roots and became Orthodox for ten years, during which time I studied the Torah and other sacred Jewish texts and commentaries at a yeshiva in Jerusalem, adhered to *halakha* and married an Orthodox man. Over time I could no longer deny my attraction to women, and I divorced. Resources were not available then (in 1986) as they are now to guide a woman who wishes to live as both Orthodox and lesbian. Rather than abandoning Orthodoxy, I would have turned to Orthodykes and the growing community of Orthodox lesbians. At the time, I felt compelled by guilt and shame to leave Orthodoxy. I was sure that if I came out of the closet some of my Orthodox friends would reject me, so I withdrew from them first. A few were completely accepting of me. Ultimately, my struggle with my own identity conflicts led me to find ways of living Jewishly other than as Orthodox. Nevertheless, because of my respect for the tradition and my intellectual interests in philosophy, law, and Jewish texts, I still desired to know what *halakha* said about lesbians. Only after I left the Orthodox world did I begin to discover and learn, if you will, *Hilchot Lesbiut*—the laws of lesbianism.

The Torah's prohibition on male homosexual activity is well known throughout the world. In contrast, how Jewish law views lesbianism is not widely known in the general Jewish or even Orthodox world. Too often, discussion of rabbinic views on homosexuality involves only the texts concerning men. Thus, there is a need for education.

The fundamental source of Jewish law, the Torah, does not ban, punish, or even refer explicitly to lesbian behavior of any kind. The first explicit mention of lesbian behavior is in the *Sifra*.[2] The *Sifra* expressly forbids same-sex marriage, but it does not explicitly impose a punishment for violators, nor does it explicitly mention lesbian sexual activity as such. The Babylonian Talmud (mid-sixth century CE), in the course of discussing a related issue, concluded that sexual activity between women constituted "mere indecency" (*pritzuta b'alma*), but it never directly dealt with the question of whether lesbian sexual activity is prohibited. In the twelfth century CE, biblical and Talmudic commentators and Jewish legal codes declared lesbian sexual activity to be forbidden and punishable by lashes of the kind imposed by rabbinical courts (versus Torah-prescribed lashes), reflecting the view that lesbian behavior was not an express Torah prohibition (an *issur d'oraita*), but at most either an inchoate Torah prohibition or a rabbinic prohibition (an *issur d'rabbanan*). Even so, the level of opprobrium and punishment (flogging) was relatively mild compared with that reserved for male homosexual acts.[3] In *Leviticus* 20:13, the Torah decrees: "A man who lies with a man as one lies with a woman, they have both done an abomination; they shall be put to death, their blood is upon them."[4]

The invisibility of lesbianism in the Torah, although it may be a source of pain for some lesbians, may give comfort and relief to others who try to reconcile disparate identities, because they are better able to remain under the radar screen of rabbinic opprobrium. Although I might wish the rabbis hadn't proclaimed any pejorative attitudes toward lesbianism, for me as well as others it felt worse to be made invisible; it is far better to be in the text and banned than not to be mentioned at all. I was thrilled to read the rabbis' discussions about women who, as we learned from subsequent texts, rubbed their genitalia together, or tempted wives to stray from their husbands. However, for some Orthodykes, who see *halakha* as binding, this creates a terrible conflict. They want to live as Torah-observant Jews, but it may mean denying an essential part of their selves.

One Orthodyke, a divorced Hassidic lesbian from the Satmar community who chose to remain living in that community to raise her children, said: "It is difficult for me by the very fact that the rabbis say that lesbian sex is nothing or a little something—by that fact they see my sexuality as less than that of a man's. It is almost like what I do doesn't count from a *halakhik* standpoint. That infuriates me." She then reflected on the irony that, although lesbian sex is a relatively minor violation of *halakha*, her community would nevertheless shun or virtually expel her if she became a visible as a lesbian: "In the Hassidic community, being a lesbian is completely unacceptable. Many of my Orthodox friends would shun me if they knew that I was sleeping with a woman, although according to *halakha*, that would not be as bad as cheating the government on my taxes, or speaking gossip, both of which activities, if I chose to do them, would not result in my expulsion." Her words cry out for Orthodox Jews to learn *Hilchot Lesbiut* and grapple with the possibility that their homophobia might reflect the dominant Christian culture's complex relationship to sexuality rather than authentically Jewish values.

I will analyze briefly only a few *halakhik* sources and offer my views, as much has been written on them already.[5] Although there is no explicit description of women engaging in lesbianism in the Torah itself, rabbinic commentators read into *Leviticus* 18:3 an oblique prohibition: "After the doings of the land of Egypt, in which you dwelt, you shall not do, and after the doings of the land of Canaan, into which I bring you, shall you not do: neither shall you walk in their laws." What did they do in Egypt and Canaan that Leviticus banned? The *Sifra* in *Acharei Mot* 8:8 answers this question as follows:

> What is the meaning of "according to the doings of the land of Egypt and according to the doings of the land of Canaan you shall not do"? Is it possible that it means that one should not build buildings like theirs or plant crops as they do? After the ways of the Egyptians you shall not go. Therefore, the Torah teaches, "and in their laws you shall not walk." Only the laws that have been established for them and their ancestors are specified. And what are they? "A man would marry a man, a woman would marry a woman, and a woman would be married to two men." Therefore, it says, "and in their laws you shall not walk."

I initially learned of the above passage while preparing for the first Orthodyke *tikkun leil Shavuot*, using a compilation and translation of *halakhik* sources produced by a member of the original Israeli Orthodykes support group (who wishes to remain anonymous). How surprised I was to discover that the rabbis discussed same-sex marriage at least 1,500 years ago. Apparently the controversy over same-sex marriage—as well as the practice itself—was alive in ancient times. In light of the current battle over legalizing same-sex marriage, it seems uncanny that the *Sifra* singles out the Egyptians' and Canaanites' unconventional marriages and marriage laws as the norms that must be rejected. As validating as it may be for lesbians today to be reflected and made visible in an early rabbinic text, nevertheless, the *Sifra*'s interpretation of the Torah's proscription may be troubling for some Orthodox lesbians. It might lead them to conclude that they should be *against* same-sex marriage.

The first mention of lesbian sexual activity in the Babylonian Talmud occurs in Tractate *Yevamot* 76a (mid-sixth century CE):

> Rav Huna said, "*nashim ha'mesolelot zoh b'zoh* are prohibited from marrying a *kohen* (male member of the priestly caste)" [because such women are considered to be *zonot*].[6]

Ravah, disagreeing with Rav Huna, says "And even for Rabbi Elazar, who says: 'if an unmarried man has sexual intercourse with any unmarried woman not for the sake of marriage, she is considered a *zonah*,' his ruling addresses [intercourse with] a man. But [even in his view], *[mesolelot]* with another woman, it is mere indecency."

(*Pritzuta b'alma*).

Orthodykes at the first *tikkun leil Shavuot* thrilled at the revelation of this beguiling Hebrew expression, "*nashim ha'mesolelot zoh b'zoh*," rendering our sexuality visible in the ancient Jewish world for the first time. The phrase refers to women (*nashim*) who are driven to do an ambiguous bodily act (*mesolelot*) by their sexual desire for each other. As the rabbis describe it, it is done *zoh b'zoh*, one woman with or inside or in relation to another, *zoh* being the feminine form of "that one." In its symmetry, the Hebrew phrase *zoh b'zoh* is a linguistic reflection of the physical act itself.[7] But what was the specific sexual act that the Talmudic rabbis were reflecting upon? Tractate *Yevamot* 76a does not explain the meaning of *mesolelot*. The key to the exact meaning of the verbal noun *mesolelot* is found in later rabbinic commentaries on this passage. The purpose of Tractate *Yevamot* 76a is to clarify who is ineligible to marry a *kohen* on account of being a *zonah* by determining whether a woman who practices *mesolelut* (the gerund form of *mesolelot*) is a *zonah*. Marrying an eligible woman is necessary to ensure that the *kohen's* priestly status is passed to his offspring.

The Torah prohibits a *kohen* from marrying a woman with the legal status of *zonah*. Rav Huna's opinion is that *nashim ha'mesolelot*[11] are prohibited from marrying a *kohen*, because he considers them to be *zonot* (*zonah*, plural). Ravah, however, dismisses Rav Huna's opinions as incorrect. He rules that *nashim ha'mesolelot* are not barred from marrying *kohenim* because the act that they engage in is not an act of completed intercourse; indeed, it is not actual intercourse at all. Ravah proves his argument by demonstrating that even Rabbi Elazar, who propounds the most stringent view as to what makes a woman a *zonah*, would agree with his conclusion. Rabbi Elazar rules that an unmarried man who has intercourse with an unmarried woman without matrimonial intent thereby renders her a *zonah* and therefore unfit to marry a *kohen*. But, Ravah points out, Rabbi Elazar's ruling addresses only the case of intercourse with a man where there is a *bona fide* act of completed intercourse. Even Rabbi Elazar did not extend his ruling beyond cases of women engaging in such intercourse to include *nashim ha'mesolelot*, because they are not engaged in an act of actual intercourse, but rather some other behavior, *mesolelut*, that is merely indecent. Hence, concludes Ravah, Rav Huna is wrong and *nashim ha'mesolelot* are not barred from marrying *kohenim*.

Ravah's view ultimately prevailed. From the Talmud's conclusion that *mesolelut* constitutes mere indecency, *pritzuta b'alma*, we can infer that the rabbis almost certainly believed it violated general societal norms but not a biblically based prohibition. The term *pritzuta b'alma* is used in the Talmud when the rabbis are expressing mere disapproval of certain conduct but are not declaring it to be forbidden (*issur d'rabbanan*). For example, the Talmud also labels as *pritzuta b'alma* the wearing of red clothing (Babylonian Talmud, Tractate *Berakhot* 20a), which today is an acceptable commonplace even among most Orthodox Jews.

We now return to discerning the exact meaning of the phrase *"nashim ha'mesolelot zoh b'zoh."* According to traditionally accepted Jewish commentaries on the Talmud, it means women (*nashim*) who do a certain sexual act with each other (*mesolelut*), one on or in, or in relation to, the other (*zoh b'zoh*). It is not obvious from the Talmud what sort of sexual activity this is.[8] What did the rabbis of the Talmud imagine that women do sexually when in bed together, with no available penis? We know that *nashim ha'mesolelot* must refer to some degree of genital-to-genital contact, because the rabbis would never have deemed a woman to be a *zonah* without at least that. Rabbi Shlomo ben Yitzhak (1040– 1105 CE), known as Rashi, explains *nashim ha'mesolelot zoh b'zoh* as follows: two women who, in the manner of male–female intercourse, rub their genitalia (*n'kavten*) together. Although lesbians surely do other things in bed, this is a rational conjecture; the root of *mesolelot, s'lul*, means to make a path or swing up (such as when one partner's hips swing up against the other's during sexual intercourse or tribadism).

Returning now to divining the precise meaning of *nashim ha'mesolelot zoh b'zoh*, Rabbi Judah ben Nathan, Rashi's son-in-law (known as the Rivan), offers an explication startlingly different from Rashi's. The Rivan thought that the phrase described two women who exchange the sperm they received from their husbands and implant it into each other's vaginas. His explication appears in the *Tosafot*'s commentary on the Talmud, Tractate *Yevamot* 76a. The *Tosafot* were certain rabbis who lived in France and Germany from the twelfth century CE to the four-teenth century CE. Not surprisingly, they concluded that the Rivan was wrong. By way of proof, the *Tosafot* refer to the following passage in the Babylonian Talmud, Tractate *Shabbat* 65a and 65b:

> Shmuel's father did not permit his daughters to sleep together. Shall we say that this supports Rav Huna, who said that *nashim ha'mesole-lot zoh b'zoh* are disqualified from marrying a *kohen*? No. Shmuel's father did not want them getting accustomed to a foreign body.

The *Tosafot* question why Shmuel's father did not permit his daughters to sleep together. Did he fear that they might engage in sexual activity with each other and thus be rendered ineligible for prestigious priestly marriage? This fear would make sense only if he believed that *nashim ha'mesolelot* were prohibited from marrying *kohenim*, which is Rav Huna's position. As the *Tosafot* did not agree with Rav Huna's position, they offered another explanation: Shmuel's father did not want them getting used to sleeping with a foreign body, i.e., a strange person, which might lead them to have intercourse with men under unsuitable circumstances.

The *Tosafot* surmise that the daughters were unmarried because they lived with their father. Therefore, whatever activity their father was worried about, it could not have been their frolicking about with their husbands' sperm.

The idea that the quintessential lesbian act is exchanging one's hus-band's sperm for another's husband's sperm and taking turns inseminating each other seems absurd; yet it is logical if you believe that the penis is the prerequisite of sex, as Jewish law affirms, and if you cannot fathom why women might want to rub their genitalia together. The Rivan must have had such a difficult time believing that women could have engaged, or would have wanted to engage, in sexual activity with each other, with no penis present or thought or possibility of pregnancy, that he was unable to envision a realistic act involving only the women's bodies. Assuming for present purposes that such a scenario had a basis in reality, these women could be seen as engaged in a daring and generous act that would have challenged one of the strictest of the Jewish laws—that which forbids a married woman to have sexual intercourse with a man other than her husband. Among other reasons for the prohibition, the adulteress might give birth to a child whose lineage cannot be determined. Such a disobedient act would have had the potential to revolutionize the social structure by usurping the power, up until then totally masculine, of deciding who gets impregnated and when. Ultimately, Rashi's sober explanation of *nashim ha'mesolelot* prevailed (see *Shulkhan Arukh, Even Ha'Ezer* 20:2, quoted below), but the Rivan's interpretation of the phrase *nashim ha'mesolelot* seems prophetic: today, centuries later, Jewish lesbians commonly bear children without men's permission, outside of marriage, using semen from a glass vial—perhaps even a married man's sperm—but certainly not from their husbands!

In summary, up to the twelfth century CE, one *halakhik* source, the *Sifra*, banned same-sex marriage. Another source, the Talmud, concluded that a certain type of sexual activity between women, namely rubbing their vulvas together—*mesolelut*—was merely indecent behavior, from which one can reasonably infer that the rabbis believed that *mesolelut* violated Jewish communal norms of behavior but not any express Torah or rabbinic prohibition. The *Midrash Halakha*, the Talmud, or any other classic textual sources of Jewish law did not explicitly forbid or prescribe any punishment for *mesolelut* or any other type of lesbian sexual activity or relationships.[9] Until the twelfth century CE, when Rabbi Moshe ben Maimon, known as the Rambam or Maimonides (1135–1204), wrote his *magnum opus*, the *Mishnah Torah*. This was the first comprehensive codification of Torah and Talmudic law. In *Sefer Kiddushah, Hilchot Issurei Be'ah* 21:8, Maimonides states:

> *Nashim ha'mesolelot zoh b'zoh* is a forbidden practice (*assur*). It is a "*ma'aseh Mitzrayim*" (one of the acts of Egypt) that we were warned about. As it is said, "the doings of Egypt you shall not do." The *Sifra* said, "What were these doings? A man would marry a man, a woman would marry a woman, and one woman would marry two men." Although *mesolelut* is forbidden, they are not given [Torah-prescribed] lashes for it because no specific negative Torah prohibition is violated and it does not involve sexual intercourse at all. Therefore, such women are not prohibited from marrying *kohenim* or remaining with their husbands because there is no *zenut* [act of prohibited sexual intercourse]. However, it is appropriate to flog them with *makot*

mardut [lashes for rebellious behavior imposed by rabbinical courts] because they did something forbidden. A man should be strict with his wife in this matter and prevent the women known for these acts from coming in for her or her from going out to them.

Here, Maimonides aims to synthesize and codify previous legal texts on the subject of *nashim ha'mesolelot*. Maimonides declares the act to be forbidden, *assur*, a term used in *halakha* to denote unquestionably banned behavior. As his proof text, Maimonides cites the *Sifra* to the effect that *mesolelut* was banned by the Torah in *Leviticus* 18:3 as a *ma'aseh Mitzrayim*—a way of Egypt. Maimonides' citation to the *Sifra* would appear to be incorrect because the *Sifra did not* include *mesolelut* as one of the Egyptian practices prohibited by the Torah. There are at least two possible explanations for what Maimonides did.

First, although the only lesbian act that the *Sifra* explicitly mentions is two women marrying each other, the *Sifra* must have implicitly understood the women to be engaging in sexual activity like *mesolelut*, because the last practice that the *Sifra* mentions, polyandry, is a profound violation of biblical law only if the wife is engaging in sexual intercourse with both of her husbands. Each act of intercourse with any husband other than her first is adulterous, and the two of them would be liable for the death penalty. It therefore must have seemed rational to Maimonides to assume that the persons included in the first category mentioned in the *Sifra*, two women marrying each other, were likewise engaging in sexual activity.

Second, Maimonides may have believed that, unless the prohibition against *nashim ha'mesolelot* was somehow linked to the Torah, it would not be taken seriously enough. The *Sifra* provided him with a basis for rooting the prohibition in the Torah without asserting that the women were violating a specific Torah prohibition. Perhaps Maimonides was aware that, historically, same-sex marriage was unknown in ancient Egyptian society, and no right to enter into such marriages was actually embodied in Egyptian law.[10] If so, Maimonides would have known that his analysis could not logically be grounded in the Torah's proscription against following the ways of Egypt. By declaring that his ban against *nashim ha'mesolelot* was under the penumbra of the *Sifra*'s decree, he was able to impose a broad prohibition that encompassed lesbian sexual activity and give it the gravitas that *halakha* bestows upon prohibitions derived from the Torah. Though this would be a creative interpretation of the *Sifra*, he found a reflection in the Torah that linked his prohibition to it, although, tantalizingly, he leaves ambiguous whether his prohibition has any basis in the Torah at all.[11]

The *halakha* as later codified in the *Shulkhan Arukh* echoed Maimonides. The *Shulkhan Arukh*, written by Rabbi Joseph Karo (1488–1575), summarized and codified the body of Jewish law in actual observance in the sixteenth century CE:

> *Nashim ha'mesolelot zoh b'zoh*, meaning rubbing and friction, are forbidden under the warning not to go after the ways of Egypt. Rabbinically decreed lashes for rebellious behavior (*makot mardut*) are appropriate since it is forbidden (*assur*). A man should be strict with his wife in this matter and prevent women known for these acts from coming in for her or her from going out to them.
>
> (*Even Ha'Ezer* 20:2)

The *Shulkhan Arukh*, codifying Maimonides' novel turn in a stricter, more authoritarian direction, calls for critical analysis by those who seek to reinterpret Jewish law in a more progressive direction by using the tradition's own *halakhik* transformational process.[12]

What led Maimonides to make this leap? Was he responding to a perceived lesbian threat to established Torah values in his community in Egypt, circa the twelfth century? This would imply at least the possibility of a group of Jewish women in Egypt living voluntarily (perhaps even happily!) without husbands, and to all appearances, married to each other.[13] In any case, although Maimonides forbade the activity implied by the phrase, *nashim ha'mesolelot zoh b'zoh*, there are indications in *Hilchot Issurei Be'ah* 21:18 that he viewed the infraction of Jewish law as relatively minor. He expressly states that there is no biblically imposed penalty of lashes for engaging in *mesolelot* because there is no express biblical prohibition that it violates. He declares the less severe *makot mardut*, lashes imposed by rabbinical courts (as opposed to biblically imposed lashes), to be the appropriate punishment for rebellion against the Rabbis' authority and societal norms. He permits errant wives to remain with their husbands.[14] Other apparent leniencies can be found in the *Mishnah Torah*, or in what is omitted from the text (whether intentional or not). Maimonides permits the flogging of women for *mesolelut*, but he does not mandate it;[15] nor does he specify a punishment for entering into same-sex marriage. Although he states that a husband should be strict (*hakpid*) about preventing his wife from socializing with *nashim ha'mesolelot*, he neither forbids nor specifies any punishment for it. Nor did he impose an unquestionable and exacting legal obligation, known in Jewish legal codes as a *chiyuv*, on the husband to prevent her from doing it. Further, Maimonides forbade only the rubbing of genitalia together, thus providing an opportunity for further *halakhik* inquiry into whether it would be permissible for unmarried lesbians to have romantic relationships and engage in sexual activity short of *mesolelut*.

What is one to make of Maimonides' novel and troubling warning against mere association between married women and *nashim ha'mesolelot*? Before Maimonides' *Mishnah Torah*, lesbian sexual conduct was viewed by Jewish legal texts as indecent but not forbidden, and the mere association of a woman with *nashim ha'mesolelot* was *neither* indecent nor forbidden. By admonishing men to keep their wives away from *nashim ha'mesolelot*, Maimonides expanded upon the kinds of lesbian relationships that Jewish law finds worthy of condemnation and made *mesolelot* punishable by lashes for the first time.

Having said this, I find some joy in Maimonides' writings. I love his assumption that women would naturally be drawn to doing *mesolelot* with each other, so much so that he had to warn men to guard their wives. Further, his main concern was not ridding his community of such women, but rather warning husbands about them. Their open existence shows they were not all forced into the closet (figuratively) by the Jewish establishment. The dangers to the existing family structure must have been terribly obvious to Maimonides. As a highly respected rabbi and scholar whose writings were known throughout the medieval Jewish world, he must have felt the need to intimidate women who might otherwise rebel against rabbinical authority, societal norms and their husbands by associating with women known for engaging in *mesolelut*. Yet, remarkably, he never decrees that the community or their families should shun or excommunicate them (i.e., put them in *cherem*) or take further punitive measures against them, than perhaps one initial optional flogging with *malkut mardut*. The proof text of this is, to quote Maimonides: *"ha'nashim ha'yidu-ot"*—the women known for these acts. Maimonides uses the definite article to refer to certain identified women who were openly known to perform *mesolelut* with each other. How wonderful and moving it is to discover in a medieval, classical Jewish text the existence of lesbian desire in twelfth-century North Africa: The recognition that Jewish women similar to us, the Orthodykes, not only existed in another place and time, many centuries ago, but whose presence was actually tolerated—albeit to a very limited extent—by the Jewish community.

Afterword

From Maimonides' writings, one is led to imagine a seductive Jewish lesbian gang in town, lurking in the shadows, outlaws who occasionally tried to recruit new members from among the Jewish wives. But even without letting one's imagination run as far as conjuring up a roving lesbian band, there is an important implication in his words *"the women known for these acts"*—that of a lesbian identity. Judaism gives the Jews an extremely strong and durable identity, one that weaves together history, religion, civilization, law, intellectualism, ethics, language, sexuality, cookery—in short, an identity that comes from every aspect of their lives and culture. For many of the women in the New York Orthodykes support group, it seemed that there was no legitimate place to incorporate lesbian relationships into their Jewish identity, let alone the specific identity of lesbian*ness*. But Maimonides' phrase, however brief, points to just such an identity. This is critical for our community, a community of women who have largely been written out of history. I am grateful that the women known to Maimonides for their lesbian acts have in turn become known to us, albeit via a text that would seek to separate us from each other. We embrace them across the centuries. If Orthodykes are also *"ha'nashim ha'yidu-ot"*—*the women known for these acts*, we do in fact have a place in the historical community and continuity of Judaism. As I have by no means exhausted the possibilities of *Hilchot Lesbiut*, the laws of lesbianism, there is, of course, much room—as always in Judaism—for further debate, discovery, interpretation, and creativity.

Notes

1   I use the word "lesbian" adjectivally to describe sex acts or relationships between women. I have avoided using "lesbian" as a noun designating a woman who engages in sexual activity with another woman before the modern era. It would be anachronistic to refer to such women as "lesbians,"

because there was no concept of lesbian identity when these sources were written. The word "lesbian" first began to be used in reference to an identity in the late nineteenth century (*Oxford English Dictionary* online, June 12, 2009).

2 The *Sifra*, a body of teachings on Leviticus, is a part of the *Midrash Halakha*, the companion literature to the Talmud. The *Midrash Halakha* contains the rabbis' analyses of various biblical verses using specific hermeneutic principles to derive rules and laws.

3 This difference in punishment and condemnation is likely due to the fact that *halakha* does not recognize sexual relations between women as sex as such, because, unlike certain male homosexual acts, lesbianism does not closely resemble *be'ah*, intercourse, i.e., the penetration of a woman's vagina by a man's penis at least to a certain degree. See, for example, Babylonian Talmud, Tractate *Yevamot* 56b.

4 Rabbi Shlomo ben Yitzhak (traditionally known as Rashi, 1040–1105 CE), universally revered throughout the learned Jewish world for his commentary on the Bible and the Talmud, comments on the act alluded to in *Leviticus* 20:13 as follows: "he enters like a paint stick into a tube."

5 See, for example, Ricetti (2005), "A break in the path: Lesbian relationships and Jewish law." Ms. Riccetti's article includes a nearly exhaustive listing of all the classical sources addressing lesbianism in Jewish law.

6 *Zonot* is the plural form of *zonah*, which is a technical *halakhik* term referring to a woman who had sexual intercourse with males to whom she is ineligible to marry because she is prohibited from having intercourse with them. A minority opinion maintains that the act of intercourse between *any* unmarried man and an unmarried woman without any marital intent would render her a *zonah*.

7 My thanks to my friend Naomi Seidman for this lovely insight.

8 There are very few other references to *mesolelot* in classical Jewish texts, and the contexts permit no inference as to what exactly *mesolelot* is. For example, see the Babylonian Talmud, Tractate *Sanhedrin* 69b, which refers to *mesolelot* between a mother and her young son.

9 In his commentary on the book of *Genesis*, R. Saadiah Gaon wrote that lesbian sexual activity is prohibited by the Torah.

10 See *Like Bread on the Seder Plate: Jewish Lesbians and the Transformation of Tradition*, p. 29. Rabbi Dr. Rebecca T. Alpert writes: "It is very likely that the author of the *Sifra* knew of same-sex marriages from the Roman culture in which he lived and interchanged the identities of Rome and Egypt without regard to historical accuracy."

11 If it is true that Maimonides elided the *Sifra*'s warnings against same-sex marriage and *nashim ha'mesolelot* in order to fortify his opposition to the latter, then his statement that the women's actions are *assur* should be taken as largely descriptive, rather than normative.

12 Serious students of *halakha* are concluding that *halakha* must and will change and adapt, as it has over the centuries in response to societal change and modernity in general. Certainly, one would think this would be called for in light of recent work suggesting an inborn predisposition to homosexuality, implying that it is not a matter of choice or willful rejection of a religious proscription (as many Orthodox Jews believe), e.g., like choosing to eat lobster instead of salmon. Perhaps this could provide Orthodoxy with a pathway to accepting lesbians as part of the Orthodox community, if not embracing them altogether.

13 They must have been Jewish; otherwise, Maimonides probably would have referred to them as "*nochriot*"—gentiles—or "*Ishmaliot*"—Muslims—so they could more easily be spotted by husbands wanting to keep their wives away from them. He never would have prescribed punishment for non-Jewish women, because they are not bound by *halakha*. Further, the question of their eligibility to marry *kohenim* would not have arisen unless they were Jewish. Maimonides' reiteration of the Talmud's ruling concerning *nashim ha'mesolelot* demonstrates his belief that it was still relevant to his era: "such women are not prohibited from marrying *kohenim*."

14 This likely is because under Jewish law, the women are technically not adulterers. To commit adultery according to *halakha*, a married woman must have intercourse with a man other than her husband. *Halakha* does not view the women's behavior as "sex" (*be'ah*), i.e., intercourse, for formal legal purposes because no penis is involved and therefore there is no possibility of a completed act of intercourse. See, for example, the Babylonian Talmud, Tractate *Yevamot* 56b.

15 The thought that Maimonides prescribed a whipping for women who engaged in consensual sex acts with each other, a right much of the western world takes for granted today, is horrifying. Nevertheless, we acknowledge that Maimonides lessened the injustice by making the penalty optional. Compare his dictate mandating that men who refuse to give their wives a divorce when they seek one for good cause be beaten until they capitulate. See *Sefer Nashim, Hilchot Gerushin*, 2:20. Whether he made the penalty optional out of compassion or because his understanding of the sources and the logical application of *halakhik* rules compelled him to do so, we do not know.

Reference

Ricetti, A. J. (2005), A break in the path: Lesbian relationships and Jewish law. In: Broyde, M. J. and Ausubel, M. (eds.), *Marriage, Sex and Family in Judaism* (pp. 262–294). Lanham, MD: Rowman & Littlefield.

Section II

Gender identity, psychoanalysis, and traditional Judaism

Introduction to Section II

Gender identity, psychoanalysis, and traditional Judaism

Alan Slomowitz

The chapters in this section provide important insights of how gender and gender identity are experienced and lived in the minds, bodies, and lives of Orthodox Jewish transgender individuals. By way of introduction we also require a contemporary understanding of gender development and identity. Therefore, the first chapter in this section, by Dr. Anne Fausto-Sterling, provides important, fundamental understandings of gender identity development and gender variability.

Dr. Fausto-Sterling explains why the concept of gender as a binary (female/male) does not work in the real world. She writes:

> that critical aspects of presymbolic gender embodiment occur during infancy as part of the synchronous interplay of caregiver–infant dyads. By 18 months, a transition to symbolic representation and the beginning of an internalization of a sense of gender can be detected and consolidation is quite evident by 3 years of age.

Her chapter clarifies the complexity of gender development and how the interplay of culture, interpersonal attachment, physiology, and hormones help create one's gender identity.

Nevertheless, I do believe there is a certain mystery as to how our minds create our own subjective gender identity.

Mark Blechner, in his book *Mindbrain and Dreams* (2018), shows the power of the mind to create fully lived realities that are not tied to the physicality of the dreamer's body. He writes "the 'I' of the dream undergoes remarkable transformations, such as changing sex" (Blechner, 2018, p. 23). He reports a patient's dream where the dreamer experiences himself as a female. Other dreamers experience themselves as animals.

Blechner also describes the concept of lucid dreaming (pp. 258–259), when the dreamer is aware that they are dreaming. Some lucid dreamers report being able to direct the outcome of their dreams. For example, in a dream in which the dreamer is feeling tired, he lies down to take a nap. Another possibility is a dreamer creating a dream within a dream. These raise questions about consciousness. For example, Blechner is curious about what it means to know one is asleep or dreaming and how does reality monitoring work when we are asleep?

From its beginnings, psychoanalysis has theorized that thought is rooted in the body and that bodily experiences form the template upon which one's psychological experiences are mapped (Blechner, 2018, p. 48). Psychoanalysis also theorized that, although the brain is individual, meaning that it has a unique individual physiological makeup, the mind is also a field and develops in relation to an other (Levenson, 2017). Therefore, our identities are not only identified by our physiology, by our physical body alone, but also by how we perceive and interpret our bodies in relation to important others (parents, siblings, peers) as well as ourselves. Blechner's research and writing (2018) demonstrate the powerful influence of one's "mind" on one's perception of one's physiological body and self. Furthermore, the debate is philosophical as well as clinical.

David Gelernter, a computer scientist at Yale, has written a book, *The Tides Of Mind: Uncovering the Spectrum of Consciousness* (2016). In his introduction he summarizes the philosophical debate between those he calls the "computationalists" and those he calls the dissenters. The former see the mind as equivalent to the software that runs a computer system. The dissenters focus on the concept of subjectivity, a concept psychoanalysts have studied since Freud. They say computers cannot create subjectivity; they do not create "your own personal experience, your mental life, your own private landscape of mind—the world inside your head that no one but you can ever wander through" (Gelernter, 2016, p. xxii).

The computationalists attempt to get rid of the mental, and to demonstrate that no mental phenomena can exist above the physical phenomena. They ignore subjectivity, partly because that is our problem—we are inside the phenomenon we are trying to study. Why is that a problem? As Gelernter (2016, p. 6) writes: "It is hard to track the rising tide when you are in the water." Unknowingly he echoes Edgar Levenson's famous quote "We don't know who discovered water, but we do know it wasn't the fish" (Levenson, 2017, p. 227). This often makes it impossible to see ourselves except as our body and biological makeup. Yet Blechner, through his study of dreams, and Gelernter, through his focus on the mind's subjectivity, demonstrate the powerful psychological mechanisms of the mind that transcend the limits of the physical body.

When we dream or perform other creative activity we are able to transform our out-of-awareness perceptions into conscious fully lived and physically felt experiences. We may now begin to understand that a person's "gender me-ness," who they are as a lived gender (female, male, or non-binary, for example), can be fully experienced and known, as different from their biologically assigned gender. Even if you believe we may be able to create software that could create consciousness, we do not yet know how or even if we truly can.

At the same time, we do have descriptive and partially explanatory models of the mind in cognitive science and psychoanalysis (see, for example, Stern, 2015; Gelernter, 2016). There is research that demonstrates how much of how we perceive ourselves and our world is completely out of our awareness.[1] Still, as much as we know about the development of gender in each individual's mind and identity, much remains mysterious.[2] This consciousness that enables us to transcend our bodies is and may always remain a mystery. This book is one attempt to confront these mysteries. The contributing authors' research and individual experiences add another layer of understanding and simultaneously evoke more mystery.

The Bible, as interpreted by the many generations of rabbis and other commentators, explicates its theory of gender: male and female. Yet even the text is ambiguous about the body(ies) created. The rabbis of the Talmud dealt with what we today call people born as intersex individuals. Dr. Fausto-Sterling presents her biological/social model of gender development. Others follow a more radically post-modern concept of socially constructed gender.[3]

If we are honest with ourselves, then I believe we must refrain from sweeping generalizations and focus on personal lived experiences. We then have a unique opportunity to find ways to understand one another across this apparent unbridgeable divide. We must find a way an Orthodox Jewish transgender person can live a fully Orthodox life, accepted by their/her/his community. We must find ways for the rabbinic and traditional community to meet the challenges of their members without believing they have abandoned their traditions. We have to begin this dialogue.

How does psychoanalysis help us? I return to Edgar Levenson, because his writings often provide us a way in without the layering of the assumption that we know what is going on. Levenson (2017), in a chapter titled "The purloined self," writes: "Many of our patients come from families where the problem was not so much the lack of affection but a narcissistic assumption that the child is who the parents want him or her to be" (Levenson, 2017, p. 186). The paradox of treatment is that, if we think we know what is "wrong" with the patient, then the patient is invaded to be cured. Importantly, "once the patient stops listening to you and starts listening to himself talking to you, change becomes possible" (Levenson, 2017, p. 187). He concludes this chapter writing: "To look with a fresh eye is to see what is obvious to everyone except the expert, with his preconceived notion of reality" (Levenson, 2017, p. 187). Listen to your self as you read these chapters. Try to pay attention to your preconceived notions and give yourself a chance to see the authors as they are and not as how you want them to be.

These key points need to be reiterated in different ways. I want to paraphrase Levenson from his chapter "The pursuit of the particular" (2017, pp. 202–203). He writes: "The Kabbalists say the mystery of God lies in the particular." The "mystery" of psychoanalysis is the pursuit of the particular—a specific deconstructed mosaic of data that emerges, not a coherent narrative. Levenson says do not try to "make sense." We must tolerate the fragmentation of meaning and the lack of coherence in our lives and experiences.

All of the above feels particularly relevant for the Orthodox transgender person. Orthodox Judaism presses us to make sense of who and what we see and who we are, especially around gender. It does this through the many daily rituals that structure even the minutest details of our lives. For example, many, such as the obligation to pray three times a day, the language of certain morning blessings, or who can be counted for a prayer quorum (10 males over the age of 13), are applied differently to women and men. It is that last structuring, of male and female, that forces a transgender person, as you will read below, to live in an incoherence that may not "make sense," or perhaps does not have to make sense. They live in a mysteriousness of being that evokes a mysterious God. Can we, the readers, who may believe we live our gender coherently, be open to and even celebrate an incoherence of being (as Ben Baader so eloquently writes in Chapter 12) without experiencing ourselves as lost and fallen apart?

Without the path-breaking dissertation of Oriol Poveda much of this section of the book may not have been written or even thought about. Dr. Poveda's (2017) dissertation was the first academic study of Orthodox transgender Jews. He gives voice to their lived experiences as Orthodox Jews. He highlights how the gendered religious practices of Judaism help us understand how deeply intertwined are the gendered and religious journeys of the participants. He shows how the participants moved, through their transitions, their gendered experiences of practice shifting from dysphoria and isolation to validation and affirmation. Their "selves" changed, what was experienced as "not-me" could be formulated into "me." Nevertheless, the other requirement for the transition to "me-ness" is a welcoming community. Without the support of such communities much of the Orthodox transgender person's transition will likely be to that of "bad-me," or to a new more welcoming community. Neither transition will likely be satisfying.

Through Dr. Poveda I was first introduced to Dr. Benjamin Baader and Dr. Joy Ladin. Dr. Poveda's chapter (11) sets the scene for the chapters of Dr. Baader (12) and Dr. Ladin (14), and Dr. Seth Aronson's commentary (Chapter 13).

Dr. Baader writes movingly and lyrically of his multiple transitions from assigned at birth female to male, from non-Jew to Jew, from non-observance to observance, and more. Dr. Baader, unknowingly echoes Levenson's writings when he concludes with the following:

> Thus, I have withdrawn from the contemporary, hegemonic ideal of a coherent, self-contained, self-determined, and fully bounded individual, whose sex and gender are in alignment with each other, producing coherence by speaking the same truth—a truth that medical experts and mental health professionals can confirm.

Dr. Seth Aronson's psychoanalytic and literary commentary on Dr. Baader's chapter provides unique insights into the felt experiences and transitions within the Orthodox Jewish community. Aronson embraces

Badder's incoherent being from the perspective of Philip Bromberg and D. W. Winnicott. He quotes Bromberg: "what underlies human growth in its broadest sense—the increased ability to stand in the spaces between self states that would otherwise be alien to each other" (Bromberg, 2011, p. 141). And Winnicott: "transitional space … permits burgeoning development and autonomy of selves while maintaining a deep sense of connection to others and the world around him" (Winnicott, 1971). As Aronson concludes, Baader's transformation is an expression of growth illuminated by his courageous journey. How true.

We are privileged to include a brilliant commentary on the Torah (Bible) by Professor Joy Ladin. Dr. Ladin's chapter (14) is an excerpt from her latest book, *The Soul of the Stranger: God and Torah from a Transgender Perspective* (2018). She combines her personal felt experiences with original commentary on how she, as a transgender woman, experiences reading the Torah, providing important insights for every reader. She finds strength in the knowledge of how difficult it is for God to have relationships with human beings. She finds comfort knowing the Israelites forget God is there. She concludes with vital advice for all of us:

> To make a place for the God who dwells invisibly and incomprehensibly among us—to show that God belongs with us, and that we belong to God—we must know, and build our lives and communities around knowing, the soul of the stranger.

Through Dr. Poveda's dissertation I was introduced to an important, relatively unknown Jewish legal work, called (in Hebrew) *Dor Tahepuchot* (2004, *A Perverse Generation*, if translated literally). This is a several hundred page legal treatise on Jewish law and transgender issues, published in 2004. This is perhaps the most detailed exposition of rabbinic thinking on transgender issues. The title is derived from a verse in *Deuteronomy* (32:20–21):

> And he [that is, the Lord] said, I will hide my face from them, I will see what their end will be, for they are a *perverse generation*, children in whom is no faithfulness. They have stirred Me to jealousy with what is no god; they have provoked Me with their idols.

Dr. Ronit Irshai from Hebrew University (speech at conference at Harvard Law School, 2017) notes that, in the book's preface, the author, Rabbi Ben Ephraim, makes this positive statement:

> Even when the Lord sees the Israelites' evil deeds, He will not punish them; He will only conceal His face so as not to behold their depravity, knowing that in the end, they will repent and change course—the Hebrew word, *tahapukhot*, rendered here as "perverse," derives from a root whose meanings include "turn back" or "change." That is, they will return to the path of virtue, because they are children who were not raised to transgress.

As she points out, although the Ben Ephraim states that sex reassignment surgery is forbidden a priori, his frequent leniency is bold and astonishing. In his Kabbalistic tradition, he describes how one's soul and body may not necessarily align. The Kabbalists believed that Isaac had the soul of a female and the body of a male; that a sixteenth-century Kabbalist's (Rabbi Vital) wife was the current metamorphosis of a man and consequently barren; but Rabbi Luria did not say that she had a man's obligation to perform the precepts. Reading Ben Ephraim, Irshai's claim is that his ambivalence, his bold leniencies are a result of his belief that "ultimately the soul, that is, a person's strong inner sense of his or her true sex, is more important." Whether one considers souls as self-states, the mysterious incoherences of dissociative experiences, or God-given realities, it would seem to me that this validates the lived experiences of Dr. Baader, Dr. Ladin, the subjects of Dr. Poveda's study, and perhaps all people, cisgendered and transgendered.

Concluding this section are chapters by two scholars who add further understanding to the importance and the nuances of *Dor Tahepuchot*. Dr. Hillel Gray, the Coordinator of the Jewish Studies Program at Miami University of Ohio, explains the differences of opinion about sex reassignment surgery and the practical implications for each opinion. He gives further depth to the *halakhic* rulings by the major rabbinic decisors. He describes how Orthodox Judaism can and does accept a person's changing their gender presentation. Dr. Gray highlights the rabbinic debates if one's phenotype (the gender I present now) and genotype (what gender I was assigned at birth) determine gender from a *halakhic* point of view. However, as Dr. Fausto-Sterling describes in her chapter (10), gender is not a simple binary.

Rabbi Hyim Shafner, rabbi of Kesher Israel, an Orthodox congregation in Washington DC, describes the challenges and rewards of his rabbinic role with transgender congregants. Rabbi Shafner demonstrates that authentic encounters with transgender congregants transforms one's own views. He writes: "It is vital that the Orthodox community recognizes and discusses the challenges and complexities which the community is facing more and more regarding gender identity. As we walk the narrow bridge between fidelity to the letter of the law and the overarching Jewish and *halakhic* value of being, '*mikabetz nidchey yisrael*,' gathering in those Jews who may feel vulnerable and alienated ... one must bring such a person as close to Judaism as they can." This would begin to fulfill Dr. Poveda's exhortation that the key for Orthodox transgender people's acceptance and validation is a community who will accept them.

My hope is that by reading this section and this book you will add to this acceptance.

Notes

1 A fascinating book addressing these issues, in an experimental and cognitive way, is by Kahenman (2011), *Thinking, Fast and Slow* (2011), the winner of the 2002 Nobel prize in Economics. Although I do not have the space here to address the research, I recommend reading it.
2 For more detailed reading some of the following are valuable sources: Fasuto-Sterling (2012), *Sex/Gender: Biology in a Social World*; Corbett (2009), *Boyhoods*; Drescher and Byne (eds) (2013), *Treating Transgender Children and Adolescents*.
3 For a more detailed discussion of this, see Poveda's (2017) dissertation: "According to whose will: The entanglements of gender and religion in the lives of transgender Jews with an Orthodox background."

References

Ben-Ephraim, E. (2004). *Dor Tahapukhot* [*A Generation of Perversions*]. (Hebrew). Jerusalem: Ben-Ephraim Family.

Blechner, M. (2018). *The Mindbrain and Dreams: An Exploration of Dreaming, Thinking, and Artistic Creation*. New York: Routledge.

Bromberg, P. (2011) *The Shadow of the Tsunami*. Hillsdale, NJ: Analytic Press.

Corbett, K. (2009). *Boyhoods: Rethinking Masculinities*. New Haven, CT, London: Yale University Press.

Drescher, J. and Byne, W. (eds.) (2013). *Treating Transgender Children and Adolescents*. Oxford, New York: Routledge.

Fasuto-Sterling, A., (2012). *Sex/gender: Biology in a Social World*. Oxon, New York: Routledge.

Gelernter, D. (2016). *The Tides of Mind: Uncovering the Spectrum of Consciousness*. New York, London: Liveright Publishing Corporation.

Irshai, R. (2017). The contemporary discourse on sex-reassignment surgery in orthodox Jewish religious law, as reflected in *Dor Tahepuchot [A Generation of Perversions]*. Conference on Transgender Persons, Harvard Law School.

Kahenman, D. (2011). *Thinking, Fast and Slow*. New York: Farrar, Strauss & Giroux.

Levenson, E. A. (2017). *The Purloined Self*. London, New York: Routledge.

Poveda, O. (2017). According to whose will: The entanglements of gender and religion in the lives of transgender Jews with an Orthodox background. *Studies in Religion and Society*, 15. Uppsala, Sweden: Acta Universitatis Upsaliensis. ISBN 978-91-554-9823-8.

Stern, D. B. (2015). *Relational Freedom*. London, New York: Routledge.

Winnicott, D.W. (1971) *Playing and Reality*. London: Karnac.

Chapter 10

The dynamic development of gender variability

Anne Fausto-Sterling

Parents of gender variant children face a multitude of questions and dilemmas. Should they discourage the gender variance? Should they "go with the flow"? How can they protect their children from harm—both physical and mental? How can they deal with their own feelings about their gender variant child? Is the gender variance treatable? Is it their fault? What will become of their child as he or she grows to adulthood? We have come a long way in terms of both knowledge and attitudes since the 1960s when Robert Stoller first analyzed children struggling with gender identity issues (Stoller, 1968; Kessler and McKenna, 1978; Green, 2010).

As I am a biologist and gender theorist, not a clinician, I do not intend in this chapter to reach conclusions about clinical practice. Rather, I am going to examine what we might and might not know about the origins of gender variance and, further, to offer some thoughts on how we might frame or model gender development in childhood.

Two housekeeping points: first, I am restricting my discussion to early presenting (within the first five years of life) gender identity issues. I do so because my own theoretical inclination is to think developmentally about the first emergence of difference and because children are the explicit topic of the focus articles. Second, because language choice betokens a theory of origin, people dispute the very language used to describe these children. The terms *gender identity disorder, gender dysphoria, gender variant children*, and *gender nonconforming* each suggest different behaviors that may or may not warrant clinical treatment. Indeed, if one views these terms as representing conditions along a continuous spectrum of gender identity and expression, then the question becomes: is there a normative line along this spectrum and where should it be drawn? The word "gender" in the context of this chapter, is the culturally local behavioral expressions of an internalized individual identity that includes understandings of masculine and feminine. In this sense, gender is not universal, but is tailored to the specific culture in which a child develops.

Extracting theories of development

The clinicians represented in this issue operate from different theoretical and practical points of view. To simplify the discussion I have assigned them to one of two kinship groups. The first joins Zucker et al. (2012) and de Vries and Cohen-Kettenis (2012) as theoretical "kissing cousins"; the second links Ehrensaft (2012) and Menvielle (2012) between whom—in my opinion—run common theoretical threads. Finally, I found it difficult to extract any theory from Edwards-Leeper and Spack (2012), although their point of view may be made clear elsewhere. The Zucker et al. kin group uses multipronged analyses, accepts pathology as part of the mix, and has published extensive numerical and qualitative details of the children visiting their clinics, including prospective follow-up studies. At the same time as they consider the possibility of multiple factors contributing to childhood gender identity variance, they seem unwilling and—due to what they view as a lack of data—unable to draw causal conclusions. Therefore, I call this kin group the "agnostics." They assume a practical, one case at a time approach to treatment.

I call the group represented by Menvielle and Ehrensaft "naturalists." Ehrensaft's (2012) notion of a true gender self that shows up to the parents "rather than being shaped by them, suggesting an innate component to gender nonconformity" (p. 340) is softened by the idea that, subsequent to showing up, the true self gets woven into a nonbinary gender web. The naturalists believe that most gender nonconformist children are mentally healthy and come from healthy families; they argue that the stress and anxiety felt by gender variant kids results from external pressures, sometimes including the inability of parents to cope with these curious children who have shown up on their doorsteps. For the naturalists, therapeutic goals include helping children to accept their true selves as they learn how to negotiate gender in a complicated and often hostile world (Ehrensaft, 2011). In addition to individual psychotherapy, an important innovation has been the development of social networks for gender variant families, providing a safe social space with others of like mind and constitution (Menvielle and Tuerk, 2002; Menvielle et al., 2005).

Finally, the agnostics and the naturalists agree on certain things. They both see biology as scaffolding on which the psyche is built. They both agree that there are probably several kinds of gender variance. And they concur that at least on occasion, psychopathology and gender variance coexist, possibly reinforcing each other.

The agnostics

Figure 10.1 stylizes the apparent elements of the agnostics' model. They propose that predisposing biological factors (e.g., genes, hormones, temperament, brain structure) provide a structural scaffolding that may precipitate other events or perpetuate other responses. In Figure 10.1,

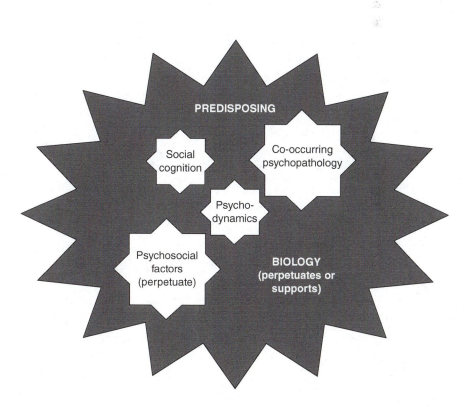

Figure 10.1 The agnostic's model of gender identity formation (based on Zucker et al., 2012)

predisposing biology appears as a background, but no arrows link biology to the other factors, nor do the other theoretical elements feed back to biology. This essential point is missed by both Zucker et al. (2012) and de Vries and Cohen-Kettenis (2012). Brain development itself, especially in children, is to a large extent directed by social and sensory experiences; so too is hormone biology and physiological regulation (Field et al., 2006; Petanjek et al., 2008; Schore, 2005). A well-developed theory of gender identity needs to place this dynamic at its center.

The biopsychosocial model conceptualizes psychosocial factors as conscious parental responses to their child's cross-gender interests. Zucker et al. (2012) view parental neutrality or encouragement of cross-gender behavior "as a perpetuating factor" (p. 377). As used by the agnostic group, social cognition seems to involve how a child applies his or her own reading of gender in his or her social world to his or her sense of self. The agnostics provide strong evidence of co-occurring psychopathology for many, but not all of the gender variant kids they see in their practice. For example, Coates (1992; Coates and Wolfe, 1995) has focused over the years on severe separation anxiety as a precursor to gender identity disorder (GID) in some boys; more recently, the Dutch group has proposed an elevated co-occurrence of autistic-like rigidity and obsessiveness in gender dysphoric kids (de Vries et al., 2010). The naturalists, it should be pointed out, also report such co-occurrences, but consider them to be rare and unrelated to mainstream (if I may call it that) gender variance. Some clinicians treat the anxiety or obsessiveness and find that the cross-gender obsessions abate. It seems likely that the succession of childhood obsessions is one of the underlying systems to be explored as we try to understand gender identity development (DeLoache et al., 2007).

Last, the biopsychosocial model proposes psychodynamic mechanisms. These mechanisms may involve the child's assumption of unresolved family conflict and traumas. In family systems lingo, the child manifests the symptoms of a distressed family system; cross-gender interests are the symptoms of a poorly functioning family, and treatment must be a family affair. Importantly, different children may have different response thresholds for similar traumatic incidents, possibly explaining why what appears to be similar family stresses could, in one case, result in a gender-focused coping response but not in another.

The biopsychosocial model contains important elements for under-standing gender development. The agnostics supply evidence from case studies to support their contention that each of these systems has the potential to play a role in the development of cross-gender identities and behaviors. Yet, they are curiously unlinked and static. It would seem the same elements ought to be a component of gender development in all kids.

The naturalists

In truth, the naturalists don't offer a theory of gender identity origins. Instead, they posit a preformed, but unexplained, true gender self, and focus on how the true self develops and takes individual shape within a particular nexus of culture, nature, and nurture. None of these terms is precisely defined, but the naturalists develop an important point: gender identity is not binary. They conceptualize it as a three-dimensional web, although neglecting that important fourth or developmental dimension. The strength in this approach is the emphasis on individual difference. The weakness is the loss of insight into how previous form shapes subsequent structure (Thelen, 2000).

Using the following passage from Ehrensaft (2012), I have created an image of the naturalist's theory of gender identity (Figure 10.2a).

> The true gender self begins as the kernel of gender identity that is there from birth, residing within us in a complex of chromosomes, gonads, hormones, hormone receptors, genitalia, secondary sex characteristics, but most importantly in our brain and mind.
>
> (Ehrensaft, 2012, p. 341)

After birth, each true gender self is "channeled through (individual) experience with the external world ... but its center always remains ... driven from within" (Ehrensaft, 2012, p. 341). This postnatal shaping is depicted in Figure 10.2b.

Two noteworthy characteristics emerge from both the agnostics' and the naturalists' theories. First, the working parts seem peculiarly unconnected. Second, gender identity is strangely disembodied and outside the world. How do the precursors of gender identity manifest

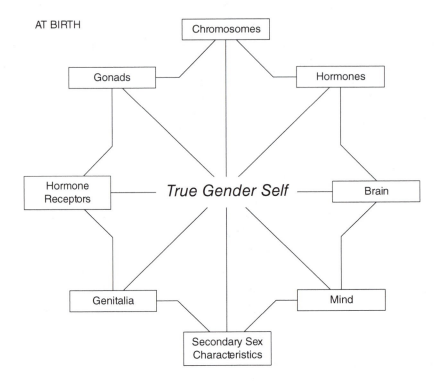

AT BIRTH

Chromosomes

Gonads

Hormones

Hormone
Receptors

True Gender Self

Brain

Genitalia

Mind

Secondary Sex
Characteristics

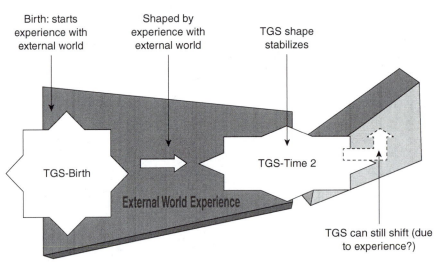

Birth: starts
experience with
external world

Shaped by
experience with
external world

TGS shape
stabilizes

TGS-Birth

External World Experience

TGS-Time 2

TGS can still shift (due
to experience?)

Figure 10.2 (a) The naturalist's theory of gender identity; (b) The naturalist's
model of gender identity formation (based on Ehrensaft, 2012)

themselves through the body—a pleasure in the soft or the pink, an aversion to rough play, for example? I argue that such signs of gender are in the body, yet these clinical theories seem to work only from the mind. Following the extraordinary lead provided by Thelen and colleagues (2000), and by psychoanalysts such as Harris (2005) and Corbett (2009), I argue that gender development be placed in a dynamic embodied systems framework. First, I provide some general principles, then I explore the presymbolic origins and early symbolic manifestations of gender identity. (Presymbolic representations are prelinguistic, physiologically embodied memories.) I end by suggesting that the transition from presymbolic to internalized symbolic representations of gender lies at the heart of the matter.

A dynamic systems framework for gender identity development

General considerations

Thelen (2000), and biologists such as Chiel and Beer (1997), insist that behaviors and cognition arise from the coupling of several contributing systems. Cognition, for example, depends on particular kinds of experiences had by particular bodies with particular perceptual and motor abilities. These sensory and motor capacities link to form a matrix within which reason, emotion, memory, language, and more reside. The developmental issue is to understand the timing, strength, and history of the coupling between these critical systems.

The world is the matrix in which all elements embed. This contrasts with predisposing factors that provide the underlying matrix (see Figure 10.1). By "the world," I intend all the experiences encountered by a child from before birth and throughout life. Postnatally, these include caregiving, touching, dressing, feeding—that is, all of the emotional and physical interactions a newborn and developing infant encounters in his or her immediate world (see, for example, Fausto-Sterling, 2010a, 2010b, 2011). The world has other people in it and the infant cannot develop without them. But, also, the infant's behaviors influence and shape how others respond. At birth an infant's behaviors relate importantly to the state of development of his or her nervous and digestive systems and physiological capacities to self-regulate. Beyond, but also reaching into the nursery, the world brings specific gender attachments—flowery wallpaper, toy trucks, pink onesies, gendered parental assumptions and expectations, and more (Feldman et al., 1980; Rheingold and Cook, 1975; Shakin et al., 1985). At birth the world subsumes what Zucker et al. (2012) call psychodynamics; in late infancy, toddlerhood and childhood it also includes social cognition.

The body is the next largest collection of systems found within the world. It is not the foundation of all things, but rather is in the middle— sustained within the world, responding to it, but also reshaping it. Obviously, as I have displaced the idea of predisposing biology (see Figure 10.1), I have also rendered it an untenable concept. To understand this, consider the work of biologist David Crews. A long and productive career analyzing the role of genes and environment in sex determination has led Crews to espouse a systems view of gonad formation and the regulation of sociosexual behavior. He understands that both complex behaviors and their genetic underpinnings (a.k.a. predisposing biology) are cumulative processes both resulting from past events and setting the stage for responses to future experience (Crews et al., 2006; Putz and Crews, 2006). Such a general framework is the appropriate starting point for thinking through the development of human gender variability.

At heart, Ehrensaft's (2012) true gender self is a biological concept, similar in many ways to the idea that one is born gay. The true gender concept is a homunculus that grows within the world and, in so growing, is shaped by it, much as, I imagine, a plant grown without enough light becomes etiolated and spindly whereas one raised with good light becomes bushy, green, and strong. But we gain little sense of the systems out of which the true gender self emerges, no sense of the multiple feedback systems that sustain or shape it.

Finally the brain/mind is integrated into the body. Through its sensory and motor abilities the exterior layers of the body bring the world into the central nervous system. Neural plasticity lies at the heart of the matter. A toddler's mind emerges from experience in a particular body and particular world. The brain's very synapses form, take shape, die back, or reconnect in response to the world and body that envelop it. The same is true of the forming neuromuscular connections—links from the central nervous system to the muscles that control motor ability and visceral responses (Thelen, 1994, 1995a, 1995b, 2001).

Chiel and Beer (1997) suggest the following metaphor. Traditionally, behaviorists think of the nervous system as the body's conductor—choosing the program for the players and influencing how they play. But consider instead that the nervous system is only one player in a jazz improv group. The music results from a continued give and take between the player, a continuous interaction among the nervous system, the rest of the body, and the environment. If gender identity were the performance piece it would succeed or fail based on the contributions of all the instruments in the band, how they integrate into a coherent system, and how the couplings ebb and flow during the time course of the performance.

Gender identity is located in all three interacting networks, a product of the coupling of critical systems—including those postulated by Zucker and colleagues (2012). I have already suggested that gender-related behaviors and identity formation emerge as a pattern of several cooperating parts; as we need each part to sustain the whole, one is not more fundamental than another. Not a thing, gender identity is a pattern in time. In any one individual, it is shaped by the preceding dynamics and becomes the basis of future identity transformations.

As a set of systems moving through time, gender identity varies in its relative stability. When the components (see following sections) cohere tightly, gender identity is stable. When the elements cohere poorly, the system becomes chaotic; more loosely bound elements are better able to make new connections out of which more stable patterns can possibly emerge. Thelen (2000, p. 8) phrases it this way:

> the components of the system are coupled in a particular way ... development consists of the progressive ability to modulate the coupling so as to meet different and changing situations .... There is no point in time when these dynamic processes stop and something else takes over.

My working premise is that enormous individual variation exists within the general processes outlined above. By individual I mean both the infant as he or she develops *in utero* and first appears outside of the womb and the adult–infant dyads, which become the units of self-regulation, mutual regulation, and learning through which infants gain an understanding of the world and of self.

I agree with Meyer-Bahlburg (2010) when he laments the lack of a general theory of gender identity development. Corbett (1996, 2009) reminds us that there can be no measurable norm without variance around it. Whether or not some variants—either in the child or in the family unit—might get labeled as productive of psychopathology is a different debate. Instead, in this chapter, I want to refocus discussion on what amounts to the previous question: How does any type of gender identity develop? Even here we confront a prior question: What is gender identity? How, clinically and experimentally, do we make it operational?

In the clinic

Clinical definitions and the criteria from the *Diagnostic and Statistical Manual of Mental Disorders* (4th edn, text revision; *DSM-IV-TR*; American Psychiatric Association, 2000) for childhood Gender Identity Disorder create, in essence, a negative film of gender identity. The supposed disorder is said to consist of some combination of: a child's insistence that he or she is the other sex, preference for cross-dressing, persistent or strong preferences for cross-sex roles in make believe or play, strong desire to participate in the stereotypical games and pastimes of the other sex, and strong wish for playmates of the other sex. The positive print of this image, then, is that gender identity in general must consist of several rather different but interwoven features. The acquisition of a gender identity usually involves the ability to self-identify as male or female, development of feelings about one's genitalia, and a set of pleasures and repulsions that concern styles of dress and play. Thus, gender identity is not a thing, but a name given to a weaving together into a subjective self of aspects of the masculine and the feminine.

Corbett's (1996, 2009) work on boyhood femininity is helpful. First, he rejects a world of binary rules. He sees gender as a dynamic of "gendered codes, behaviors, and traits circulate and transform ... within modern families" (Corbett, 2009, p. 103) which reside in a larger, social field of relatives, schools, television, social workers, and more. The family, in this view, is the locale of concrescence for the gender rules and representations encountered in the outside world. "The 'outside' society is indelibly 'inside' the family" (Corbett, 2009, p. 103). Such a notion of the outside has not seriously penetrated the skin of attachment or social learning theory.

Developmental timing

Operationally, gender identity lies partly inside the body—in the shape of sensitivities, desires, preferences, and interests; but it is partly outside the body in that it is always an oppositional concept. Corbett (2009), for example, quotes Robert Stoller that "The first order of business in being a man is don't be a woman" (Corbett, 2009, p. 91). A version of that web we call gender identity is first visible in early toddlerhood and transforms over a period of years. That which we call gender identity in a three year old differs in important ways from that which we call gender identity in a seven year old. As Harris (2005) has so aptly put it, gender is a softly assembled system. In the first five or so years of life, the system itself develops fairly rapidly; thereafter, it usually stabilizes even as it transforms more modestly. Occasionally, the systems that stabilize gender identity fall into chaos and reorganize on a substantially new plain (Martin, as cited in Meyer-Bahlburg, 2010).

Soft assembly contrasts with the "developmental, biopsychosocial model" of Zucker and colleagues (2012) which asserts that in the majority gender identity is a "fixed and unalterable" (Zucker et al., 2012, p. 375) trait. Zucker et al. contrast this fixity with a lack of stability in gender variant kids. Agnostics seem to set up a binary division between majority development, and that which must be explained, i.e., deviation from the majority. In contrast, by understanding the acquisition of gender identity and gender expression as a process common to all people, we can weave elements of the agnostics' model into an account in which the processes for both gender variant and gender congruent kids are similar in kind, but differ in timing and or execution. In a process model, gender identity may be stable, but it is never fixed.

The presymbolic phase of gender identity formation

A better understanding of the many and complex pathways that lead to human variation can produce a greater tolerance for variability in children and adults alike. Offering families a deeper conceptualization of the dynamics of gender identity formation in childhood may well be the best therapy of all. The framework developed in the following pages sets us on the path toward that end.

The newborn infant does not have a self-concept as either male or female. Indeed, on the surface of things, the foremost agenda item for an infant is to attract the adult attention needed for survival. In the first few months all children have a set of tasks, the successful accomplishment of which provides a sound physiological and emotional basis for the emergence of individual gender identity. We postulate that the building blocks that enable gender identity differentiation, including a developing awareness of symbolic and culturally specific gender knowledge, takes shape during the first year of life, whereas gender identity itself becomes increasingly evident to adult observers during the second.

The achievement of universal developmental tasks (e.g., dyad competence and physiological regulation) provides the skills needed to internalize and symbolize gender; these universal tasks are, however, always individually and culturally specific. The developmental state of the newborn, the emotional and skill states of the parents, their financial resources, and the cultural accoutrements of parenthood structured by social gender norms all matter (Fausto-Sterling et al., 2018a, 2018b).

In the beginning there is touch. Through skin-to-skin contact the infant gains hold of temperature regulation. Through touch, the infant develops control of crying and sleeping (de Weerth et al., 2003; Korner and Thoman, 1970; Sadeh et al., 1996; Weller and Bell, 1965). Early affectional touch improves the quality of reciprocal communication in the adult–infant dyad. Infants who are held and touched have lower circulating stress hormones and careful massage of preterm infants decreases metabolic rate, improves sleep, decreases stress behaviors, and improves immune function. Proper touch is essential to the embodiment of emotions and the development of self (Ferber et al., 2008; Field, 2010; Field, Diego, and Hernandez-Reif, 2006; Field, Hernandez-Reif, and Diego, 2006).

Touch co-occurs with vocalizations, facial expressions, body tone, and movement. All these come from the caring adult—usually called the mother, but the importance of other adult–infant contact requires a great deal more study (Lamb, 1977); these behaviors are a response to infant demands but also meet infant needs and enable infant development. The dyadic exchanges affect and attune autonomic, neurological, and hormonal systems of each partner in the dyad (Schore, 1994). By two to three months, parent–infant interactions have a clear structure and timing; Observers note cycles of behavior that include looking, touching, and affective expression. At four months, the direct social gaze becomes all important. Periods of synchronous gazing are often integrated with affectionate touch and vocalization. Importantly, this pattern is culturally specific, more typical of North America and western Europe. Parents from other parts of the world offer more bodily contact but less gaze, voice, and object use. As development passes the half-year mark, objects become the center of adult–child play; with this transition gaze synchrony lessens and shared attention turns toward an object (R. Feldman, 2007a, 2007b).

In this pas-de-deux, sex and gender matter. From birth to six months most studies focus on behaviors related to the function of the mother–infant dyad. In addition to differences in weight, brain size, and motor and sensory development (Fausto-Sterling, 2011), neonatal starting points may include greater average brain cortical maturity in girls (Thordstein et al., 2006) and average differences in crying and fussing at birth, three to six months (Moss, 1967; Phillips et al., 1978; Sadeh et al., 1996).

A study of the mother–infant dyad from birth to three months reveals sex-related variability in dyadic communication (Lavelli and Fogel, 2002). If, for example, the critical factors that shape early dyadic communication include levels of neural development, sleep and fuss patterns, and physical size, these variables might correlate with the development of dyadic communication patterns. If these variables, in turn, correlated with the sex of the infant, as suggested by the findings of et al. (1999), then a process by which the development of early sex differences is initiated might be identified. Studies of the gender dynamics of adult–infant dyad formation and coordination suggest that at three to nine months a mutually engaged state has stabilized in mother–daughter dyads but is more likely to still be unilateral in mother–son dyads (Hsu and Fogel, 2003; Malatesta et al., 1989; Tronick and Cohn, 1989; Weinberg et al., 1999).

Parents also bring sex and gender to the nursery. R. Feldman (2007b) found that first time mothers and their five-month-old infants cycled between low and medium peaks of arousal, with the occasional peak of high positive emotion. The father–infant dyad involved greater emotional and physical arousal. Peaks of laughter and exuberance became more frequent as play progressed. Although, father and infant achieved the same degree of synchrony as mother and child, when dyads were gender matched (father–son or mother–daughter) synchrony was at its highest. Such differing dyad interactions provide infants with the opportunity to form presymbolic representations, or models, for masculine and feminine styles of activity and emotional output.

To sum up our argument to this point: (a) from the beginning (possibly even before birth) the dyadic interaction shapes individual nervous systems in such a way that groups with overlapping but statistically differentiable behaviors start to emerge; (b) at birth great individual variability in developmental parameters exists, some of which rises to the level of average group differences between male and female infants; and (c) from birth on, average sex-related differences in (parent–infant) communication take shape, developing into varied patterns of vocal, physical, and emotional interactions. Between three and six months other dyadic patterns emerge, some of which appear to be sex differentiated.

Presymbolic representations of difference

Piaget defined the presymbolic stage as lasting roughly from birth to 18 months (Piaget and Inhelder, 1972). Relying primarily on sensorimotor representations, the infant in this period interacts with the world through actions such as crying and regulated gestures. Infants enter the world with surprisingly advanced capabilities. Using auditory, visual, motor, touch, and circadian insights, infants take the measure of their surroundings even *in utero*. As they measure, they also learn to manipulate the adults whose care they need, and begin the life-long process of honing a capacity for self-regulation (Beebe et al., 1997). The environmental trappings of gender, from the voices, faces, modes of holding and touching, dress, hair, and grooming, to the colors in the room, the toys offered, and the baby clothing used, are ever present. From birth or before, an infant absorbs them, commits them to memory, develops expectations about them, and receives bodily messages about their own sex and gender.

Beebe and Lachmann (1994) articulate three working hypotheses about how presymbolic representations of social relatedness form in infancy. First, ongoing regulations in adult–infant interactions create regularities that organize an infant's experience. Second, infants further learn to regulate their environment through a process of disruption and repair. An expectancy (e.g., feeding at a certain hour) may be disrupted, the infant expresses distress, and adults repair the disruption by (belatedly) feeding or otherwise attempting to comfort the infant. Finally, during heightened affective moments infants respond to heightened adult emotion evident in facial or vocal expression, with an arousal pattern measured physiologically as changes in brain waves, heart rates, and/or respiration. The high moments of excitement in father–infant dyad play is one example. The differential between maternal and paternal interactive styles could be one of the early inputs that shapes presymbolic representations of gender and links them to emotional development.

Beebe and Lachmann (1994) believe that both self-representation (obviously relevant to the emergence of a sense of oneself as male or female) and object representations (with regard to gender, an understanding of familial and cultural gender categories), result from "the expected moment to moment interplay of the two partners" (p. 131). Representations are "persistent, organized classifications of information about an expected interactive sequence" (p. 131). Infants and children base representations on past interactions, but continuously modify and restructure them as the environment—including the human interactions within it—transforms.

How might the idea that infancy involves a continuous organizing process based on developing expectancies, their disruption, and their repair apply to gender development? The experiences that organize gender might include, first, the daily physicalities of care. How do parents carry, touch, sooth, and play with their children, and how do specific infant nervous systems experience the resulting physical sensations? What pleasurable or discomforting expectations develop from sensory input, including emotive faces, voice timbre and expression, touching while playing, bathing (including genital touch), and feeding? Are these linked in ways that differentiate gender? At a more removed level, male and female adults in the infant environment shape infant expectations. From the start, toys are available in different types and quantities, and the colors and tactile features of clothing and stuffed animals also shape infant expectations and are highly differentiated even for neonates (Rheingold and Cook, 1975; Shakin et al., 1985). Thus, taking seriously Beebe and Lachmann's (1994) framework for the infant phase of representing and individualizing opens a little-explored field of study for those interested in the emergence of gender identity in toddlers and beyond.

As infants perceive regularities in their experience they begin to form categories. In the case of gender, both visual and auditory categories can be noted by 6–9 months (faces and voices) and by 12 months cross-modal abilities emerge including an association of male and female voices with gender-related objects (Fausto-Sterling et al., 2018b). By the time an infant has become a toddler, gender knowledge has progressed from presymbolic representations such as recognition and association of voice pitch and faces to a far more sophisticated, increasingly symbolic representation of gender in self and others. It seems likely that this transition from presymbolic to symbolic and to increasingly internalized representations of gender, which must start in the vicinity of one year of age and carry on for several years, is an especially important period for understanding the developmental dynamics of gender identity.

From presymbolic to symbolic representations of gender

R. Feldman (2007a) and others (see, for example, Beebe and Lachmann, 1994) argue that symbolic representations emerge toward the end of year one as specific infant responses to the training afforded by perceptual, affective, and motor experiences organize into coherent structures Early synchrony between parent and child correlates positively with more complex symbolic play at age three years. At three and nine months it correlates with how well a child can use words to refer to mental states such as thoughts or feelings attributed to self or others, whereas parent–infant synchrony at three months predicts how well a five year old can perceive that his or her own emotions might differ from those of others.

Gender differentiation becomes most evident as children develop symbolic representations. Gender-specific toy preference, for example, begins to emerge at about one year of age (Jadva et al., 2010). At 18 months, children are startled at culturally gender inappropriate images (e.g., a man putting on makeup) and have also developed a system of gender-related metaphors (Poulin-Dubois et al., 2002). Gender identity itself—which lies at the heart of the discussion— comes on line gradually. Before two years of age, children learn to label others as boy or girl—using external (symbolic?) features such as hair length or dress. They next develop the ability to self-label and can exhibit a nonverbal gender identity. However, the notion that gender itself is stable and sex constant as children grow to adulthood does not usually take root until a child is five or six years old (Fagot, 1995; Fagot and Leinbach, 1989, 1993; Fagot et al., 1986, 1992).

Gender metaphors and words

Zosuls et al. (2009) studied the development in toddlers of the ability to utter basic gender labels (girl, boy, man, woman). At 17 months, about a quarter of the kids they studied had used at least one verbal label, and by 21 months this number had increased to 68%. However, boys developed this ability more slowly. In this same time period, children accurately associate gendered objects such as a fire hat or a tiara with male or female faces and they have acquired a view about what links, symbolically, to one or the other sex (Eichstedt et al., 2002). Such symbolic knowledge seems to affect children's belief systems about which sex should play with which toys. Eichstedt et al. (2002) suggest that symbolic gender knowledge in the pre-two-year-old set can drive or enhance the acquisition of a variety of gender stereotypes.

Oppositional knowledge

In this same time period, we first detect a surprisingly sophisticated understanding of gender roles. When asked to choose either male or female dolls to act out activities deemed by adults to be masculine stereotyped, feminine stereotyped, or gender neutral, 2-year-old girls used the male dolls to play act masculine activities 70% of the time. For neutral activities, they used the male doll 30% of the time and for feminine-stereotyped activities they used the male dolls 48% of the time. Despite a range of variability from 23% to 95%, these 2-year-old girls clearly had some knowledge about gender-stereotyped behavior. The same cannot be said for the boys, who used male and female dolls pretty much equally regardless of the task's stereotypy (Poulin-Dubois and Forbes, 2002). In studies using a looking rather than a playing method, however, both male and female two year olds looked longer at photos of women behaving in gender-inappropriate ways, such as hammering a nail, fixing a toy, or taking out the garbage, but seemed unimpressed by photos of a man putting on lipstick, feeding a baby, or ironing (Serbin et al., 2002). These studies suggest that even two year olds know some pretty complicated things about gender roles. As they also develop the capacity to label themselves according to gender, they may put this knowledge to use in building their own identities.

Self-labeling

Zosuls et al. (2009) found a significant relationship in months 17–21 between the ability of kids to label themselves as a boy or a girl and increased levels of gender-typed play. Thus, the application of some knowledge of gender in the world to a sense of self happens between the second and third years of life and provides self-feedback on behavioral preferences. Some argue that this is the moment in which a child acquires a gender identity. For Ehrensaft (2012), this might be the point in time in which a child presents his or her parents with a true gender self. But, clearly, this version of gender identity, gradually acquired as knowledge about experienced gender roles, forms a dynamic network that gradually ensnares the child.

Internalizing a gender self

Harris (2005, p. 181) states it beautifully:

> Brought into an intense, embodied responsiveness and contact with the material world, caught up in the conscious and unconscious reverie of parents, prenatally already an object of intense fantasy, a child finds the experience of self within a relationship in which he or she is already seen …. The internalization … of the gender/body mirror becomes a part of the child's procedural knowing, available

for many complex remappings and reassemblies in the course of development.

Children with individualized nervous systems, genes, hormone levels, and physiologies are born into a gender-differentiated world. Even during the last weeks of uterine life, fetuses can perceive gender outside the womb. These differences take shape or disappear at first through the dyadic formations of early infancy and, with time, through increasingly independent knowledge acquisition and behavioral patterns. Gender is never absent. There is never a point at which it begins. Still, the $64,000 question remains: How do increasing levels of gendered embodiment, knowledge about gender in the world, and the growing abilities to self-label and modulate behaviors to correlate with labels become part of an internal sense of self?

In Figure 10.3, we recap the elements contributing to presymbolic gender embodiment and representation, indicating a period of transition—critically mediated by language development—to symbolic gender knowledge. Such knowledge builds on previous embodiment and enmeshes in a web of behavior, self-labeling, and preferences that are the subsystems of that dynamic web we call *internalized gender identity*. In each developmental phase, there are dynamically interacting subsystems, but the developmental time line is unidirectional.

Psychoanalyst Susan Coates distilled several important characteristics from a study of over 130 young boys (aged 2–4 years) brought to therapeutic attention because of their cross-gendered behaviors, interests, or identities. First, the boys' cross-gendered behaviors emerged during a critical period of development (2–4 years). Second, GID in children often appeared and consolidated quite suddenly and, for the boys who came to Coates' practice, frequently (but not always) in the context of some kind of psychic trauma. Coates associated several biopsychological markers with these boys including a sense of physical fragility, the avoidance of highly physical play, anxiety in new situations, high sensitivity to others' emotional states, high vulnerability to separation or loss, an unusually acute ability to imitate others, and extraordinary sensory sensitivity to sound, color, texture, smell, and pain (S. Coates, 1992; S. W. Coates and Wolfe, 1995).

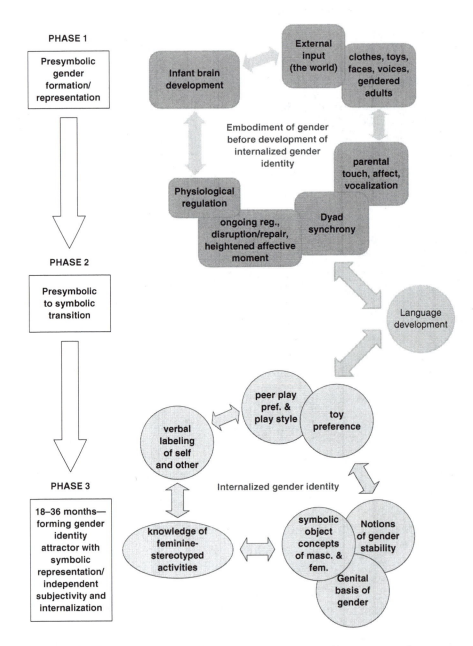

Figure 10.3 Three phases of gender representation and identity internalization

Analyst Ken Corbett (1996) argues that boyhood gender nonconformity does not represent a continuum of femininity. Instead, he suggests these boys fall on "a continuum of ego integration and psychic structure" in which GID and gender-nonconforming boys may be equally feminine, but in the latter group "the femininity is contained within a more stable psychic structure" (p. 438). Corbett insists that the very category of GID demands that we develop theoretical approaches that explain how the psyche, the soma, and the social build one another.

As should be clear, I agree with Harris and Corbett (and thank Coates for her expanded framing, which initially broadened my own perspective on early gender identity development) that to understand the emergence of gendered behaviors and their attachment (or not) to natal sex we need first to become more knowledgeable about the presymbolic, dyadic processes through which gender becomes embodied in infancy. Such embodiment forms the basis for the transition to symbolic understandings of gender as a relational and oppositional concept coincident with the internalization and dynamic stabilization of gender as a component of the self.

What next?

A lot of work remains to fully develop and shape these ideas. Beebe and colleagues (Beebe and Lachmann, 1994; Beebe et al., 1997, 2010) have published a series of studies of dyad formation and interactions. What must still be done here is to incorporate the sex of infant as a variable into such studies. Some such work exists, but more is needed (Fogel and Thelen, 1987; Fogel et al., 1987, 1997). To understand the dynamics of gendered embodiment, investigations of presymbolic gender formations must be longitudinal.

Dyad formation and input from the physical environment likely affect brain development, but neither has been studied in relation to neural growth and development. Although the measurement of functional brain activity in infants is still fairly crude, the development of noninvasive scanning methods seems to be coming into its own (Bell and Fox, 1992; Dawson et al., 1999; Kuhl, 2010). It should be possible to link the development of dyad synchrony to brain development both generally and with regard to gender. Similarly, studies testing the importance of exposure to a skewed physical environment (e.g., many toy cars, few dolls) to brain activity and development during the first year of life should illuminate gendered developmental systems.

More detailed knowledge of gender formations and embodiment during infancy should enrich our thinking about the transition from presymbolic to symbolic gender representation and the concomitant internalization of identity. Writ large this is a question about how sense memories and bodily knowledge transform into psychic knowledge. In terms of gender, for the time being, it makes sense to operationalize identity via the study of gendered behaviors and self-assessments. If the transformation really is a dynamic system, then we might expect this period to be chaotic and unstable relative to the stability of well-formed dyadic synchrony that precedes, and the relative rigidity of gender identity evidenced by, children by the time they are four to five years of age (Hollenstein, 2007).

As the developmental details and dynamic interactions of phase 1, the transition, and phase 2 come into clearer focus, a supportable theory of gender identity development will emerge, allowing us to get a handle on individual variations in identity formation and expression. Given the number of subsystems contributing to the outcome as seen by age five or so, it seems likely that several roads can lead to similar-appearing variations in gender identity. Furthermore, no single item—be it parental behavior or infant genes—can be held responsible for the outcome. Improved understandings of the many and complex pathways that underlie human variation can lead to a greater tolerance for variability in children and adults alike. Offering families a more profound knowledge of the dynamics of gender identity formation in childhood may well be the best therapy of all.

References

American Psychiatric Association. (2000). *Diagnostic and Statistical Manual of Mental Disorders* (4th edn, text revision). Washington, DC: American Psychiatric Association.

Beebe, B., Jaffe, J., Markese, S., Buck, K., Chen, H., Cohen, P., et al. (2010). The origins of 12-month attachment: A microanalysis of 4-month mother–infant interaction. *Attachment and Human Development*, 12:3–141.

Beebe, B. and Lachmann, F. M. (1994). Representation and internalization in infancy: Three principles of salience. *Psychoanalytic Psychology*, 11:127–165.

Beebe, B., Lachmann, F. M., and Jaffe, J. (1997). Mother–infant interaction structures and presymbolic self-and object representations. *Psychoanalytic Dialogues*, 7:133–182.

Bell, M. A. and Fox, N. A. (1992). The relations between frontal brain electrical activity and cognitive development during infancy. *Child Development*, 3:1142–1163.

Chiel, H. J., and Beer, R. D. (1997). The brain has a body: Adaptive behavior emerges from interactions of nervous system, body and environment. *Trends in Neuroscience*, 20:553–557.

Coates, S. W. (1992). The etiology of boyhood gender identity disorder: An integrative model. In J. W. Barron, M. N. Eagle, and D. L. Wolitzky (eds.), *The Interface of Psychoanalysis and Psychology* (pp. 245–265). Washington, DC: American Psychological Association.

Coates, S. W. and Wolfe, S. M. (1995). Gender identity disorder in boys: The interface of constitution and early experience. *Psychoanalytic Inquiry*, 15:6–38.

Corbett, K. (1996). Homosexual boyhood: Notes on girlyboys. *Gender and Psychoanalysis*, 1:429–461.

Corbett, K. (2009). *Boyhoods: Rethinking Masculinities*. New Haven, CT: Yale University Press.

Crews, D., Lou, W., Fleming, A., and Ogawa, S. (2006). From gene networks underlying sex determination and gonadal differentiation to the development of neural networks regulating sociosexual behavior. *Brain Research*, 1126:109–121.

Dawson, G., Frey, K., Panagiotides, H., Yamada, E., Hessl, D., and Osterling, J. (1999). Infants of depressed mothers exhibit atypical frontal electrical brain activity during interactions with mother and with a familiar, nondepressed adult. *Child Development*, 70:1058–1066.

de Vries, A. L. C. and Cohen-Kettenis, P. T. (2012). Clinical management of gender dysphoria in children and adolescents: The Dutch approach. *Journal of Homosexuality*, 59:301–320.

de Vries, A. L. C., Noens, I. L., Cohen-Kettenis, P. T., van Berckelaer-Onnes, I. A., and Doreleijers, T. A. (2010). Autism spectrum disorders in gender dysphoric children and adolescents. *Journal of Autism and Developmental Disorders*, 40:930–936.

de Weerth, C., Zijl, R. H., and Buitelaar, J. K. (2003). Development of cortisol circadian rhythm in infancy. *Early Human Development*, 73:39–52.

DeLoache, J. S., Simcock, G., and Macari, S. (2007). Planes, trains, automobiles— And tea sets: Extremely intense interests in very young children. *Developmental Psychology*, 43:1579–1586.

Edwards-Leeper, L. and Spack, N. (2012). Psychological evaluation and medical treatment of transgender youth in an interdisciplinary "gender management service" (GeMS) in a major pediatric center. *Journal of Homosexuality*, 59:321–336.

Ehrensaft, D. (2011). "I'm a Prius": A child case of a gender/ethnic hybrid. *Journal of Gay and Lesbian Mental Health*, 15:46–57.

Ehrensaft, D. (2012). From gender identity disorder to gender identity creativity: True gender self child therapy. *Journal of Homosexuality*, 59:337–356.

Eichstedt, J. A., Serbin, L. A., Poulin-Dubois, D., and Sen, M. G. (2002). Of bears and men: Infants' knowledge of conventional and metaphorical gender stereotypes. *Infant Behavior and Development*, 25:296–310.

Fagot, B. I. (1995). Psychosocial and cognitive determinants of early gender-role development. *Annual Review of Sex Research*, 6:1–31.

Fagot, B. I. and Leinbach, M. D. (1989). The young child's gender schema: Environmental input, internal organization. *Child Development*, *60*, 663–672.

Fagot, B. I., and Leinbach, M. D. (1993). Gender-role development in young children: From discrimination to labeling. *Developmental Review*, 13:205–224.

Fagot, B. I., Leinbach, M. D., and Hagan, R. (1986). Gender labeling and the adoption of sex-typed behaviors. *Developmental Psychology*, 22:440–443.

Fagot, B. I., Leinbach, M. D., and O'Boyle, C. (1992). Gender labeling, gender stereotyping, and parenting behaviors. *Developmental Psychology*, 28:225–230.

Fausto-Sterling, A. (2010a). Nature versus nurture (part 1): It's time to with- draw from this war! Sexing the body: The dynamic development of gender and sexuality. *Psychology Today*. Retrieved February 15, 2012 from: www.psychologytoday.com/blog/sexing-the-body/201007/nature-versus-nurture-part-1-it-s-time-withdraw-war

Fausto-Sterling, A. (2010b). Nature versus nurture (part 2): Building brains. Sexing the body: The dynamic development of gender and sexuality. *Psychology Today*. Retrieved February 15, 2012 from www.psychologytoday.com/blog/sexing-the-body/201008/nature-versus-nurture-part-2-building-brains

Fausto-Sterling, A. (2011). Nature versus nurture (part 3): QUACK? Sexing the body: The dynamic development of gender and sexuality. *Psychology Today*. Retrieved February 15, 2012 from www.psychologytoday.com/blog/sexing-the-body/201103/nature-versus-nurture-part-3-quack

Fausto-Sterling, A., García Coll, C., and Lamarre, M. (2018a). Sexing the baby: Part 1—What do we really know about sex differentiation in the first year of life? *Social Science and Medicine*, in press.

Fausto-Sterling, A., García Coll, C., and Lamarre, M. (2018b). Sexing the baby: Part 2 Applying dynamic systems theory to the emergences of sex-related differences in infants and toddlers. *Social Science and Medicine*, in press.

Feldman, J. F., Brody, N., and Miller, S. A. (1980). Sex differences in non-elicited neonatal behaviors. *Merrill Palmer Quarterly*, 26:63–73.

Feldman, R. (2007a). On the origins of background emotions: From affect synchrony to symbolic expression. *Emotion*, 7:601–611.

Feldman, R. (2007b). Parent–infant synchrony and the construction of shared timing; physiological precursors, developmental outcomes, and risk conditions. *Journal of Child Psychology and Psychiatry and Allied Disciplines*, 48:329–354.

Ferber, S. G., Feldman, R., and Makhoul, I. R. (2008). The development of maternal touch across the first year of life. *Early Human Development*, 84:363–370.

Field, T. (2010). Touch for socioemotional and physical well-being: A review. *Developmental Review*, 30:367–383.

Field, T., Diego, M., and Hernandez-Reif, M. (2006). Prenatal depression effects on the fetus and newborn: A review. *Infant Behavior and Development*, 29:445–455.

Field, T., Hernandez-Reif, M., and Diego, M. (2006). Newborns of depressed mothers who received moderate versus light pressure massage during pregnancy. *Infant Behavior and Development*, 29:54–58.

Fogel, A., Dickson, L., Hsu, H.-C., Messinger, D., Nelson-Goens, G. C., and Nwokah, E. (1997). Communication of smiling and laughter in mother-infant play: Research on emotion from a dynamic systems perspective. *New Directions in Child Development*, 77:5–24.

Fogel, A. and Thelen, E. (1987). Development of early expressive and communicative action: Reinterpreting the evidence from a dynamic systems perspective. *Developmental Psychology*, 23:747–761.

Fogel, A., Garvey, A., Hsu, H.-C., and West-Stroming, D. (2006). *Change Processes in Relationships: A Relational–Historical Research Approach*. Cambridge: Cambridge University Press.

Green, R. (2010). Robert Stoller's sex and gender: 40 years on. *Archives of Sexual Behavior*, 39:1457–1465.

Harris, A. (2005). *Gender as Soft Assembly*. Hillsdale, NJ: The Analytic Press.

Hollenstein, T. (2007). State space grids: Analyzing dynamics across development. *International Journal of Behavioral Development*, 31:384–396.

Hsu, H.-C. and Fogel, A. (2003). Stability and transitions in mother-infant face-to-face communication during the first 6 months: A microhistorical approach. *Developmental Psychology*, 39:1061–1082.

Jadva, V., Hines, M., and Golombok, S. (2010). Infants' preferences for toys, colors, and shapes: Sex differences and similarities. *Archives of Sexual Behavior*, 39:1261–1273.

Kessler, S. J. and McKenna, W. (1978). *Gender: An Ethnomethodological Approach*. New York: Wiley.

Korner, A. F. and Thoman, E. B. (1970). Visual alertness in neonates as evoked by maternal care. *Journal of Experimental Child Psychology*, 10:67–78.

Kuhl, P. K. (2010). Brain mechanisms in early language acquisition. *Neuron*, 67:713–727.

Lamb, M. E. (1977). Father-infant and mother-infant interaction in the first year of life. *Child Development*, 48:167–181.

Lavelli, M. and Fogel, A. (2002). Developmental changes in mother-infant face-to-face communication: Birth to 3 months. *Developmental Psychology*, 38:288–305.

Malatesta, C. Z., Culver, C., Tesman, J. R., and Shepard, B. (1989). The development of emotion expression during the first two years of life. *Monographs of the Society for Research in Child Development*, 54:1–104.

Menvielle, E. (2012). A comprehensive program for children with gender variant behaviors and gender identity disorders. *Journal of Homosexuality*, 59:357–368.

Menvielle, E. and Tuerk, C. (2002). A support group for parents of gender-nonconforming boys. *Journal of the American Academy of Child and Adolescent Psychiatry*, 41:1010–1013.

Menvielle, E. J., Tuerk, C., and Perrin, E. C. (2005). To the beat of a different drummer: The gender variant child. *Contemporary Pediatrics*, 22:38–39.

Meyer-Bahlburg, H. F. (2010). From mental disorder to iatrogenic hypogonadism: Dilemmas in conceptualizing gender identity variants as psychiatric conditions. *Archives of Sexual Behavior*, 39:461–476.

Moss, H. A. (1967). Sex, age, and state as determinants of mother–infant interaction. *Merrill Palmer Quarterly*, 13:119–135.

Petanjek, Z., Judaš, M., Kostovic, I., and Uylings, H. B. (2008). Lifespan alterations of basal dendritic trees of pyramidal neurons in the human prefrontal cortex: A layer-specific pattern. *Cerebral Cortex*, 18(4):915–929.

Phillips, S., King, S., and DuBois, L. (1978). Spontaneous activities of female versus male newborns. *Child Development*, 49:590–597.

Piaget, J. and Inhelder, B. (1972). *The Psychology of the Child*. New York: Basic Books.

Poulin-Dubois, D. and Forbes, J. N. (2002). Toddlers' attention to intentions-in-action in learning novel action words. *Developmental Psychology*, 38:104–114.

Poulin-Dubois, D., Serbin, L. A., Eichstedt, J. A., Sen, M. G., and Beissel, C. F. (2002). Men don't put on make-up: Toddlers' knowledge of the gender stereotyping of household activities. *Social Development*, 11:166–181.

Putz, O. and Crews, D. (2006). Embryonic origin of mate choice in a lizard with temperature-dependent sex determination. *Developmental Psychobiology*, 48:29–38.

Rheingold, H. L. and Cook, K. V. (1975). The contents of boys' and girls' rooms as an index of parents' behavior. *Child Development*, 46:459–463.

Sadeh, A., Dark, I., and Vohr, B. R. (1996). Newborns' sleep–wake patterns: The role of maternal, delivery and infant factors. *Early Human Development*, 44:113–126.

Schore, A. N. (1994). *Affect Regulation and the Origin of the Self: The Neurobiology of Emotional Development*. Hillsdale, NJ: Lawrence Erlbaum.

Schore, A. N. (2005). Back to basics: Attachment, affect regulation, and the developing right brain: Linking developmental neuroscience to pediatrics. *Pediatric Review*, 26:204–217.

Serbin, L. A., Poulin Dubois, D., and Eichstedt, J. A. (2002). Infants' response to gender- inconsistent events. *Infancy*, 3:531–542.

Shakin, M., Shakin, D., and Sternglanz, S. H. (1985). Infant clothing: Sex labeling for strangers. *Sex Roles*, 12:955–964.

Stoller, R. (1968). *Sex and Gender: On the Development of Masculinity and Femininity*. New York: Science House.

Thelen, E. (1994). Three-month-old infants can learn task-specific patterns of interlimb coordination. *Psychological Bulletin*, 5(5):280–285.

Thelen, E. (1995a). Motor development: A new synthesis. *American Psychologist*, 50(2):79–95.

Thelen, E. (1995b). Origins of motor control. *Behavioral and Brain Sciences*, 18:780–783.

Thelen, E. (2000). Grounded in the world: Developmental origins of the embodied mind. *Infancy*, 1:3–28.

Thelen, E. (2001). Dynamic mechanisms of change in early perceptual-motor development. In J. L. McClelland and R. S. Siegler (eds.), *Mechanisms of cognitive development: Behavioral and Neural Perspectives* (pp. 161–184). Mahwah, NJ: Lawrence Erlbaum.

Thordstein, M., Lofgren, N., Flisberg, A., Lindecrantz, K., and Kjellmer, I. (2006). Sex differences in electrocortical activity in human neonates. *NeuroReport*, 17:1165–1168.

Tronick, E. Z. and Cohn, J. F. (1989). Infant–mother face-to-face interaction: Age and gender differences in coordination and the occurrence of miscoordination. *Child Development*, 60:85–92.

Weinberg, M. K., Tronick, E. Z., Cohn, J. F., and Olson, K. L. (1999). Gender differences in emotional expressivity and self-regulation during early infancy. *Developmental Psychology*, 35:175–188.

Weller, G. M. and Bell, R. Q. (1965). Basal skin conductance and neonatal state. *Child Development*, 36:647–657.

Zosuls, K. M., Ruble, D. N., Tamis-Lemonda, C. S., Shrout, P. E., Bornstein, M. H., and Greulich, F. K. (2009). The acquisition of gender labels in infancy: Implications for gender-typed play. *Developmental Psychology*, 45:688–701.

Zucker, K. J., Wood, H., Singh, D., and Bradley, S. J. (2012). A developmental, biopsychosocial model for the treatment of children with gender identity disorder. *Journal of Homosexuality*, 59:369–397.

Chapter 11

Negotiating gendered religious practices among transgender Jews with an Orthodox Jewish background

Summary of findings[1]

Oriol Poveda

This chapter presents part of the findings from the first study in its scope of transgender religiosity in general and transgender with a Jewish Orthodox background in particular. My intervention focus on the ways participants negotiated gendered religious practices in three key periods of their lives: pre-transition, transition, and post-transition. The research was mostly based on in-depth, semi-structured interviews with three participants (six female-to-male (FTM), six male-to-female (MTF),[2] and one who presented as male but had a nonbinary gender identity) located in either Israel or North America. Given the qualitative nature of the research and the number of participants involved, the findings cannot be said to be representative of the general transgender population with a Jewish Orthodox background. Furthermore, the fact that a significant number of participants were contacted through the Dina list, an email list devoted to offer a platform for transgender Jews who retain a positive view of Orthodox Judaism, introduced a certain bias in the selection. With one possible exception, the group of participants reflects the views of people who were still connected to Orthodoxy in one way or another, because either they were part of the community or were struggling to find their way in, or they decided to stay out but close by. According to Beth, one of the participants in the study and moderator of the Dina list, most transgender Jews seldom stay in touch with Orthodox Judaism. As Beth put it:

> [T]he vast majority of people who are *frum* [observant] and trans stop being *frum* [observant]. A big chunk refuse to transition. Some of those may even survive.

Maybe one day someone will write about the stories of those who decided to leave for good. In my study and in this chapter I write mostly about those who, at the time of our meetings, were still sticking around, often defying the stereotypes of what it was to be Orthodox and what it was to be transgender. This does not mean, however, that several of the themes illustrated in the findings might not resonate with other transgender with an Orthodox background who became fully secular or assimilated. Hopefully future research will contribute to assess the representativeness of these findings as well as add new nuance and depth to our understanding of transgender religiosity.

The gendering of religious practice in Orthodox Judaism

In order to better appreciate the findings that are presented below, it is important to understand the ways in which religious practices are deeply gendered in Orthodox Judaism, i.e., in which instances the gender of its adherents is decisive in determining a significant number of religious roles and practices. Although the rabbinical sages recognized a diversity of body configurations including intersex and *tumtum* (someone who's biological sex is not clearly visible to the naked eye) (Fonrobert, 2010; Dzmura, 2010b), for practical purposes Jewish law follows the gender binary and distinguishes between women and men on the basis of the genitalia. Although a handful of communities have made attempts at including gender variance,[3] the gender binary continues to be the main organizing principle for the community and religious life of Orthodox Jews. Through interaction with the participants and my own observations in Orthodox settings, I noticed that the gendering of Orthodox religious practice works at least at five levels, which are frequently intertwined.

1. *Spatial: separation of genders*

In Orthodox synagogues, for instance, women's and men's sections are separated at times by architectonic arrangements but also by a physical barrier known as *mechitzah*. Among ultra-Orthodox communities, the physical separation of genders outside the family extends to almost every facet of life.

2. *Performative: who does what and how*

2.1.   Different practices for each gender

Certain practices, like keeping dietary laws, are equal and obligatory for both genders. Other practices are, however, associated with either women or men. This association can be a matter of Jewish law, barring members of a particular gender from performing that practice, or due to custom. There is, for instance, no law prohibiting men from lighting candles on the eve of the Sabbath, but the commandment applies specifically to women. The opposite can be said of donning phylacteries, which is strongly associated with men (for whom the commandment is obligatory), although there is no explicit prohibition against women doing the same. On the other hand, being counted in a *minyan* (a quorum of 10 necessary to perform certain rituals) is permitted only to adult males.

2.2.   Same practices with variations according to gender

Certain practices are common to both women and men, but are inflected in different ways according to the gender of who is performing them. The morning blessings, which both Orthodox women and men are commanded to recite every morning, present variations in the text depending on the gender of the worshipper (more on the same topic below).

3. *Material: gendered religious items*

Orthodox Judaism has a gendered material culture, which, in relation to gender religious practices, takes particular expression in the use of gendered religious items. Skullcaps, phylacteries, and prayer shawls, for example, are strongly male-inflected items. In the case of women, the commandment to dress modestly influences their dress code (skirts and long sleeves) and for those who are married it makes head covering compulsory (usually with a wig, a cap, or a headscarf).

4. *Linguistic: Hebrew as a gendered language*

Hebrew has only two grammatical genders, feminine and masculine. As the main ritual language, Hebrew contributes significantly to the gendering of religious practice and experience (see Cohen and Berkowitz, 2005). This can be found, for instance, in the way that Orthodox Jews address God and themselves in prayer.

5. *Ideological: a gender hierarchy*

The question "Is there a gender hierarchy in Orthodox Judaism?" has different answers depending on who is responding. One possible view, often advanced by Orthodox commentators, is that Orthodox Judaism sees women and men as different but equal: they have different tasks and play different roles, but both are equally necessary for the wellbeing of the community. According to this view, women were relieved from many of the duties that men perform so that they could focus on the rearing of children. Another view, also popular in Orthodox circles, is that women are actually more attuned to spirituality than men and for this reason they are subjected to fewer commandments. Contrary to men, they would not need to be frequently reminded of their connection with God. Other commentators espouse the opposite views. The fact that in Orthodox Judaism women are generally barred from becoming rabbis has been interpreted as clear evidence of a gender hierarchy (Israel-Cohen, 2012). As the argument goes, given that rabbis have a large influence in the way the religious affairs of the community are conducted, the fact that women are barred from ordination would put them at an important disadvantage when it comes to asserting leadership. Furthermore, the fact that women are subjected to fewer commandments has also resulted in some Orthodox women feeling relegated to a secondary role in the religious life of the community (Israel-Cohen, 2012). This can, however, greatly vary from community to community, with a small but growing number of women's prayer groups and egalitarian synagogues striving to include women more fully within the bounds of the Jewish law (Israel-Cohen, 2012).

(Some additional gendered hierarchy examples: heterosexual marriage effected only by the man, though with the woman's permission; divorce effected only by the man; qualifying as a legal witness, only men except in some extraordinary circumstances.)

As illustrated above, the gendering of religious practice in Orthodox Judaism operates at different levels. Moreover, Jewish law should be understood as a comprehensive system of commandments that extends to every facet of an Orthodox life. The comprehensive character of Jewish law, combined with the multilayered gendering of religious practice, offered a particularly fertile ground for understanding the intersection of gender and religion, particularly as experienced by the participants.

Negotiating gendered religious practices: from dysphoria to affirmation

The findings I am about to present illustrate the different ways in which participants negotiated gendered religious practices over the course of their lives. During analysis of the material, it became apparent that the different themes that emerged in relation to gendered religious practices tended to cluster toward particular periods of the participants' lives, which were more related to transition (or lack thereof) than age. For this reason, I present the following findings according to a tripartite time division of pre-transition, transition, and post-transition.

Pre-transition: hard beginnings

One of the main themes that emerged in relation to the pre-transitional period was the role of gendered religious practices in the religious and gender journeys of the participants. It is important to remark that the distinction between religious and gender journeys – as two separate biographical trajectories – is done more for analytical clarity than anything else. Often those journeys were so intertwined that their boundaries blurred and they merged seamlessly into each other. Taking this into account, gendered religious practices emerged as the most promising place in which to study the intersection of gender and religion in the lives of the participants.

The accounts of several participants illustrate how the gendering aspects of religious practice might have contributed to their gender dysphoria. By religiously validating and repeatedly underscoring the gender assigned at birth, those religious practices constituted an obstacle in the early stages of the[ir] journey to accept and give expression to their own gender identity. The fact that the gendering aspects of religious practice were not conducive to accepting and expressing their gender identity does not mean that the participants' relationship to Orthodox Judaism as a whole was negative.

Their religious attachments could also be a source of spiritual nourishment or provide a sense of purpose, identity, and community (including family ties), which constituted powerful motivations to remain Orthodox. As a result, religious practices that were at odds with the participants' gender identity were negotiated as part of a larger scheme of things which included both positive and negative aspects of living an Orthodox life. Furthermore, the extent to which participants could actively opt in or out of an Orthodox lifestyle at the onset of gender dysphoria depended very much on their personal circumstances. No participant, however, reported feeling trapped in Orthodox Judaism against their will. On the other hand, several participants spoke in unambiguous terms of their feelings of struggling with religion, both [as] a source of nourishment and distress. This resulted in negotiations and compromises to mitigate the detrimental aspects of their religious lives.

The morning blessings and dressing up for the Sabbath

Among MTF participants, one of the clearest examples of how gendered religious practices were negotiated was the way they recited the morning blessings before they transitioned. The morning blessings for Orthodox women and men share all but one verse. That verse takes the following form for Orthodox men:

Hebrew original	ברוך אתה ה' אלוקינו מלך העולם שלא עשני אישה
Transliteration	*Barukh atah Adonai Elokeinu melekh ha-olam she-lo asani ishah.*
Translation	Blessed are You, LORD our God, King of the Universe, who has not made me a woman.

As for the corresponding blessing for Orthodox women, the form it takes varies from one Orthodox stream to another. The *Koren Sacks Siddur* (2009), popular among modern Orthodox communities, offers the following blessing for women:

Hebrew original	ברוך אתה ה' אלוקינו מלך העולם שעשני כרצונו
Transliteration	*Barukh atah Adonai Elokeinu melekh ha-olam she-asani kirtzono.*
Translation	Blessed are You, LORD our God, King of the Universe, who has made me according to His will.

Noam, who was raised in a Sephardic household, was familiar with a shortened version of the same verse for women that leaves out the name of God followed by the kingly attributes:

Hebrew original	ברוך שעשני כרצונו
Transliteration	*Barukh she-asani kirtzono.*
Translation	Blessed be [the One] who has made me according to His will.

Finally, Yiscah reported that in the Chasidic movement *Chabad* there is no corresponding verse for women, only the verse for men is recited. At least three MTF participants reported struggling with the special verse for men. Yael, for instance, commented:

> I said [the blessing], but my *kavanah* [intention] was *afilu she-lo asani ishah* [even though you did not make me a woman]. I did not actually say it that way, because that's what I talked to myself. Even though, even though you did this to me. [...] Sometimes you have to make *brakhot* [blessing] to *Hashem* [God] even when He does things to hurt you.

Along similar lines, Belinda reported:

> The morning prayers were a problem for me, from the get-go. [...] When I pray it myself, I say modified versions to myself. When I am called upon to say blessings [...] I say what is in the prayer book because that is what people are expecting and, if I modify it, people will get very upset and I don't want to rock that boat. [...]. I always had a problem with *she-lo asani ishah*, that It did not create me a woman. First of all, I am very angry that that is the case; I wish it were not the case. I am taking steps to remedy that, in so far as one can take steps to remedy that, and a number of years ago I simply stopped saying it. I said instead the women's blessing, Who has created me by His will, which is gender neutral, positive, and there is no actual *halakhic* [referring to the Jewish law] problem saying that.

In the case of Noam, the difficulty with this blessing was compounded by the fact that as a child she was asking God to change her body to female:

> The only thing that was hard for me to say was *she-lo asani ishah*
> [who did not make me a woman]. Because I was praying that He
> will make me a woman, that God would make me a woman. And
> this is the one thing that it was very hard for me to say but I said it
> because this is part of the siddur, we were praying every morning
> and noon [. . .] in the school where I was studying and putting on
> *tefillin* [phylacteries].

FTM participants also reported on their struggles with the morning
blessings and the different approaches they developed to deal with
them. Yonatan, for instance, commented:

> I always did say the two of them [the verse for men and the verse for
> women] actually, even before my transition [. . .] one after the other. [. . .]
> Because I did not feel He created me a woman and He did not create me
> the way I see, like, I wanted it, but He created me the way He wanted.

Amichai and James, on the other hand, reported skipping the blessing
"she-asani kirtzono" (who made me according to His will) altogether. As
the examples above suggest, the special verses for women and men in the
morning blessings were often the site of conflicted feelings among the
participants, which led them to develop different strategies.

Among the five FTM participants who were Orthodox before transitioning,
there was considerable agreement about the gendered religious practices they
had been struggling with. Four of them reported that dressing up for the
Sabbath was something that bothered them. Wearing special clothes on the
Sabbath is a religious custom devised to honor the day of rest.

Amichai, for instance, did not want to wear skirts, whereas James felt
uncomfortable wearing clothes that revealed too much and opted for
wearing trousers under a tunic. Likewise, Moshe did not like to wear
"girly clothes" on the Sabbath and for a period of time he wore just
white shirts and black skirts because, as he put it, "that is what boys did,
boys just wore white and black pants, so, I felt, why do I have to choose
colors?" Ethan stopped wearing dresses altogether.[4]

Taking the group of participants as a whole, there are grounds to
believe that certain gendered religious practices, most notably the morning blessings for MTFs and dressing up for the Sabbath for FTMs, were

potentially detrimental to the acceptance and affirmation of their gender identity. Other gendered religious practices seemed to have uneven effects, which suggests that each practice needs to be looked into on a case-by-case basis. In relation to this, it is important to point out that not all gendered religious practices triggered a negative reaction and that even those that triggered a negative reaction did not affect all participants in the same way. MTF participants, for instance, did not report any distress before their transition as a result of wearing particular religious items associated with men such as skullcaps or ritual tassels. Furthermore, at least one participant (Moshe) reported a practice (religious either by definition or by association) that allowed the expression of his gender identity: dressing as a boy on *Purim*.[5] This opens the possibility, marginal as it may be, that other gendered religious practices could be deployed to express other gender identities to those assigned at birth. Likewise, this also calls for a nuanced approach to a religion such as Orthodox Judaism which, at face value, seems to provide no outlets for the expression of gender identities outside the norm.

Another important insight is that gendered religious practices cut both ways, laying down not only what each gender is expected to do but also – and more crucially in the case of FTMs – what one gender is barred from doing. For transgender Orthodox Jews, gendered religious practices have the potential to include them in a group they do not want to belong or to exclude them from the group they feel they are a part of. Although the predicaments for FTMs and MTFs may vary, in the final analysis both groups agreed that before their transition they felt they were standing on the wrong side of the separation barrier (*mechitzah*).

Transition: dislocation of religious practice

In the long term, the strategies devised by several participants to negotiate the mismatch between their gender identity and the demands of living as an Orthodox Jew did not work, the gender dysphoria did not go away, and binary transition became a vital necessity. By binary transition we could understand the process by which a transgender person moves from one side of the gender binary to the other and, by doing so, aligns their gender identity with their gender expression (i.e., the way they present to themselves and others).[6] Transition may include one or more of the following steps: changing name and gender pronouns, dressing according to the code of the preferred gender, taking hormones, changing hairstyle, voice training, or undergoing different kinds of surgeries (hair removal, top surgery, Adam's apple removal, bottom surgery, etc.). Transition is often bound up with the sensitive topic of passing. Basically, passing occurs when a transgender person is perceived ("passes") as cisgender in the eyes of others. The ability to pass among transitioned people often depends on a range of factors: age at the time of transition, bone structure, availability of financial resources to undergo medical procedures, etc. The fact that not all transitioned people "pass" has led commentators to talk about "passing privilege" (Hansbury, 2005; Sawyer, 2013). In the framework of this study, passing was often considered a requirement in order to safely function within an Orthodox context. As a result, the length of transition for some of the participants depended on how long it took for them until they felt passable enough to be safe. An added element in the picture is that, at least until fairly recently, the low awareness about transgender issues in the Orthodox world arguably made it easier to pass, because most Orthodox people would not have entertained the possibility that a transgender person could be part of their community.[7]

Concerning the focus of this chapter on gendered religious practices, transition often meant for the participants dislocating their religious practices, particularly those performed in communal spaces. For Orthodox transgender Jews, the possibility of participating in the religious life of the community – primarily synagogue services – cannot always be taken for granted. The question of to which side of the *mechitzah* they belong – according to the rabbi of the synagogue, the community, and themselves – might become a particularly thorny issue during the process of transition. The moment in which transition is completed may vary from person to person, depending on their religious beliefs and understandings of gender. Some may consider transition completed the day a person starts to consistently present in the preferred gender. Others, especially those who would like to abide by the ruling of the Tzitz Eliezer,[8] may consider transition completed when, in addition to changing the way they present themselves, they have also undergone "bottom surgery."[9] In the latter case, if there is a considerable gap between the time when that person started to present as female and the bottom surgery, the person in question may feel that their gender status is compromised. In other words, they might perceive that there is a mismatch between how they present and the status of their gender according to Jewish law. Regardless the question of bottom surgery, a degree of indeterminacy is built into the concept of transition. Depending on personal circumstances, the indeterminacy of their transitional status may put practicing Orthodox transgender in a situation in which they find themselves "balancing on the *mechitzah*" (Dzmura, 2010a, p. xviii), unable to resolve with certainty to what side of the *mechitzah* they belong during their transitional period. The fact that, with very few exceptions, most Orthodox synagogues do not have gender-neutral areas that could function as transitional spaces is a potential factor contributing to the dislocation of Orthodox transgender people during their transition. Another way to avoid the dislocation of practice would be to facilitate a sharp transition from one side to the other of the *mechitzah* (this was the preferred alternative of Belinda and Yael), but even that option would require significant support from the community as well as education on transgender issues. As Yael put it:

> There are people who never stopped being religious through transition, a lot more people did stop, but they stopped because they felt there was no place for them and I think to a great extent that is a flaw of the community.

Under the dislocation of practice, communal religious practices are either no longer performed or confined to the private sphere of the home. In relation to this, Amichai and Ethan, for instance, considered themselves Orthodox in terms of basic beliefs but did not lead orthopractic lifestyles. In their cases, the withdrawal from public worship already started years before they began transitioning and constituted one of the main signs of their gender dysphoria. For others, the fact that they were forced to leave their community, particularly when a non-Orthodox setting was chosen to resettle, often brought by itself a dislocation of practice because Orthodox Judaism is not a religion that is amenable to being practiced alone. Without a community to rely on for the provision of a wide range of needs and services, from kosher food to a synagogue within walking distance, the practice of Orthodox Judaism becomes a major challenge if not an impossibility. Beth's story illustrated one particular instance of dislocation of practice, which, in her case, was not related to feeling rejected by the community but rather by practical considerations concerning how passable she thought she was during a particular period in her transition:

> One of the problems during transition was that, during electrolysis, I had to put on this gunky make-up and I could not put that on on *shabbes* [the Sabbath] because it was too thick, so I stayed inside on *shabbes* [the Sabbath]. [. . .] I made *shabbes* [the Sabbath] by myself and I spent *Rosh Hashanah* [the Jewish New Year] and *Yom Kippur* [the Jewish Day of Atonement] in my room by myself, which, okay, I am a loner, but that was a little too much even for me.

Due to unexpected circumstances, Beth was once forced to leave her apartment on the Sabbath and she realized that she was passing, so she decided to resume regular attendance to synagogue.

Post-transition: a reversal story

The way in which participants navigated their own transitions was an important factor in the outlook of their religious lives after transition. One shared element in the narratives of the participants who had already transitioned, and who felt the need to leave religion either during or in the process leading to transition, was that, after transitioning, all of them attempted to return to an observant life. Yonatan, on the other hand, did not cease to be Orthodox in the course of his transition but transitioning enabled him to live his religious life more fully. In the case of Ben and Dov, they became Orthodox for the first time after transitioning.

Gendered religious practices were a key element in the re-engagement with religion of the transitioned participants. The dislocation of practice referred to above, for instance, was due in no small measure to the fact that those practices subjected to dislocation were gendered in such a way that participants felt that they could not take part in them as long as they would not "pass." Below, I take a look at some of the implications of gendered religious practices for those participants who had already transitioned.

Learning and unlearning gendered religious practices

Except for Ben and Dov, who became religious for the first time after their transition, all the other participants were socialized into Orthodoxy in the gender assigned at birth. This included the gendered religious practices that they were expected to perform. As a result, once they transitioned they had to go through a process of learning new gendered religious practices and unlearning previous ones. The adjustment, though, was different for FTM and MTF participants. In Orthodox Judaism, a significant number of religious commandments apply only to men and for that reason FTM participants had significantly more to learn. Finding someone willing to teach those skills was not a minor issue, particularly for someone who had grown up religious and, thus, was supposed to know those kinds of things. Yonatan found an ingenious way to get around some of those problems:

> I say thank you to *Hashem* [God] that put me in this generation because we got YouTube! [laughs] [...] That was my school actually, that is how I learnt the first time to put *tefillin* [phylacteries] on. I bought myself *tefillin* [phylacteries] and I did not know how to put them, I remembered a bit how my father used to do it every morning, but it is different, plus ... I could have not ... I did not know that ... I mean they put it there [points to the biceps] and I remember I used to see it but I did not know that it is supposed to be inside, inside [points under the armpit]. It says in YouTube that you are supposed to put it here [points to the biceps] but when I came to the *shul* [synagogue] the first time the guy was telling me "in! in!" He put it inside and I could not figure why. But yeah, it was a process to learn how to be a religious man.

As the quote shows, Yonatan taught himself to don phylacteries through a YouTube video and what he learnt was enough to pass as observant but not sufficient to get it completely right. Moshe was another participant who mentioned using online resources (YouTube, Ask-the-Rabbi websites, etc.) to learn how to perform male religious practices. In spite of the different resources and support from friends, who taught him how to put phylacteries, he commented:

I feel I am still in that process [of learning how to act religiously as a man]. When I go to *shul* [synagogue], I still sometimes feel like, I do not really know what we do now because on the women's side you do not always see what's happening, so like when it comes, when they take the Torah out or put the Torah in, what you say at what point, I still when I go to *shul* [synagogue], even a conservative *shul* [synagogue], I am still a little behind and I do not know exactly what's gonna happen when they read in the scroll.

In the case of Ben he learnt to put on phylacteries from a Renewal woman cantor, but otherwise his socialization as an Orthodox man was facilitated by the fact that he could introduce himself as a previously unaffiliated Jew. Furthermore, the task of teaching someone to become observant was at the core of *Chabad*, the outreach group he had turned to at the beginning of his religious journey. Among the FTM participants who were at the threshold or initial stages of their transitions, they had already been thinking about similar questions. James, for instance, was hoping that his brother would teach him to don phylacteries, although he was concerned that his brother might find that awkward at first. Ethan, on the other hand, would love to learn how to don phylacteries from his father, but a friend had already offered to teach him who happened to be an older FTM man also from an Orthodox background.

Among the MTF participants the situation was different. Beth and Yiscah reported that they learned all they needed to do through living together with their ex-wives. In the case of Yiscah, she mentioned that she and her ex-wife became Orthodox at the same time and that they were socialized from the beginning as a couple. In the case of Yael, she mentioned that it took her rabbi five minutes to explain to her all the implications in terms of the Jewish law of being an Orthodox woman. Finally, Belinda also reported having learned through her marriage and a balanced division of household tasks, particularly concerning questions of religious dietary laws in the kitchen. In her case, however, a different issue came to the fore: the importance not only of learning new skills but also of unlearning previous ones. For someone who spent decades routinely performing certain practices which, although somehow gendered did not trigger gender dysphoria, it is reasonable to think that in the early stages of transition it would take a degree of self-consciousness to avoid performing those practices unwittingly. Belinda, for instance, had been to an event organized for the Orthodox LGBTQ community presenting as female and she remembered that she had to hold herself back not to say the blessing over wine at the table, something that women are allowed to do but that traditionally is performed by men.

Gendered religious practices after transition: validation and affirmation

Returning to an observant life after transition had a potential benefit related to the gendering aspect of religious practice. If, before transition, several of the gendered religious practices of Orthodox Judaism had the effect of undermining the gender identity of the participants, the reverse was often the case in a post-transitional situation. After transition, the fact that religious practices were significantly gendered was often a powerful source of validation. By performing these practices, the participants were not only recovering the religious aspect of their identities but also reaffirming their gender in front of themselves, the community, and God. This is an important element to take into account, because feminist discourses about gendered religious practices often highlight their potential for disenfranchisement without considering how those practices can also enable identity and community (Reilly and Scriver, 2014). Gendered religious practices cut both ways. Compared with the gender journeys of secular transgender people, the gendered religious practices of Orthodox Judaism had the potential to become an obstacle during growing up. After their transition, however, gendered religious practices could become a valuable resource for affirmation and cosmic validation.[10] Belinda and Yiscah, for instance, reported feelings of elation the first time they took part in a religious service on the women's side of the *mechitzah*. Belinda reported the following in relation to an Orthodox LGBTQ event she took part in:

> Friday night I attended the regular service and I stood on the women's side and that felt great, I felt right, the amount of right that I felt was perfect.

It is important to point out, however, that not all participants felt the same way. Noam for instance, reported:

> The times that I was in the women's section of the *mechitzah*, when I was praying in [name of the synagogue], [. . .] there I knew why some transwomen are saying that they like to sit in the women's section and also religious women that are saying that they like to sit in the women's section because you feel more secure, you feel somewhat sisterhood. I didn't, I never felt this sisterhood. Maybe because I am not passing so well.

Noam's concerns about her passing removed any gender-affirming quality from the experience but still she understood why that practice could be particularly meaningful to other women, MTF or otherwise. Among the MTF participants, another of the gendered religious practices that stood out was the ritual bath. Yiscah, for instance, reported:

> [W]hen I was able to be in a women's *mikvah* [ritual bath], where all the other women went, I felt such a sense of wholeness and sisterhood. [. . .] It was just so spiritual, experiencing my woman-ness, my femaleness, and it felt so right, it was so natural for me, it was everything like the other side of the *mechitzah* that was negative, this was the positive side for me. [. . .] [G]oing into the *mikvah* [ritual bath] was affirming. It really was so wonderful to affirm my sisterhood that way through spiritual tradition, spiritual ritual.

Other practices that were reported as gender affirmative were lighting candles (Beth and Yiscah) and being called by their names to the Torah (Beth and Yonatan, the former in the context of a women's prayer group). Finally, Belinda had been reflecting about two practices in particular (the prohibition to touch members of the opposite gender and the prohibition for a woman and a man who are not spouses to be together in a secluded place) in relation to her ongoing transition. The first practice became relevant when she attended the Orthodox LGBTQ event I have referred to. She mentioned that the women at the event, who were fully aware of her MTF status, had no problem being physical with her and this sort of interaction helped her to feel accepted as a woman. Concerning the prohibition for a woman to be alone with a man other than her husband, she felt that enforcing that practice, although not always convenient, would have gender-affirming effects:

> I imagine that there will be a sort of societal pressure, which I have no problem accepting, to avoid [infringement of the prohibition], I actually think that from an emotional standpoint that would be preferable, because it would mean a level of acceptance of my new gender expression that previously was unavailable.

As we have seen, religious practices in Orthodox Judaism are gendered to a significant extend and that could be detrimental to the participants' gender identity before transition but, by the same token, that gendering aspect could also become a source of validation and affirmation after transition.

Two qualifications: re-engaging on their own terms and gray areas

The examples provided above concerning how gendered religious practices had potentially beneficial outcomes require two important qualifications. The first concerns the way in which participants re-engaged with religion. In the case of several MTF participants, the exhilaration over living a religious life as women did not always last. For Yael and Yiscah, once the novelty waned they started to feel uneasy about what they perceived in certain contexts as the marginalization of women from Orthodox religious life. The gender division in the synagogue was, again, a case in point. The women's section in several synagogues they knew about was built in such a way that women could not see the altar or the Holy Ark. Furthermore, the women's section was often not big enough to accommodate a large number of congregants. As a result, the participants who raised such concerns felt that women were being discouraged from leading an active religious life at synagogue. This example suggests that returning to a religious life after transitioning was not synonymous with an uncritical acceptance of Orthodox custom and practice. In several cases, such as Noam's, their gender journeys helped them to become sensitized about other groups who they perceived as being excluded and discriminated, such as lesbian, gay, or Jews of Sephardic descent like Noam herself. In relation to the last, Noam started to learn the Jewish law of Sephardic rabbis. She particularly appreciated that the Sephardic tradition of Jewish law was more flexible and less of a dichotomy than its Ashkenazi counterpart. As a result, Sephardic Judaism appeared to be much more inclusive of difference and varying degrees of observance to Noam. Therefore, re-engaging with religion was also a way to reclaim her cultural roots which, growing up within the religious Zionist educational system, she had not been able to fully explore. At the same time, Noam's renewed interest in Sephardic Judaism was not uncritical. At the time of our meeting, for instance, she was not reciting the morning prayers according to the Sephardic tradition but rather adding the name of God followed by the kingly attributes before reciting "who made me according to His will."

The reclaiming of Orthodox Judaism went beyond introducing small changes in the liturgy. The re-engagement with religion frequently led also to a re-evaluation of the relationship with rabbis. Although observant participants generally accepted the mainstream rabbinical opinions in questions of Jewish law, they frequently made an exception when the issue at stake was transition or the place of transgender in the Orthodox community. The re-engagement with Judaism often also meant looking for new spaces in which to live religion more fully. Beth, for instance, reported that after she transitioned she greatly missed being able to chant verses from the Torah. Fortunately, in the area where she lived she was able to join a women's prayer group where she was able to chant again. It is significant that the acceptability of women's prayer groups is a contentious issue in the Orthodox world, with a considerable number of rabbis expressing disapproval (Israel-Cohen, 2012). Beth reported that her engagement with prayer groups had nothing to do with the rabbinical criticism, namely, that women's prayer groups had a covert feminist–egalitarian agenda. She mentioned joining those groups simply because she loved to chant, but women's prayer groups were still controversial in some quarters.

The examples discussed above suggest that the process of transitioning had potential far-reaching effects on the participants' outlook of religion. In that process something seemed to have changed and their understanding and practice of Orthodoxy was not uncritical or devoid of personal expressivity. That certainly applied to those who did not self-identify as observant (Moshe, Noam, and Yael) but also to those who did (Ben, Beth, Dov, and Yiscah).

The second important qualification concerns the role of gendered religious practices. Although certain gendered religious practices had the potential to provide a sense of validation and gender affirmation (and that was indeed the case among several participants, as illustrated in the previous section), other religious practices fell in a rather gray area in terms of their gendering effects on the participants. The prohibition to touch members of the opposite gender was a case in point. The issue with that prohibition is that, ideally, those having physical contact read each other's gender as being the same. If only one does so, that might become a problem. Furthermore, how should transgender people interact with Orthodox people who abide by different understandings of how the Jewish law determines gender than their own? We have already seen how Belinda felt that having physical contact with other women in the Orthodox LGBTQ event she attended was gender affirming. Other participants, however, reported different and often complicated relations to the issue of the prohibition to touch members of the opposite gender. Noam, for instance, mentioned that in a group of Orthodox lesbian women where she used to be active everyone accepted her as female, but some of the group members refrained from touching her because, in terms of the Jewish law, they believed that there was a possibility that she might still be considered male. Moshe also found himself in a similar situation on a few occasions:

> Usually I am never the first one to put my hand out to shake [the hands of Orthodox men], because there have been a couple of times when I have and then I get embarrassed because they won't shake my hand. So usually I just try not to and if they put their hand out to me or try to give me a hug, I'll go with it. I try not to be the first one. I made that mistake with the rabbi here. He is a very accepting, wonderful rabbi in a lot of ways, but he will not touch me.

However, Moshe also reported that his status as FTM concerning the prohibition to touch members of the opposite gender had its advantages:

> [W]omen, especially women who were my good friends, they will
> ask me [if they have to observe the prohibition to touch members of
> the opposite gender with me] and I say, listen, the rabbis you would
> listen to would classify me as a woman, so I am happy if you give
> me a hug. [. . .] I like hugs. I don't care what their belief system is
> that allows them to hug me.

In relation to this, James also expressed having thoughts about drop-
ping the prohibition to touch members of the opposite gender after his
transition because he wanted to be able to continue showing affection
with his female friends and, anyway, as a gay FTM man being
physical with women was less of an issue for him. Finally, Ben had
also had thoughts about that prohibition. At the Chabad synagogue
where he had been going, the rabbis stopped being physical with him
once they knew about his background. On the other hand, his rabbi at
the time of our meeting was aware of Ben's story and did not hesitate
to shake his hand. In spite of his rabbi's forthcomingness, Ben
pondered that, given the fact that his gender with regard to Jewish
law was undetermined, this could put him at least in theory in an
untenable position concerning the prohibition to touch members of the
opposite gender:

> [T]echnically if you take the most stringent approach, I should touch
> neither men nor women [. . .]. But, yeah, when I travel, when I go to
> an Orthodox *shul* [synagogue] or something, or to a chasidic *shul*
> [synagogue] somewhere, I act as a man and shake hands with men
> and, you know, if this is sexual temptation for them, then they are
> not being tempted by my feminine charms [laughs].

As the cases above suggest, the prohibition to touch members of the
opposite gender was one gendered religious practice that was not clearly
gender affirming or undermining; it revealed a gray area that depended
very much on how the interaction with the other person(s) was resolved.
Moreover, the fact that some participants were at times misgendered
through that prohibition did not have, at least in Moshe's case, only
detrimental effects. For Moshe, that also provided a way to show
affection with old friends.

Conclusion

As this chapter hopefully illustrates, gendered religious practices are a fruitful site to study the religiosity of transgender people in general and transgender Jews in Orthodox contexts in particular. The focus on gendered religious practices helps us understand how deeply intertwined the gendered and religious journeys of the participants are. As they move through different periods in their lives (pre-transition, transition, and post-transition) their relationship to gendered religious practices tends to change accordingly. From often being a source of dysphoria and isolation in the pre-transitional and transitional periods, respectively, gendered religious practices reveal a potential in the post-transitional period to become a source for validation and affirmation.

An important caveat is that the validating potential of gendered religious practices ultimately depends on finding welcoming communities. Given the gendering aspect of these practices, they could also lead to misgendering, particularly when those practices are not performed individually but are negotiated in interaction with other Orthodox Jews who might have different understandings of gender, both socially and with regard to Jewish law. For this reason, whatever medical and social advances are put in place by society at large, allowing transgender people to get better and earlier care, full transgender inclusion will not happen until Orthodox communities change and become more welcoming. A few bold, courageous rabbis could lead the way in that change, but it is more likely that, once lay community members become more welcoming towards transgender Jews, rabbis will follow suit. As in generations passed, willing rabbis should be able to tap the wealth of Jewish law to find ways to respond to new and changing realities.

Notes

1 This chapter is based on my PhD dissertation "According to Whose Will: The Entanglements of Gender & Religion in the Lives of Transgender Jews with an Orthodox Background" defended on May 2017 at Uppsala University, Sweden.
2 Hereafter, I use FTM instead of female-to-male and MTF instead of male-to-female for reasons of language economy.

3 See, for instance, the case of the *trichitzah* as reported by Dzmura (2010a, p. xxvii, note 3), in the modern Orthodox synagogue of Mission Minyan in San Francisco. The *trichitzah* presents three instead of two praying areas: One for women, one for men, and one "for those who wish not to *daven* [pray] in segregated space, or belong to another gender category."

4 *Editors' note*: in Orthodox Judaism, the dress/skirt vs pants becomes another issue. Not only one of the commandments not to cross-dress, but also one of customs of modesty, which are focused mostly on women. So even if pants might be considered today a woman's clothing, pants in many Orthodox circles are not considered modest clothing because of their form-fitting nature. This adds to the dysphoric gendered states and behaviors. Making it all so confusing and, I would say, enraging to both FTM and MTF, because it does so in cisgender Orthodox too).

5 A holiday that commemorates the story told in the book of Esther and in which masquerading is customary.

6 There also exists the possibility of a nonbinary transition, but that option was not relevant given that all participants (with the exception of Ben) had a binary gender identity. In Ben's case, although his gender identity did not neatly fit the gender binary (with female and male understood as mutually exclusive options) he functioned outwardly as a male. (See Chapter 12 by Ben Baader, pages 206–231).

7 In spite of the fact that the gender binary is one of the main structuring principles of Orthodox Judaism, towards the end of my research I became aware of a small but apparently thriving community of young, genderqueer Orthodox Jews. The way genderqueer and gender-fluid Jews practice Orthodox Judaism would be a fascinating and very timely follow-up to my study.

8 The Tzitz Eliezer, also known as Rabbi Eliezer Waldenberg (1915–2006) was a widely respected Israeli Orthodox rabbi specialized in medical Jewish law. The name Tzitz Eliezer came to refer to him after he published his main treatise of that name. Without going into the subtleties of his argument, Rabbi Waldenberg ruled in that treatise that a MTF woman who had undergone bottom surgery was to be considered female for any purposes related to Jewish law.

9 I decided to use this colloquial expression, frequently used by the participants themselves, to avoid more medico-technical terms such as "sex correction surgery" or "sex reassignment surgery." The reason I am avoiding those terms is that for some people they might imply value judgments on questions of correct gender presentation and body configuration. I am using "bottom surgery" as an inclusive and neutral term aimed at referring to the medical procedure alone.

10 By cosmic validation I mean that, whereas in a secular setting validation is often considered a socially constructed concept derived from changing gender mores, in a religious setting validation has the potential of acquiring an ontological quality warranted by God, which aligns the worshipper with the created universe or cosmos. Here I am also relying on the Greek

etymology of *kosmos* as referring to the perfect order and arrangement of the universe (Retrieved from https://en.oxforddictionaries.com.)

References

Cohen, D. and Berkowitz, N. (2005). Gender, Hebrew language acquisitions and religious values in Jewish high schools in North America. In A. Joulé (ed.), *Gender and the Language of Religion*. Basingstoke: Palgrave Macmillan.

Dzmura, N. (2010a). Introduction: The literal and metaphorical *mechitza*. In N. Dzmura (ed.), *Balancing on the Mechitza: Transgender in Jewish Community* p. xviii. Berkeley, CA: North Atlantic Books.

Dzmura, N. (2010b) An ancient strategy for managing gender ambiguity. In Dzmura N. (ed.), *Balancing on the Mechitza: Transgender in Jewish Community* (pp. 170–181). Berkeley, CA: North Atlantic Books.

Fonrobert, C. (2010). Regulating the human body: Rabbinic legal discourse and the making of Jewish gender. In Dzmura N. (ed.), *Balancing on the Mechitza: Transgender in Jewish Community*. Berkeley, CA: North Atlantic Books.

Hansbury, G. (2005) The middle men: An introduction to the transmasculine identities. *Studies in Gender and Sexuality*, 6(3):241–264.

Israel-Cohen, Y. (2012). *Between Feminism and Orthodox Judaism*. Boston, MA: Brill.

Reilly, N. and Scriver, S. (2014). Conclusion: Gender justice and the "postsecular" public sphere: Toward nonoppressive reconfigurations. In N. Reilly and S. Scriver (eds.), *Religion, Gender, and the Public Sphere*. New York: Routledge.

Sacks, J. (2009). *The Koren Siddur*. New Milford, CT: Koren Publishers.

Sawyer, K. (2013). Explorations in trans subjectivity. *International Journal of Narrative Therapy & Community Work*, (3):33–38.

Chapter 12

Genocide, transsexuality, the limits of coherence, and the radiance of the universe

Benjamin M. Baader

This text has grown and changed over the past few years. I have given early versions of it as talks in Jewish community – mostly religious – settings, but then I was asked in the winter of 2016–17 by the Faith and Spirituality Center of the University of Calgary to speak about my experience at the university's Sex and Gender Wellness Week. I found this to be a challenge, due to the gap between my personal experience and my scholarly voice, my spiritual self and my academic persona. Yet I took on the challenge, and in the narrative that I present here I build on what I did in Calgary.[1] I tell my story the way I would or did in a religious setting, and then weave my critical, scholarly voice into the text, reflecting and commenting on the narrative that I present.

I begin with what I consider to be most fundamental to the fabric of my life.
> I was born in Germany, 1959, in the shadow of the Shoah,
>> when the killings were still very close.
Sitting across people in the subway,
> we – those who had been persecuted in the Nazi period for political reasons or as Jews, and their children –
always wondered what they had done, just a few years earlier.
My teachers,
> the doctors we had to see in emergencies,
> the policemen who directed the traffic
were not necessarily all Nazis, but at best
> they had grown up and had been trained in the Nazi period.
The military culture of fascism and murder   shaped their choice of words
> and colored their tone of voice, their body language and posture,
>> their attitude, and their approach to the world.

When I met another child,

I knew within a few minutes whether her or his father had been in
the German army

or worse (the SS),

or whether his or her parents had been in the camps or had just returned
from exile,

as Jews or as socialists.

References to experiences and realities in the war, the army, the ghettos,
camps, or exile

belonged to children's talk.

And the murderous past was still very real, it was all around us.

Murder was inscribed in the buildings,

some of which had been deportation centers or Nazi police
stations,

into physical objects, and into the gestures and words of humans.

The past was not over yet.

It became present every time the doorbell rang,

and my father's face turned white   with terror.

I lived in multiple worlds,

the world of a safe childhood with my sisters, at the outskirts of
Munich,

with love, play, strawberry bushes in the garden, open fields behind the
house,

and the smell of grass.

And I lived in a world in which children just like me had been picked up
in the early morning,

the voices of SS men in the folds of my daydreams on the way to the
station,

the sound of the trains going East,

and the smell of gas.

It was hard for me to feel at home in either reality,

and to accept a life that I did not seem to deserve.

Why me? Why was I alive and others had been killed?

The world of my childhood in the 1960s in postwar Germany lacked
coherence,

and it seems to me, it was multiple worlds:

There was the world of terror that was not inhabitable,
and the other world that did not feel fully real and certainly not safe,
and that could not be a home.
No place for me. No place to live.

Yet it seems to me today, that the first world was actually two worlds,
    which were mapped onto each other, on the dream level below my
    consciousness.
First, my father's memories, stories, and his terror in my body.
And secondly, the presence of unredeemed souls, whose distress
absorbed the Light.
    A recent conversation with old friends in Berlin on a long Shabbat
    summer evening,
as the light was turning in the room with the open windows above the trees,
    has confirmed my recollection:
There was not only the terror, the nightmares, anxieties, strange habits,
    and frozenness of our parents,
    the things that they told us and that they did not tell us,
but there was also the visceral presence of the dead,
    that restricted the freedom of our breath.

As a child, I could not hold this.
    I did not grow a skin that was of one piece.
Disorientation and dread made me numb,   many days of my life.

So it appears to me that the original and primary rupture in my life stems
from having grown up in the shadow of the Nazi genocide. And indeed,
when people have asked me to speak about my gender, I have always
talked first about the echoes of the mass murder that surrounded me,
when I was a child. That rupture and this experience has always seemed
much more fundamental to me than any struggles about my gender. The
saying of children of survivors "The most important thing in my life
happened before I was born" certainly applies to me.

Growing up, my Jewish identity was a persecution identity:
    There was not much religion in my family,
but my father is a camp survivor, born in Vienna,

and my mother was from Moravia, Czechoslovakia, not Jewish.
As a socialist, my father was not affiliated Jewishly, when I was a child,
 and he passed to me only faint echoes of a Jewish practice.
My sense of Jewishness was based on the ways
 in which the still recent Nazi persecution colored our every-day lives,
and in which it echoed differently in our family
 than in the homes of the non-Jewish families around us.
Yet this was not the only way in which we were different.
 We were different by the fact that one of my sisters was severely
 disabled,
different because of all sorts of cultural differences,
 including being Austrian rather than German,
and spending an unusually high proportion of the small family budget on
books,
 rather than on cars and clothing.
And among the numerous aspects of our being strange and not quite
belonging,
 was the unsettledness of my gender.
Today I would say, I was a bi-gendered child,
 though there was of course no such language at the time.
Assigned female at birth,
 I was a girl according to my anatomy and documents.
On the one hand, I enjoyed girlhood in some settings, especially with my
sisters.
 It was lovely being one of three girls, part of our delightful girl club,
  and until today, I cherish the female to female register,
  when I am allowed to engage in it.
On the other hand, I behaved like a boy and I thought of myself as a boy.
 I played and hung out with boys at school and on the street,
and when other children insulted, teased, or tormented my disabled
sister,
 I beat up those kids as a boy.
So I could be both, boy and girl, girl and boy,
 my gender was fluid, and it was fine that way.
However, at the deepest level of my sense of self, my personhood,
 my sense of purpose in the world, I was my father's first-born son.
My sense of responsibility towards the dead,

my sense of loyalty to something larger
> that I did not understand and did not know about
was gendered male.

I was extremely lucky
> that my parents supported the way in which my gender was unanchored.

It was one aspect of our family being odd.
> And my mother held that since this is who I was,
>> I must be meant to be that way,
>>> no matter what the neighbors said.

Yet in puberty, she could no longer protect me
> from the expectation of having to be fully a girl,

and growing into a woman was an extremely difficult and alienating experience for me.
> For years, I was deeply unhappy, desperate, and full of rage at the world.
> I hated being a woman towards men.

When I started living as a lesbian in my twenties, things became easier.
> Living as a lesbian allowed me to be more male again.

Melting like a girl,   and taking the place of a man in the bed of a woman,
> I could inhabit the gap between male and female,
> I could be tough and sweet, and sing and live on both sides of the

gender divide.

I remember how the cells in my body realigned
> (a sensation, similar to what I felt when I started taking testosterone later),

how the meaning of my body and its soul changed,
> when I came to inhabit this boyish, dykish place in the world,

when I recovered my childhood pleasure of gender playfulness
> and laced it with adult joy.

In my twenties I also made another transition that was at least as significant
> as starting to live as a lesbian:

I began searching for what Judaism was beyond concentration camps.
> I knew that this Jewishness to which I was bound reached deep
> into the past,

but my actual knowledge was only about the abyss of death and destruction,
    that had engulfed us just a few years before I was born.
So I began learning Hebrew and enrolled in a Judaic Studies university
program.

    I underwent a Reform conversion,
and formally joined the Jewish community of Berlin,
    to which I had not belonged previously.

Then the Berlin Wall fell, in the fall of 1989,
    and I was afraid to remain in a proud, strong, reunited Germany,
    that seemed to reassert German-ness.
And, after years of psychoanalysis, I could give myself permission to
abandon the dead,
    for a life of my own,
    on a continent, where the streets did not reverberate with the
    sounds of Nazi boots.[2]
Thus in the early 1990s, I left Berlin for New York   with a lesbian
partner,
    and on my quest for a content and a positive meaning of my
    Jewishness,
    I pursued a doctorate in Jewish history.
I had started to fall in love with the richness and complexity of Jewish
texts,
    the shiny fabric of Jewish learning delighted and enchanted me
    like nothing else in the world.
All I wanted was Torah, I would say today,
    and where I came from, this meant academic learning.
So I became a scholar of Jewish history,
    and increasingly embraced Jewish practice.
However, the years in New York were not easy.
    I could not shake off my sense of alienation, dread,
    and the numbness into which I had fled.
For one, my partner wanted (and needed) me to be a woman.
    And so the male aspects of myself was only welcome in closely
    circumscribed ways.
We were part of lesbian separatist circles,

and I felt deeply guilty about having secret male impulses and
identifications

that turned me into the male oppressor.

Yet equally, if not more serious was

that my emigration to North America had not solved my most
fundamental issue.

The geographical distance to the persecution and the genocide of
European Jewry

in New York was an immense relief.

I relished the intensely Jewish character of the city,

and the fact

that neither the stones nor the interactions between humans

resonated with the echo of mass murder,   like they did across
the ocean,

made my step lighter.

The air was less heavy in New York, and the light more transparent.

But my partner was also the daughter of a survivor,

and in our household we cultivated the half-shade culture of guilt
and melancholy,

in the cracks between our hugs and our laughter.

The weight of the dead still suffocated our present and future.

I had escaped but I had not escaped,

numbness still enveloped me.

I still did not experience the world around me as fully real.

My life and my skin still painfully lacked coherence.

So one day I left my partner and fled into my wilderness.

What came now were years of utter uncertainty, barrenness,
exposure, exile,

a year of dissertation research in Jerusalem,

(yes, ironically in exile from a livable life in Jerusalem),

fellowships, postdocs, temporary employment in Los Angeles, Bloo-
mington (Indiana),

Toronto, Halifax,

always on one-year fellowships, short-term visas,   never knowing where
I would be next year,

on the job market as a female, much too early,

because my gender had cracked open,
and I did not know how much longer I would be able to operate in this social space of a woman.

>But I could not transition before I had attained an academic appointment.

I was in an impossible position,

>she in the mornings on the university campus in Toronto,
>and he in the evenings with my friends.

Literally, the only two stable and reliable things in my life were my e-mail address,

>and the telephone contact with Janet Clogston, my psychoanalyst in New York.

In fact, in the depth of my exile, my body had lost its meaning,

>or its meanings were proliferating into Nothingness.

My body was not legible anymore.

>Its soul had gone on vacation and I did not know whether it would return.

In fear and desperation,

>I took vows, lit candles, gave up unkosher meat,
>>begged for protection,

and one evening, at a small neo-Chasidic Kabbalat Shabbat *minyan* (prayer circle)

>that my friend Rabbi David Seidenberg led in Los Angeles,
>>I felt a connection and a presence that changed my life.

Finally, I received an academic position in Winnipeg, Manitoba, was allowed to settle,

>and fully transitioned to live as a man.

I had reached a shore,

>and my gender regained enough coherence

that I could operate in the world   with some ease,

>while I also mischievously   held on to the indeterminacy of my gender.

At this juncture, as I gained some existential stability

>in a city far removed from the genocide nightmare land of my childhood,[3]

I came to feel a little more at home in the world.
> I had arrived in a place that wanted me,
> a city and major research university that invited me to stay,

and where I had a contribution to make.
> Winnipeg, with its widely open sky and its awesome light.

And I began to feel safe – an entirely new and unknown experience.
> Thus, I started to slip out of my father's terror.

My numbness and much of my anxious tension lifted,
> and a new type of joy emerged.

I had known passion and pleasure in intellectual and physical engagements,
> when exertion produced sensations that were strong enough
> to break through my numbness.

Yet now I noticed with astonishment that I could feel joy
> just because breath flowed through my body and I was alive,

and the sun and wind greeted me in the morning,
> and I could teach students about the complexities of Jewish life
> in Biblical and Roman times, Muslim Spain, and 19th-century Germany,

and the magnificent dance Jews do, when they are both Hellenistic, French, or American,
> and hold on to Jewish distinctiveness.

In Winnipeg, life ceased to be primarily a burden and a struggle.

However, rather than my ruptured soul, skin, and life fully growing together
> and closing the gaps by entirely settling in this world,

my slow yet sustained move into Jewish practice culminated in a series of new openings.
> The dread lifted,

but my sensitivity to what I have called since the years of my adolescence, the world of the dead,
> did not fade.

And as I was no longer pushing against the shadow of the great death – the Shoah,
> and against the dead,

as I was no longer running and hiding from them,
> I began to make friends with them – the dead,

and with the realm of what we might call the spiritual.

And now we are about to move into a part of my story that is utterly beyond of what is acceptable in academic discourse. I am talking about my spiritual experiences.

At the *shivah* for my stepmother Lilith Schlesinger in Berlin, in the summer of 2008,

> I laid *tefillin* (phylacteries) for the first time, in a masorti,[4] egalitarian setting.

My father had met Lilith in a child survivor group,

> when he, like many of us Jews on the Left,

in the 1980s had followed the call to look for one's roots,

> after the dream of the socialist utopia was shattered.

Like my father, Lilith was from Vienna,

> fiercely feminist, beautiful, red haired, with a strong and unconventional spirituality.

She had survived with a group of partisans in the forests of Belgium,

> and after the war gave birth to three sons on a kibbutz.

I loved her very much,

> and even though she herself was somewhat suspicious
>
> of what she considered patriarchal institutions, such as ritual prayer and phylacteries,

wrapping *tefillin* at her *shivah* and standing in prayer

> was a most powerful experience.

Months later, when my friends in Winnipeg asked me

> what I wanted for my fiftieth birthday,

the only thing I could think about was

> having my friend David Seidenberg lead Kabbalat Shabbat for me.

So my friends flew him in,

> and again I felt a strong connection during the *amidah* (central standing prayer),
>
> and I felt Lilith's presence.

In the following weeks, I had the sense that Lilith wanted me to do something

> – to say prayers?

But her sons and my father were saying *kaddish*,

and I did not understand what she might want from me.
Yet she did not let go, and I kept thinking about the morning in Berlin,
  when I had laid *tefillin*, – but of course I did not have any.
After weeks, during the Passover days, I could not wait any longer,
  and I started davening (praying) *shacharit* without *tefillin*.
I was not at home in the liturgy, which seemed rather confusing to me,
  I sought help on the internet,
and in the beginning, I probably only said a few central prayers,
  the *sh'ma*, the *amidah*, *aleinu*.
But from the first day on, the world around me looked different.
  The color of all things seemed deeper and more intense – more
  shiny.
I had passed through a gate,
  and it seemed to me that Lilith relaxed and left.
I have missed morning prayers less than a handful of times, since.
  I do not want to be without this door to radiance.

In a religious context, I say that prayer had changed my access to light.
Is there another explanation? Did the meditative practice, on the background of my new sense of safety and ease, cause a physical relaxation
that altered my perception of things around me? Certainly, as Alan
Slomowitz suggested in informal comments to this text, the effects of
trauma had receded in the preceding years. Yet it seems to me that this
healing and an underlying structural change in the make-up of my
emotional eco-system did not form more than the background for the
pathway to radiance that my davening opened. The impact of the
davening that morning was powerful and immediate, and it established
a connection to an enormous flow of Light that has not faded since.
  An astounding, entirely unearned gift.
And more than a year later, my mother died in Berlin. She had dementia,
and I had organized her care from far for years, which was terrible,
inadequate, and never enough. But then, my sister and I were able to
move her into a truly wonderful care home, and the last years were
beautiful. Every summer, I took my books and my work and spent six
weeks in Berlin with her. She had left intellectually, but she was emotionally present. One summer, she said that it was good, and it was enough,
and it was time for her to die. I told her that this was out of the question

and that I wanted to see her again the next summer. But I knew that I
should not tie her to this world in such a manner, and in the following
summer of 2010, I gave her permission to leave. She had kidney failure
just a few days after I had said good bye and had departed from Berlin.

My mother, Charlotte Kasten, died in peace at the exact time, when I
was saying *shacharit*
    (morning prayers)
    and laying *tefillin* in Winnipeg.
And everywhere, except in a scholarly setting, I would now talk about
my sense
    that she ascended on the connection that I was holding,
that I felt her giggling with pleasure
    about how light she was   without the weight of her body,   as
    she rose.

And the day after her funeral,
    for which I had come to Berlin,
        I was bathed in light.

It was a grey and rainy day, but the room where I stayed was breath-
takingly illuminated
    by a magic and translucent light,
    and filled with a deep peace, an enormous, still joy.
In an e-mail I sent to friends that day, I wrote:
    "The color of her death is not blackness but radiance,
    playful and tender like a summer meadow.
    So much gentle light!"

This light remained with me for months,
    it shone from behind or through trees and bushes,
        it was a little overwhelming.
            Being in astonishment and awe, I hardly mourned.
In these weeks, I was able to distinguish between the light of the sun and
the other light,
    except at dawn and dusk, when something happened that puzzled me.

In the winter, the sun rises late in Winnipeg,
    and as I came to pray at that time before sunrise,
when dark and light both mingle and separate,
    breathing into the Hebrew words   made me lower myself
    into an opening
        in that space between light and dark,
and I learned how to slide down the *ayin* and the *dalet* of the *sh'ma*,
    a little less than an hour before sunrise,
and to lower myself into a tremendous flow of radiance and joy.
    At times in the depths of depths, my connection to High caught
    fire – too frightening!
Today, I ride Splendor less dramatically and more humbly,
    I love to open myself to the stream of de-light   gently.
  Rather than descending very deep, I let joy and laughter rise through me.
But at the time, I found my access to brilliance and enchantment in
ecstatic innocence,
    and when I had made my own connections, my mother stopped
    channeling light.

That winter, I also became increasingly aware of the shininess and the
glow in food,
    in particular in fruit, berries, and nuts,   but really in
    everything.
Therefore, I began saying blessings over food,
    and I learned that speaking the words of *b'rakhot* (blessings),
        magnifies the radiance in an apple or in broccoli.
In fact, I observed how the song and the light
    that flows between the twigs of the trees and bushes, the blades of the
    grass,
  the petals of flowers and leaves of plants, the particles of rocks,
    the grains of sand and dirt, and more, are the same (or of the same
    kind)
    as what flows in the spaces between the Hebrew letters of liturgy
    and Torah.
And in prayer, one can tie them all together.

All of this is not in line with the reality of western modernity. However, in the course of the past years I have discovered that my observations and experiences are very similar to what is described in various mystical texts. The Zohar (foundational compendium of Jewish mysticism from the Spanish Middle Ages) in fact has precise descriptions of that light at the onset of dawn which it calls "*or kadmon*," the primordial light, and that, according to the Zohar is the light from before creation. The Sefer Bahir (an even earlier text) records observations about letters, light, and wind (*ruach*) that match my own. And when I was still very baffled and disoriented about my experiences, a visiting scholar at our university's Department for German and Slavic Studies, gave a talk about mystical poetry from Renaissance Poland, which described experiences of light in nature that resembled mine. Chasidic texts are full of similar descriptions, relating mostly to text and Torah, but also to nature. I have also read a little about ideas and practices involving light and illumination in Hindu, Yogic, and Tibetan systems.[5] And I belong to a Sufism study group, where I encounter familiar patterns and observations in Ibn al-'Arabi's texts from medieval Islam. So in some ways, my experiences are not extraordinary at all. I have stumbled across a well-trodden path that humans before me, in a variety of cultures, have walked for centuries.

And in that same winter in which I developed this pre-sunrise prayer practice
     of *davening nez* (prayer at dawn, before sunrise),
       I started keeping Shabbat, too.
It was just too strange not to do so,
     even though I did not have community for it,
     and I had only a very general understanding of what keeping Shabbat entails.
Yet from the first week, I fell in love with her, like with nothing else.
     I adore her transparency,
when eternal time shines through the fabric of the day,
     shimmers through the surface of the apparently linear sequence of hours.
I have learned that the space/time pattern that we call reality
     is not more than a particular mode of apparent coherence.

One could say, that in this period, my failure to be sufficiently of and in this world my inability to feel fully real and coherent started to turn from a liability into a strength (or in religious parlance, from a curse into a blessing).

In the summer after my mother had died,
    I sat in the grass at my mother's grave for a long time,
in stillness and widely open,
    when a small red fox came and stood across the grave, facing me.
For a time beyond time, we looked at each other and shared consciousness.
    And I could feel the fox listening to the stream of the universe,
        without being constrained by the boundedness of the human
        psyche.
Under the fox's guidance, and later in a similar encounter with two owls in Colorado,
    I learned how to withdraw my soul from coherence and meaning,
        and to listen
            to the Flow itself,
                to the deep murmur and the exhilarating stream
                of joy and light
                    that illuminates
                        every snow flake.

Today I listen to and with trees and rocks,
    and the teaching that *domim* (silent ones, meaning minerals),
    plants, and animals
are closer to God than we are, appears right to me.[6]
    It seems that rocks and trees, for instance, always face God,
while we know how to turn our gaze away.

Thus, my spontaneous watching of light
    has expanded
        into a practice of
            listening.

And I have come to cherish Halakhah (Jewish law) as a fabric of light.
It seems to me that Halakhah is a structure that creates distinctions
    (between pure and impure, sacred and profane, Jew and Gentile,
    day and night, and many more),
and distinctions create a space between one thing and the other,
    in which radiance can flow.
Halakhah restrains. It turns of a realm in which all is allowed, for instance,
    into a fabric in which the allowed and the forbidden are separated.
Forbidden in Hebrew is assur (aleph – samech – vav – resh)
    and (aleph – vav – resh) is *or* – Light!
And I'd say that the samech stems from and leads us to
    the center of chesed (chet-samech-dalet) – God's kindness or grace.
Thus, *mitzvot* (Jewish ritual commandments) are conduits of luminosity,
    from the root tsadeh-vav-hey,
    containing half of the tetragrammaton – the revealed aspect of God.
And Halakhah and *mitzvot* allow me to align myself
    with the flow of Light in the universe,
    and with the infinite shaping and reshaping of all.

And what had frightened me for so many years,
    that the curtain between the world of the living and the world of the dead
        is thin and transparent a veil
            has ceased to alarm me.
The souls of the dead have become my friends.
    Rather than abandoning and interring them,
    in the way in which modern thought prescribes that ghosts should be laid to rest
    and should be banned from a disenchanted world,
I aim at loving ghosts
    with a love
        that redeems their souls.[7]
When this happens their distress turns into a light
    that illuminates my days.
The souls of the dead have become my companions and teachers
as I learn

how to watch the Beloved   and to wrap
   in the arc of my hammer,   all day long
     when I work,[8]   the surface of my soul
                                   around the radiance
                                      of Hir kiss.

And I have found an enormous flow of Love and Trust,
    listening and sleeping in the grass
    next to the grave of Reb Shmuel Shmelke of Nikolsburg,   in
Moravia
    one of the early Chasidic masters.
All the world's tenderness,
    sorrow,
      forgiveness,
        and deliverance
          stream from the earth.

Reb Zalman had suggested I go to Shmuel Shmelke's *kever* (grave)
        in the town that is called Mikulov today, in the
        Czech Republic,
        near where my mother was born,
when I asked him for advice about the soul of my grandfather,
    my mother's father, who had killed himself during the war.

And in the summer of 2012, before I went to Nikolsburg and from there
    to Uman,
    I underwent an Orthodox conversion.
By now my Berlin Reform conversion was just not good enough any
more,
    and I had the enormous good fortune to find an Orthodox *beit din*
    (rabbinical court)
    that considered me despite my non-normative gender.
In fact in an extraordinary move, the rabbi who presided over the
conversion
    honored my gender indeterminacy
    and thereby gave me permission to cultivate it.

My gender had not been an important topic in the conversations, leading up to the conversion,

> and the rabbis felt no need to rule on my halakhic gender,
>> as I thought they might do.

> I was willing to submit to such a ruling, but I did not pursue it.

Rather, in order to avoid a gender designation in the Hebrew text of the conversion certificate,

> the document refers to me only by my name, without adding *bat* or *ben*,

> and it uses the grammatically passive voice,

not "has immersed and has accepted *mitzvot*,"

> – which would be grammatically gendered in Hebrew–,

but "immersion and acceptance of *mitzvot* has taken place and been witnessed,"

> which is grammatically gender-neutral.

I am now living an Orthodox life in the social space of a man,

> but in a place of halakhic gender indeterminacy
>> (This means, no rabbi has made a decision
>> about whether I am male of female according to Jewish law,
>> and my gender status is thus undetermined).

However, since the setting in an Orthodox synagogue and Orthodox life,

> is highly gendered and strictly binary,

the *beit din* and the rabbi in my local modern Orthodox synagogue,

> needed to make some practical decisions

about my position in this gendered social and ritual world.

> Thus, women and men sit separately, and I sit with the men,

not because I AM a man,

> but because me sitting with the women would violate modesty, the way I look.

Likewise, I can receive *aliyot*, meaning I can be called to the Torah,

> which is a male privilege in Orthodox synagogues.

And again, I can be called to publically read from the Torah,

> not because I am a man,

but because nothing speaks against women reading from the Torah,

> and the restrictions that apply to women, do not apply to me.

However, I cannot be counted in a *minyan* (prayer quorum of 10 men) in

the Orthodox setting,
> not because it has been established that I am a woman,
but because it is Torah law that only men count in a *minyan*,
> and there is too much doubt
> about whether I am halakhically male or female or something else.

Thus, I can be counted in a regular *zimun*.
> I can count as a man when three men are needed.
But I cannot be counted for saying the additional words, when ten men
are needed,
> because this is like a *minyan*, and that's where I am not counted.
I love this.   I am counted here,   and I am not counted there.
> Like a particle in quantum physics, I inhabit two places
> that are usually thought of as mutually exclusive.

I also love not being implicated into the full set of privileges
> that come with being halakhically male.
I am little like a woman, and I embrace this as a reminder of my
femaleness,
> and as a place of humility.
I rather not possess full social and halakhic male authority.

But most importantly, I have come to embrace my lack of coherence.
> my failure to be of one piece, my brokenness, my peculiar
> positioning
> and the fragility of my attachment to the world,
all of which have been a source of pain and distress.
> which is what other trans people describe, too.

When I transitioned, I still hoped for a home in this world,
> I still was on the quest for some true and coherent self.
Yet even then, I remember saying that when nobody will mistake me for
a woman any more,
> I will wear skirts again in the summer, when it is hot.
> I will not be my own gender police.
Well, now that I live in an Orthodox context, I don't do this in public.
> But it seems to me that instead of anchoring me,

transitioning unmoored me from whatever illusion I had
    of having a real and coherent gender.

And, as in the teaching according to which,
    the answer to longing is not in the object of our longing,
  but in the opening within the longing,
        I have not attained cure and release by overcoming my condition,
        but by inhabiting it.
Condition, such as in "human condition" and "spiritual condition,"
    not as in "medical condition" – more about this below.

So according to how I have told my story,
        one could say that my lack of gender coherence, my being
        transgender,
is more symptom than cause,
        stemming from the rupture of trauma in a post-Holocaust
        childhood.
Yet, it has turned out that this incoherence and lack has created openings
        not only into pain and suffering,
        but also into radiance and joy.

Like in Halakhah, where most light flows in the spaces
        before the fabric of sacred law settles into rulings,
            when things are open,
I experience the status of gender indeterminacy as a place of magnificent
illumination,
        like in:
While the status of gender uncertainty can be a place of terror,

while living across genders is disorienting and frightening,

while living across genders means being vulnerable, lost, in pain,

while living across genders can mean shame, rejection, – even violence,

living across genders
        means having your guts perched on a ray of light across an abyss,

living across genders
    means trusting the song more than the instrument,

living across genders shimmers with the promise of a world
    unyoked from narrow regimes of meaning, knowledge, and order.

Dancing across genders means
    praising the exhilarating richness and beauty of a universe that is
    alive.

In the embrace of gender indeterminacy,
    I map myself on the radical contingency of the Divine.

So allow me some final reflections. I have offered you a narrative about transsexuality that is both similar to and different from the more common story of transsexuality as pathology. It is similar to a narrative that traces a journey from suffering and alienation to redemption. Trans stories (and the story we all need to tell when we wish to access medical services and get hormones, for instance) are stories about an existential dissonance between the gender of one's body and the gender of one's soul.

Gender dysphoria, in the language of pathology,
    is a place of alienation, dissociation, suffering, and pain,
and transitioning with the help of medical intervention
    brings the healing of the condition, in this version of the story.
Only transitioning leads to the relief of tremendous distress.
    And communities that bar transition drive people into suicide.
Attaining a whole self, a true self, an unbroken self, a coherent self, an authentic self
    can be a matter of life and death.

For many transsexuals and other trans and non-trans people,
    authenticity is a tremendously important concept.

My narrative is similar to this story, as is it also a story
    about a journey from a narrow place of suffering to redemption.[9]

But my account is different as it leads not to more self but to less.
>   The vision of fulfilment it propagates
>   is the opposite of the attainment of an authentic self,
> or in the language of my narrative:
>   I tell the story of redemption by retreat from self,
> and by a release into the splendor of the open sky,
>   as is being taught by mystical traditions.

In fact, to my knowledge, mystical teachings and practices have a strong emphasis on disengagement from the self. In Sufism, practitioners have to overcome multiple levels of the ego or *nafs* to reach a stage of complete surrender and dissolution of self, in which they are able to unconditionally manifest God's qualities in the world.[10] Along similar lines, Chasidut propagates *bitul ha-yesh*, the nullification of being, a spiritual practice that aims at reaching the level of *ayin* (nothing), where "man is as naught" so that "God can dwell within him."[11]

>   fasting, sleep deprivation, humility to the extent of self-erasure,
> serving God, the Rebbe or Sheikh, and other humans,
>   in the pursuit of subduing the ego and systematically disassem-
>   bling the self,
> undoing the boundaries
>   that separate the human from the flow of the Sacred.

I do not engage in extensive ascetic practices, and I am certainly not the world's most humble person. My emotional economy knows anger and pride. Yet I wonder whether my childhood trauma and my failure to erect a coherent, self-contained self has led me to the state of spiritual sensitivity that mystics seek to achieve, when they purposefully dismantle their ego.

And here is another observation:
>   When the world of terror released its grip on me,
>   when I settled in Winnipeg and emerged from the most dramatic
>   effects of trauma,
> I could have fully entered the world of the living, the material, real world around me.

Yet strangely, the opposite happened.
As I became more alive and somewhat at home in this world,
> I did not retreat from the liminal space of souls to the solid
> grounds of physical existence.
Rather, under the guidance of Lilith and my mother,
> the world of souls and of the flow of primordial light became
> alive to me, too.
Death ceased to be synonymous with dread,
> and I have come to be at ease and at home in both, this world and
> the one beyond.
The cultivation of spiritual alignment has become the center of my life,
> and I understand my gender practice as an aspect of it.
The disinvestement in boundaries, indeterminacy, the embrace of contingency,
> and the renunciation of full coherence, in the framework of
> halakhic observance
>> tie me to the Sacred.

Thus, I have withdrawn from the contemporary, hegemonic ideal of a coherent, self-contained, self-determined, and fully bounded individual, whose sex and gender are in alignment with each other, producing coherence by speaking the same truth – a truth that medical experts and mental health professionals can confirm.

However, these ideals and norms are not universal. They are distinct to western modernity. In pre-modern Europe, for instance (the non-modern western setting that I understand most about as a historian), gender was more fluid, the boundaries of selfhood were less starkly demarcated, and the mechanics of human coherence worked differently. Selfhood was not tied to the same regime of unitary, absolutist conceptions of truth and knowledge about gender and about personhood, as we take to be normative in western modernity.[12] And western modernity is also the only culture I know that demarcates reality by a strictly rationalist regime of a unitary and exclusivist truth. It cordons off what is part of reality in all other cultures – the world of souls, spirits, the experience of light or God, or whatever names humans have given to their encounter and entanglement with a large range of presences. What cannot be measured with the tools of western science and accounted for within the parameters of Enlightenment rationality is relegated to the realm of "religion" at best. Or, in other instances, it is understood as mental illness, as incoherent, as rupturing or exceeding the symbolic order that defines the parameters of our existence, and that determines what we consider coherent and real.

So one could say that in the narrative about my experience,

> trauma has disrupted the surface of how this society fashions reality,

has undermined gender coherence in my life

> and has ruptured the regime of truth

by which our society both establishes and forecloses insight and awareness.

> And it has released me
>> into Light.

Notes

1 I am indebted to Jessica Burke for inviting me to Calgary and for hosting me there most generously. I am also deeply grateful to many others who encouraged me to share my experience in the past years, and whose feedback and comments helped making this text stronger, including my dear friends Rabbi David Seidenberg, Daniel Thau Eleff, Joy Ladin, Oriol Poveda, Méli Solomon, Karen Barad, Rabbi Fern Feldman, and Rabbi Micah Buck Yael and Aviva Buck Yael, Rabbi Jeff Fox, the women at Yeshivat Maharat, Seth Aronson, and of course most of all Alan Slomowitz.

2 For an account of how I experienced the events of 1989 and came to the decision to leave Germany, see Maria T. Baader (1994). And the North American continent has its own ghosts, of course. Living in New York, I was very aware of the tensions between white Americans and African–Americans and the echoes of slavery. Likewise, the North American landscape reverberates with genocide and the ongoing subjugation of remaining indigenous populations, though to me the sounds of physical decimation and spiritual dispossession are more discernable in Canada than they are on the American East Coast. The erasure of Native Americans seems more complete there.

3 As I noted above, this province has its own history of exterminatory politics. Yet as a newcomer here, I am privileged to not have them weigh on me in the way the Nazi genocide does.

4 Traditional.

5　My favorite text is Kapstein (2004), *The Presence of Light: Divine Radiance and Religious Experience*. I am grateful to Oriol Poveda for making me aware of this book and also for introducing me to Alan Slomowitz.

6　See www.neohasid.org/torah/mute_world/

7　In fact, my mother left behind a manuscript in which she describes doing this.

8　I believe that this wording is inspired by a line from Rumi or Hafiz, but I am unable to locate the reference.

9　Let me be clear: None of these two narratives or the many other possible ways in which humans might want to tell the story of their gender journey, is better or more true than the others. Experience is not a hard fact. We fashion who we are in the process of telling our stories, with the tools of the cultural repertoire that is available to us, and we create meaning and establish our personhood as we tell them.

10　See, for instance, Dickson (2013, pp. 92–102). "The Sufi way." In *Ways of the Spirit: Celebrating Dialogue, Diversity, and Spirituality*.

11　Koretz (1999), in Norman Lamm, *The Religious Thought of Hasidism: Text and Commentary*. And for a contemporary example, see Schochet at: https://www.chabad.org/library/article_cdo/aid/114921/jewish/Nullification.htm. For more on *bittul* in Chabad theology, see Wolfson (2009, especially pp. 49, 75–76, 111–113, 146, and 247). I am grateful to Justin Jaron Lewis and Don Seeman for directing me to Lamm's and Wolfson's books.

12　For literature on premodern personhood and gender fluidity (and its limits) in medieval and early modern Europe, see Dinshaw (1994), "A kiss is just a kiss: Heterosexuality and its consolations in *Sir Gawain and the Green Knight*; Karras and Boyd (2002), "'Ut Cum Muliere': A male transvestite prostitute in fourteenth-century London" Lindemann (2002), "Gender Tales: The Multiple Identities of Maiden Heinrich, Hamburg 1700"; Puff (2000), "Female sodomy: The trial of Katharina Hetzeldorfer (1477); Watt (2014), "Behaving like a man? Incest, lesbian desire, and gender play in *Yde Et Olive* and its adaptations". For the classical text on the rise of the concept of truth about a person's gender, determined by medical experts, see Foucault (1980), *Herculine Barbin: Being the Recently Discovered Memoirs of a Nineteenth-Century French Hermaphrodite*.

References

Baader, M. T. (1994) Zweierlei Befreiung. In J. Jacoby, C. Schoppmann and W. Zena-Henry (eds.,*Nach Der Shoa Geboren: Jüdische Frauen in Deutschland* (pp. 11–20). Berlin: Elefanten Press.

Dickson, R. (2013) The Sufi way. In D. Bryant ed. *Ways of the Spirit: Celebrating Dialogue, Diversity, and Spirituality*, (pp. 92–102). Kitchener: Pandora Press).

Dinshaw, C. (1994) A kiss is just a kiss: Heterosexuality and its consolations in *Sir Gawain and the Green Knight*. *Diacritics* 242/3:204–26.

Foucault, M. (1980) *Herculine Barbin: Being the Recently Discovered Memoirs of a Nineteenth-Century French Hermaphrodite*pp. viii–xvii. New York, NY: Pantheon Books.

Kapstein, M., (2004) *The Presence of Light: Divine Radiance and Religious Experience*. Chicago, IL: University of Chicago Press.

Karras, R. M. and Boyd, D. L. (2002) Ut Cum Muliere: A male transvestite prostitute in fourteenth-century London. In K. M. Phillips and B. Reay (eds. *Sexualities in History: A Reader* (pp. 90–104). New York, NY: Routledge).

Koretz, Rabbi P. (1999).In *The Religious Thought of Hasidism: Text and Commentary*(p. 445. New York, NY, Hoboken, NJ: Michael Scharf Publication Trust of Yeshiva University Press.

Lindemann, M. (2002) Gender tales: The multiple identities of Maiden Heinrich, Hamburg 1700. In Ulinka Rublack (ed. *Gender in Early Modern German History* (pp. 131–51). Cambridge: Cambridge University Press).

Puff, H. (2000) Female sodomy: The trial of Katharina Hetzeldorfer (1477). *Journal of Medieval and Early Modern Studies* 30(1):41–61.

Watt, D. (2014) Behaving like a man? Incest, lesbian desire, and gender play in *Yde Et Olive* and its adaptations. *Comparative Literature* 504:265–285.

Wolfson, E. (2009). *Open Secret: Postmessianic Messianism and the Mystical Revision of Menachem Mendel Schneerson*. New York, NY: Columbia University Press.

Chapter 13

Border crossings

Commentary on Dr. Ben Baader's chapter

Seth Aronson

One of the earliest things that my brain retained recalls one of the protagonists of Nicole Krauss's novel *Forest Dark*, which is that she—by virtue of her being human—might inhabit two separate planes of existence concurrently, that it could be possible for her to be both here and there (Krauss, 2017).

Benjamin Baader, in his fierce, yet gentle, bold and subtle chapter, poignantly describes being both here and there—as Jew and non-Jew, male and female, German and Canadian, and, of course, describing experiences and realities that belong to the Shoah and the post-Shoah (if one can say such a thing) experience. Baader lyrically writes of multiple worlds, describing them as "each possessing a competing definition of reality" (Shagar, 2017, p. 28).

Shagar (2017), in his book *Faith Shattered and Restored: Judaism in the Post-Modern Age*, describes two contradictory roads to faith:

> the first is a return to innocence, to self acceptance—faith is where one accepts one's identity ... the second path is the opposite one. It is a path of choice, of creativity. Its point of departure is one not of identity but freedom, such as ethical freedom, which does not rely on facts but rather establishes them
>
> (p. 34)

Baader's courageous and difficult journey to transcendence (and, in essence, faith) lives on and in the spaces between these two roads.

Trauma permeates Baader's experience. He is born in the shadow of the Shoah, in a country described by the psychoanalyst and philosopher

Roger Frie (2017), among others, as struggling with a narrative of victimization, namely that Germans suffered too, during the war. But:

> by putting one's suffering on a parallel with Nazi victims and identifying with them, one can avoid confronting the perpetrator aspects of one's family past on the one hand and protect oneself from empathizing and taking on the perspective of Nazi persecution on the other
>
> (Rosenthal, 2010, as quoted by Frie, 2017, p. 136).

In an attempt to counter dissociation, as a child, Baader tries to quickly create categories—for example, Nazi/concentration camp survivor: asking himself was this child's parents in the German army, or had his or her parents been in the camps—to begin to make sense of experience. It is, initially, a reflection of what Bateman and Fonagy (2012) refer to as psychic equivalence, that is, a more concrete understanding of events, e.g., because I think this, it must be true. For example, a Jewish identity must be a persecution identity, or Judaism equals concentration camp. Such thinking is inflexible and not open to other perspectives.

Trauma is often shrouded in silence and yet, as Bromberg (2011) writes, for the trauma survivor, within the silence, the shadow of the tsunami looms (Bromberg, 2011, p. 17). The past never disappears, but is enacted, making itself known in verbal and non-verbal ways, dysregulating, haunting, and shaping the present. As Frie writes:

> History is conferred on us before we are born. Our identities are historically and culturally grounded (I would add and biologically, an idea to be discussed below, see vander Kolk and Bick) and in this sense, unbidden, a function of narratives, traditions and language that we inherit through family and community
>
> (Frie, 2017, p. 160)

If trauma and history exert too strong an influence on the present, parts of the self must remain unmetabolized, kept from awareness:

> If parts of the self were systematically disconfirmed early in life, the task of continuing to exist in the mind of another person (and thereby in one's own eyes) as the same self that was 'his parents' child' is a much

more complicated and difficult task because it includes having to dissociate those self states that are disjunctive with it.

(Bromberg, 2011, p. 58)

Traumatized, unsymbolized aspects of experience remain out of awareness, but, although unbidden, continue to exert pressure on any illusion of coherence of self and other.

What did this mean for one growing up "among the echoes of the mass murder that surrounded me," or one who was assigned female at birth whose "sense of responsibility towards the dead, my sense of loyalty to something larger *that I didn't understand and did not know about* [italics mine] . . . was gendered male"?

"We now know that trauma compromises the brain area that communicates the physical, embodied feeling of being alive . . . it is an imprint left by that experience on mind, brain and body" (Van Der Kolk, 2014, p. 3).

This physical manifestation of trauma is encapsulated in Baader's experiences ("my father's memories, stories and terror in my body") or when his body begins to betray him at puberty when his mother can no longer protect him from the realization/expectation of having to "be fully a girl." Rosemary Balsam, in her book *Women's Bodies in Psychoanalysis* (2012), argues how important it is for the individual to "appreciate for one's self how elements of both gender and body work and don't work in a composite picture of a person's life" (Balsam, 2012, p. 7). The difficulty Baader faced at puberty was integrating gender with a body that was proceeding predictably along the lines of development and was being perceived "objectively," while he simultaneously perceived and experienced subjectively his physical self in a very different way (Balsam, 2012, p. 7).

As Baader reminds us, trauma is not only imprinted on our physical selves, but also inscribed on our physical surroundings, "inscribed in the buildings some of which had been deportation centers" or, for example in the displaced persons camp building in Hanover in close proximity to his grandparents' home in Hanover (and about which Frie's mother has no recollection) or the "striking modernist building in Berlin" that Frie admires—until he comes to know that it was a Jewish school for girls—whose pupils and staff were deported to death camps (Frie, 2017).

What, then, are the tasks to help ameliorate the impact of trauma, to lessen the terror and dissociation?

Enduring personality growth is interwoven with ability to increase the threshold for affective hyperarousal ... it derives its power from two essential qualities—safety and risk. Through the creation of a dyadic space that includes the subjectivities of both patient and analyst but isn't the exclusive property of either, a growth process can occur

(Bromberg, 2011, p. 33).

For Baader, this begins with both "recovering the childhood pleasure of gender playfulness" and escaping the "suffocating weight of the dead," creating space in his experience for all those dissociated elements that have haunted him and his family for generations.

Initially, he describes his life and skin "as lacking coherence". Esther Bick (1968), in a seminal paper, described the "primal function of the skin" as helping to bind together parts of the self. By gradually experiencing the introjection of an external object that contains and holds the infant's experience, and identifying with this object, the un-integrated state is superseded and space within the self is born. This leads to the development of a skin, which can then contain disparate aspects of experience and allow for the creation of a self.

Baader discovers these containing objects and experiences in people and places, and through safety—a prerequisite for therapeutic action in Bromberg's thinking (2011). But it is not safety alone that therapeutic change is driven, but rather through unanticipated relational events that straddle safety and some danger, a "new reality—a space between spontaneity and safety—is coconstructed and infused with an energy of its own" (Bromberg, 2011, p. 56). As he writes: "it is the interpersonal foundation of 'safe surprises' that allows the synthesis of old and new meanings through the paradoxical co-existence of safety and otherness" (Bromberg, 2011, p. 106). Disjunctive mental states can then become more amenable to recognition.

Living in a city far removed from "the genocidal nightmare land of my childhood," he begins to feel more "at home, safe, secure" and makes room for joy. Baader must literally move away from the very buildings "inscribed" with death in order to free himself and begin to acknowledge the traumatic experiences that he reports were so dysregu-lating and destabilizing, thus allowing room for the development of a more secure, safe base.

This new sense of self sustains Baader's move into Jewish practice which culminates, paradoxically, in a series of new openings. Instead of "pushing against the shadow of the great death—the Shoah .... I began to make friends with them—the dead," truly turning ghosts into ancestors (Loewald, 2000). Loewald believed that "resolution in the analytic process is due to the blood of recognition, which the patient's unconscious is given to taste so that the old ghosts may reawake to life—those who know ghosts tell us that they long to be released from their ghost life and led to rest as ancestors. As ancestors, they live forth in the present generation, while as ghosts they are compelled to haunt the present generation with their shadow life ... in the daylight of analysis, the ghosts of the unconscious are laid and led to rest as ancestors" (Loewald, 2000, pp. 248–249). But perhaps the goal is not so much to lay the ancestors to rest, but, rather, to discover the ways in which they "live forth in the present generation," guiding, shaping, and even enriching those who live on. The aim is not burial and detachment, but continuity and use of those who came before to enliven the present. Baader's engagement with the dead then allows him to truly begin to live.

Safety, "an entirely new and unknown experience," allows Baader to slip out of the vise-like grip of his father's terror. Joy, laughter, light, and transcendence begin to permeate and color his experience. Instead of being "frightened by the [thinness of] the curtain between the world of the living and the world of the dead," Baader comes to see how "eternal time shines through the fabric of the day, shimmer[ing] through the surface of the apparently linear sequence of hours, much like the verse in Song of Songs [midrashically explained as referring to the Divine]: 'My beloved standing behind our wall, gazing through the windows, peering through the lattices'<TH>" (*Cant.* 2:9).

In the Babylonian Talmud, *Makkot* 24b, we are told of the story of four rabbis who walk among the ruins of the Holy Temple in Jerusalem. They spy a fox walking among the rubble. Three of the rabbis begin crying; Rabbi Akiva laughs.

The three ask him, "Why are you laughing?"
He asks them,

"Why are you crying?"

They reply, if an animal such as a fox now lives among the ruins of the
Holy of Holies, how can we not cry?

Rabbi Akiba then explains how the sighting of the fox is an indication
that the prophesy regarding the rebuilding of Jerusalem will now
come true.

The three rabbis then thank him, saying,

"Akiba, you have consoled us."

The story is reminiscent of Baader's experience sighting a fox at his
mother's grave—an event he interprets as a sign to give up trying to
achieve coherence (an "illusion") and to begin "to listen to the flow
itself, to the deep murmur and exhilarating stream of joy and light that
illuminates every snow flake."

The laughter of Akiba is life affirming—there will be a redemption
and rebuilding. It is a "fully human affirmation of affinity" (Zornberg,
1995, p. 100) and one that Baader allows himself to feel at his mother's
death, knowing "the color of her death is not blackness but radiance,
playful and tender like of summer meadow—so much gentle light."

The engine driving Baader's quest to turn the lack of coherence into a
strength is described by Bromberg as "what underlies human growth in
its broadest sense—the increased ability to stand in the spaces between
self states that would otherwise be alien to each other" (Bromberg, 2011,
p. 141). It allows Baader to live in "the social space of a man but in a
place of *halakhic* gender indeterminacy" and to "embrace my lack of
coherence."

This living across spaces and genders reflects the imaginative capacity
to play: Baader engages in an exchange of ideas and affects "across a
transitional space" (Winnicott, 1971) that permits burgeoning development and autonomy of selves while maintaining a deep sense of
connection to others and the world around him (Winnicott, 1971).

And Baader gratefully names the family, friends and rabbis who have
allowed him to find them and, in doing so, begin to discover himself.

This journey to self-discovery is hinted at by Baader in his allusions
to the Zohar. One kabbalistic concept is the notion of the shattering of
the vessels (*shvirat ha'kelim*) that hold Divine light. As Rabbi Kook
wrote:

> Why does the shattering of the vessels occur? ... the recipient cannot receive the light without shattering completely himself and then rebuilding himself through his desire to return to his unbounded source ... thus the created can make himself and attain the perfection of the creator, and transcend the limitations of the created.
>
> (quoted in Shagar, 2017, p. 127).

Shattering the vessels endows humanity with creative freedom, the freedom to play and create.

Ronald Britton writes of the dangers of rigidity and achievement of coherence. "Such a state [of rigid adherence] can lead to a refuge in a pathological organization which offers coherence on a basis of dogma or delusion" Britton, 1998, p. 73). The cost of appearing to achieve coherence is becoming stuck and immovable, unable to play or experience joy. It is only the embracing of creative chaos, the unmooring of fixed psychic structures that allows for true creativity and growth.

Transitioning, Baader writes, "unmoored me from whatever illusion I had of having a real and coherent gender." It allows for play, give, between the states of experience, and ultimately, creative transcendence. Baader's gender indeterminacy becomes experienced as a "place of magnificent illumination."

In place of dogma and psychic equivalence, there is a tenuous excitement of approaching the unknown, of embracing uncertainty, of renouncing the quest for full coherence. While in states of psychic equivalence as a result of trauma, Baader remained rooted in the concrete, the fixed, the feeling of immovability, unable to acknowledge or begin to make sense of traumatic experience. As a result of his journey, this state has now been replaced with symbolization—a way to represent experience that recognizes and mourns the losses while recreating lost experience and past traumas in personally meaningful and vitalizing ways.

In contemplating the multiplicity of realities (and self-states), Krauss (2017) suggests that the awe that we are filled with when we must confront the unknown stems from understanding that we have the potential to be altered. In our view of the world, we may discover a measure of our own incompleteness, our still-yet unfinishedness, which is to say, the potential we all harbor for change, even transformation. In a world where multiple realities exist, the concepts of known and unknown are rendered useless, for, ultimately, everything is equally both known and unknown. If multiple worlds and realities exist, then nothing is essential and, perhaps, we no longer have to struggle with the limits of our immediate reality and comprehension (Krauss, 2017).

In Baader's brave writing, he beautifully describes this awe, taking measure of his and our incompleteness, and the beautiful and mysterious potential for some small degree of redemption and transformation, transformation as an expression of growth illuminated by his courageous (and ongoing) journey.

References

Balsam, R. (2012). *Women's Bodies in Psychoanalysis*. New York: Routledge.

Bateman, A. and Fonagy,P., eds. (2012). *Handbook of Mentalizing in Mental Health Practice*. Arlington, VA: American Psychiatric Press.

Bick, E. (1968). The experience of the skin in early object relations. *International Journal of Psychoanalysis*, 49:484–486.

Britton, R. (1998). *Belief and Imagination*. London: Routledge.

Bromberg, P. (2011). *The Shadow of the Tsunami*. Hillsdale, NJ: Analytic Press.

Frie, R. (2017). *Not in my Family*. Oxford, New York: Oxford University Press.

Krauss, N. (2017). *Forest Dark*. New York: HarperCollins.

Loewald, H. (2000). *The Essential Loewald*. Hagerstown, MD: University Publishing Group.

Shagar, R. (2017). *Faith Shattered and Restored: Judaism in the Post-modern Age*. Jerusalem: Maggid.

Van Der Kolk, B. (2014). *The Body keeps Score*. New York: W.W. Norton.

Winnicott, D. (1971). *Playing and Reality*. London: Karnac.

Zornberg, A. (1995). *Genesis: The Beginning of Desire*. Philadelphia, PA: Jewish Publication Society.

Chapter 14

Knowing the soul of the stranger

Joy Ladin

"How long will this people spurn me?"

When I first turned to the Torah as a child, I read it as a series of stories about how hard it is for God to have relationships with human beings. Like me, I believed, God was too different, too strange, for human beings to relate to, and that belief, despairing as it was, made me feel less alone.

Before my gender transition, I had never experienced a relationship in which my differences were accepted, because I hid the ways in which I was different. But as I got older, it became hard to ignore the fact that the Torah portrays relationships in which individual human beings (notably Abraham and Moses) accept God's differences and are able to relate to God even though, like me, God does not fit human categories like gender.

However, when it came to being recognized and accepted not by individuals but by human communities, it still seemed to me that the Torah portrays God as being a little more successful than I was. From *Exodus* to the end of *II Chronicles*, the Torah is filled with examples of the Israelites' failures to recognize and remember that God is there, dwelling among them.

Nowhere are those failures more striking than those that occur after the Exodus, when God's place in the Israelite community should be absolutely clear. God creates the Israelite community by bringing them out of Egypt, maintains it by giving them manna every day, and rules it not only through the laws God gives through Moses, but through the pillars of smoke and fire whose movements guide the community on its journey.

But after Moses disappears into the cloud that covers Mount Sinai, the Israelites no longer recognize the God whose presence is blazing on the peak above them. Instead:

> When the people saw that Moses was so long in coming down from the mountain, the people gathered against Aaron and said to him, "Come, make us a god who shall go before us, for that man Moses, who brought us from the land of Egypt – we do not know what has happened to him ...
>
> [Aaron] made ... a molten calf. And they exclaimed, "This is your god, O Israel, who brought you out of the land of Egypt!"
>
> (*Exodus* 32:1, 4)

The Israelites don't just fail to recognize that God is there; they seem to have forgotten God's role in their history and their lives, first claiming that Moses brought them out of Egypt, and then creating an idol – the infamous Golden Calf – to worship as the divinity who delivered them from Egypt. Despite all that God has done for them, it seems to the Israelites as though God was never there.

Even though God's presence is blazing before them, God, unlike Moses, has no place in Israelite society, no fixed role or identity, not even a form, like Moses' body or the Golden Calf, by which to be recognized or remembered. In fact, once Moses is out of sight, they don't remember God's role in the Exodus.

In the Torah's telling, it is clear that it is God, not Moses, who brings the Israelites out of Egypt. This makes the Israelites' inability to recognize and even remember God's presence seem willful, as though they are turning their backs on God, denying that God is and was with them.[1]

But when I think of my family when I was growing up, I see another explanation. I have no place in my family's history of my childhood. The real me – me as I knew myself when I was a child – doesn't appear in my family's snapshots or stories. I was there, with my fear and misery and longing to be loved, but no one could recognize and so no one can remember the girl who had no body, the invisible daughter and sister who, as far as my family was concerned, didn't exist because she had never been born.

The child I showed my family, the one who appears in their memories, stories, and photographs, was the boy I pretended to be, an image I knew they could recognize, relate to, and love because it fit their ideas of gender, just as the Israelites could recognize, relate to, and worship the Golden Calf because, unlike the God whose presence is blazing on the mountain, it fit their ideas of divinity.

I gave my family an image of a child they could understand and because, I loved them, I tried to pretend, to myself and to them, that when they loved that image they were loving me. They, in turn, gave that image a clear, secure place in our family. They fed and clothed it, sent it to school, took it on vacations, and framed photos of it (several still hang on my mother's wall).

But as God makes clear at the beginning of the Ten Commandments, God will not settle for that kind of relationship with the Israelites. God demands that the Israelites recognize and give a place not to an image that fits their ideas of divinity, but to God's formless, incomprehensible, category-disrupting Presence:

> I the LORD am your God who brought you out of the land of Egypt, the house of bondage: You shall have no other gods besides Me. You shall not make for yourself a sculptured image, or any likeness of what is in the heavens above, or on the earth below, or in the waters under the earth. You shall not bow down to them or serve them
>
> (*Exodus* 20:2–5)

These words are so familiar that it is easy to forget that, even as God prohibits the Israelites from making or worshiping images of divinity, God is also demonstrating how utterly different God is, not just from other, more familiar deities, but from everything the Israelites know. God's voice emerges not from a body but from thunder and flame; God's presence shakes the mountain. As God's self-introduction reminds the Israelites, this is the God who turned water into blood, day into night, dust into swarming lice; who split a sea in half and led them across on dry land. Not only is God unlike anything in the heavens, the earth, or the waters, God does not fit and has no place in any human or natural order.

No wonder the Israelites find it hard to recognize or remember God when Moses is not there to remind them. God insists on being known and worshiped only as a being they cannot imagine.

The Golden Calf, however, gives the Israelites a version of divinity that makes sense: it looks the way they expect it to look, it means what they say it means, it goes where they take it, stays where they put it, and fits the roles they assign it. The Golden Calf will never disrupt the laws of nature or the order of the community; it will never lead the Israelites beyond what they know and understand; it will never shake the foundations of their world by saying to them, "I am."

The image of a boy I fashioned fit my family's ideas so well that they never missed me. The Golden Calf fits the Israelites' ideas of divinity so well that, even though it is made out of their own jewelry, before their eyes, they immediately embrace it as the god who brought them out of Egypt. The Golden Calf fills the empty place in their history and their lives where they know divinity should be and, if God and Moses had not intervened, there is no sign that the Israelites would have ever missed God's presence.

To me, this is the most horrifying aspect of the Israelites' idolatry: not their disobedience, but the fact that, like my family, they prefer a relationship with an image they understand to a relationship with a real being they can't.

But though God is enraged by the Golden Calf, God does not give up on having a place in Israelite society and, despite their flirtation with idolatry, the Israelites make it clear that they want God's presence to remain among them. They not only repent but go into mourning when God, after punishing them with a plague, says, "I will not go in your midst . . . lest I destroy you" (Exodus 33:3, 4). They now prefer to live with an incomprehensible God who might destroy them than to accept a safer, smaller version of divinity, such as the angel God offers to lead them (Exodus 33:2).

When God summons Moses back into the cloud covering Mount Sinai, the Israelites wait faithfully below (*Exodus* 34:28–33). When Moses returns, they are so eager for God to dwell among them that, as the last five chapters of *Exodus* detail, they enthusiastically contribute the materials and labor necessary to fulfill God's design for the Tabernacle, the portable sanctuary that gives God's presence a clear, well-defined place in their camp.

The Tabernacle represents the most complete integration of God into a human community recorded in the Torah.[2] But despite God's and the Israelites' joint efforts to give God a place in the Israelite community, even after the Tabernacle is completed, the Israelites continue to complain, cower, and despair as though they don't know or remember the God who dwells in their midst. To take the most infamous of many examples, the Israelites refuse God's command to occupy Canaan. "Why is the LORD taking us to that land to fall by the sword? Our wives and children will be carried off," they wail, after hearing the spies' descriptions of the strength of Canaan's inhabitants (*Numbers* 14:2–3). "If only we had died in the land of Egypt ... or if only we might die in the wilderness," they shout. "It would be better for us to go back to Egypt!" (*Numbers* 14:2–3). They would rather be dead or enslaved than count on God to help them.

God takes the Israelites' refusal as a personal rejection, asking Moses, "How long will this people spurn Me, and how long will they have no faith in Me despite all the signs that I have performed in their midst?" (Numbers 14:11). As God says, the Israelites are acting as though they don't know and can't trust the God who visibly dwells at the center of their community and is intimately involved in their lives.

Unlike their behavior in making the Golden Calf, the Israelites do not refuse to enter Canaan because they have forgotten God's presence. They acknowledge in their wailing that they know the God telling them to occupy Canaan is the God who brought them out of Egypt. But they also know that they don't understand God and can't predict what God will do.

God can, and does, threaten and punish the Israelites into obedience, but God's threats and punishments cannot change the fact that, even while dwelling in their midst, God remains a stranger to them, a being whose motives, feelings, and perspectives they cannot understand, who cannot be counted on to share their values (even values as simple as the desire to protect their families from heavily armed Canaanites), a being so different that, despite the Tabernacle and their shared history, they do not see God as part of their community. The Israelites treat God as a stranger not because they don't know God, but because they do.

The Torah makes it hard to side with the Israelites in these confrontations, but their treatment of God fit my life-long assumption that God and I were simply too different to fit into human communities. If God had asked me, "How long will this people spurn Me?," I would have answered, sometimes in rage, often in anguish, always in despair, "Forever." The Israelites spurn God, I thought, because people are people, and neither God nor I could ever find a place among them.

However, Moses and the Biblical prophets who followed him disagree with me. In *Deuteronomy*, Moses claims that it is not hard for the Israelites to give God a place at the center of Israelite community: "And now, O Israel, what does the LORD your God demand of you? Only this: to revere the LORD your God, to walk only in [God's] paths, to love [God], and to serve the LORD your God with all your heart and soul, keeping the LORD's commandments and laws" (*Deut.* 10:12–13). According to this view, which is echoed in different variations by later prophets, God's place in Israelite community is clear, and relating to God is simple: God is to be revered, followed, loved, and served by following the laws and commandments. No understanding of God, no negotiation of God's differences is required for the Israelites to relate to God. As long as the Israelites do as they have been told to do, they will be living in ways that show that they recognize, remember, acknowledge, and accept the God in their midst. According to this view, because it is so simple for the Israelites to give God a place at the center of their community, when they don't it is not because God is too different to fit in, or because God makes demands (such as invading the heavily armed land of Canaan) that make no sense from the Israelites' perspective, but because they are too sinful, stubborn, ungrateful, stupid, greedy, or otherwise damnably determined not to do so.[3]

Many of the prophets express a dim view of human beings in general and Israelites in particular, but even their most passionate condemnations of the Israelites' treatment of God reflect an optimism that I couldn't share or even understand. To me, it was obvious that God could never have a place in human community; the prophets insist that God can, that as soon as human beings turn away from our sins, we will find that it is easy to recognize and remember and act as though that God is there, dwelling among us.

I loved the prophets' idealism, but what they said didn't seem to have much to do with the people I knew. I didn't see the human beings around me as choosing to reject or turn away from God. Though they didn't seem to know that God was there, it wasn't because they were evil or consumed by sin, or that they deserved the kinds of plagues, exiles, and other punishments the prophets prescribe as cures for neglecting God's presence. They didn't know that God was there because God was invisible and incomprehensible, with no body to make room for, no role in their lives, not even a shadow they might notice stretching beside their own.

God's estrangement from human communities is not a moral or modern or secular problem; it isn't caused by mass media, the internet, the rise of science, the decline of the traditional family, or defects in faith or worship or theology; it is built into God's relationships with human beings. Being a member of a human community means taking on roles and identities, acting consistently and being seen and known in ways that are understandable and predictable. God can't do that. As God says at the beginning of the Ten Commandments, God can only be known as someone − something − human beings do not and cannot know. If communities treat God as a deity we can understand, a deity who fulfills the roles we assign, and appears in forms we recognize, we are repeating our own version of the making of the Golden Calf. If we don't recognize God's incomprehensible strangeness, we aren't recognizing God. God is a stranger who dwells apart.

Though my identification with God helped me recognize God's inherent strangeness, it also represented a kind of private idolatry. Just as the Golden Calf gave the Israelites a deity that fit comfortably into their ideas and lives, my image of God's incurable isolation from human community gave me a deity who fit comfortably into mine. I liked imagining God as being as hopelessly stranded outside humanity as I was, because I didn't want to be alone, and couldn't believe that humanity might have room for someone as different as I was. Accepting isolation and despair seemed far safer to me than risking the kind of rejection and heartbreak God experiences in the Torah over and over again when God tries to find a place among the Israelites.

But the God I found it comfortable to imagine − a God who, as I did, gives up on finding a place in human community, who sobs or sulks alone in a haze of disembodied difference − is not the God we see in the Torah. The God we see there never gives up on finding a place in human community. Even in the midst of the genocidal rages that lead God to imagine wiping out the Israelites after they make the Golden Calf and refuse to occupy Canaan, God is still determined to try again with a new people descended solely from Moses. Despite all the heartbreak and recrimination God expresses through the Biblical prophets, God never stops believing that human communities can make a place for a God who is incomprehensibly strange and utterly different, a God who cannot fit into human roles and categories, but whose presence, like the cloud and fire that surrounded the Tabernacle, is recognized and embraced at the very heart of their lives – not only their lives as isolated individuals, but the lives they live together.

"How does it feel to be a problem?" God, transgender people, and other hyper-minorities

Before my transition, I thought it was impossible to do what God tries to do throughout the Torah: find a place in human community as someone who clearly does not fit in. Now that I live as an openly transgender person, I see that I was wrong. Communities can and do include individuals who are too different to fit established roles and categories.

Social scientists call people in that position "hyper-minorities." W.E. B. Du Bois (2009), the great African–American sociologist and activist, used a simpler term, saying that his own position as a Harvard-educated African American with a PhD at the turn of the twentieth century made him "a problem":

> Between me and the other world there is ever an unasked question: unasked by some through feelings of delicacy; by others through the difficulty of rightly framing it. All, nevertheless, flutter round it. They approach me in a half-hesitant sort of way, eye me curiously or compassionately, and then, instead of saying directly, How does it feel to be a problem? they say, I know an excellent colored man in my town; or, I fought at Mechanicsville; or, Do not these Southern outrages make your blood boil? At these I smile, or am interested, or reduce the boiling to a simmer, as the occasion may require. To the real question, How does it feel to be a problem? I answer seldom a word.

(p. 5)

Like God among the Israelites, Du Bois here is surrounded by a society – a white society – to which he can never belong. The people who belong to that society can see that Du Bois is not only different from them but different from anyone they know, different in ways that make it impossible for them to understand him, because he doesn't fit the roles and categories assigned to people of color by the brutal early twentieth-century version of America's racial binary. They don't want to be unfriendly, insult, or otherwise spurn him, but they know they don't know how Du Bois sees himself or them or the society they do and do not share. His difference is impossible to ignore and impossible to for them to comprehend, a center of attention that not only makes it hard to relate to him but also disrupts their usual ways of relating to each other. That makes Du Bois, to them, a problem.

To white people, Du Bois is a problem they don't know what to do with; to the Israelites, God is a problem who may at any moment do something to them (*Number* 11:20, 33).

Now that I live as myself, I often feel like a problem. I live in communities where I am the only one who is different in the way I am different, the only person who doesn't fit or make sense in what Du Bois would call the other world of binary gender. Like Du Bois among white northerners, I have a place in that other world or, rather, I have places in a few of the communities, which, though otherwise quite unlike one another, are part of the world of binary gender: I have tenure at my Orthodox university, membership in my not-Orthodox synagogue, and have lived in the same small-town New England area for the past 15 years. Like Du Bois, I know how it feels to be treated by those around me as too different to fit in: as someone they don't want to exclude but can't understand, someone whose feelings, they fear, might be unintentionally hurt by what, to them, is their normal way of relating to each other. They are always polite, and often kind. No one tells me that they know, and know that I know, that I am a problem.[4]

How does it feel to be a problem? As Du Bois (2009) suggests, it can feel lonely, awkward, and uncomfortable. In a later passage describing growing up as a hyper-minority, he talks about feeling "shut out from [others'] world by a vast veil." Being seen as too different to understand by those we dwell among can also make us feel frustrated, overlooked, unappreciated, disregarded, deliberately spurned, despairing, and sometimes very angry. When we express those feelings, inexplicable to those around us, we become even more of a problem.

But to me, being seen as a problem by a community that acknowledges and makes a place, however uncomfortable, for my difference, feels better than believing, as I used to believe, that I had to choose between concealing my difference from those around me or being exiled forever – a devastating choice that many transgender people still face. God's persistence in dwelling among the Israelites suggests that God makes a similar decision: God prefers to be seen as a problem – to be recognized as a being the Israelites cannot understand – than not to be seen at all.

Like me and many people who are so different from others in our communities that we are seen as problems, Du Bois treads carefully when negotiating the ways the people from the other world respond, and fail to respond, to him.[5] He does not insist that the white people talking about their race-related feelings and experiences listen to his. He says nothing about what it is like to be black in America or to be seen as a problem by them. He has a place among them, but it is a tenuous place, a bubble defined by difference and maintained by silence. He isn't sure, or perhaps is all too sure, whether he would still have a place among them if he spoke his mind.

I find myself behaving similarly at my university. I do not hide my difference – everyone knows that I'm trans – but I never talk about it either. If others say nothing about it, I say nothing. If someone says they know an excellent transgender person, I smile; if they tell me they participated in some action to support LGBT rights, I show interest and encouragement; if they express anger at the university's hostility to LGBT people, I, like Du Bois, try to reduce the boiling to a simmer. No one ever asks, and I never say, how it feels to be a problem. I accept whatever signs I am given that others accept my presence among them without expecting or demanding that others accommodate, or even hear about, the feelings and experiences that go with being different in the ways that I am different. Like many people in the position of being hyper-minorities, I fear that if I burst the bubble of silence – if I turn the problem I am into a problem others have to reckon with – I will no longer have a place in my community.

Needless to say, God in the Torah is not willing to settle for dwelling among the Israelites in silence. Many people in the position of being hyper-minorities keep their anger to themselves, choosing either to hide their feelings or leave the community whose failure of understanding has hurt them. God not only expresses God's anger but demands that the Israelites change their lives to accommodate God.

As far as God and the Torah are concerned, God is a problem that is easily solved: everyone should always accommodate God, no matter how strange or burdensome God's demands may seem.

However, as God finds in the Torah, communities can find it hard to accommodate hyper-minorities, particularly when those accommodations require them to do things that do not make sense to them.

The Israelites' difficulties in accommodating God may seem familiar to traditional religious communities struggling with how to accommodate openly transgender members.[6] Like people who are openly trans, God refuses to conform to the community's ideas of what God should do or be, and insists that the community change to accommodate God's differences. And like God among the Israelites, openly trans people expect to be recognized no matter how we appear, to be treated with respect no matter how disruptive our presence may seem, and for our feelings to be acknowledged and accommodated, no matter how unusual, hard to understand, or inconvenient they may seem to others in the community.

As people who are hyper-minorities are by definition different in ways communities find hard to understand, it can be hard for them to anticipate and respond to our feelings, and it is easy for us to feel rejected when they do not. For example, the rabbi of the progressive Jewish community to which I belonged before, during, and after my gender transition didn't understand why I was angry when I learned that he planned to call my daughter to the Torah at her *bat mitzvah* using my old male Hebrew name, rather than the name I took when I began living as myself.[7] To the rabbi, calling my daughter using my male name was simply a matter of custom; he called all children to the Torah using the names their parents had when they were born. But to me, using my male name when calling my daughter to the Torah would amount to a public rejection of my identity, an announcement that, as far as the rabbi and the congregation were concerned, I was still a man.

The rabbi didn't mean to reject me by planning to call my daughter to the Torah by my former male name any more than the Israelites meant to reject God by complaining about manna. But it was hard for me not to feel rejected when the rabbi made it clear that he and the community would prefer to follow their usual practices without worrying about how I felt about them, and to go ahead with my daughter's *bat mitzvah* as though I weren't there.

Like most people, I live on both sides of this situation. In some communities, I am the disregarded, misunderstood minority who is seen as a problem, whereas, in others, I am part of the majority who do not understand the feelings of those who do not fit in. At my university, I am both at once: in the majority, as a relatively able-bodied white person of Ashkenazi Jewish descent, and, as an openly transgender person, the only one of my kind.

Living as myself has taught me not only what it is like to be a hyper-minority, but also that the experience of being incomprehensibly different is one of the things most people have in common. Whether we are the only openly transgender person in an Orthodox Jewish university, the only black Jew in an otherwise white synagogue, the only white member of a black church, the first blind person at a seminary where everyone can see – no matter who or what we are, we each may find ourselves in the position of being problematic hyper-minorities in some communities, no matter how well we fit into others.

To the extent that God's difficulties dwelling among the Israelites reflect the common difficulties hyper-minorities face, this means that most of us have something in common with God. At some time in our lives, we too have felt invisible and incomprehensible to those we live with and love, and felt rejected by words and actions that, to most members of the community, are simply routine. We too have had to choose between withdrawing from communities that do not understand us and staying and being a problem.

However problematic God's position among the Israelites may be, the relationship between God and Israel portrayed in the Hebrew Bible makes it clear that both God and the Torah reject my long-held belief that human communities cannot make a place for those who are seen as too different to fit in. No matter how often the Israelites fall short, God continues to dwell among them. And despite the trouble the Israelites have in understanding and accommodating God's differences, they still give, and risk their lives to give, God a place among them.

Knowing the soul of the stranger

> You shall not oppress a stranger, for you know the [soul] of the stranger, having yourselves been strangers in the land of Egypt
> (*Exodus* 23:9)[8]

Thinking of God as a hyper-minority has helped me move beyond my childhood assumption that, because God is too different to fit into human communities, God cannot have any place among them. It has also helped me see that the conflicts between God and the Israelites in the wilderness do not reflect the Israelites' rejection of God, and that the Israelites' failures to anticipate and accommodate God's feelings happen only because the Israelites, after the incident of the Golden Calf, dedicate themselves to making a place for a God they know they cannot understand.

Although the hyper-minority model offers a pragmatic way of understanding why the Israelites' relationship with God goes wrong, when it comes to thinking positively about how human communities can make a place for God, it does not get us very far. As I and many others who have lived as hyper-minorities have found, communities tend to treat those who are seen as too different to fit in not just as strange, but as strangers. We have a place in the community, but the place we are given is defined by our difference from other members. Even in communities in which our differences are accommodated, our differences from others tend to remain the focus of the community's attention, the first and sometimes the only thing about us that people think and talk about. No matter how long we have been part of our communities, we are not seen as one of *us*.

In the commandment not to oppress the stranger, God offers a different model for how communities should relate to members who are seen as too different to fit in, a model that rejects the idea that there is an unbridgeable gulf between those who are embraced as *us* and those who are treated as *them*:

> You shall not oppress a stranger, for you know the soul of the stranger, having yourselves been strangers in the land of Egypt.
> (*Exodus* 23:9)

This commandment combines hard-headed realism, the acknowledgment that even Israelites who were oppressed as strangers in the land of Egypt are likely to oppress others when they have a chance, with the idealistic belief that people who enjoy the privilege and power of being *us* can, and will, identify with those whom they see as *them*.

I have thrilled to those words since I first read them as a child who feared that even other members of my family would not identify with me if they realized how different I was from them. But I had my doubts about the practicality of this commandment. After all, I hid my female gender identification for most of my life because I was sure that, if others knew I was too different to fit into the gender roles on which my family was based, they would treat me as a stranger, someone they didn't know and didn't want to know. My skepticism that anyone would ever live up to this commandment was reinforced every time someone in my family reacted to a man they saw as "queer," that is, a man who didn't fit their ideas of how men are supposed to look or act. No one ever responded to seeing a man as queer the way the commandment not to oppress the stranger imagines: by affirming that because, as everyone in my family knew, Jewish men have often been mocked for not meeting non-Jewish standards of masculinity, we, as Jews, knew the soul of the queer. Instead, they made it clear that queer men were people we didn't understand, and didn't want to have anything to do with.

Of course, the commandment not to oppress the stranger does not order the Israelites to identify with the experience of not fitting gender norms; it commands them to identify with an experience – being oppressed as strangers in Egypt – that all of them at that time (the commandment is given shortly after the Ten Commandments) could remember. But the commandment is not only directed at Israelites who had lived in Egypt: this law also speaks to the future, when Israelites would be settled in their own society in the land of Canaan. By the time the Israelites invade and occupy Canaan, few of them could remember life in Egypt. Most had been born free in the wilderness, and grown up in a community in which Israelites were the ruling majority. They had never set foot in Egypt, and had never known what it was to be seen as strangers, to be treated as one of *them* instead of one of *us*, by those among whom they dwelt. To fulfill this commandment, the Israelites of the future (a category I saw as including me) would have to identify not just with those we saw as strangers, but with the experience of Israelites who lived in Egypt long before we were born. How, I wondered, could anyone do that?

I was also puzzled by the fact that even the Israelites who *had* been slaves seem to forget their lives as strangers in the land of Egypt. The only times the Torah portrays the Israelites recalling life in Egypt, as they do when complaining about manna, they remember their old life fondly, like nostalgic exiles. The Israelites had lived in Egypt for many generations before they were enslaved, and in the wilderness they miss their old lives. Their nostalgia suggests that, even when they were enslaved, the Israelites hadn't seen themselves as strangers; no matter how they were treated by the Egyptians, to them, Egypt was home.

That – the experience of being treated as strangers in the society they felt to be their own – is what God orders the Israelites to recall in the commandment not to oppress the stranger. That is what *ger*, the Hebrew word translated as "stranger" in this commandment, means: not someone who is a foreigner, with no permanent ties to Israelite society (the Torah has a different term, *ben-nachar*, for the foreigner), but what US immigration law calls a "resident alien," and the Torah often refers to as "the stranger [*ger*] who dwells among you," a person who lives in and is part of the Israelite community but is seen as too different to be considered one of us.[9]

The Israelites in Egypt officially become *gerim*, resident aliens, when Pharaoh, at the beginning of the *Book of Exodus*, declares that Israelites who have lived in Egypt for generations are not members of Egyptian society but a threat to it: "Look, the Israelite people are much too numerous for us. Let us deal shrewdly with them, so that they may not increase; otherwise in the event of war they may join our enemies in fighting against us" (Exodus 1:10). As Pharaoh, pioneering a line of anti-Semitic propaganda that continues to this day, makes clear, the Israelites are now to be treated as "them" rather than "us" by the Egyptians they dwell among.[10]

God not only commands the Israelites to keep alive the memory of being treated as strangers by their fellow Egyptians; throughout the laws establishing Israelite rituals and festivals, God reminds the Israelites to include and make a place for the stranger. In fact, from the outset, *gerim* are built into God's idea of community and religion. Shortly after the killing of the first-born and before the parting of the Red Sea, God commands the Israelites to include strangers in the Passover sacrifice – a ritual that defines Israelite identity:

> The LORD said to Moses and Aaron: This is the law of the Passover offering: No foreigner [*ben-nachar*] shall eat of it . . . .
> But i]f a stranger [*ger*] who dwells with you would offer the Passover [sacrifice] to the LORD, all his males must be circumcised; then he shall be admitted to offer it; he shall then be as a citizen of the country.
>
> (*Exodus* 12:43, 48)

It seems unlikely that Moses and Aaron, still in the midst of escaping Egypt, were thinking about how the Israelites would one day treat minorities they see as strangers. But God is. To God, acknowledging and accommodating *gerim* – non-Israelites who identify with the Israelite community so strongly that they not only want to offer the Passover sacrifice but are willing to be circumcised to do so – is so important that this is among the first commandments God gives after the Israelites begin to leave Egypt.

Here and elsewhere, God insists that all *gerim* who undergo circumcision be treated equally – as citizens – in terms of ritual and civil law. Later Jewish tradition recognized two different kinds of *gerim*: the *ger toshav*, the stranger who lives with you, who commits to observing some but not all of the commandments Israelites are obligated to observe; and the *ger tzedek* or "righteous stranger," who not only lives in and follows the laws of the community of Israel but identifies as a Jew and formally converts to Judaism.

Rabbinic law requires that communities treat those who convert to Judaism as Jews, and tries to protect them from discrimination by, for example, forbidding other Jews to refer to the fact that a *ger tzaddik* was not born Jewish. But as the term *ger tzedek* shows, no matter how strongly those who are not born Jewish identify as Jews, no matter how fully they embrace Judaism and Jewishness, and no matter how much they have sacrificed to join the Jewish people, the rabbis assume that they will always be seen as *gerim*, strangers.[11] In fact, the Hebrew word for converting to Judaism is *l'hitgayer*, which literally means "to make oneself a stranger":

to become a Jew when you are not born a Jew is to identify yourself with a community in which you will always be considered a stranger.[12]

Converting to Judaism is far from the only way people *hitgayer*, estrange themselves from the communities they consider their own. Immigrants make strangers of themselves when they leave their native lands and start new lives in countries where their accents and origins will always mark them as different from those who are born there, and I made a stranger of myself when I stopped living as a man and started living as a woman who is openly transgender.

Of course, even before my transition, I always *felt* like a stranger, because I always knew I didn't fit into a world where everyone had to be either and only male or female. But feeling different didn't make me what the Torah and the rabbis call a *ger*, because the people I dwelt among, the family and communities I considered mine, didn't see me as different. As far as they were concerned, I was one of *us*, a heterosexual male, with all the privileges accorded to people who fit into those categories. To me, living as a male was the opposite of privilege: it was a form of enslavement I endured in order to avoid exile and oppression. But miserable as I was about living as a male, I still received the benefits that went with it. When I was a child, my mother cleaned up for me; she expected my sister to clean up for herself. When I grew up, I took it for granted that I would be listened to when I spoke up in synagogue or meetings, and that I could walk alone down the darkest, emptiest streets without fear of being raped. As someone seen as a heterosexual man, I never hesitated to hold hands with or kiss a woman in public – things my wife and I now only do when we are sure we are safe. When, in 1982, my now-ex-wife and I decided to get married, we knew we could walk into any city hall and get a marriage license. I never worried, as I have since my transition, that my status as a spouse or a parent would be questioned. The IRS gave me tax deductions; my employer automatically included my wife and children in our health insurance; and when my children or wife were in the hospital, I had the unquestioned right to see them, day or night. My kids never worried about being teased or bullied if their friends found out that I was their parent; they were proud to be known as my children.[13]

In short, before my transition, though I lived my life in fear of others finding out that I was different, I wasn't seen or treated as a *ger*. But when I began living as myself, I experienced what it means to *hitgayer*, to make oneself a stranger. Members of my family, my university, my synagogue, my small-town community who, when I was a man, had considered me one of them, now saw me as someone they didn't know or understand. People who had always greeted me on the street or at synagogue walked by without a sign of recognition. They weren't trying to slight me. They had known me as a man. Now I was a stranger.

But *ger* and *l'hitgayer* do not refer to the kind of sudden estrangement I experienced as a result of gender transition. They refer to the long-term social situation of living in a community in which, no matter how long or how well we are known, we are always seen as too different to fully fit in or be considered one of us. After the shock of transition wears off, that is the position I and many openly transgender people find ourselves in, and that is the position that the rabbis expect people who convert to Judaism to face in Jewish communities. The price for living as whom we truly are is that we are seen as *gerim*, strangers, perhaps as righteous strangers, admired for our courage, honesty, and commitment, but strangers none-the-less.[14]

But God makes clear in the laws of Passover and throughout the Torah that, though they are seen as strangers, *gerim* are part of the Israelite community. For example, the laws about the rituals for absolving the Israelite community leave no doubt that *gerim* too are stained by communal sins: "The whole Israelite community and the stranger residing among them shall be forgiven, for it happened to the entire people through error" (*Numbers* 15:26). Such laws show both that God considers *gerim* part of the Israelite people and that God knows that the Israelites must be constantly reminded that their community includes those they see as strangers. Indeed, God repeatedly tells the Israelites that "[t]here shall be one law for you and for the resident stranger . . .. You and the stranger shall be alike before the LORD; the same ritual and the same rule shall apply to you and the stranger who resides among you" (*Numbers* 15:15–16).

But in the commandment not to oppress the stranger, God goes beyond reminding the Israelites to acknowledge and include the strangers who dwell among them. Though God does not use the term *hitgayer*, that commandment effectively requires every Israelite to identify as strangers, both collectively, as members of a people who were treated as strangers, and individually, by knowing, and acknowledging that they know the soul, the experience, of being a stranger.

This commandment does not presume or require that we know how any individual stranger feels. For that, we would have to get to know those we see as strangers as individuals, and God does not, here or elsewhere, command the Israelites to do that. Rather, God commands that we respond to seeing someone as a stranger by remembering the ways in which we too have felt or been seen as too strange to fit in with communities we consider our own.

How can those who have always fit in with those around them know – how can God insist they know, and why does it matter so much to God that they know – the soul of those who are seen as *them*?

When I was growing up, I was sure that God and I were the only strangers in a world of human beings who fit in and identified with each other – and who would not, and could not, understand or identify with strangers like us. I know now how wrong I was. Few of us identify as transgender, but most of us are aware of being different in ways that might be hard for other members of our communities to understand or accept. No one perfectly fits the roles our communities assign us, or the categories that define who is *us* and who is *them*. Each of us is made in the image of the God who does not fit human categories or roles. All of us, like God, dwell among and love those who cannot fully know or understand us. God's assumption is right: because the sense of being different is part of being human, whether or not we have had the experience of being treated as *gerim*, we all know – and, whether or not we wish to admit it, we all have – the soul of the stranger.

Those of us who are hyper-minorities in religious communities don't need to dredge up painful memories of feeling different, steep ourselves in histories of times when our communities were oppressed, or engage in other psychological or spiritual work to know the soul of the stranger. Being seen as different from those among whom we dwell is the price we pay for belonging to our communities. Like the non-Israelites who, as God anticipates during the Exodus, willingly circumcise themselves and all the males in their households to participate in the Passover offering, we willingly, if not happily, *hitgayer*, accept the pain of being seen as strangers in our communities, because, to us, those communities are home. But even though we are hyper-minorities, we too need to do the work of identifying with others *we* see as different – of knowing the souls of those who, to us, are strangers.

Whatever the differences that set hyper-minorities apart, our differences are dwarfed by what we have in common with others in our communities. Our needs are human needs, our loneliness is human loneliness, our love is human love. We can form friendships, serve on committees, greet people at the door, study sacred texts, dance at weddings, hold mourners in our arms, raise our voices in song. And so, however hard our differences may be for our communities to reckon with, we will always be easier to include than God. Our differences from other people, as Maimonides might say, are differences of degree; God's differences are absolute.

God is not just a stranger in this or that community: God is the ultimate *ger*, a singular Presence who, as Judaism and other traditions that grew out of the Torah teach, dwells among human beings, sharing our lives, caring about our actions, knowing our sorrows and our struggles, but who can never fit in or be seen as one of us. That perhaps is why God worried about making a place for the *ger* even while the Israelites are still leaving Egypt: because to make a place for God, the Israelites, and the other religious communities that have grown out of the Torah, must make a place for a stranger who dwells among them.

From this perspective, the commandment to know the soul of the stranger is more than a summons to social justice or a reminder not to do to others the evil that others have done to us. Knowing the soul of the stranger is part of the spiritual discipline required for a community to make a place for God. In the Torah, God constantly prompts the Israelites to practice this spiritual discipline. God institutes rituals, like that of Passover, that keep the memory of being strangers in Egypt alive and central to Israelite identity; God gives laws that demand that those who are seen as strangers be treated equally and included fully in communal life; and God commands the Israelites to *hitgayer*, to identify with the experience of being strangers so that they know the soul of the stranger – the stranger who dwells among them, the strangers they are, the stranger who is God.

Though these laws are specific to the Israelites, the spiritual discipline they represent is not. Regardless of our religious tradition or affiliation, to welcome God into our communities is to welcome a stranger who will never assimilate, who will not go along to get along, will not follow our rules, accept our judgments, embrace our values, affirm our doctrines, confirm our biases, or look or behave the way we expect – a stranger who may bless us or curse us, who is responsible for all the good and all the evil that befalls us, who takes without asking and gives without explanation. To love God, we must learn to love someone who will always be a stranger. To serve God, we must serve the needs of a stranger. To grow close to God, we must become intimate with a stranger. To open ourselves to God, we must open ourselves to a stranger. To make a place for the God who dwells invisibly and incomprehensibly among us – to show that God belongs with us, and that we belong to God – we must know, and build our lives and communities around knowing, the soul of the stranger.

Notes

1 As is often noted, the Haggadah – the text that is the basis for the ritual retelling of the Exodus at the Passover seder – mentions only God when recounting the Exodus, and does not mention Moses at all. When we juxtapose the Haggadah's version of the story with the Israelites' revisionist history at Sinai, it looks as though later tradition is responding to the Israelites' amnesia about God by telling the story in a way that prevents later generations from making the same mistake.

2 The first and second temples were designed by human beings, built through taxes and forced labor, and represented the power of the state as well as devotion to God. The Tabernacle was a joint effort, designed by God and built through the generosity of the Israelites, who willingly contributed materials and labor in order to give God a place among them.

3 Abraham Joshua Heschel's *The Prophets* (1962), eloquently and exhaustively explores the repeated failures of God to find a place in Israelite society, and of Israelites to remember, recognize, and be faithful to the fact that God is there. Like God and the prophets, Heschel gives little consideration to any difficulties the Israelites might have had in relating to God.

4 I don't want to imply that people of color and transgender people face the same struggles, or to equate Du Bois's life as a pioneering African–American intellectual and activist with my personal struggles. Being openly transgender in the Jewish world in the early twenty-first century is not at all like being a black intellectual and activist in America 115 years ago. But when I read Du Bois's description of the isolation and social

awkwardness that go with being a hyper-minority, I feel a deep sense of familiarity and recognition – and because Du Bois writes his description without marking himself as black or his interlocutors as white, I suspect that he hoped that even readers who were not black would, like me, identify with his situation, despite our awareness of how different our lives are from his.

5 I am speaking here only of the way Du Bois portrays himself in this paragraph. In his life, Du Bois was a fierce, courageous activist who fought for decades to empower African Americans and to tear down the veil that kept white people safe from knowing African–American experiences, perspectives, and feelings.

6 By saying "openly transgender people," I am referring to people who want others to know that we don't fit binary gender categories. That excludes trans people who, like me when I lived as a man, do not want others to know that we are transgender, as well as transsexuals who, after gender transition, want to be seen not as transgender but as men or women.

7 When people are called up during the public reading of the Torah at religious services, they are named, in Hebrew, as "X [their Hebrew first name], son or daughter of Y [the Hebrew names of their parents]."

8 Though the new JPS translation renders this as "you know the **feelings** of the stranger" – a translation that captures the colloquial meaning of the text – the Hebrew word is actually *nefesh*, "soul."

9 The phrase "the stranger who dwells among you" makes explicit the connotations of the word *ger*, which is derived from a root that means "to dwell."

10 Though the Israelites were not hyper-minorities in the land of Egypt – there were a lot of them – the term *ger* includes people who are hyper-minorities, because hyper-minorities are those who, like me at my university, are seen as too different to fit in by a community that we consider our own.

11 For more on the treatment of the ger tzedek, see, for example, *Talmud Bavli Bava Metzia* 58b–59b.

12 As Jews have not generally sought to convert others to Judaism, most Jews who convert are in the position of being hyper-minorities – not only being seen as different from other Jews in their community, as *gerim*, but being among few who are different the way they are different.

13 Though I now worry about and occasionally experience harassment for being seen as transgender, as before, my white skin enables me to walk through the world without being marked for discrimination or police attention.

14 It is important to note that, contrary to the assumption built into the term *ger tzedek*, neither all Jews who have converted nor all transgender people are seen as strangers in their communities. Communities *can* embrace those who are different as *us*, though I suspect most communities find this harder

to do with regard to members who are visibly different, or trans people whose appearance doesn't fit binary norms.

I explore the parallels between gender transition and Jewish conversion in Ladin (2018), How we become real: "The making of Jewish and transsexual identities."

References

Du Bois, W. E. B. (2009), The souls of black folk. *Journal of Pan African Studies*. 5:6.

Heschel, A. J. (1962). *The Prophets*. New York:Harper & Row.

Ladin, J. (2018). How we become real: The making of Jewish and transsexual identities. *Journal of Jewish Identities*, 11(1):67–74.

Chapter 15

Rabbinic and *halakhic* discourse on sex-change surgery and gender definition

Hillel Gray

A new introduction

Since this chapter was written, Orthodox discourse has paid increasing attention to transgender people, particularly those who have had gender (re)assignment surgeries. As anticipated, writers on Orthodox *halakhah* are drawing on the in-depth monograph *Dor Tehapuchot*, which is cited for conventional as well as more lenient approaches. The monograph is also being used as a research resource, it seems, even when not directly cited.[1] *Halakhic* discourse continues to bring up new legal and inter-personal implications, or consequences, as more transgender Jews inter-act with Orthodox communities. To date, no major decisor (*posek*) has published an approval of genital surgery for transitioning, though it is becoming more common for rabbis to openly discuss whether surgery could be warranted as a matter of preserving life (*piku'akh nefesh*).

Orthodox *halakhic* discourse continues to emphasize that gender (re) assignment surgery is a violation of Jewish law.[2] In their rhetoric, speakers may avow the need for compassion while expressing a rejec-tionist policy toward transgender persons insofar as they present differ-ently to their birth sex assignment.

An exemplary statement of Orthodox opposition can be seen in Alfred Cohen's *Transgenders in Jewish Thought and Law* (Cohen, 2017). To a degree he finds transgender people exotic, as with his opening anecdote of a couple that divorced after the husband transitioned to female, which Cohen describes as a "bizarre" case. Cohen's wording is rather unsym-pathetic, expressed in an indirect or perhaps uninformed way.[3]

Consistent with the dominant genotypic view, Cohen states that *halakhic* gender does not change with surgery. Yet he does raise the question of whether transgender persons may be permitted to do Jewish rituals in line with their current gender presentation. For instance, Cohen sees a dilemma with the gendered morning blessing of the divine will, because he finds the original formula for men ("who has not made me a female") unacceptable for female-to-male (FTM) trans people who, he contends, were created by God as female. As Cohen treats the FTM person as a woman under Jewish law, he examines whether a woman can put on tallis and tefillin (i.e., perhaps in some circumstances). He also raises the problem of burial in light of the separate rows for men and women in some Jewish cemeteries. As with the living, Cohen gives no indication that a deceased trans person should be accorded formal recognition for their gender reassignment. None the less, his text does refer repeatedly to the (male-to-female or MTF) person as a "woman," i.e., albeit one with male *halakhic* status, who troubles the gravesites of neighboring men to the imagined distress of relatives and mourners. To his credit, Cohen considers whether intense distress over gender identity could be grounds for setting aside the *halakhic* prohibitions on genital surgery. He also mentions non-surgical means of transitioning, e.g., hormonal treatment.

Similar views may be found on the flagship modern Orthodox website, YUTorah. In one recorded teaching, the rabbi holds by the genotype view and mentions psychological issues. He mentions the elevated suicide rate among transgender people and notes the need for sensitivity. Like Cohen, he discusses whether gender reassignment surgery could be permissible as *piku'akh nefesh* (preservation of life). However, he is challenged by one congregant as insensitive, for mocking trans people and dead naming.

None the less, new voices continue to shift *halakhic* discourse, at least at the margins of Orthodoxy, toward more lenient approaches to the status of transgender people. A notably trans-sympathetic, if not trans-affirmative, talk was delivered by Rabbi Tzvi Hersh Weinreb, the former Executive Director of the Orthodox Union, a psychotherapist. Though not a *posek*, he opined that the genital surgeries could be justified under Jewish law in cases where gender dysphoria is deemed life threatening. (Weinreb, 2016) Meanwhile, Rabbi Jeffrey Fox and others associated with the more liberal Yeshivat Chovevei Torah and Yeshivat Maharat have made an effort to serve as allies to Orthodox trans Jews.

To be sure, Orthodox *halakhah* still contrasts with the non-Orthodox Jewish rabbinic groups, especially with the wide-ranging 2017 responsum of the Jewish Theological Seminary of the Conservative movement. This responsum appears to fully permit gender alignment surgeries as well as full ritual acceptance of transgender persons (Sharzer, 2017).

In the last half-dozen years, it seems that a small but increasing number of Modern Orthodox synagogues are finding ways to accommodate transgender Jews, enabling them to participate in line with their gender presentation. If these rabbis are not relying on a phenotypic assignment of gender as such, they at least are adopting *Dor Tehapuchot*'s hybrid adaptation for Jewish rituals and communal interactions. Such adjustments are not apparent in the very diverse ultra-Orthodox world, though there are exceptions of trans-supportive efforts.[4]

In the near future, there will likely be much greater Orthodox discourse on transgender persons and gender reassignment surgery. *Halakhic* decisors are reportedly fielding an increasing number of questions on these topics. For example, Rabbi Asher Weiss recently published a responsum that allowed a groom to sign his marriage document (*ketubah*) with the female name of his biological father, now a transgender woman, despite the sin involved. Weiss contrasted the transgender case to the severe sin of apostasy; he also stressed that people with gender reassignment surgery should be treated with compassion. In addition, the rabbinic courts in Israel will face a variety of cases; for example, a *beit din* in Haifa ruled in 2017 that a transwoman remains a *halakhic* male and ordered her to grant a *get* (divorce document) as the husband. (Domb, 2017)

In short, there are ongoing developments in Jewish legal discourse that can be better understood and contextualized using the chapter presented in this volume. Western culture is rapidly shifting on LGBT issues and, although Orthodox Jewish law changes at a far slower pace, rabbinic decisors are facing new questions, responding in diverse ways, and opening up new lines of legal discourse. The chapter and its analysis are even more important during this changing time.

Original introduction

Orthodox resistance to changes in Jewish law is, arguably, a strategic self-representation. Orthodox communities are responsive at times to the preferences of the larger society, even in relation to gender issues that distinguish Orthodoxy from non-Orthodox Judaism. To fully understand the permeability of rabbinic discourse on gender, it is helpful to examine attitudes toward transsexuality—that is, toward persons who, previously known as males or females, present themselves following hormonal treatment and sex-change surgery (SCS) as the other sex, male-to-female (MTF) or female-to-male (FTM).[5]

Transsexuality challenges, profoundly, the theological assumption of a created human nature: men are men, women are women. Sexual dimorphism is an inescapable, naturalized presupposition of western (if not all) societies.[6] One might well say that this binary is what makes the entire sex-differentiated map of Orthodox Judaism workable. To be sure, rabbinic discourse has ancient categories (e.g., *androginos*) that could make space for gender variance. Yet, epitomized throughout Orthodoxy, especially in its ultra-Orthodox (*ḥaredi*) forms, the gender binary is foundational to individual duties and aspirations, to the regulation of family and communal life, and to the allocation of ritual practices and spaces. It is hard to imagine how Orthodoxy could tolerate SCS and integrate transsexuals into such a gender-differentiated formation. Likewise, rabbinic views of SCS are tied to struggles within Orthodox culture to control sexuality. As scholars have shown, attitudes toward transsexuality intersect with the history and regulation of homosexuality, even though the linkages are seldom articulated in rabbinic texts.[7] Accordingly, Orthodox approaches to transsexuality can help us understand the resilience of traditionalist rabbinic law on gender and sexuality. Although scholars have delved deeply into SCS in the general society, much less attention has been paid to the reception of SCS and transsexuals in Orthodox Judaism. Hence, the purpose of this chapter is to examine Orthodox legal discourse on SCS, a corpus overlooked in Jewish gender studies, notwithstanding its significant repercussions. To identify shifts in the history of Orthodox approaches to SCS, this analysis encompasses *halakhic* texts from the 1970s to the past decade.[8] The aim is to look carefully and below the surface, to characterize the repertoire of rhetorical and practical Jewish legal stances on SCS and transsexuality. The texts I peruse include published responsa, articles in rabbinic journals, and *halakhic* pronouncements on the internet. Above all, I analyze an extensive 2004 monograph published by an Israeli Orthodox rabbi, Edan Ben-Ephraim, entitled *Dor Tahepukhot* (*Generation of Perversions*).[9]

Ben-Ephraim has put a formidable document into play within the Orthodox Jewish community. *Dor Tahepukhot* differs from other rabbinic texts on SCS in three significant ways. First, Ben-Ephraim is based in the Sefardi religious community, which differs in some of its views from the Ashkenazi yeshiva system that has largely dominated *halakhic* discourse in North America and Israel. He studied at Yeshivat Ḥazon Ovadia under Yitzḥak Yosef, son of the late renowned *halakhic* scholar and Sefardi Chief Rabbi of Israel Ovadia Yosef and now himself the Sefardi Chief Rabbi.[10] Second, perhaps on account of his Sefardi perspective, he makes extensive use of rabbinic lore (*agadah*) and mysticism (*kabalah*; see below) in discussing what is essentially a legal issue. Third, Ben-Ephraim offers the first book-length treatment of SCS, framed as a systematic guide to practical *halakhah* (e.g., Ben-Ephraim, 2004, pp. 9ff.) To be sure, his mixing of senior rabbinic opinions with his own more novice interpretations makes the book come across more as a scholarly exercise than as an authoritative text; it received approbations from major rabbinic authorities, but such approbations are common, and Ben-Ephraim himself has neither the discursive clout nor the reputation of their authors.[11] None the less, in its scope and analytical intensity, his tome outdoes the preceding responsa and incidental Orthodox writings on SCS. Ben-Ephraim's curiosity leaves no law sacrosanct, no viewpoint or ruling beyond reproach; even established opinions are tested and retested. This thorough engagement with the topic is a rabbinic practice that opens up conversations rather than shutting them down.

In subtle ways, Ben-Ephraim's work marks a nascent shift in Orthodox thinking about SCS. This chapter explores these shifts in rabbinic legal discourse in three sections on, respectively, the legality of SCS, the postoperative assignment of sex for the purposes of Jewish law, and the regulation of transsexuality in day-to-day Orthodox life. In each case, to highlight the transitions under way in Orthodox discourse, my analysis contrasts previous *halakhic* texts with the approaches taken in Ben-Ephraim's pioneering monograph. As shown in two further sections, potential changes in rabbinic law are shaped by the psychiatric perspective on transsexuality, which decouples biological sex and gender, and by popular conceptions of the gendered soul. These sections compare Ben-Ephraim's views with the innovative opinion of modern Orthodox Rabbi Dror Brama.

Lest the reader harbor unrealistic expectations, make no mistake: none of the transitions in Orthodox discourse are as revolutionary as those propagated by queer theory or the contemporary struggle for legal rights for transsexuals. I ask, rather, whether Orthodoxy's small ripples reveal an instability, a dialogical response to the waves of change set in motion by SCS. In its own terms, perhaps traditionalist Judaism is also queering gender identities for Jewish law purposes. Although not seeking directly to overturn *halakhic* rules against SCS, this emerging Orthodox discourse may have opened up interpretive space for sympathetic responses to transsexual persons.

Legality of SCS: prohibition and its rhetorical expression

Early rhetorical responses

Every Orthodox rabbinic text on SCS deems it prohibited under Jewish law.[12] According to these texts, Jews who willingly undergo SCS or perform it on others have committed serious transgressions of biblical rules, as understood in Jewish law and ethics. Nevertheless, the reasoning and rhetorical expression of this judgment have varied in several important ways.

When SCS first came to the attention of Orthodox *halakhic* commentators, their reactions ran a gamut. During the 1960s to the 70s, several rabbinic decisors and Jewish medical ethicists—J. David Bleich, Lev Grossnass, Avraham Hirsch, Avraham Steinberg, and others—wrote neutrally or even sympathetically about transsexuals.[13] To be sure, such sympathy is attained by pathologizing the transsexual. For instance, Bleich speaks kindly of Jan Morris's *Conundrum* and refers to transsexuality as a "tragic condition."[14]

By contrast, most authors of a series of responses compiled by the Hebrew ultra-Orthodox rabbinic journal *Hama'or* in 1972 were shocked by SCS, denied its relevance to their community, and called for an uncompromising stance against any future Jewish transsexuals. A hasidic rabbi, Shalom Krausz, opened his response by questioning the need for any response at all: "In my opinion, this is beyond the bounds of abomination, and it is not worthwhile wasting time suitable for studying Torah to clarify this disgusting matter for them in a responsum."[15] Such rhetoric condemns transsexuality by way of a "politics of disgust," specifically allusion to biblical language on homosexuality.[16] Another responder with roots in the rabbinic leadership of the Satmar hasidic community, R. Hananya Yom Tov Lipa Teitelbaum, used aptly surgical imagery: "If this plague [*makah*] spreads, God forbid, among Jews, we need to gather teachers and rabbis together, to unify, all as one, in mind and soul ... with a sharp knife [*sakina ḥarifta*] against this outbreak."

Though articulating an opinion on the law, these rabbis exhorted in a theological vein by characterizing SCS as an attack on the divinely ordained natural order—a more subjective and discretionary principle than, say, the biblical prohibition of castration. Teitelbaum (1972) wrote: "God created the world and made all forms appropriate and complete. One should not change it at all, and any change is against the will of the Creator."[17] Krausz compared SCS with the forbidden mixing of seeds, which he saw as grounded in the divine concern for the natural order,[18] and to sorcery, which also contravenes "the natural way that was established at the beginning of creation."[19] Condemnation of SCS could mean utter rejection of transsexual persons themselves.

Teitelbaum stated that Jewish transsexuals should be considered no longer Jewish and subjected to a rare banning from the Jewish community:

> In my humble opinion, anyone who acts thusly to surgically remove the male organs, in order to change to female, is in the category of a person who leaves Judaism. [The person] is no longer classified as a Jew and is legally considered ... an apostate to the entire Torah ... and thereby governed by the laws for non-Jews. ... If the state allows us to issue [a *ḥerem*, a religious ban] then it is a mitzvah to ban and separate from and expel this person completely from the community of Israel.[20]

However, *Hama'or* editor Meir Amsel, who had solicited his colleagues' responsa, explained why, in his view, Orthodox rabbis should respond seriously to SCS in Jewish legal terms. The ultra-Orthodox (*haredi*) world should not lock itself up like a fortress and pretend that "our Jews" would never be involved with transsexuality. Amsel predicted that "the licentious and derelict influence [of society] would also enter the [*haredi*] camp," so that rabbis would eventually have to rule on the issue. To justify his rabbinic analysis of a hypothetical future with Orthodox postsurgery transsexuals, he mentioned other situations that merit *halakhic* deliberations for anticipated problems and argued that SCS, from a *halakhic* point of view, is no worse than apostasy or forbidden marriage. Anticipating that some transsexuals would repent of their error and seek a *halakhic*, observant life, Amsel argued that Orthodoxy should welcome these "unusual creatures," provided they repent, and educate them about how to conduct themselves according to *halakhah*. Such sinners could participate in the Orthodox community, and MTF transsexuals, even without repentance, could perform such male-specific religious duties as the priestly benediction, because otherwise they would always be adding sins for dereliction of duty.[21]

In the 1970s, Orthodox Judaism was confronting a new reality, a new plateau in the capabilities of medical science. Yet, Orthodox rabbis were comfortable with the trope of claiming that SCS is actually not new but eerily familiar, and that it had already been anticipated and competently addressed by ancient and medieval rabbinic thought. With a kind of perverse pride, they cited ancient precursors, pointing, for example, to the midrashim according to which Adam and Eve were created as a single, androgynous being, not unlike Siamese twins who are later separated,[22] and Dinah, sister of Jacob's twelve sons, was changed *in utero* from a male to a female on account of her mother Leah's prayer;[23] and to the Talmudic story of the sage Rava creating a *golem*, a new kind of being—though this comparison implies a criticism.[24] In a similar, albeit harsher, vein, Amsel (1972) was convinced that "if we knew all the details of the abominations of Egypt and Canaan, there is no doubt ... that this monstrosity [i.e., transsexuality] was one of their lewd ways."[25]

With this not uncommon hermeneutic, the bodies of transsexuals merge in the rabbinic imagination with bodies imagined by ancient Jewish lore. For most authors, these legendary precursors to transsexuality do not function formally in legal argumentation but rather lend an air of competency to the rabbis' handling of a seeming medical innovation. Avraham Hirsch, an Orthodox rabbi associated for many decades with World Agudath Israel, also reinforces rabbinic competency in citing the *Kuzari* (4:25) on the similar structure of male and female sexual organs[26] and, in referring along with other commentators, to the early modern responsa of Ḥayim Pelaggi and Ḥayim Miranda on persons with intersex conditions.[27] Although thus demonstrating their virtuosity with rabbinic literature, the Orthodox rabbis who discussed SCS in the 1970s listed these analogous cases and principles haphazardly. A more nuanced use of these variegated cases would have to wait a few more decades.

Dor Tahepukhot

To this day, Orthodox rabbinic authorities oppose efforts by transsexual persons to change their sex organs or secondary sexual characteristics, whether through surgery or through hormonal treatment. No Orthodox authority accepts sexual transition as the proper management of gender dysphoria. SCS is said to violate biblical law, the strictest category of prohibition—especially the rule against castration, but also the prohibitions on cross-dressing and changing the natural order. Over time, rabbinic authors have invoked additional Jewish legal principles that they believe would prohibit SCS, but the conclusion has remained constant. In 2002, for instance, Israeli Orthodox medical ethicist Yigal Shafran emphasized that the surgery is not only forbidden and ugly, but also a "severe abomination."[28]

Now let us consider Ben-Ephraim's *Dor Tahepukhot*, the most creative and comprehensive work in the 50-year history of Jewish law on SCS. In its 307 pages, *Dor Tahepukhot* covers an unexpectedly wide spectrum of SCS topics, including surgeries, the rabbinic approach to scientific "novelties," the prohibition on SCS, dozens of laws that might govern postoperative transsexuals, secular laws, relationships with non-Jews, homosexuality, the status of *androginos* (a person with an intersex condition), genetic engineering, the maternity of cloned persons, women in religious rituals, the marriage of two transsexuals, and debates about rabbinic sources.[29] Ben-Ephraim also describes how he came to investigate the topic, when he befriended a newly observant friend (a *ba'al teshuvah*) who had a transsexual (FTM) sister. Through his monograph, Ben-Ephraim undertakes to identify and analyze each Jewish law that might prohibit SCS. Although it is a theoretical work rather than an authoritative rabbinic ruling, it may set the intellectual and rhetorical stage for future directions in *halakhic* discourse.

At first glance, *Dor Tahepukhot* comes across as a no-holds-barred attack on transsexuality, as Ben-Ephraim examines a dozen distinct prohibitions against SCS. None the less, it might strike an observer that the more his list of violations expands, the less definitive it appears. After all, if SCS were irrefutably outlawed by any single biblical rule, why would *halakhic* texts need to creatively propose more laws that might prohibit it? Perhaps the cumulative recitation of violations is expected to resonate with some readers, but those attentive to legal argumentation may be left unpersuaded.

In reviewing the intricacies of each apparent prohibition, moreover, Ben-Ephraim manages to dig up or hint at leniencies—at reasons why the prohibition might not apply to some or all types of SCS. For instance, the biblical castration rule applies most clearly to the *surgeon*—not to the patient, though the latter might be liable for the previous arrangements that put the surgery in place. Transsexual patients could still be forbidden to abet the surgeon's sin, but their own sin might be limited, insofar as they are anesthetized at the time of the prohibited action (p. 57).[30] Ben-Ephraim further asks if the injunction against the surgeon might be malleable if a *non-Jewish* surgeon is involved.

Furthermore, Ben-Ephraim shows that the strongest legal rationale for a clear-cut ban on SCS, the biblical prohibition of castration, applies differently to women, who are not punished for what the rabbis consider the female equivalent of castration—a nuance that had already drawn attention.[31] Although it might seem to derive solely from longstanding Jewish law, this asymmetry in the rabbinic treatment of FTM transsexuality echoes the asymmetry, in the general population, between the transition experiences of birth males as opposed to females. Birth females (FTMs) are more inclined toward nonsurgical options, adjust more smoothly to transition regardless of surgery, and are less likely, medically, socially, and psychologically, to be perceived as needing surgery.[32] Jewish law applies a severe injunction against MTF surgery, in effect matching the greater demand by MTF transsexuals, while adopting a far more lenient approach to FTM persons, seemingly in line with their lesser need or demand for genital surgery.

Ben-Ephraim uncovers additional leniencies. For instance, SCS is often said to be prohibited on account of the biblical ban on wearing garments of the opposite sex. Ben-Ephraim shows how this ban's application to SCS could be disputed. After all, the surgery itself does not involve any items to be worn,[33] and if SCS reassigns a person's sex, then the rule would be moot.[34] Likewise, he questions whether SCS would contravene the *halakhic* prohibition against changing the created order. He points out that the rule might apply only to changes brought about by sorcery (*kishuf*), and he doubts that the divine fiat (*hok*) against mixed species can be adapted to cover SCS merely by speculative reasoning. By the same token, *Dor Tahepukhot* seems to undermine efforts to prohibit SCS as profaning God's name (so does soccer, notes Ben-Ephraim—p. 58) and as transgressing the biblical laws regarding damaged male genitalia (*patzua 'daka'* and *kerut shofkhah*), which would regulate only postoperative relations and would not apply to FTM transsexuals (p. 671).

The book also touches on the prohibition against causing grief to one's parents and family, derived by rabbinic authorities from the obligation to honor one's parents and from other biblical laws (e.g., *Deut.* 27.16). Ben-Ephraim asserts that SCS causes grief and shame, even if the parents are not observant Jews. But he offers no evidence for this assertion, an omission that may implicitly index a leniency. Indeed, anticipating that some parents would accept their transsexual child, Ben-Ephraim asserts that such acceptance is irrelevant because the parents' shame is built into the situation. By making such flat and unsupported assertions, his relatively weak argument here opens the door to opposing arguments for leniency (e.g., that the Jewish law against causing parental grief might not apply under various contingencies).

To be sure, Ben-Ephraim presents several undiluted or unqualified prohibitions against SCS. In one short section, for instance, he argues that the surgery would violate the Jewish law against self-wounding. He states: "Though there is no concern about the prohibition against self-wounding whenever there is medical need . . . however, in our case [of SCS], since there is no medical need whatsoever," the prohibition applies (p. 55).[35] Still, one wonders whether his brief treatment of self-wounding might be read as implicitly pointing to the opportunity for an exemption based on "medical need"—as has been claimed.[36] A second clear violation, according to *Dor Tahepukhot*, is that of nullifying the ability to procreate. Ben-Ephraim's analysis does not seem to leave much room to maneuver in this regard, save an exception for a person who has already fulfilled the commandment of procreation before undergoing SCS (p. 63). A third, related violation noted by Ben-Ephraim is that SCS might be considered to void the fulfillment of the procreation commandment by the transsexual's *father*. In explaining the problem, however, Ben-Ephraim of course points out that the father could fulfill this commandment through his other children.

Thus, if the basic thrust of Ben-Ephraim's book, and its upfront summary, affirm the prohibition of SCS, upon close examination the book in subtle ways undermines its own apparent condemnation. Perhaps this is an unavoidable outcome, to be expected of any in-depth mono-graph on a matter of rabbinic law, because the deep structure of Talmudic reasoning is multivocal and pluralistic. Still, it means that in-depth "insider" knowledge shaves away at the unwavering public face of prohibition. If Ben-Ephraim is partly subverting the law against SCS, he does so by chipping away at the multiplicity of reasons posed in its support—a death by a thousand paper cuts. These leniencies are not the kind of sweeping exemption invoked by rabbinic authorities to permit outright other, even related, surgeries. Notably, rabbis have authorized cosmetic surgery for a patient's greater good, or the removal of repro-ductive organs (hysterectomy or orchiectomy) in cases of uterine or testicular cancer.[37]

This is not to say that Ben-Ephraim is unaware of the potential relevance of a *piku'akh nefesh* ("saving a life") exemption for SCS. Without any trace of irony, he applies that very principle in one instance: penitent transsexual persons are allowed to *surgically reverse* their previous sex change (p. 126). Such surgery on the genitalia might be considered forbidden as an unnecessary medical risk, yet it could be justified, Ben-Ephraim argues, if a psychiatrist verified that its denial would cause so much mental anguish as to constitute a danger. He goes on to adduce a series of *halakhic* rulings to justify reversal in cases of mental anguish.[38]

For the reader who favors SCS, this section of *Dor Tahepukhot* seems counterintuitive, because, for the sake of lending rabbinic support to the possibility of reversal, a relatively rare event, Ben-Ephraim offers precisely those rulings that could be cited to justify SCS in the first place, as medically necessary to alleviate the mental anguish produced by gender dysphoria. Such reasoning also could conceivably be applied, retrospectively, to mitigate the illegality of SCS. One Orthodox transsex-ual told me that a prominent Orthodox rabbi had indicated privately that

SCS can be understood as a kind of desperate act, committed under the duress (*'ones*) of emotional suffering.[39] This understanding of duress could be invoked to absolve the postoperative Jew of guilt for transgressing the rules against surgery. However, mental anguish would not suffice to condone or permit SCS from the start. Nor would such an interpretation of duress go uncontested, if it were to be published.[40]

Rabbinic debate on postoperative sex assignments

Does SCS effectively reassign sex under Jewish law?

Once rabbinic thinkers faced the issue of SCS, an early and central question was whether the surgery would actually *reassign* patients' *halakhic* sex, i.e., their sex identity for the purpose of Jewish law. Two contrary legal views soon emerged in this regard. One view accepts that the surgery *does* reassign *halakhic* sex, because the latter depends on outward appearances, especially external genitalia, i.e., on *phenotype*.[41] The second view does not concede, retrospectively, that a man can become a woman, or vice versa, because it sees *halakhic* sex as depending, in effect, on one's underlying genetic situation, i.e., on *genotype*. As we shall see, Ben-Ephraim supports a hybrid of these dichotomous approaches to *halakhic* sex assignment.

A key figure in the *halakhic* dispute over sex reassignment was R. Eliezer Waldenberg, a prominent Jewish medical ethicist in Israel. Over the course of a few years, Waldenberg wrote responsa on both SCS and pediatric intersex surgery, in both cases relying on the phenotypic argument. In a 1967 responsum, Waldenberg opined that SCS would alter a person's *halakhic* sex and marital situation. As precedents, he invoked two premodern responsa annulling the marriages of women who reportedly had been changed into men by natural causes.[42] Similarly, reasoned Waldenberg, as two persons of the same sex cannot be married to each other under Jewish law, SCS would automatically dissolve a transsexual's marriage, without the need for a *get*, a traditional Jewish divorce document.[43] In 1970, Waldenberg stated the phenotype rule explicitly in a responsum on a neonatal intersex case: "it is clear that only the external organs, which are different in males and females, determine [a person's assigned] sex in practice."[44] Several other rabbis have favored Waldenberg's (1970) position of assigning *halakhic* sex according to phenotype.[45]

By contrast, a number of prominent Orthodox rabbis have ruled that, when physical sex is ambiguous or disputed, *halakhic* sex should be based on genotype. In other words, bodies with XY chromosomes are male, and those with XX are female. The genotype view (or its equivalent) has been dominant in Orthodox Jewish legal discourse; prominent supporters include leading Israeli medical ethicist Avraham Sofer Abraham and the late preeminent American *halakhic* authority Moshe Feinstein (2012).[46] From the genotype standpoint, surgery cannot change a person's sex for the purposes of Jewish law. Orthodox rabbis who favor genotype avoid the appearance of encouraging or validating SCS retrospectively. The Catholic Church has similarly rejected the surgical reassignment of sex, as have several US states.[47]

As could be expected, the two competing approaches to *halakhic* sex assignment (phenotype vs. genotype) are not based on the voluntary *choice* or self-identification of transsexual patients and their physicians. In contemporary secular biomedical law and ethics, patient choice is often the decisive factor. However, rabbinic medical ethics typically subordinates patient choice to such principles as the preservation of human life, the minimization of pain and suffering, beneficence and nonmaleficence, human dignity, the fulfillment of biblical command-ments, respect for rabbinic teachings, and so on. As a result, as a pivotal Jewish law question sex assignment is unlikely to hinge on patient choice. Understandably, Orthodox Jewish transsexuals oppose the assignment of a person's sex by genotype. Many postoperative transsex-uals favor deciding sex by external appearance, because this approach recognizes the sex reassignment sought by surgery.[48]

Two more recent developments favor the genotype view among Orthodox *halakhic* experts. First, Waldenberg's support for phenotypic sex assignment has been called into question, especially after a 1997 opinion in which he apparently treated a specific transsexual as an *androginos*.[49] Several rabbis have argued that the external appearances rule formulated by Waldenberg, who died in 2006, has been miscon-strued, and that it should not apply to SCS, because the bodies of transsexuals have reconstructed genitalia, not their original, *functioning* genitalia.[50] Second, in a responsum relying largely on Waldenberg's approach based on external appearance, the Committee on Law and Standards of the Conservative Movement's Rabbinical Assembly has approved phenotypic reassignment of sex after SCS.[51] As Orthodox authorities tend to distance themselves from the views of the more modernist conservative movement, the latter's endorsement of Waldenberg could further undermine support for phenotypic sex assignment within Orthodox *halakhic* views.

If followed rigorously, the immutability of genotypic sex would certainly deter SCS and transsexuality. However, genotypic assignment of *halakhic* sex also has its drawbacks. It can hardly describe historical understandings of *halakhic* sex in the era before chromosomal testing. It also does not suitably assign (*halakhic*) sex for certain intersex conditions.[52] Moreover, some Orthodox rabbis have started to rethink a flat genotypic formula for sex assignment with regard to persons with intersex conditions. For example, Asher Weiss states that phenotype is primary, though he partly accommodates the use of genetic testing.[53]

Citing legal precedents, Ben-Ephraim rejects the majority view that *halakhic* sex should be determined by genotype; like Waldenberg, he accepts that sex should be determined by a person's outward appearance, i.e., their genitalia. But, unlike Waldenberg in his 1967 statement, Ben-Ephraim rejects the notion that surgical reshaping of genitalia would matter. In contrast to the two leading views, Ben-Ephraim argues that only a person's *birth phenotype* matters. He thereby differentiates a person's original genitalia from their surgical reconstruction. (He also claims that each person's *halakhic* sex is an attribute of the soul at birth; see below.) Hence, though Ben-Ephraim does not say this outright, his birth phenotype view is functionally equivalent to a genotypic assignment for transsexuals.[54] Before explaining why Ben-Ephraim advocates this hybrid birth phenotype approach, it is instructive to see how he would adjust the rabbinic regulatory regime for people whose *halakhic* sex does not match their postoperative presentation.

Regulation: how should Jewish law treat postoperative transsexuals in practice?

Whichever way transsexuals are assigned a sex for *halakhic* purposes, they can bring complex challenges into any Orthodox Jewish community in which they hope to participate. Women and men are distinguished throughout Jewish marriage and family law, of course, but also in numerous other areas of Orthodox Jewish life. Orthodox social space is choreographed by informal rules and by Jewish law governing physical contact, ritual segregation, the seclusion of individuals of opposite sexes together in closed spaces, text study, and the interaction between the sexes. In religious practices, men's obligations and ritual roles differ markedly from women's. Adherents of Jewish praxis are expected to act in line with their assigned sex and, accordingly, face strong incentives to resolve any uncertainties. In short, any Jew who does not conform to conventional sexual dimorphism will have a hard time fitting into Orthodox social spaces and religious practices.

Gradually, however, some Orthodox clergy and communities are encountering postoperative transsexuals who seek tolerance and inclusion. Accordingly, rabbinic scholars are endeavoring to figure out the repercussions of SCS for the religious observances of the individuals involved, as well as their families and communities. In view of the fundamental dispute over the sex assignment of transsexuals, postoperative transsexuals could face at least three regulatory schemes, depending on whether their community's approach favors the assignment of sex by genotype, by phenotype, or perhaps by a hybrid view of the type suggested by Ben-Ephraim.

In communities where the view that assignment of *halakhic* sex is determined by genotype prevails, it is fair to assume that an MTF transsexual who appeared as female would not be allowed to function as a woman, and if they dressed in clothes typically worn by women, which would be understood as cross-dressing in violation of Jewish law, they would likely be excluded from men's roles as well. A community could still welcome violators of the cross-dressing law, but they might be excluded from most ritual and other religious activities. This is the majority view.

Alternatively, if the community accepts the assignation of sexual identity by phenotype (genitalia), transsexuals might be permitted to participate in line with their reassigned sexual identity. With phenotypic sex assignment, the postoperative transsexual has both a new *halakhic* sex and, in effect, the status of a new legal person—a status that may be unsettling, or worse.[55] Not only would a marriage be annulled, according to Waldenberg, after one partner undergoes SCS, but, as Michael Broyde (1988) pointed out, this could imply that the transsexual loses their parental rights and duties, too.[56] Still, as the assigned sex would match the person's desired appearance, the phenotype approach offers transsexuals the least complicated entrée into communal Orthodox life. By recognizing the reassigned sex, an Orthodox community could allow the transsexual to participate in nearly all ritual practices and social interactions. For better or worse, Jewish transsexuals confirm that the genotype vs. phenotype divide has resulted in polarized communal reactions to their presence. Several MTF transwomen told me about rabbis who would accept them in their synagogues only if they appeared as men.[57] Michelle spoke of feeling extremely humiliated by one Orthodox rabbi who addressed her in the synagogue, publicly, as a male. By contrast, another rabbi invited her home for Sabbath dinner and sat her among his daughters and other women in segregated seating. Similarly, Naomi told me that one rabbi called her crazy and insisted that she dress as a man if she wished to go to his synagogue. But another Orthodox rabbi told her that he is "LGBT positive." (I am not aware of any transsexual persons who participate in Jewish life by appearing as their genotypic or birth sex rather than their transitioned identity.)

Even in Jewish communities where rabbis technically recognize a reassigned sex, transsexuals may not feel welcome, because they are subjected to ostracism or prejudice outside the purview of Jewish law. Two transsexuals told me about receiving rabbinic advice to live their lives as new persons, presumably in line with their phenotypic sex, and one was advised to relocate to a new Orthodox community and keep their past as the other sex secret.[58] Nevertheless, in the sex-divided world of Jewish Orthodoxy, if genotype implies rejection, phenotype implies acceptance.

Ben-Ephraim, however, shows that Jewish law need not be collapsed into a binary choice between rejection and acceptance. As he would assign *halakhic* sex by birth phenotype, we might expect that he would have communities exclude transsexuals who present as their surgically reconstructed sex. Instead, Ben-Ephraim advances a key regulatory principle for absorbing transsexuals into Jewish life: while they retain their preoperative *halakhic* sexual identity, they may, in effect, be treated consistently with their postoperative, transitioned appearance for the purpose of Jewish laws governing the public sphere and social relations.[59] This socializing principle modulates the rejectionist impulse of genotypic and birth phenotypic sex assignment.[60]

With this discretionary principle in hand, Ben-Ephraim makes a herculean effort to figure out when and how the conventional sex roles can be waived for the transsexual. He reevaluates about two dozen areas of Jewish law where a transsexual's sex assignment would matter. The list of Jewish legal topics is itself revealing, as seen in the topics covered by Ben Ephraim's book, *Dor Tahepuchot* (2004). Although questions about marriage, divorce, and sexual relations have received the most sustained attention, Ben-Ephraim's list shows the extent to which religious law might claim to regulate the bodies of transsexuals, with respect to their physical contact with other bodies, the company they keep, their voices and clothing, private ritual non-performance (blessings, circumcision, and numerous other *mitzvot*), participation in public ritual (prayer leading, Torah reading, synagogue seating, mourner's kaddish), their legal and economic rights and roles (inheritance, witnessing), and even disposal of their earthly remains.

Rabbinic discourse is gradually making special accommodations for transsexuals, as either imagined or genuine participants in Orthodox life. Ben-Ephraim explores creatively—and unflinchingly—how *halakhic* regulations for transsexuality may be refined and justified.[61] For example, to avoid impropriety, the seclusion of unmarried individuals of opposite sexes is forbidden. However, Ben-Ephraim states that an MTF transwoman may be secluded with a woman but not with a man, even though the MTF is a genotypic and hence a *halakhic* male. Ben-Ephraim's social interactions principle can have curious results. For instance, although women in Orthodoxy generally are not given the honor of an *'aliyah* during public reading of the Torah, Ben-Ephraim states that FTM persons may be given this honor, despite their *halakhic* status as females, because they pass as men publicly.[62]

This innovative regulatory scheme is rooted, I believe, in Ben-Ephraim's commitment to birth phenotype as a new *halakhic* sexual identity marker. How does he justify this approach to sexual identity in *halakhic* and Jewish terms?

The souls of transsexuals

To better understand Ben-Ephraim's hybrid approach to transsexual identity, let us delve into the heart of *Dor Tahepukhot*. As I hinted above, even as Ben-Ephraim details the *halakhic* prohibitions against SCS, in subtle and perhaps unintended ways he shows that most prohibitions might be unraveled. In other words, the book states that SCS is completely sinful from the start, and yet, in the fine print, Ben-Ephraim finds ways to qualify, limit, or undermine the rabbinic law on transsexuals.

In one remarkable section (pp. 69–82), Ben-Ephraim seeks to settle the question of *halakhic* sex by examining the human soul from a kabbalistic perspective.[63] Questions about the soul have been raised by Catholic ethicist Bernard Guevin, too, on the basis of the belief of many transsexuals that they have the soul of a female in a male body, or vice versa. Guevin argues against the notion of a sexed soul.[64] However, Ben-Ephraim treats the soul as sexually identified from the time of its creation and as the basis for determining *halakhic* sex.[65]

Ben-Ephraim begins with the kabbalistic view that the body is merely the garment of the soul. Moreover, it is the Jewish soul that is instructed to observe the commandments (p. 72). Non-Jews, he asserts, do not have a *neshamah*—the highest level of soul—but rather a *nefesh ḥayah* (roughly: a life force); hence God sends each convert a *neshamah* upon conversion (p. 73). There is a strong kabbalistic tie between the character of the soul and the degree of one's obligation for commandments (*mitzvot*). As women are not obligated to fulfill as many commandments as men, it can be inferred that women have different souls (p. 74). Moreover, Ben-Ephraim adduces kabbalistic sources to show that no bodily changes can disrupt the commandments laid upon a soul (p. 75). He states an interim conclusion: "It is clear that humans do not change sex through surgical means, and surgery does not raise or lower one's obligation to Torah commandments, because the essence of the obligation of commandments is derived from the unchanging human soul" (p. 76). In other words, he posits that Jewish law governs only the soul, which is untouched by surgery.

Delving further into the Jewish mysteries of the soul, however, Ben-Ephraim finds an apparently conflicting kabbalistic view. What if a soul does not match its body's sex? Ben-Ephraim points to a series of rabbinic texts indicating that a man might occasionally be given a feminine soul and consequently would act like a woman. Nevertheless, he would still be fully obligated as a man, due to his unaltered male body. *Dor Tahepukhot* (pp. 76f.) analyzes a series of rabbinic references to a soul's sex changes or sex reversal, based mainly on kabbalistic interpretations of biblical and Talmudic texts.[66] He also brings the case of the masculine soul of the wife of Ḥayim Vital, a founder of Lurianic kabbalah. These cases would seem to disprove his previous hypothesis that Jewish law governs only the soul:

> Certainly, in such a case, we do not say that this man is obligated for commandments like women, since his soul is the soul of a woman, but rather he is [still] obligated for commandments like a man, in every matter.
>
> (p. 77)

Regardless of the femininity of his soul, a man's obligations are those of a man. Consequently, Ben-Ephraim shifts directions:

> It is clear from this discussion that the obligatoriness of commandments depends not on the soul but on the body. We should not gauge the behavior and activities of a person in order to declare that he has a feminine soul (as is done [in non-Jewish discourse] with men who have sex-change surgeries). .... Apparently, the [situation] is not like what I wrote at the beginning [of this section], that the principle [of obligation] follows the person's soul.
>
> (p. 81)

With this rhetorical about-face, which the text does not foreshadow in its preceding emphasis on the soul, Ben-Ephraim shifts to the body as the locus of Jewish norms.

At this juncture, *Dor Tahepukhot* brings rabbinic texts to show how the commandments may be grounded in the body, not the soul. Ben-Ephraim tries to reconcile the competing kabbalistic views. He is persuaded that, although it was the soul that received the fundamental order to obey the commandments, it is the ensouled *body* (male or female) that serves to determine the concrete, sex-differentiated law for each person.[67] Thus, he concludes, because the body's original sex is unchanged, SCS cannot alter *halakhic* obligations and sexual identity (p. 81). Yet *Dor Tahepukhot* seems tentative about this chain of inferences, because the author declares that truth is elusive: more needs to be revealed; man is unable to discern God's secrets; even the masters of kabbalah felt they had not totally grasped the truth; and so on.[68]

Ben-Ephraim then tackles evidence about bodily changes that could trip up the last step in his argument. Assuming now that *halakhic* duties are bound up with the body, Ben-Ephraim turns to analyzing a hodgepodge of body transformations in rabbinic literature, including (pp. 82–85):

- Pelaggi's responsum about a married woman who changed into a man;
- the "natural transformations" of one species into another, such as hyenas turning into bats after seven years, per BT *Bava kama* 16a;
- the monthly change in sex of an *androginos*;
- lycanthropy and other transformations of humans into animals, including cat, donkey and monkey, caused by divine intervention or sorcery;
- the aforementioned sex reassignment *in utero* of the biblical character of Dinah;
- the transformation of Nebuchadnezzar into a beast and back again, based on Dan. 4:29f, and instances of people who were changed by living among or being raised by monkeys or wolves.

Although these cases may appear legendary, they serve Ben-Ephraim as precedents, because in some of them the applicable Jewish law could be said to have shifted with the bodily transformations.

As rabbinic texts could thus be shown to recognize that *halakhic* sex can vary with transformations in the body, one might suppose that Jewish law could likewise shift with the body as transformed by SCS. However, Ben-Ephraim argues that there is a difference between "natural" or "divine" transformations and those wrought surgically. He asserts that, as the above sex or species transitions were natural and divinely ordained, they do not disprove his claim that artificial, unnatural surgery cannot truly alter a person's *halakhic* sex. In the end, he concludes that "the human soul and the original form of its creation" determine Jewish law's obligations and its concomitant assignment of sex (pp. 34, 69, 115).

Although such kabbalistic beliefs rarely enter into a *halakhic* analysis of SCS, Ben-Ephraim's ideas can be taken further. In an unpublished manuscript, another Israeli Orthodox rabbi, Dror Brama, has raised the possibility that a transsexual might be correct in claiming to be placed in the wrong body. Brama, who has worked in London for Torah MiTzion, a religious Zionist institution, and is affiliated with the religious Zionist rabbinic organization Tzohar, compares transsexuality with a form of prophecy, in that a prophetic role may be attributed to people who correctly figure out that their bodies do not match their souls. He does not point to any concrete implications for rabbinic law.[69]

In emphasizing the disjuncture between the transsexual person's soul and body, Ben-Ephraim's and Brama's texts resonate with the "wrong body" motif so common in secular discourse by and about transsexuals. In secular settings, it has been typical for a preoperative transsexual to aver that he or she is a woman or man, or a woman's or man's soul, trapped in a body of the opposite sex.[70] This motif became widely known through the story of Christine Jorgensen, the first famous transsexual in the United States. In medical discourse, the "wrong body" construct was highlighted in 1966 by Harry Benjamin, a pioneer in the diagnosis of transsexuality:

> [The fully developed transsexual] lives only for the day when his "female soul" is no longer being outraged by his male body, when he can function as a female—socially, legally, and sexually.[71]

In self-disclosures that helped justify their diagnosis and subsequent surgery, transsexuals have frequently voiced this notion of a gendered soul in the wrong body, and Ben-Ephraim adduces it, too (p. 23).[72] Though he does not say so overtly, readers may infer that his in-depth analysis of the kabbalah's concept of a gendered soul is unexpectedly responsive to popular and diagnostic conceptions of transsexuality as a condition of a gendered soul in the wrong body.

Sympathy for the different? *Halakhic* innovations in transition

Not surprisingly, both the phenotype and the genotype approaches to *halakhic* sex are developing some mechanisms, albeit limited, to absorb transsexuals into Orthodox Jewish life. Taking either approach, it is feasible under Jewish law to allow transsexual persons to participate in Jewish prayer and ritual activities in their chosen sexual identity. Yet, even when their participation is considered technically allowed by Jewish law, social ostracism can make it unworkable. In practice, Jewish transsexuals report that they are welcomed with their reassigned sex in some Orthodox synagogues but not in others. It is unclear whether the practical rule making for transsexuals, and their occasional integration into Orthodox life, may help alter anti-transsexual rhetoric. In any case, the public now has access to a slow trickle of Orthodox rabbinic viewpoints about transsexuals and their real-life situations.[73]

In a concrete route toward leniency, Orthodox Jewish legal discourse has increasingly spoken of transsexuality as a pathology, a form of rabbinically defined mental illness.[74] The medicalization of transsexuality puts seemingly insular Orthodox writings in conversation with non-Jewish discourses, such as those of secular psychology and Catholic bioethics.[75] In a 2008 statement, Brama, who strikes me as one of the more sympathetic Orthodox commentators on SCS, discussed the psychological challenges for preoperative transsexuals. He has written the only Orthodox responsum in my dataset to refer specifically to a psychiatric diagnosis such as gender dysphoria.[76] Brama frames this diagnosis in the pre-modern rabbinic vocabulary for psychological conditions, arguing that the desire to change one's sex fits the rabbinic category of a person who, though otherwise functional and healthy, is obsessively disturbed about a single matter (*shoteh ledavar ehad*). He appreciates ("I write in sorrow") that transsexuals may feel hurt by this rabbinic mental health designation, regardless of the diagnosis they may have received from their doctors. In addition, Brama takes a fascinating stance toward the biological underpinnings of transsexuality. He anticipates that it may well be found to be a biophysical problem rather than a (merely) psychological one, and that it may be treatable by way of medication. In debates over homosexuality, such biological determinism has muted moral criticisms predicated on viewing homosexuality as a preference rather than as a neurophysical condition.

Brama's categorization of transsexuality within Jewish law as a psychological disorder has implications that may be meaningful and beneficial to Orthodox transsexuals. He emphasizes that the obsessive status might exempt transsexuals from sex-differentiated commandments relating to their psychological condition,[77] such as donning *tefillin* (phylacteries) for a *halakhic* male, and might open up options for them to participate freely in various sex-segregated practices.[78] He insists, moreover, that transsexuals should be treated like anyone with an illness, i.e., with kindness.[79] It seems that a route to compassion, if not to acceptance, is through pathologizing transsexuality.

It is instructive in this regard to compare Brama's views with those taken by *halakhic* experts within the conservative movement. Not surprisingly, conservative Judaism has also moved toward a less restrictive stance toward transsexuals, and its scholars, too, have done so by defining their status as pathological. In the 2003 responsum endorsed by the Committee on Law and Standards of the Rabbinical Assembly, Mayer Rabinowitz defined transsexuality as gender dysphoria, a psychiatric diagnosis described in the *Diagnostic and Statistical Manual of Mental Disorders* (DSM). In an appendix, Rabinowitz argued that there may be grounds under Jewish law to allow SCS from the start, on the basis of the principle of beneficence—of permitting an intervention "for the good of the ill person" (*letovat haholeh*). This dispensation would apply on the basis of the assumption, or even stipulation, that the transsexual suffers from a dysphoria that SCS would treat. In a cautionary tone, Rabinowitz's responsum concludes that the "long-term effectiveness" of SCS has not yet adequately been studied, and preoperative transsexuals should be counseled to take this lack of sufficient evidence into account.[80]

Another conservative scholar advocates a further step in accepting transsexuals by virtue of their medical condition. Leonard A. Sharzer has proposed that transsexuals be assigned *halakhic* sex based not merely on postoperative genitalia, as the Rabinowitz responsum had stipulated. Instead, Sharzer would assign *halakhic* sex purely on the basis of the diagnosis of a psychological condition, gender dysphoria, without requiring SCS.[81] Sharzer's as-yet-unpublished proposal has had little effect on rabbinic discourse on SCS, but it merges conceptually with Ben-Ephraim's approach to transsexuality in *halakhah*. In both views, sex assignment and transitioning should be evaluated by attention to the psyche or soul.

Conclusion

Over the past 40 years, Orthodox Jewish legal discourse has not been static in responding to SCS. Early commentators expressed the most shock at SCS, disparaged transsexuality harshly, and denied its relevance to observant Jews. However, although deprecating sentiments continue to be expressed, rabbinic writings have emerged that approach SCS with more equanimity and take for granted the need to offer guidance.

SCS is increasingly analyzed in practical terms. There has been detailed *halakhic* analysis of how to regulate the religious observance and social conduct of transsexuals. Over the years, some Orthodox authors have found ways to express sympathy for them. Exposure to other religious and secular medical discourses has led some rabbis and *halakhic* experts to begin treating transsexuality less as a "deviant" lifestyle choice and more as a severe psychological disorder. This shift is opening up interpretive space for further sympathetic responses. In effect, the rabbinic élite within traditionalist Judaism has begun showing its dexterity at conceptualizing the regulatory regime for postoperative transsexual bodies.

To date, the prohibition against SCS remains intact within Orthodox Jewish circles. This bright-line prohibition of SCS is backed up by authoritative precedents, justified by multiple *halakhic* rules and reinforced by a cross-cultural discourse linking transsexuality to the thorny issue of homosexuality. Most Orthodox rabbis are unlikely to jeopardize their reputation for strict opposition to the latter by showing any leniency toward the former. Nevertheless, a groundwork for change is being laid by recent rabbinic writings, such as Ben-Ephraim's exploration of potential leniencies, Brama's attention to transsexuality as a psychological dysphoria, and a few non-Orthodox arguments for permitting SCS from the start. Orthodox transsexuals are aware that SCS might be condoned retrospectively as an inexorable compulsion, even if it is never officially condoned from the start.[82] To be sure, these incremental moves at the margins of Orthodox *halakhic* discourse have so far had a minimal impact on the prevailing authorities in North America and Israel.

Although Orthodox Jewish discourse rarely acknowledges any explicit influence from non-Jewish moral discourses, the deliberations over SCS can readily be seen as alluding to outside concerns and responding to non-Jewish norms. Notably, as described above, Jewish law has begun to engage with the pathologizing of transsexuality as a psychological condition. To be sure, from the perspective of transgender persons and their allies, a medicalizing Orthodox rabbinic discourse is trailing recent efforts to depathologize SCS and transsexuality in mainstream society. Yet, within the current context of Orthodox Jewish law, pathologizing is innovative, especially as it appears to echo non-Jewish moral concerns. Other dialogical Jewish interactions with outside views may be inferred from rabbinic conversations about "passing" by transsexuals, from the "the wrong body" discourse that has permeated Orthodox texts, and, arguably, from the asymmetry in Jewish handling of MTF versus FTM transitions. Although it is premature to predict the impact of opinions like those of Ben-Ephraim and Brama, these developments suggest that Orthodox *halakhic* thinking on SCS is gradually transitioning in its responsiveness to the broader social dynamics around transsexuality.

Acknowledgments

I appreciate the suggestions of a variety of readers, including Michael Broyde, Mara Cohen, Diane Klein, Winnifred Fallers Sullivan, Shmuel Weinberger, Louise Kertesz, and Nashim's two anonymous peer reviewers, as well as the participants in a panel of the American Academy of Religion, Atlanta, 2010.

Notes

1 Sources include 2015–2016 talks by modern Orthodox rabbis Efrem Goldberg, Tzvi Sinensky, and Michael Taubes.
2 For example, there are online responsa on the topic by Israeli rabbis Baruch Efrati, Hanan Shokron on Kipa.co.il, and Hillel Mayers and Binyamin Shmuli on Hidabroot.org (2015–2017).
3 For instance, trans people are referred to as "transgenders," a deprecated usage. He puts "transition" in scare quotes. He also states that "It is claimed that transgender is not the same homosexuality," as if it were an arguable hypothesis rather than two distinct phenomena. He believes that transgenderism may be a "product of the modern lifestyle, where gender lines tend to get blurred." (7) Compare "Our interest is to find out what Hashem

wants, not to be moved or swayed by every new phenomenon that the winds of change blow our way." (10)

4 Hanau (2017) reports on Rabbi Mike Moskowitz, an unexpected ally who shifted from campus outreach for yeshivish (ultra-Orthodox) Aish HaTorah to trans advocacy for Uri L'Tzedek, a left-leaning Orthodox social justice group. Another trans activist, Abby Stein, is also from right-leaning Orthodoxy; however, she is no longer affiliated with Hasidism or Orthodoxy. (Katz, 2016)

5 For the purposes of this paper, "transsexual/ity" refers to people who seek or have obtained SCS. "Sex-change surgery" refers to various surgeries and related medical treatments that Jewish legal discourse would regard as removing or altering sexual organs in order to change sex for an MTF or FTM transsexual. For better or worse, Jewish sources do not clarify precisely which surgeries are under discussion. This chapter avoids the terms "gender" and "reassignment" in discussing these surgeries, because they are often absent, ill-defined, or contested in the rabbinic discourse under investigation. SCS herein does *not* include medical interventions for persons with intersex conditions (i.e., disorders of sexual development).

6 Suzanne J. Kessler (1985); Judith Butler (1999).

7 For *halakhic* authorities who believe that surgery does not change one's sex, staunch opposition to homosexuality can be taken for granted. In US society, opposition to transsexuality is linked to homophobia; see Gross (2009) and Nagoshi et al. (2008). But see also Talia Mae Bettcher (2007).

8 There are gaps in my effort to gather a complete dataset. This chapter focuses on statements of rabbinic law with regard to SCS, not on actual practices within Orthodox communities.

9 Edan Ben-Ephraim (2004), *Dor Tahepukhot* (Hebrew; Jerusalem: [Ben-Ephraim Family], 2004; henceforth: *Dor Tahepukhot*). The title, drawn from *Deut*. 32:20, could be rendered as the more neutral "Generation of reversals," but "perversions" fits the introduction's tone, which refers to SCS as an abomination and a loathsome affair (*to'evah, shikutz*). As a caveat, it is difficult to place any given rabbinic text within the social, medical, and legal context of SCS, because authors rarely cite non-Jewish sources or reveal their awareness of contemporaneous sources on transsexuality. Moreover, as many writings deal with SCS in the abstract, the published discourse may not reflect rabbinic deliberations on concrete cases. Nothing in this chapter should be construed as providing Jewish law guidance for any personal decisions.

10 Ben-Ephraim has also written two monographs on family purity (2002, 2003).

11 The approbations in the book are signed by Rabbis Shlomo Moshe Amar, formerly the Sefardi Chief Rabbi of Israel, Zalman Nehemiah Goldberg of the Rabbinical High Court, Jerusalem, and the Jerusalem College of Technology, Yosef Lieberman, who held leadership positions in a yeshiva and a

synagogue in Jerusalem, Asher Zelig Weiss, a yeshiva head, communal rabbi and senior judge of rabbinic civil law in Jerusalem, and Yitzḥak Yosef and Ovadiah Yosef.

12 One exception is an unpublished paper by Hillel Lavery-Yisraeli, an Orthodox rabbi working for a non-Orthodox synagogue in Sweden; see below, notes 45 and 65. I first learned of Lavery-Yisraeli's views from an article published in the *YU Observer* (October 2008).

13 Sex-change surgery is described matter of factly by, among others, Sofer (2007); Bleich (1981); Grossnass (1973); Hirsch (undated) "Artificial transformation of male to female and female to male," pp. 152–155; Steinberg (1994). Excerpted English translation in *Mordechai Halperin* (1998), "Transexuality," *Jewish Medical Ethics*, 3/2 (1998), pp. 74–75; and Eliezer Waldenberg, *Tzitz Eli'ezer*, I–XXII, n.d. (see below, notes 35, 40, and 46).

14 Bleich (1981), p. 98.

15 Krausz (1972)."On the new abomination of changing from men to women," compare Yitzḥak Liebes, *Beit Avi*, III, §158:5, as cited in *Dor Tahepukhot*, p. 8.

16 Martha Nussbaum (2010)

17 Teitelbaum (1972). "A question regarding the present-day effrontery of changing from male to female and vice versa."

18 Citing *Sefer Haḥinukh* §244 on Lev. 19:19.

19 Krausz (1972)."New abomination." However, his formulation implies that cosmetic surgery, as a change in creation, might be forbidden as sorcery. Ben-Ephraim, in *Dor Tahepukhot*, pp. 61ff., argues that the mixed seed and sorcery rules ought not to be stretched creatively to cover SCS.

20 Teitelbaum (1972), "A question". Although Teitelbaum opposes SCS for FTM transsexuals, it is noteworthy that much of his analysis focuses on MTF situations.

21 Amsel (1972). Amsel compares the issue of SCS with the future need for rulings on people with *mamzer* status, Siamese twins, faking death with a near-double, and artificial insemination.

22 In this analogy, the androgynous being reflects transsexuality, and the divine separation presages surgery.

23 Amsel (1972), citing Rashi on Gen. 30:21, who refers to BT *Berakhot* 60a; Krausz (1972), citing the Talmudic text directly. The *Hama'or* articles also shed light on the authors' conceptions of sex, nature, and gender.

24 Amsel (1972), citing *Sefer yetzirah* as the means for creating a golem, as stated in BT *Sanhedrin* 65b.

25 Ibid, p. 21.

26 Hirsch, "Artificial transformation" (see above, note 9), p. 153.

27 Ḥayim Miranda (1784), *Yad ne'eman*; Ḥayim Pelaggi (1896). The latter addressed the status of a marriage involving a woman who apparently changed into a man.

28 Yigal Shafran (2002), "*Nituaḥ lehaḥlafat hamin* (Sex-change surgery)."

29 For example, the authorship of the mystical works *Sefer Yetzirah* and *Besamim rosh.*

30 Ben-Ephraim also says the patient would be liable for prior arrangements. He cites Teitelbaum, "A question" (see above, note 20), pp. 10–13.

31 *Shulkhan 'arukh, Even ha'ezer* 5:11. For diverse rabbinic views, see Shaul Weinreb (2000), "Tubal ligation and the prohibition of *Sirus.*" As noted by Ben-Ephraim in *Dor Tahepukhot* (pp. 261ff.), authorities waive the castration prohibition for women on the basis of suffering, substantial need or family harmony, e.g., Moshe Steinberg, "Sex change for an *androginos* [hermaphrodite]," *Assia*, 1/1 (n.d.), pp. 144ff. [Hebrew]. Some rabbis hold that the prohibition of castration applies to women as a rabbinic edict only (and thus is less stringent than a prohibition ascribed directly to the Pentateuch) or even not at all. Ben-Ephraim (p. 44) points out that sterilization of women by means of a potion was permitted (*Shulkhan 'arukh, Even ha'ezer* 5:12), because it was not a tangible action. Weinreb also notes that here is no specific prohibition of passive sterilization. Accordingly, Ben-Ephraim may in effect be opening interpretive room for leniency with preoperative hormonal treatments that aid an FTM transition. See also *Dor Tahepukhot*, p. 67f. Another question is whether the castration law depends on fertility. If so, hormonal treatments that cause infertility arguably may be prohibited only by rabbinic law.

32 Points made by Klein et al. (2009). Kockott and Fahrner (1988), Rachlin (1999), Verschoor and Poortinga (1988); and Weitze and Osburg (1996).

33 *Dor Tahepukhot*, pp. 52f. and 128f.

34 The rule might, however, restrict the preoperative transition known as the "real life experience."

35 Ben-Ephraim (2004) notes that the prohibition is considered rabbinic, not biblical, by some authorities; p. 55.

36 Avraham Steinberg, for instance, refers to self-wounding, while mentioning as well that approval of SCS in Israel depends on a diagnosis of "appropriate psychological problems"; see idem, "*Nituaḥ haḥlafat min*" (see above, note 9). Due to self-endangerment concerns, Ben-Ephraim states that both the patient and the Jewish doctor should refrain from surgery and anesthesia unless it is necessary or urgent. But this assumes that SCS does not qualify as needed treatment; see *Dor Tahepukhot*, pp. 56–57. Ben-Ephraim later shows that the self-endangerment issue is more complex; see his footnote, ibid, p. 124.

37 On hysterectomies see the sources cited in *Dor Tahepukhot*, pp. 261ff.

38 Ben-Ephraim (2004) cites Yekutiel Yehuda Teitelbaum, *Avnei tzedek* (1992); Weiss, *Minḥat Yitzḥak*, I, §115; Feinstein, *Igerot Moshe, Even ha'ezer*, III, §22 (on contraception), IV, §§36 (on *Sirus*—castration or excision of the sexual organs) and 69 (on contraception) and *Oraḥ ḥayim*, II, §85 (on *Sirus* for an institutionalized girl). He also cites, among others, Waldenberg, *Tzitz Eli'ezer*, IV, §13, VIII, §15:12:1 (p. 124); Yitzḥal Yosef, *Yalkut Yosef*, V, p. 98, note 19;

Yitzḥak Tzioni, *'Olat Yitzḥak*, II, §235:3 (p. 391); and Yisroel Dovid Harfenes, *Nishmat shabat*, §5:310 (p. 289). Medical protocols authorize SCS based on the patient's mental health. See Meyer-Bahlburg (2009).

39 Private conversation with "Michelle." This possibility was also expressed by an Orthodox rabbi at Merḥavim: Institute for the Advancement of Shared Citizenship in Israel; see Efrati (2009). For the lenient views of Hillel Lavery-Yisraeli and non-Orthodox rabbis, see note 65 below and the text there.

40 Biblical sexual prohibitions are not incontestably absolved if committed under duress (Michael Broyde, telephone conversation, 2010).

41 In this chapter, phenotype refers to external appearances only, especially the primary sexual characteristics, and genotype to the genetic and chromosomal basis for sex identity.

42 For persons with male chromosomes whose phenotype changes during puberty, see, for example, Cohen-Kettenis (2005). For a popular account, see Jeffrey Eugenides' novel *Middlesex* (2002).

43 *Tzitz Eli'ezer*, X, §25:26:6 (20 Shevat, 5727 [January 30, 1967]). But see below, at note 46, for a different view expressed by R. Waldenberg in (1997).

44 *Tzitz Eli'ezer*, XI, §78 (11 Marcheshvan 5731 [November 10, 1970]). Translation by the author and Joshua Schreier. Compare Mayer Rabinowitz, "Status of transsexuals," Committee on Jewish Law and Standards of the Rabbinical Assembly (December 3, 2003).

45 See Amsel (1972); *Dor Tahepukhot*, pp. 112ff. Ben-Ephraim appends a letter by Asher Weiss and also cites Ḥayim Greiniman, *Sefer ḥidushim ube'urim, Kidushin, Even ha'ezer*, §44:3, p. 104, s.v. *vehineh*; Shaul Breisch, *She'ilat Sha'ul, Even ha'ezer*, §9:1–2; and Yehoshua Neuwirth, oral communication cited in Sofer Abraham, *Nishmat Avraham* (above, note 9), *Yoreh de'ah*, §262:11, p. 326, though Neuwirth objects to Waldenberg's reasoning (*Nishmat Avraham, Even ha'ezer*, §44:2, p. 268).

46 Gray (2012); Sofer Abraham, *Nishmat Avraham* (see above, note 13), *Even ha'ezer* §44:4.3.1; Bleich (1974).

47 Fitzgibbons et al. (2009); Guevin (2005); and Norton (2003).

48 Based on communications with Orthodox Jewish transsexuals, including Beth Orens. For non-Orthodox transsexuals, see Noach Dzmura (2010), *Balancing on the Mechitza: Transgender in Jewish*. However, as Diane Klein pointed out, an FTM transsexual who does not have reconstructive surgery (phalloplasty or metoidioplasty) would not appear to have male genitalia and, presumably, would reject *halakhic* sex assignment by either phenotype or genotype.

49 *Tzitz Eli'ezer*, XXII, §2 (22 Shevat 5757 [January 29, 1997]). Waldenberg's first opinion can be read as a conjecture, not a ruling on an actual case, as noted by Hillel Ḥayim Lavery-Yisraeli, "The transsexual and transgender in Halakhah" (unpublished manuscript). In the 1997 ruling, Waldenberg

reconsiders MTF transsexuality and invokes the laws of *androginos* and *tumtum*, which involve dubious *halakhic* gender. He thus seems to have shifted away from his earlier stance based on phenotype alone. Compare the stance published by the American Reform movement's rabbinic organization: CCAR Responsa (1990).

50 Bleich (1981); Shafran (2002); *Dor Tahepukhot*, p. 113. They suggest that Waldenberg rested on a valid legal principle in assigning sex by external appearance, but that he applied it incorrectly to the reconstructed genitalia of postoperative transsexuals. Alternatively, as suggested by Lavery-Yisraeli ("Transsexual," see above, note 45), Waldenberg doubted that phenotype could serve as a reliable criterion for transsexuals. Still, Lavery-Yisraeli attributes a comparable, phenotypic position to R. Ovadiah Hedaya (*Yaskil 'avdi*, §7:4), who was a leading Sephardi kabbalist and rabbinic judge in Israel (d. 1969).

51 Rabinowitz (2003).

52 A genotypic assignment would be wrong for XY persons who develop primarily female bodies due to conditions such as complete androgen insensitivity syndrome (CAIS). See Ben-Ephraim's analysis in *Dor Tahepukhot*, pp. 112–115, and Gray, "Not judging by appearances" (see above, note 46).

53 Asher Weiss, letter appended in *Dor Tahepukhot*, pp. 280–282.

54 For CAIS and other sex-reversal intersex conditions, the birth phenotype approach enables Jewish law to proceed with sex assignment against genotype, while reinforcing genotypic assignment for transsexuals. *Dor Tahepukhot*, pp. 113–115.

55 In this it resembles the legal status of converts to Judaism.

56 Michael J. Broyde (1988). "The establishment of maternity & paternity in Jewish and American law, Appendix: Sex change operations and their effect on marital status—A brief comparison,"

57 Private communications, October 2010. Michelle and Naomi are pseudonyms.

58 Naomi was given the latter suggestion explicitly. The suggestion to pass as heteronormative may conform with Jewish law and the lived practice of many transsexuals.

59 Ben-Ephraim does not define his approach as a social relations principle as such, except to explain it as designed to prevent transgressions by either the transsexual or others around them; *Dor Tahepukhot*, pp. 34–36. He cites two opposing views, those of Raphael Evers (1994) (*Shut Veshav verafa*) and Shafran (2002), and justifies his view at length (e.g., pp. 136, 140–148), though with limited support (e.g., Amsel (1972). I do not claim that Ben-Ephraim originated this principle.

60 The principle is generally grounded on concerns for sexual and interpersonal impropriety as well as recognition of the social ramifications of "passing" as another gender.

61 One future avenue may be marriage: Michelle reported that an Orthodox rabbi had privately offered to officiate were she to get married. This offer has not been confirmed and otherwise would seem to be prohibited.

62 Compare *Dor Tahepukhot*, p. 163, with Amsel (1972).

63 Kabbalah is a non-legal discourse with mystical elements. Leaving no stone unturned in seeking analogies to SCS, Ben-Ephraim deploys kabbalah and other rabbinic lore (*agadah*), a genre that tends to be downplayed in *halakhic* writings. See Shafran, "Nituaḥ lehaḥlafat hamin" (see above, note 28).

64 Against a view of the soul as form and the body as matter, Guevin (2005) argues that the soul is "a spiritual nature that informs the [gendered] body." As a result, Ben-Ephraim refers not to "natal sex" but rather to "original sex."

65 His examples of such reversals include: anal intercourse by a married couple (BT *Nedarim* 20a); homosexual or other sins (per Ḥayim Vital's *Gate of Reincarnations*); the measure-for-measure principle (per Natan Shapira's *Matzat shimurim*); Yael, the biblical slayer of Sisera (Judges 4–5); Isaac at the time of his sacrificial binding; the wife of Ḥayim Vital, who had a male soul and gave birth only to daughters; and Saul's daughter Michal, who was said to have donned phylacteries (BT *Eruvin* 96a). He also mentions souls who changed their status as priests or as Hebrew slaves. *Dor Tahepukhot*, p. 78.

66 See p. 81, where he is not citing any rabbinic sources.

67 It is not clear why Ben-Ephraim wrote in this way. Perhaps the book served as a way for him to work out his own ruminations about SCS; or, as he indicated in a private communication, perhaps he was merely pursuing a rhetorical argument.

68 Brama (2010)."Analysis of the definition of 'incompetent for one matter' in the case of transsexuality" in "The transsexual and transgender in Halakhah" by H. H. Lavery-Yisraeli [Hebrew, unpublished document]. He views his analysis as purely legal, not sympathetic as such (private communication, October 2010). The more ambitious claim advanced by Lavery-Yisraeli (2008) is that, on the basis of kabbalistic thought, *halakhah* could assign gender identity based on psychological examination and personal self-reflection. His view posits *halakhic* approval for the surgery itself. See also *YU Observer* (above, note 8).

69 On the "wrong body" narrative, see: Darryl Hill (2008), Mason-Schrock (1996), and Sandy Stone (1993). See also King (1984).

70 Benjamin (1966); electronic edition: Düsseldorf: Symposium (1967).

71 The trapped body concept is also mentioned by Dror Brama (2008).

72 In order to participate in Orthodox Jewish life, some transsexuals have received oral or written guidance in private. As far as I know, all transsexuals discussed in public statements have remained anonymous.

73 To be sure, some rabbis have long held a medical view of transsexuality. Bleich (1974); Shafran treats an FTM transsexual as having a psychological illness, as

against the natural, innate desire of women to be mothers and wives. But he also treats it as a decision from within a corrupt, modern society.

74 For example, King (1984); Fitzgibbons et al. (2009).
75 Brama (2010). On the history of the DSM diagnosis, see Meyer-Bahlburg (2009).
76 Brama associates this possible exemption with Ezekiel Landau, *Or hayashar* §30.
77 On the other hand, Brama believes that an obsessive disorder could disqualify a postoperative transsexual from conversion to Judaism.
78 Compare the concern for "compassion, mercy and connection" mentioned in a response by Cherlow (2007).
79 Rabinowitz (2003).
80 Sharzer (2017), argues in an unpublished responsum that transsexuality is similar to a rare intersex condition, because the transsexual is a hybrid with a male body and a female psyche, or vice versa.
81 Arguably, SCS might be excused when done not as a willful sin but under the duress (*'ones*) of a psychological compulsion. Orthodox transsexuals told me that such acceptance has been expressed privately by an influential rabbi, and it is conjectured of Cherlow (2007). From a technical standpoint, an excuse of duress (were it justified) need not be confirmed by a rabbinic opinion, though it may have pastoral value (Broyde, telephone conversation, 2010).
82 Based largely on *Dor Tahepukhot*.

References

American Reform Movement Rabbinic Organization. (1990). Conversion and Marriage after Transsexual Surgery, CCAR Responsa, §8. Available at: www.ccarnet.org/responsa/tfn-no-5750-8-191-196 (accessed June 18, 2015).

Amsel, M. (1972). A male transgressor who was surgically changed into a female, or vice versa—if they wished to revert, what would be the law regarding their social and sexual relations, and all the other commandments, *Hama'or*, 25/2:14–15 [Hebrew].

Baruch Efrati, B. (2009). Sex Change. In: Ask the Rabbi. Available at: www.kipa.co.il/ask/show/191457, (accessed July 9, 2015).

Ben-Ephraim, E. (2003). *Kuntres 'Et milḥamah* [Hebrew]. Jerusalem: self-published.

Ben-Ephraim, E. (2002). *Sefer 'Edan hathorah* [Hebrew]. Jerusalem: self-published.

Ben-Ephraim, E. (2004). *Dor Tahepukhot* [Hebrew] (*A Generation of Perversions*). Jerusalem: Ben-Ephraim Family.

Benjamin, H. (1966). *The Transsexual Phenomenon*. New York: Julian Press.

Bettcher, T. M. (2007). Evil deceivers and make-believers: On transphobic violence and the politics of illusion. *Hypatia*, 22/3:43–65.

Bleich, J.D. (1974). Survey of recent Halakhic periodical literature: transsexual surgery. *Tradition*, 14(3):96.

Bleich, J. D. (1981). *Transsexual Surgery and Ambiguous Genitalia, Judaism and Healing: Halakhic Perspectives* (pp. 74–79). Hoboken, NJ: Ktav.

Brama, D. (2008). What Is the Relation of Jewish Law to Transgender Persons? Ynet. Available at: www.ynet.co.il/Ext/Comp/ArticleLayout/CdaArticlePrint Preview/1,2506,L-3564862,00.html [Hebrew] (accessed June 25, 2015).

Brama, D. (2010). Analysis of the Definition of 'Incompetent for One Matter' in the Case of Transsexuality, [Hebrew; unpublished manuscript. He views his analysis as purely legal, not sympathetic per se (private communication, October 2010).

Breisch, S. (n.d.). She'ilat Sha'ul, Even ha'ezer, §9:1–2.

Broyde, M. J. (1988). The establishment of maternity and paternity in Jewish and American law, Appendix: Sex change operations and their effect on marital status—a brief comparison. *National Jewish Law Review* 3:117–158. Available at: www.jlaw.com/Articles/maternity_appendix.html (accessed July 8, 2015).

Butler, J. (1999). *Gender Trouble: Feminism and the Subversion of Identity*. New York: Routledge.

Cherlow, Y. (2007). Transsexual. Available at: www.kipa.co.il/ask/show/115532 [Hebrew] (accessed July 9, 2015).

Cohen, A. (2017). Transgenders in Jewish law and thought. *Journal of Contemporary Halacha and Society*, 74:5–41.

Cohen-Kettenis, P.T. (2005). Gender Change in 46,XY persons with 5α-reductase-2 deficiency and 17β-hydroxysteroid dehydrogenase-3 deficiency, *Archives of Sexual Behavior*, 34(4):399–410.

Domb, Y. (2017). Transgender refuses to grant divorce, claims he is a woman: Haifa Rabbinical court forces transgender person to grant wife a get, despite his claiming he could not give it as he is a woman. Arutz Sheva. Available at: www.israelnationalnews.com/News/News.aspx/227012

Düsseldorf: Symposium. (1967). Transvestism and transsexualism in the male and female. *Journal of Sex Research*, 3(2):107–127.

Dzmura, N. (2010). *Balancing on the Mechitza: Transgender in Jewish Community*. Berkeley, CA: North Atlantic Books.

Eugenides, J. (2002). *Middlesex*. New York: Picador.

Evers, R. (1994). *Shut Veshav verafa* (pp. §79). Jerusalem: Eliezer Fisher.

Feinstein, M. (2012). Igerot Moshe, Even ha'ezer, III, §22 (on contraception), IV, §§36 (on Sirus—Castration or excision of the sexual organs) and 69 (on contraception) and Orah hayim, II, §85 (on Sirus for an institutionalized girl).

Fitzgibbons, R. P., Sutton, P. M., and O'Leary, D. (2009). The psychopathology of 'sex reassignment' surgery: Assessing its medical, psychological, and ethical appropriateness. *National Catholic Bioethics Quarterly*, 9(1):97–125.

Gray, H. (2012). Not judging by appearances: The role of genotype in Jewish law on intersex conditions. *Shofar*, 30(4):126–148, notes 13–16.

Gross, A. M. (2009). Gender outlaws before the law: The courts of the borderlands, *Harvard Journal of Law & Gender*, 32:165–231.

Grossnass, A. L. (1973). *Lev Aryeh, Part II* (no. 49, p. 166). London: Hamadpis,.

Guevin, B. (2005). Sex reassignment surgery for transsexuals: An ethical conundrum? *National Catholic Bioethics Quarterly*, 5(4):719–734.

Hanau, S. (2017). From black hat to trans ally, and paying a price: The unlikely journey of an Orthodox rabbi who lost a pulpit and an outreach post but gained a cause. Available at: http://jewishweek.timesofisrael.com/from-black-hat-to-trans-ally-and-paying-a-price.

Harfenes, Y. D. (n.d.). Nishmat shabat, §5:310, p. 289.

Hill, D. (2008). Dear Doctor Benjamin: Letters from transsexual youth (1963–1976). *International Journal of Transgenderism*, 10(3):149–170.

Hirsch, A. (n.d.). Artificial transformation of male to female and female to male. *No'Am*, 16:152–155.

Katz, B. (2016). Amid a shifting tide of tolerance, transgender Jews search for faith and community. *The New York Times*. Available at: https://womenintheworld.com/2016/02/23/finding-faith-and-community-as-a-transgender-jew

Kessler, S. J. (1985). *Gender: An Ethnomethodological Approach*. Chicago, IL: University of Chicago Press,.

King, D. (1984). Condition, orientation, role or false consciousness? Models of homosexuality and transsexualism. *Sociological Review*, 32(1):38–56.

Klein, D., Bockting, W., Benner, A., and Coleman, E. (2009). Gay and bisexual identity development among female-to-male transsexuals in North America: Emergence of a transgender sexuality. *Archives of Sexual Behavior*, 38(5):688–701.

Klein, M. (2003/2004). *Mishneh halakhot, Machon Mishne Halakhot Gedolot*, Brooklyn: Machon Mishne Halakhot Gedolo [Hebrew].

Kockott, G. and Fahrner, E.M. (1988). Male-to-female and female-to-male transsexuals: A comparison. *Archives of Sexual Behavior*, 17(6):539–546.

Krausz, S. (1972). On the new abomination of changing from men to women. *Hama'or*, 25(2):pp. 12–13 Kislev–Tevet 5733 [Hebrew].

Lavery-Yisraeli, H. (2008). *YU Observer*, October.

Mason-Schrock, D. (1996). Transsexuals' narrative construction of the "true self." *Social Psychology Quarterly*, 59(3):176–192.

Meyer-Bahlburg, H. F. L. (2009). From mental disorder to iatrogenic hypogonadism: Dilemmas in conceptualizing gender identity variants as psychiatric conditions. *Archives of Sexual Behavior*, 39(2):461–476.

Miranda, H. (1784). Yad ne'eman, Salonika, p. 62a [Hebrew]

Nagoshi, J. L. et al. (2008). Gender differences in correlates of homophobia and transphobia, *Sex Roles*, 59(7–8):521–531.

Norton, J. (2003). Vatican says 'sex-change' operation does not change person's gender. Catholic News Service. Available at: http://ai.eecs.umich.edu/people/conway/TS/CatholicTSDecision.html (accessed July 9, 2015).

Nussbaum, M. (2010). *From Disgust to Humanity: Sexual Orientation and Constitutional Law*. New York: Oxford University Press.

Pelaggi, H. (1896). Yosef et 'eḥav. *Izmir*, 3:5.

Rabinowitz, M. (2003). Status of transsexuals. Committee on Jewish Law and Standards of the Rabbinical Assembly, December 3, 2003.

Rachlin, K. (1999). Factors which influence individual's decisions when considering female- to-male genital reconstructive surgery. *International Journal of Transgenderism*, 3(3). Available at: www.iiav.nl/ezines/web/ijt/97-03/numbers/symposion/ijt990302.htm.

Rapoport, C. (2004). Conversion of an uncircumcised male who underwent treatments to change his bodily form and his sex. Kesher: Platform for European Rabbis to Research Jewish Law.

Shafran, Y. (2002). *Nituaḥ lehaḥlafat hamin* (Sex-change surgery). *Teḥumin*, 21:117–120.

Sharzer, L. A. (2017). "Transgender Jews and halakhah." (Committee on Jewish Law and Standards). Rabbinical Assembly.

Shaul Weinreb, S. (2000). Tubal ligation and the prohibition of Sirus, *Journal of Halacha & Contemporary Society*, 40/Fall. Available at: www.daat.ac.il/daat/english/journal/weinreb-1.htm.

Sofer, A. (2007). *Nishmat Avraham: Hilkhot ḥolim rof'im urefu'ah 'al arba'at ḥelkei haShulḥan 'arukh, I–IV* [Hebrew], Jerusalem: Machon Hadrat Yerushalayim.

Steinberg, A. (1994). *Nituaḥ haḥlafat min* [Hebrew], Entziklopediya hilkhatit refu'it.

Steinberg, M. (n.d.). Sex change for an *androginos* [hermaphrodite]. *Assia*, 1 (1):144ff. [Hebrew].

Stone, S. (1993). The 'empire' strikes back: A posttranssexual manifesto. Available at: http://pendientedemigracion.ucm.es/info/rqtr/biblioteca/Transexualidad/trans%20manifesto.pdf (accessed July 8, 2015).

Teitelbaum, H. Y. L. (1972). A question regarding the present-day effrontery of changing from male to female and vice versa. *Hama'or*, 25(2):10–13 [Hebrew].

Tzioni, Y. (n.d.). Olat Yitzḥak, II, §235:3, p. 391.

Verschoor, A. M. and Poortinga, J. (1988). Psychosocial differences between Dutch male and female transsexuals, *Archives of Sexual Behavior*. 17(2):173–178.

Waldenberg, E. Y. (1967). Tzitz Eli'ezer, X, §25:26:6.

Waldenberg, E. Y. (1970). Tzitz Eli'ezer, XI, §78, Translation by the author and Joshua Schreier.

Waldenberg, E. Y. (1997). Tzitz Eli'ezer, XXII, §2.

Weinreb, T. H. (2016). Transgender in the Jewish Community, Beth Jacob Congregation.Available at: www.youtube.com/watch?v=BTylRVBFZok&t=4s

Weiss, A. (2014). Questions regarding names on a ketubah, Minchat Asher [Hebrew responsa], *II:87*, Jerusalem: Machon Minchat Asher.

Weitze, C. and Osburg, S. (1996). Transsexualism in Germany: Empirical data on epidemiology and application of the German Transsexuals' Act during its first ten years. *Archives of Sexual Behavior*, 25(4):409–425. [Hebrew] (accessed December 10, 2015).

Chapter 16

Orthodox Judaism and its transgender members

Rabbi Hyim Shafner

Real people

My first experience with a transgender individual took place over 10 years ago, soon after I became a pulpit rabbi. A man with a beard, *kippah* (yarmulke), and *tzitit* (ritual fringes), came into my office and told me the story of his life. He had grown up as a non-Jew in a rural location with no Jewish people, but from his youth knew two things: he was a woman and he was a Jew. He moved to a bigger city where he successfully became a woman and converted to Reform Judaism. All was well until, a few years later, during a trip to Israel he had an epiphany: he was really a man and was really Orthodox.

He sat across from me unfurling his complex and to me novel, personal narrative as I attempted to assimilate it all. This was my first exposure to someone transgender. Suddenly he concluded: "Rabbi, I have just one question." "What side of the *mechitza* [partition in Orthodox synagogues which separate the men's and women's sections] should I sit on?"

At that moment I experienced several realizations:

- Gender is a much more serious issue for many than I had realized;
- People who care deeply about their religious life, the Torah, and *halakhah* (Jewish law) are among those who are transgender;
- Judaism needs to quickly formulate some answers and approaches for the members of our communities who are transgender and serious about their Jewish life.

Orthodox communities are by definition more insular and less diverse than the general society. What we do not have contact with is often scary, an anathema, and perplexing. Though we may not be able to relate personally or culturally to the transgender among us, we must conclude that, if people are willing to change their lives in such dramatic and often painful ways, such as undergoing surgery, then this is a level of pain and seriousness that is life changing. If conflicts between one's gender as assigned at birth and one's personal gender identity lead people to depression and suicide, then those of us without such experiences must conclude that, even though we may not personally relate to such feelings, these feelings are powerful life-and-death issues that go much deeper than most of us can fathom.

Since that initial encounter I have known several Orthodox transgender people. When I encounter Orthodox people who are transgender (or gay or other ways of being considered outside the Orthodox mainstream) and yet choose to stay within the Orthodox community, I am inspired by their commitment. We should be inspired by people who love Judaism so much they stay within communities that are wary of them, and into which they do not comfortably fit. Our mission as a community, I believe, is to work hard to embrace all Jews. One should not have to leave the community and the Torah just because one is transgender or gay.

After my discussion with the above questioner it became clear to me that the correct answer was that the function of *mechitza* (the physical barrier in a synagogue that separates the genders) is to facilitate personal prayer and concentration even while praying in a communal forum. If one looks like a woman one should sit on the women's side and if one looks like a man one should sit on the men's side. I told him this and he began attending services and sitting on the men's side. Though some had known him as a woman, in Judaism not shaming others is paramount, and so he was treated as the male he felt himself to be, and indeed, in this case, as the male gender he was assigned at birth.

A culture of welcoming

In the winter of 2017 I spoke on a panel at Columbia University in New York City sponsored by the Jewish Orthodox Feminist Alliance (JOFA) dealing with the topic of transgender Orthodox Jews. The audience was mostly composed of members of the modern Orthodox community and the panel consisted of me, another Orthodox Rabbi, and an Orthodox woman who had once been an Orthodox man. I spoke about the way in which my congregation in St. Louis welcomed transgender people into the community, generally welcoming them as any other community member, when someone in the audience asked, "But why are they only in St. Louis?"

I replied that of course transgender Orthodox Jews were not only in St. Louis. They are not seen in most synagogues because, although all synagogues generally call themselves warm and welcoming, in reality they are often welcoming only to those they want to welcome, to those who fit in and are like them. At the synagogue in St. Louis, I explained, we had instead cultivated a *culture of welcoming* that pervaded the community. This meant that everyone, no matter who they were, would be welcomed: the LGBTQ individual, the intermarried, the non-Jew, it did not matter. Like Abraham who leaves God's presence in the book of *Genesis* to run into the desert and welcome the three idolater nomads in the desert, so too we must welcome all, even those whom we find culturally difficult to see as one of us.

In the case of transgender Jews who transition while they are part of the community there is often some discomfort on the part of members that must be overcome. Community members may have known the individual for perhaps years as one gender and now this person presents as another gender. Especially in an Orthodox synagogue, where men and women sit in different sections of the sanctuary, the presence of someone "crossing over" the *mechitza* may feel shocking and transgressive.

In one instance of a woman becoming a man in our synagogue, I anticipated that some individuals might feel uncomfortable. When the transitioning individual asked me if he could sit on the men's side I replied that, though he had been thinking about this for many years, for those around him it was new. I told the transitioning individual that, aside from the technical Jewish legal question of whether biology, appearance, or perception should govern where one sits, the interpersonal question of being sensitive to other's feelings, realizing that for them this may be shocking, is also a very important *halakhic* factor.

In the end it was very important for this person to begin sitting on the men's side; I asked him to sit next to me so others would not be too uncomfortable and would have time to get used to this congregant's changed gender presentation. The rabbi's attitude in a synagogue is paramount in making it a welcoming place for those who may feel left out. Even in the absence of *halakhic* permission to treat the individual as a new gender, a general attitude of welcoming and non-judgmentalism in a community goes a long way in helping trans individuals feel included.

The Baal Shem Tov (1962) famously said that the Torah records in *Genesis* Abraham leaving God's presence to welcome three people in the desert, not only to teach us that welcoming guests is more important than receiving the Divine presence as the Talmud concludes, but that even if we think welcoming someone will take its toll on our personal religious life, we should welcome them. Even if it may take our time from Torah study or that our guest will speak *lashon hara*, slander, nevertheless the Baal Shem Tov says the Torah wants us to welcome them. Welcoming the stranger is vital even if we worry that it will threaten our religious life (Baal Shem Tov, 1962).

It is also important for the rabbi to give those who run the service clear *halakhic* (Jewish legal) guidelines with regard to which honors may be given to transgender people. Cases of male-to-female transitions will be different to female-to-male ones with regard to Jewish law, as well as the stage of transition in which the person is currently found. These decisions will no doubt be different for different rabbis and different synagogues within Orthodoxy (see Chapter 5 for further discussion and examples).

Does gender change from a *halakhic* perspective?

Judaism has always had more than just a binary understanding of gender. The Talmud in fact describes four genders. The *halakha* is most interested not in the moral or social implications of gender but in practical *halakhic* questions. Judaism and Jewish law are gendered at their core. For example, who may perform a particular *mitzvah*, such as blowing the shofar, and for whom. Would an androgynous person, one who has both male and female genitalia, be permitted to blow the shofar for a man, a woman, or only another androgynous individual? A *tumtum*, one whose gender is either male or female but we are unsure which, for whom may they blow the shofar?

Within more traditional religious Jewish communities the question of communal LGBTQ integration cannot be explored without recourse to *halakha*, Jewish law, because it is deeply interwoven within all aspects of Orthodox Jewish life. Nevertheless only a few rabbis have written about gender transition and the questions that evolve from it. Though far from a comprehensive analysis, the following is a short summary of key opinions about the Jewish legal implications of gender transition (for a more in-depth analysis see Chapter 15).

Rabbi Eliezer Waldenberg

The great twentieth-century *posek*, decisor, of Jewish law, Rabbi Eliezer Waldenberg (1967, 1971), was one of the first to address this issue in modern times. In a responsa he quotes from Rabbi Yosef Philacci of Izmir, who was asked about a married man and woman who had consummated their marriage and lived as husband and wife, when: "The wife became fully a male." The original question was, does the wife who became a male require a *get*, a religious divorce, in order to remarry, or, as in Jewish law two males are not considered married, perhaps this, now male spouse does not need a *get*? Rabbi Philacci ruled that he does not need a religious divorce because he is now a man and concludes, "Do not be surprised by this occurrence, for everything is possible, there is nothing new under the sun ... for others have written of such occurrences" (Tzitz Eliezer, 1967, 22:2)

In addition, adds Rabbi Philacci, even though this person now has a penis he does not need a *bris*, a circumcision, because he was not born male but female, and a *bris* is specifically given only to one who is born male.

Though this person's change in gender seems to be a spontaneous, and to us a perhaps shocking and questionable, happening, what I find informative about the passage is the lack of value judgment. The event is a human phenomenon and must be viewed as such, with all of its *halakhic* implications. In addition, what is striking is the interested wonder with which he writes the response. There is a feeling of mystery and awe about the world with which Rabbi Waldenberg reports these transgender *halakhic* writings.

Rabbi Waldenberg also writes that a person who was a woman and became a man does not say the traditional blessing, "Who has not made me a woman." Indeed, God did make them a woman. Rather he formulates a new blessing for such a person: "Blessed are You Lord our God King of the universe who has transformed me into a man."

Although Rabbi Waldenberg did not permit gender reassignment surgery from the outset, in contrast to many others, he ruled that such a person who has had gender reassignment surgery is indeed now a different gender than they were before.

Rabbi Zev Farber

Rabbi Zev Farber (2015), in a *halakhic* article on the blog Morethodoxy, distinguishes between genitals and other outward characteristics. He argues that for marriage and sexual questions we determine gender based on an individual's genitals, but for obligations in *mitzvot* and social implications he suggests we let their personal gender identity be determinative.

Rabbi Edan Ben-Ephraim

In a fairly recent and comprehensive, *halakhic* work on the subject, *Dor Tahepukhot* (in Hebrew, English translation of the title: *A Perverted Generation*, 2004) the author, Rabbi Edan Ben-Ephraim, writes that the soul is gendered and this does not change when the body is changed (Ben-Ephraim, 2004, p. 81). Thus one's obligation in *mitzvot* would not be affected by gender change, but social behaviors such as *kol isha* (the prohibition of men hearing the voice of a woman singing) or *negia* (the prohibition that men and women who are not married are not permitted to have any physical contact with each other) or *yichud* (laws circumscribing private meetings with the opposite gender) would change with a gender operation (pp. 68–70).

This is very different from Rabbi Zev Farber who rules that one's outward appearance does change one for reasons of *mitzvot* and that "bottom surgery" would fully change someone for all issues of *halakha* – social, ritual, and with regard to marriage and sexuality.

Rabbi Ben-Ephraim does in theory recognize the decisions of Rabbi Philacci and Rabbi Waldenberg that one who is transformed into another gender is considered that new gender. At the same time Rabbi Ben Ephraim distinguishes between Rabbi Philacci's case and cases of gender reassignment surgery. He rules that, if one is suddenly transformed, "by the hand of heaven," into a new gender, then Rabbi Philacci would be correct. On the other hand, surgery performed to achieve a new gender would not fully change a person's gender with regard to *halakhah*.

Rabbi Ben-Ephraim believes that a non-miraculous change in the body does not change the person's gendered soul or transform them into a new person (p. 103). He writes that if one's arms are cut off they are exempt from the commandment of *tefillin* (phylacteries), but this is not because they are now a new person to whom *tefillin* does not apply, but for rather a more technical reason, because they do not have arms they are practically prevented from doing the *mitzvah*.

In contrast Rabbi Waldenberg would rule that one who physically changes their gender (through surgery) has changed their gender. According to Rabbi Waldenberg genitals define us completely differently than other limbs or organs. Thus changing one's genitals changes our gender.

Selected *halakhic* repercussions of gender change

Rabbi Ben-Ephraim's writing is very helpful for those *halakhic* communities who wish to welcome transgender individuals. In an Orthodox community Jewish law is paramount. Questions about synagogue honors, obligations, and permissions, as well as many other *halakhic* questions are impacted by gender. Thus clarity with regard to the details of how gender transition intersects with Jewish law is vital so they do not become obstacles in integrating trans individuals into the Orthodox community.

Rabbi Ben-Ephraim generally distinguishes between the *halakhic* status of an individual who has changed their gender, which he rules does not change, and their "social" identity with regard to *halakhah*, which does. This has many practical implications.

Dress

May a person who has undergone gender reassignment dress as their new gender or is this a violation of the biblical prohibition of cross-dressing (*Deuteronomy* 22:5)? Though Rabbi Ben-Ephraim is very clear that an operation to change one's gender is forbidden and such change does not essentially transform one's gender from a *halakhic* perspective, none the less he does rule that after gender reassignment it is not problematic to dress as one's new gender. Rabbi Ben-Ephraim argues that wearing the clothing of the opposite gender is Biblically forbidden when it is done specifically to dwell within the realm of the opposite gender, in order to entice them to sexual activity (p. 131). In this case that is not the intention.

Although with most commandments, even when the Biblical reason does not apply, we still retain the commandment, here he argues, and cites sources to that effect, the reason for the commandment itself is part of its definition and application. For instance, he cites as a precedent, the *halakhic* decision that, if one is wearing the clothing of the opposite gender in order to keep warm, it is not forbidden.

Tzitzit, tefillin, and talit (wearing ritual fringes and phylacteries)

Rabbi Ben-Ephraim rules that, if a woman has transitioned to being a man, he is permitted to wear *tzitzit, talitot,* and *tefillin* (p. 151). This is because according to the strict definition of the law a woman may also wear these items. Even in communities in which women do not wear these items publicly, because this individual's public persona is now male, they may. In a similar vein he rules that that one should sit in the section of the synagogue that applies to their new post-reassignment gender.

With regard to *tzitzit* and *tefillin*, however, he does make the qualification that a person who was female and is now male may wear these religious garments but should not recite a blessing on them. If they were male and have now transitioned to be female, they should still wear these religious articles but only in private.

Minyan (quorum required for public prayer)

With regard to a *minyan* Rabbi Ben-Ephraim writes that a transgender individual who was female and is now male should not be counted in a *minyan*, and that one who was male and is now female should also not be counted in a *minyan*.

Aliyah (being called to the Torah)

Rabbi Ben-Ephraim writes that a woman who becomes a man may be called up to the Torah because essentially women may receive *aliyot* (this honor) according to the Talmud and codes of Jewish law. The

Talmud does state that we do not apply this practice due to the "honor of the congregation." In this case, however, as this individual looks like a man and sits with the men there is no such violation of the congregation's norms (p. 163). He adds that the application of these decisions lies in the eyes of the local rabbi or spiritual guide, which is important because, when it comes to issues of a congregation, its honor and cohesion, one must be familiar with the particular congregation's social and religious sensitivities (see Chapter 5 in Section 1).

Birkat hamazon (grace after meals)

With regard to grace after meals, Rabbi Ben-Ephraim rules that a woman who has become a man may be counted in a *mizuman* (the quorum of three people required to say the grace publicly) with two men because the Talmud seems to hold that women really can be counted in a *mizuman*, but that this is not done for reasons of modesty (*BT Berachot* 45b). Thus, in our situation this would not apply and they could be counted (p. 171).

Conclusion

It is vital that the Orthodox community recognizes and discusses the challenges and complexities that the community is facing more and more with regard to gender identity. As we walk the narrow bridge between fidelity to the letter of the law and the overarching Jewish and *halakhic* value of being, "*mikabetz nidchey yisrael*," gathering in those Jews who may feel vulnerable and alienated, may the words of Rabbi Eliezer Waldenberg help to guide our way, so that, even if we conclude that gender reassignment brings along with is a whole host of *halakhic* problems, "nevertheless one must bring such a person as close to Judaism as they can" (quoted in *Dor Tahepukhot*, p. 9)."

References

Baal Shem Tov, Y. (1962). *Al HaTorah*. Jerusalem: Parshat Vayera [Hebrew)].
Ben-Ephraim, E. (2004). *Dor Tahepukhot* [*A Generation of Perversions*], [Hebrew], Jerusalem: Ben-Ephraim Family.

Farber, R.Z. (2015). Transgender orthodox Jews. In: *Morethodoxy*. Available at: https://morethodoxy.org/2015/08/06/transgender-orthodox-jews.

Waldenberg, E. Y. (1967). Responsa dealing with body alterations. In *Tzitz Eliezer*, Volume X, Part 25, Chapter 26, Section 6, Jerusalem.

Waldenberg, E. Y. (1971). Case of androgen insensitivity syndrome. In *Tzitz Eliezer* [Hebrew], Volume XI, Part 78, Jerusalem.

Index